MICROFOUNDATIONS
OF INSTITUTIONS

RESEARCH IN THE SOCIOLOGY OF ORGANIZATIONS

Series Editor: Michael Lounsbury

RESEARCH IN THE SOCIOLOGY OF
ORGANIZATIONS   VOLUME 65A

MICROFOUNDATIONS OF INSTITUTIONS

EDITED BY

PATRICK HAACK

University of Lausanne, Switzerland

JOST SIEWEKE

Vrije Universiteit Amsterdam, The Netherlands

LAURI WESSEL

University of Bremen, Germany

emerald
PUBLISHING

United Kingdom -- North America – Japan
India – Malaysia – China

Emerald Publishing Limited
Howard House, Wagon Lane, Bingley BD16 1WA, UK

First edition 2020

Reprints and permissions service
Contact: permissions@emeraldinsight.com

British Library Cataloguing in Publication Data
A catalogue record for this book is available from the British Library

ISBN: 978-1-78769-124-7 (Print)
ISBN: 978-1-78769-123-0 (Online)
ISBN: 978-1-78769-125-4 (Epub)

ISSN: 0733-558X (Series)

Printed and bound by CPI Group (UK) Ltd, Croydon, CR0 4YY

ISOQAR certified
Management System,
awarded to Emerald
for adherence to
Environmental
standard
ISO 14001:2004.

ISOQAR
REGISTERED

Certificate Number 1985
ISO 14001

INVESTOR IN PEOPLE

CONTENTS

SECTION 1
PROLOGUE

SECTION 2
INTRODUCTION

SECTION 3
COGNITIVE PERSPECTIVE ON MICROFOUNDATIONS

Chapters in this section are related to the cognitive perspective on microfoundations of institutions. This perspective applies a broad understanding of cognition and thus also covers the emotional underpinnings of institutions. Therefore, chapters in this section investigate how thought structures and emotions contribute to institutional change and maintenance.

LISTS OF FIGURES AND TABLES

FIGURES

TABLES

LIST OF CONTRIBUTORS

Mattia Anesa	The University of Sydney, Australia
Alex Bitektine	Concordia University, Canada
Romain Boulongne	HEC Paris, France
Eva Boxenbaum	Copenhagen Business School, Denmark
Julia Brandl	University of Innsbruck, Austria
Konstantinos Chalkias	University of London, UK
Magdalena Cholakova	Rotterdam School of Management, Erasmus University, The Netherlands
Jeannette Colyvas	Northwestern University, USA
W. E. Douglas Creed	University of Rhode Island, USA
Arnaud Cudennec	HEC Paris, France
Tiffany Darabi	Cornell University, USA
Rich DeJordy	California State University, USA
Jochen Dreher	University of Konstanz, Germany
Rodolphe Durand	HEC Paris, France
Nina Eliasoph	University of Southern California, USA
Teppo Felin	Oxford University, UK
Emamdeen Fohim	University of St. Gallen, Switzerland
Nicolai Foss	Bocconi University, Italy
Santi Furnari	University of London, UK
Claudia Gabbioneta	Newcastle University, UK
Vern L. Glaser	University of Alberta, Canada
Mary Ann Glynn	Boston College, USA
Jan Goldenstein	Friedrich Schiller University Jena, Germany
Royston Greenwood	University of Alberta, Canada

Tim Hallett	Indiana University, USA
Derek Harmon	University of Michigan, USA
Amelia Hawbaker	Indiana University, USA
Osnat Hazan	Hebrew University of Jerusalem, Israel
Yanfei Hu	University of Surrey, UK
Hokyu Hwang	UNSW Business School, UNSW Sydney, Australia
Benjamin D. Innis	Boston College, USA
Gazi Islam	Grenoble Ecole de Management, France
Paula Jarzabkowski	Cass Business School, UK
Candace Jones	University of Edinburgh, UK
Joshua Keller	UNSW Business School, UNSW Sydney, Australia
Ju Young Lee	Boston College, USA
Taehyun Lee	Boston College, USA
Lianne M. Lefsrud	University of Alberta, Canada
Omar Lizardo	UCLA, USA
Jade Y. Lo	Drexel University, USA
Jaco Lok	Macquarie University, Australia
Namrata Malhotra	Imperial College London, UK
John W. Meyer	Stanford University, USA
Daniel Muzio	University of York, UK
Robert Nason	Concordia University, Canada
Lionel Paolella	Judge Business School, UK
Raissa Pershina	University of Oslo, Norway
Nelson Phillips	Imperial College London, UK
Walter W. Powell	Stanford University, USA
Davide Ravasi	UCL School of Management, UK
Trish Reay	University of Alberta, Canada
Claus Rerup	Frankfurt School of Finance and Management, Germany

Anna E. Roberts	The Pennsylvania State University, USA
Thomas J. Roulet	University of Cambridge, UK
Charles-Clemens Rüling	Grenoble Ecole de Management, France
Riku Ruotsalainen	Vrije Universiteit Amsterdam, The Netherlands
Oliver Schilke	University of Arizona, USA
Anna Schneider	University of Innsbruck, Austria
Elke Schüßler	Johannes Kepler University Linz, Austria
Birthe Soppe	University of Innsbruck, Austria
Andreas Paul Spee	The University of Queensland, Australia
Christopher Steele	University of Alberta, Canada
Panita Surachaikulwattana	University of the Thai Chamber of Commerce, Thailand
Hovig Tchalian	Claremont Graduate University, USA
Pamela S. Tolbert	Cornell University, USA
Madeline Toubiana	University of Alberta, Canada
Eero Vaara	Aalto University, Finland
Peter Walgenbach	Friedrich Schiller University Jena, Germany
Tammar B. Zilber	Hebrew University of Jerusalem, Israel
Lynne G. Zucker	UCLA, USA

ABOUT THE CONTRIBUTORS

Mattia Anesa is a Lecturer in Ethics at the University of Sydney Business School. His research adopts a sociological lens to understand ethical dilemmas within organizational settings. He employs qualitative research methods to investigate the legitimation process of highly contested institutionalized practices with a particular focus on the tax domain. Mattia's work is published on *Accounting, Organization & Society* and *Journal of Business Research.*

Alex Bitektine is Professor of Management at the John Molson School of Business at Concordia University, Montreal, Canada. His research interests include entrepreneurship, institutional theory, social judgments (legitimacy, status, reputation, trust, and others), non-market strategies, sustainable development, as well as application of experimental methods in organizational research.

Romain Boulongne is an Assistant Professor in the Strategic Management Department at IESE Business school and affiliated member of the Society and Organizations Center at HEC Paris. His primary research focus is on how categorization processes – the various cognitive mechanisms that people use to make sense of the social world – shape social evaluation and performance of organizations in markets.

Eva Boxenbaum is Professor of Organization and Management Theory at Copenhagen Business School from where she also obtained her PhD. She conducts research on how organizational actors shape the innovation and spread of management practices and organizational forms. Her most recent work focuses on the role of verbal, visual, and material modes of communication in institutionalization processes.

Julia Brandl is a Professor of HRM & Employment Relations at the University of Innsbruck, Austria. Julia's research aims to promote a pluralist HRM paradigm with particular attention to the role of the state for HRM policies and careers. Her current research projects examine the effectiveness of salary transparency legislation in Austria and developments in the HRM profession.

Konstantinos Chalkias is a Lecturer in Management at Birkbeck, University of London. His research interest revolves around the practices and strategic dynamics of organizations and markets. Drawing from social-practice theory, he studies how strategy is done inside organizations and how financial markets are constructed.

Magdalena Cholakova is an Associate Professor of Entrepreneurship in the Department of Strategic Management and Entrepreneurship at the Rotterdam School of Management, Erasmus University. Magdalena's work focuses on several core strands including entrepreneurial reasoning and learning during idea validation, decision-making heuristics under Knightian uncertainty, and micro-foundations of institutional complexity. Magdalena obtained her PhD from Bocconi University, Italy.

Jeannette Colyvas is an Associate Professor at the School of Education and Social Policy at Northwestern University. She received her PhD from Stanford University in 2007.

W. E. Douglas Creed is Professor at University of Rhode Island. He received his PhD and MBA from the Haas School of Business at the University of California, Berkeley. His work focuses on social identity, change agency, and micro-politics in contested organizational and institutional change processes.

Arnaud Cudennec is a PhD candidate at HEC Paris and affiliated member of the Society and Organizations Center at HEC Paris. His research mainly focuses on expertise, categorization processes and the evaluation of organizations in markets.

Tiffany Darabi is a PhD student in Organizational Behavior at Cornell University's ILR School. Her research explores how organizations generate social value. Previously, she worked as an organizational development specialist in the international development sector. She holds a BA in International Relations from Johns Hopkins University.

Rich DeJordy is Assistant Professor of Management at California State University, Fresno. His research interests are at the intersection of institutions, networks, and identity, exploring how individuals and organizations construct and manage their identities as they navigate their institutional environment.

Jochen Dreher is Chief Executive Officer of the Social Science Archive Konstanz (Alfred Schutz Memorial Archive), University of Konstanz, Germany, and Lecturer in Sociology, University of Konstanz and University of St. Gallen, Switzerland. His research interests are sociology of knowledge, sociology of culture, phenomenology, social theory, sociology of organization, qualitative social research, intercultural communication, sociology of power, and the sociological theory of the symbol.

Rodolphe Durand is the Joly Family Professor of Purposeful Leadership at HEC Paris and the Founder and Academic Director of the Society and Organizations Center. He studies the multiple sources of conformity and deviation that weigh on organizations and their impact on organizational advantage and performance.

Nina Eliasoph is a Professor of Sociology at the University of Southern California. She is the author of three books (*Avoiding politics: How Americans produce apathy in everyday life*; *Making volunteers*; and *The politics of volunteering*), as well as numerous articles about everyday interaction in voluntary associations and nonprofits.

Teppo Felin is Professor of Strategy at Saïd Business School, University of Oxford. His current research focuses on strategy, rationality, perception and cognition, entrepreneurship, and markets.

Emamdeen Fohim is a PhD student at the Institute for Systemic Management and Public Governance at the University of St. Gallen. His research investigates institutional change processes in a public sector context.

Nicolai Foss is the Rodolfo Debenedetti Chaired Professor of Entrepreneurship at the Bocconi University. His main research interests are strategic management, entrepreneurship, and the methodology of social science.

Santi Furnari is Professor of Strategy at Cass Business School, City, University of London. His research interests include the emergence of new fields and practices as well as the microfoundations of institutional logics. His paper titled "Interstitial Spaces" received the Academy of Management Review Best Paper Award in 2014.

Claudia Gabbioneta is Senior Lecturer in Accounting at Newcastle University Business School. Her current research focuses on professions and organizational and professional misconduct. Her research has been published in a number of journals including *Accounting, Organization and Society, Long Range Planning*, and the *Journal of Management Inquiry*.

Vern L. Glaser is an Assistant Professor at the Alberta School of Business, University of Alberta. He received his PhD from the University of Southern California. His research investigates how organizations strategically change practices and culture.

Mary Ann Glynn is Joseph F. Cotter Professor of Management and Organization at Boston College and 73rd President of the Academy of Management. Her research studies social cognition writ large, as organizational identity and creativity, mapping its embeddedness in systems of meaning attending market categories, institutional fields, and cultural forces.

Jan Goldenstein is Postdoctoral Researcher at the Chair of Organization, Leadership, and Human Resource Management, at the Friedrich Schiller University Jena, Germany. His primary research interests include institutional and glocalization theory, institutional change, organizational actorhood, and research methodology such as natural language processing.

Royston Greenwood graduated from the University of Birmingham in the UK. He is a Professor Emeritus at the University of Alberta, Canada; and Visiting Professor at the University of Edinburgh, UK. He is a Fellow of the Academy of Management and Honorary Member of the European Group for Organization Studies.

Patrick Haack is Professor of Strategy at HEC Lausanne, University of Lausanne. His current research focuses on social judgment formation, practice adoption, and the application of experiments and formal modeling approaches to the study of institutionalization and legitimation.

Tim Hallett is Associate Professor of Sociology at Indiana University. He has published extensively on inhabited institutions. He is currently working on developing an inhabited institutional approach to understanding professional socialization via an ethnographic study of a Masters of Public Affairs program. Another line of research examines how social science ideas become public ideas.

Derek J. Harmon is an Assistant Professor of Strategy at the Ross School of Business, University of Michigan. His research leverages language as a theoretical and empirical lens to explore social evaluations, collective meaning making in markets, and the microfoundations of institutions.

Amelia Hawbaker is a PhD candidate in the Department of Sociology at Indiana University. Her scholarly work includes research on organizational sociology, institutional theory, and health policy. Her current research focuses on organizations and medicine, in which she examines medical decision making in the context of hospital-based care.

Osnat Hazan is a Teaching Fellow at the Jerusalem School of Business, Hebrew University of Jerusalem, Israel. She is interested in organizational theories and social construction. Her research focuses on the patterns in which institutions infuse individuals' thought and at the same time depend on individuals to sustain them.

Yanfei Hu is a Lecturer in Sustainability at the Surrey Business School, University of Surrey, United Kingdom. Yanfei's research explores organizational strategies and tactics in changing entrenched cultural and political institutions. She explores this question with institutional theory, social movement theory, and the sensemaking perspective.

Hokyu Hwang is an Associate Professor in the School of Management at the Business School, UNSW Sydney. He received his PhD in Sociology from Stanford University.

Benjamin D. Innis is a Doctoral student in Management and Organization at Boston College. His research focuses on processes whereby organizations both influence, and are influenced by, broader meaning systems, such as categories, institutions, and culture. Currently, his research setting is that of cultural industries and institutions.

Gazi Islam is Professor of People, Organizations and Society at Grenoble Ecole de Management, and has served as faculty at Insper, Tulane University, and the University of New Orleans. He is currently Editor for the Psychology and Business Ethics section at the *Journal of Business Ethics*. His current research interests revolve around the contemporary meanings of work, and the relations between identity, group dynamics, and the production of group and organizational cultures.

Paula Jarzabkowski is a Professor of Strategic Management at City, University of London, UK, and University of Queensland, Australia. Her research on strategy-as-practice in pluralistic contexts is published in *Academy of Management Journal,*

Journal of Management Studies, Organization Science, Organization Studies, and *Strategic Management Journal*. Her latest co-authored book, *Making a Market for Acts of God*, was published by Oxford University Press in 2015.

Candace Jones is the Chair of Global Creative Enterprise at the University of Edinburgh Business School, UK. Her research uses theoretical lenses of institutional logics, networks, vocabularies, and materiality to explore the symbolic, material, and social relationships of cultural products in architecture, film, and music. She is past division chair for Organization and Management Theory Division, Academy of Management.

Joshua Keller is Associate Professor of Management at the School of Management at the Business School, UNSW Sydney, Australia. His core research interests are in the cultural and cognitive foundations of organizations, using theories from cognitive psychology, cognitive linguistics, and cognitive anthropology. His work has been published in numerous organizational journals, including *Academy of Management Journal, Organization Science*, and *Organization Studies*.

Ju Young Lee is a doctoral candidate in Management and Organization at Boston College. His research examines the processes of institutional change with a special focus on changes that address social problems. He is currently exploring these issues in the context of socially responsible and impact investment.

Taehyun Lee is a doctoral candidate in Management and Organization at Boston College. His research focuses on how actors employ meaning systems to open up avenues for and to legitimate innovations and new markets, and how actors embedded in different meaning systems interact in various emergence and change processes.

Lianne M. Lefsrud is an Assistant Professor in Engineering Safety and Risk Management. She draws from institutional theory, framing, emotion, and visual/ multimodal rhetoric to equip organizations to better recognize, evaluate, and manage risks (climate change, workplace fatalities, mine tailings, energy development/transitions, and pipeline corrosion).

Omar Lizardo is the LeRoy Neiman Term Chair Professor in the Department of Sociology at the University of California, Los Angeles. His areas of research interest include the sociology of culture, social networks, the sociology of emotion, social stratification, cognitive social science, and organization theory. He is currently a member of the editorial advisory board of six journals, and with Rory McVeigh and Sarah Mustillo, he is one of the current co-editors of *American Sociological Review*.

Jade Y. Lo is an Assistant Professor at the LeBow College of Business, Drexel University. She received her PhD from the University of Southern California. She is an organizational theorist with interests in innovation and emerging phenomena, as well as sensemaking and sensegiving in a dynamic environment.

Jaco Lok is Professor of Strategy at Macquarie Business School in Sydney, Australia. He received his PhD from Judge Business School at the University of

Cambridge. His research interests include further developing the microfoundations of institutional theory by exploring the complex relations between institutions and the people who live them.

Namrata Malhotra is Associate Professor in Strategy at Imperial College Business School, Imperial College London, UK. Her research interests include organizational and institutional change with a focus on professional services organizations.

John W. Meyer is Professor of Sociology, Emeritus, at Stanford. He has contributed to organizational theory, comparative education, and the sociology of education. He has studied the impact of global models of society (*World Society: The Writings of John W. Meyer*, Oxford; Bromley and Meyer, Hyper-Organization, Oxford 2015).

Daniel Muzio is a Professor of Management at the University of York. He is an Associate Editor of the *Journal of Management Studies* and a Founding Editor for the *Journal of Professions and Organization*. Daniel's research interests include the organization and management of professional services firms, wrongdoing, and diversity.

Robert Nason is the Concordia University Research Chair in Entrepreneurship and Society and Associate Professor in Management at the John Molson School of Business in Montréal. He received his PhD in Entrepreneurship from Syracuse University. His broad research interests examine the role of entrepreneurship in society.

Lionel Paolella is an Assistant Professor of Strategy and Organization at the Cambridge Judge Business School, University of Cambridge, and affiliated with the Center on the Legal Profession at Harvard Law School. He obtained his PhD from HEC Paris. His main line of work explores the categorization processes in markets.

Raissa Pershina is a Doctoral Research Fellow at the University of Oslo, Norway, research section Digitalization and Entrepreneurship. Her research interests include organizational and institutional processes involved in creation of innovative products, particularly in the context of the creative and cultural industries.

Nelson Phillips is the Abu Dhabi Chamber Chair in Strategy and Innovation at Imperial College Business School in London, UK. Originally from Canada, he completed his PhD at the University of Alberta in 1995. His research interests include institutional theory, innovation, and entrepreneurship. He has also written extensively about qualitative methods, in particular discourse analysis and other linguistic approaches to the study of social phenomena.

Walter W. Powell is Professor of Education, Sociology, Organizational Behavior, Management Science and Engineering, and Communication at Stanford University, where he is a faculty co-director of the Center on Philanthropy and Civil Society. His interests focus on the processes through which ideas and practices move across organizations, and the role of networks in facilitating or hindering the transfer of ideas.

Davide Ravasi is Professor of Strategy and Entrepreneurship at the UCL School of Management, University College London. His research primarily examines strategic and organizational changes, with particular emphasis on changes that challenge or otherwise affect the organizational culture or identity. He is interested more generally in socio-cognitive processes shaping entrepreneurship, design, and innovation.

Trish Reay is Professor in Strategic Management and Organization at the University of Alberta School of Business in Edmonton, Canada. She is also Visiting Distinguished Professor at Warwick Business School. She is Editor-in-Chief at *Organization Studies*. Her research interests include organizational and institutional change, professions and professional identity.

Claus Rerup is a Professor of Management at the Frankfurt School of Finance and Management, Germany. Claus studies organizational routines, attention/sensemaking and learning from a process perspective. His work has been published in *Administrative Science Quarterly, Academy of Management Journal, Journal of Management, Organization Science*, and several other journals and handbooks.

Anna E. Roberts is a Doctoral candidate in the Management and Organization Department at the Smeal College of Business, The Pennsylvania State University. Anna studies the future of work, new organizational forms, and the microfoundations of institutions. She earned her BA from Rice University, graduating magna cum laude and was the sole recipient of the Muhammad Yunus Commencement Award for Humanitarian Leadership. Prior to joining academia, she led the West Coast Regulatory Practice Area at Gerson Lehrman Group.

Thomas J. Roulet is a Senior Lecturer in Organization Theory at the Judge Business School and the Fellow in Sociology and Management Studies at Girton College, both at the University of Cambridge. His work focuses on negative social evaluations (stigma, disapproval, and scandals) and institutions.

Charles-Clemens Rüling is a Professor of Organization Theory and the Associate Dean for Research at Grenoble Ecole de Management. His research addresses institutional maintenance and change.

Riku Ruotsalainen (D.Sc., Aalto University) is an Assistant Professor of Organization Theory at Vrije Universiteit Amsterdam in the Netherlands. His research focuses on how organizations can lead complex change processes through which they can initiate, foster, and strengthen organizational innovation paths that bring about organizational renewal.

Oliver Schilke is an Assistant Professor of Management and Organizations at the Eller College of Management, University of Arizona. He previously received a PhD in Sociology from UCLA and was a Research Fellow at Stanford University's Department of Sociology. His research focuses on micro-institutional processes including routines, trust, and legitimacy.

Anna Schneider is an Assistant Professor of HRM and Employment Relations at the University of Innsbruck, Austria. Anna has a longstanding interest in managing the workforce as she previously held several HRM positions in a multinational retail company. Her research focuses on tensions and (e)valuations in new forms of organizing work.

Elke Schüßler is Professor of Business Administration and Head of the Institute of Organization Science at Johannes Kepler Universität Linz. Her research deals with societal challenges such as climate change, decent work or digitalization, as well as with the organization of creative work and innovation.

Jost Sieweke is Associate Professor of Management and Organization at the Vrije Universiteit Amsterdam. His research focuses on human errors and legitimacy. He is also working in the application of natural experiments in management research.

Birthe Soppe is Professor of Business Administration at the University of Innsbruck, Austria. She is also affiliated with the University of Oslo. Birthe bridges institutional and organization theories to understand the fundamental societal, institutional, and organizational underpinnings that shape new fields and organizational transitions in the context of sustainability.

Andreas Paul Spee is Associate Professor in Strategy at the University of Queensland Business School. Paul's research is grounded in social practice theory, particularly known for advocating strategy-as-practice as an alternative perspective to traditional strategy theory. Some of his work appeared in the *Academy of Management Journal, Accounting, Organization & Society, British Journal of Management, Organization Science, Organization Studies*, and in influential handbooks. Paul currently serves as Senior Editor for *Organization Studies*, and as Outgoing Chair for the Strategizing, Activities & Practices Interest Group within the *Academy of Management*.

Christopher Steele is an Assistant Professor of Strategic Management and Organizations at the University of Alberta. His research interests are focused on the social production of truth, the dynamics of individual and collective identity, and the everyday generation of social order. Institutional theory helps casts light on all three topics.

Panita Surachaikulwattana is an Assistant Professor of Organization and Management at the School of Business, University of the Thai Chamber of Commerce (UTCC), in Thailand. She is also a research fellow at the Research Institute for Policy Evaluation and Design, UTCC. She completed her PhD at Imperial College Business School in London, UK. Her research interests include institutionalization and agency, translation, theorization, and organizational form and practices, primarily investigated with the use of qualitative methodologies. Her current research projects focus on translation processes of managerial and social innovations across national boundaries in diverse settings, including the health care industry, the software industry, and the education industry.

Hovig Tchalian studies the impact of language and language-based processes on social and institutional innovation. He uses a mixed-methods approach combining qualitative and computational methods to study the re-emergence of the modern electric vehicle market, the values that underlie corporate governance, and the upscaling of the Canadian whisky category.

Pamela S. Tolbert is the Lois S. Gray Professor of ILR and Social Sciences, and a member of the Organizational Behavior Department in the ILR School at Cornell University. She joined the ILR faculty after receiving her PhD in sociology from UCLA. She is broadly interested in organizational change, culture and entrepreneurship, and organizational practices and social inequality.

Madeline Toubiana is an Assistant Professor of Strategic Management and Organizations at the University of Alberta. Her research focuses on the role emotions, complexity, and stigmatization play in processes of social change. To understand the dynamics of social change, she examines the intersection and interaction between individuals and institutional systems.

Eero Vaara is a Professor of Organization and Management at Aalto University School of Business, a Permanent Visiting Professor at EMLYON Business School, and a Distinguished Visiting Scholar at Lancaster University, UK. His research focuses on organizational, strategic and institutional change that he examines from discursive and narrative perspectives.

Peter Walgenbach is Professor of Organization, Leadership, and Human Resource Management at Friedrich Schiller University Jena, Germany. His research interests include institutional theory. Currently, he is a Senior Editor of *Organization Studies*.

Lauri Wessel is Associate Professor of Management and Organization at the University of Bremen, Germany. His research spawns the domains of organization theory and information systems research by applying sociological theories such as institutional theory to understand digital technology.

Tammar B. Zilber is Associate Professor of Organization Theory at the Jerusalem School of Business, Hebrew University of Jerusalem, Israel. She is interested in the microfoundations of institutions, and how individual-, organizational-, and field-level dynamics involve meanings, emotions, and power relations that take part in constructing and maintaining institutional realities.

Lynne G. Zucker received her PhD at Stanford University and is a Professor of Sociology and Public Policy at UCLA. Her research focuses on micro-institutional processes including trust, legitimacy, and common understandings (standard practices and routines), and the development and protection of tacit knowledge, using quasi-experimental designs.

SECTION 1

PROLOGUE

WHAT ARE MICROFOUNDATIONS? WHY AND HOW TO STUDY THEM?

Pamela S. Tolbert and Lynne G. Zucker

Since the publication of foundational analyses in the late 1970s and early 1980s (DiMaggio & Powell, 1983; Meyer & Rowan, 1977; Zucker, 1977), neo-institutional theory (NIT) has provided a platform for an enormous body of work in organizational studies. Its enduring vitality is attested both by the very large number of citations to these works and the steady stream of special issues in journals and edited volumes focusing on this theoretical tradition (e.g., Greenwood, Oliver, Lawrence, & Meyer, 2017; Powell & DiMaggio, 1991; Zucker, 1988).

Despite its generativity, the NIT has drawn fire from many critics over the years as well, and one of the most frequent criticisms is its "lack of agency" (see DiMaggio, 1988). What, exactly, this often-used phrase means is not always clear – inadequate specification of causal mechanisms, independent action given conformity pressures, or something else? At the most general, it appears to connote critics' dissatisfaction with early formulations, perhaps deriving from inattention to how institutions function as a feature of collectivities that demand institutional acceptance by individuals for entry and continued participation.[1] Lurking in the background may also be the longstanding tensions about over-socialized conceptions of persons.

Over time, such dissatisfaction has fueled a steadily increasing number of calls for research on what is dubbed the "microfoundations of institutional theory" (see Lawrence, Suddaby, & Leca, 2011; Powell & Colyvas, 2008; Thornton & Ocasio, 2008; Zilber, 2016; Zucker, 1983, 1987, 1991). While some progress has been made on this front, as the editors of these two volumes note, research on this topic remains fragmented by what could be called "conversational groups" (e.g., those studying "institutional entrepreneurship," "logics," "institutional work," and "institutional discourse," among other labels). Dialogues across these groups have been surprisingly limited and causal mechanisms too often obscured in these conversations. While "logics" sound causal, few studies of logics have

Microfoundations of Institutions
Research in the Sociology of Organizations, Volume 65A, 3–8
Copyright © 2020 by Emerald Publishing Limited
All rights of reproduction in any form reserved
ISSN: 0733-558X/doi:10.1108/S0733-558X2019000065A004

causal specificity. Logics focus on different organizational types that behave differently, rather than on the roots of these differences. Thus, similar to our plaint about the state of NIT research 20 years ago (Tolbert & Zucker, 1996), research on NIT's microfoundations shows few signs of becoming institutionalized.

By bringing together a significant body of work on issues related to this topic, written by a variety of authors with different theoretical and methodological approaches, these two volumes aim to help scholars identify core questions that cut across such "conversational groups," ones that need to be explored if we are to understand the key links between institutions and individuals. The chapters in these volumes also serve to illustrate the range of theoretical frameworks and methods that can be used and, we think, should be used together to address these questions. Distillation of guiding questions and reflection on the range of methods needed to address these effectively are critical for synthesizing and producing a coherent, "institutionalized" body of academic research.

WHAT ARE MICRO-FOUNDATIONS?

The first step, in our view, entails defining what the research on "microfoundations" constitutes. As implied by our discussion above, we are inclined to define it as research focused on explaining the links between patterns of behavior in a collectivity and individual-level cognitions and behaviors that produce and change those collective patterns. Note that the term "institution" is regularly used to denote *both* general patterns of behavior that characterize a collectivity *and* cognitions and values shared by the individual members of the collectivity that presumably produce the patterns. "Institutional microfoundations" focuses attention on the latter, in particular. Exploring this, we think, requires answering a number of questions, including: (1) what conditions foster individuals' cognitive and normative acceptance of and adherence to existing institutions; and (2) what individual cognitive processes and social interactions are involved in producing changes in shared cognitions and thus patterns of behavior? The latter set of processes may produce new and transformed institutions over time based on new – or blended – sets of cognitions.

The first general question is often the one addressed by work taking what the editors of these volumes refer to as cognitive and behavioral perspectives. More specifically, it is concerned with understanding what conditions makes individuals more compliant with or resistant to institutional pressures, and in the latter case, able to convince others to resist as well. The second question is commonly identified with work that the editors characterize as behavioral and communication perspectives. The more specific concerns here include understanding the nature of communication processes and interpretations of others' behavior that are most likely to affect individual acceptance or rejection of existing shared cognitions and thus understanding how this affects the spread of new schema or action choices. In this latter case, we can examine directly the processes involved in the formation, and potential proliferation, of new institutions. Not only "institutional entrepreneurs" but also anyone who has on-going interactions with others can form these new cultural/societal elements. Hence, many participate in redefining and improving the social contexts we live and work in.

WHY STUDY MICRO-FOUNDATIONS?

We see these questions as both intriguing and almost intuitively obvious ones to ask by institutional theorists. Hence, it is interesting to speculate on the sources of institutional inertia, as it were, in terms of addressing them. One set of explanations might rest on finally exhausting the most interesting and rich macro-level themes in institutional theory, leaving room for micro-institutional theory and research. Relatedly, when macro-foundations involve diffusion as the main mechanism of institutional transmission, the role of the individual as change-agent is obscured, even rendered invisible. Another might point out how often, possibly with increasing frequency, self-interest underlies macro-institutions, de-legitimating them.

Another potential explanation, perhaps most convincing for the early history of institutional theory, points to old turf wars between sociology and psychology, amplifying disciplinary biases. Durkheim's (1938) canonical attempt to define the then-fledgling field of sociology emphasized outcomes describing collectives, and supra-individual influences on behavior, as its appropriate domain. That is, patterns that distinguish one group from others were posed as the appropriate explanandum, and characteristics of group relations and shared beliefs, or structure and culture, as the explanans. Some early work on institutions, however, drew directly from social psychology including use of experiments that derived in part from early work by Sherif and others (e.g., Zucker, 1977) and the development of new vocabularies of motives prior to and during an institutional shift (Tolbert & Zucker, 1983). In carving out a distinctive domain, however, questions of how the two social sciences might relate to one another were sometimes side-stepped, a pattern that has only recently been broken (see DiMaggio, 1997, for an early exception).

HOW TO STUDY MICRO-FOUNDATIONS?

We are beginning to see a growing number of empirical studies examining social influences on cognition and decision making, explicitly designed to illuminate the mechanisms underpinning well-documented patterns of organizational-level adoption, diffusion, and abandonment of practices and formal structures (e.g., Haack, Schoenborn, & Wickert, 2012; Raaijmakers, Vermeulen, Meeus, & Zietsmas, 2015; Schilke, 2018).

We also see that social psychological processes such as trust production have been explicitly embraced by those building new, more process-based, theories of microfoundations of institutions (Zucker, 1986; Zucker & Schilke, 2019), and, in fact, it is providing a means of linking changes at one level of analysis to changes at a different level. We frequently find parallel concepts at the different levels.

For example, we often measure trust in institutions. Trust in the US Congress is conceptualized and measured alongside trust in the President of the United States. At the same time, we often use individual-level trust measures to decide with whom we will interact or engage in trade. Thus, it has been traditional to look at some institutional level practices and groups through much the same lens as we look at some individual practices.

Under some conditions, though, it can be difficult to link changes at one level of analysis to changes at a different level. It is sometimes easier to study how change in the institutional level – societal, organizational, or even subunit or group level – affects changes at the individual level, particularly when the higher level change is discrete, such as the passage of a law, or the formal adoption of an organizational policy. In those cases, there is a temporal marker that researchers can use that to begin an investigation of its filtered impact through individual-level phenomena. Still, the actual link is sometimes difficult to identify. The reverse research problem is sometimes more difficult. This requires two things: the emergence of alternatives to accepted, taken-for-granted arrangements becoming cognitively accessible to a large number of individuals within a given time span; and the acceptance of such alternatives by a larger number of individuals, rather than collectively ignored and/or sanctioned. Some of these methodological issues have had solutions proposed, but these remain difficult to execute (Barley & Tolbert, 1997).

Also note that institutional processes are not always straightforward. Sometimes, it is not all exactly as it seems. We sometimes try to trace effects from one level to the next only to find they are a cover for practices never implemented at all; or an action that was performed violated the criteria expected. "Say one thing and do another" seems to be enshrined as a basic method of obscuring illegitimate action under an institutionalized cover. While we often think of institutions as automatically legitimate, we find that the unfolding story is quite different and there is considerable pressure for change in the functioning of existing institutions.

MICRO-FOUNDATIONS OF INSTITUTIONAL THEORY, METHODS, AND RESEARCH

Insights stemming from taking a new look at the roots of institutional theory in the assembled chapters in these volumes will produce stronger theory and method. With this sturdy foundation, illumination by juxtaposition of the assembled chapters in these volumes will open our collective "eyes" to new opportunities in strong and varied theoretical development and synthesis and to "new-to-institutions" methodologies. All are critical to the continued influence and generativity of microfoundations that, once fully integrated into institutional research as a whole, will offer significant contributions to the continued influence of institutional perspectives.

NOTE

1. Zucker's (1977) work represents a notable exception to this.

REFERENCES

Barley, S. R., & Tolbert, P.S. (1997). Institutionalization and structuration: Studying the links between action and institution. *Organization Studies, 18*, 93–118.

DiMaggio, P. D. (1997). Culture and cognition. *Annual Review of Sociology, 23*, 263–287.

DiMaggio, P. D., & Powell, W. W. (1983). The iron cage revisited: Institutional isomorphism and collective rationality in organizational fields. *American Sociological Review, 48*, 147–160.

DiMaggio, P. J. (1983). Interest and agency in institutional theory. In L. G. Zucker (Ed.), *Institutional Patterns and Organizations* (pp. 3–20). Cambridge MA: Ballinger.

Durkheim, E. (1938). *Rules of the sociological method*. Chicago, IL: University of Chicago.

Greenwood, R., Oliver, C., Lawrence, T. B., & Meyer, R. (2017). *The Sage handbook of organizational institutionalism*. London: Sage Publishing.

Haack, P., Schoeneborn, D., & Wickert, C. (2012). Talking the talk, moral entrapment, creeping commitment? Exploring narrative dynamics in corporate responsibility standardization. *Organization Studies, 33*(5), 815–845.

Lawrence, T., Suddaby, R. & Leca, B. (2011). Institutional work: Refocusing institutional studies of organization. *Journal of Management Inquiry, 20*, 52–58.

Meyer, J. W., & Rowan, B. (1977). Institutionalized organizations: Formal organizations as myth and ceremony. *American Journal of Sociology, 83*, 340–363.

Powell, W. W., & Colyvas, J. A. (2008). Microfoundations of Institutional Theory. In R. Greenwood, C. Oliver, R. Suddaby & K. Sahlin (Eds.), *the SAGE handbook of organizational institutionalism* (pp. 276–297). London: Sage.

Powell, W. W., & DiMaggio, P. D. (1991) *The new institutionalism in organizational analysis*. Chicago, IL: University of Chicago.

Raaijmakers, A. G. M., Vermeulen, P. A. M., Meeus, M. T. H., & Zietsmas, C. (2015). I need time! Exploring pathways to compliance under institutional complexity. *Academy of Management Journal, 58*(1), 85–115.

Schilke, O. (2018). A micro-institutional inquiry into resistance to environmental pressures. *Academy of Management Journal, 61*(4), 1435–1466.

Thorton, P. H., & Ocasio, W. (2008). Institutional logics. In R. Greenwood, C. Oliver, R. Suddaby, K. Sahlin (Eds.), *The SAGE handbook of organizational institutionalism* (pp. 99–129). London: Sage.

Tolbert, P. S., & Zucker, L. G. (1983). Institutional sources of change in the formal structure of organizations: The diffusion of civil service reform, 1880–1935. *Administrative Science Quarterly, 28*, 22–39.

Tolbert, P. S., & Zucker, L. G. (1996). The institutionalization of institutional theory. In S. Clegg, C. Hardy, & W. Nord (Eds.), *Handbook of organization studies* (pp. 175–190). London: Sage.

Zilber, T. B. (2016). How institutional logics matter: A bottom-up exploration. In M. Lounsbury (Ed.), *Research in the sociology of organizations* (Vol. 48A, pp. 137–155). Bingley: Emerald Publishing.

Zucker, L. G. (1977). The role of institutionalization in cultural persistence. *American Sociological Review, 42*, 726–772.

Zucker, L. G. (1983). Organizations as institutions. In S. B. Bacharach (Ed.), *Research in the sociology of organizations*, (Vol. 2, pp. 1–47). Greenwich, CT: JAI Press.

Zucker, L. G. (1986). Production of trust: Institutional sources of economic structure, 1840–1920. *Research in Organizational Behavior, 8*, 53–111.

Zucker, L. G. (1987). Institutional theories of organization. *Annual Review of Sociology, 13*, 443–464.

Zucker, L. G. (1988). *Institutional patterns and organizations: Culture and environment*. Boston, MA: Ballinger Press.

Zucker, L. G. (1991). Postscript: Microfoundations of institutional thought. In W.W. Powell & P. DiMaggio (Eds.), *The new institutionalism in organizational analyses* (pp. 103–106). Chicago, IL: University of Chicago.

Zucker, L. G., & Schilke, O. (2019). Toward a Theory of Micro-institutional processes: Forgotten roots, links to social-psychological research, and new ideas. In P. Haack, J. Sieweke, L. Wessel (Eds.), *Microfoundations of Institutions (Research in the Sociology of Organizations*, Vol. 65B, pp. 371–389). Bingley: Emerald Publishing.

SECTION 2

INTRODUCTION

MICROFOUNDATIONS AND MULTI-LEVEL RESEARCH ON INSTITUTIONS

Patrick Haack, Jost Sieweke and Lauri Wessel

ABSTRACT

This double volume presents the state of the art in research on the microfoundations of institutions. In this introductory chapter, we develop an overview of where the emerging microfoundational agenda in institutional theory stands and in which direction it is moving. We discuss the questions of what microfoundations of institutions are, what the "micro" in microfoundations represents, why we use the plural form (microfoundations vs microfoundation), why microfoundations of institutions are needed, and how microfoundations can be studied. Specifically, we highlight that there are several traditions of microfoundational research, and we outline a cognitive, a communicative and a behavioral perspective. In addition, we explain that scholars tend to think of microfoundations in terms of an agency, levels, or mechanisms argument. We delineate key challenges and opportunities for future research and explain why we believe that the debate on microfoundations will become a defining element in the further development of institutional theory.

INTRODUCTION

The last decade has seen growing interest in the topic of "microfoundations of institutions" (Powell & Rerup, 2017), with the term "microfoundations" appearing in several important journal publications (e.g., Cardinale, 2018; Chandler & Hwang, 2015; Harmon, 2018; Schilke, 2018; Tracey, 2016). These developments in institutional theory[1] are taking place alongside a more general "microfoundations movement" in strategy and organization theory (Felin, Foss, & Ployhart, 2015).

Microfoundations of Institutions
Research in the Sociology of Organizations, Volume 65A, 11–40
Copyright © 2020 by Emerald Publishing Limited
All rights of reproduction in any form reserved
ISSN: 0733-558X/doi:10.1108/S0733-558X2019000065A005

The growing popularity of microfoundations can be seen in Fig. 1, which is based on a Web of Science search and plots articles published in journals in the disciplines of business and management, economics, political science, and sociology that refer to ("Microfoundation*" OR "Microfoundation*") AND "Institution*" in their title, keywords, or abstract. While the total number of articles is still fairly manageable, the number of references has significantly increased over time across disciplines.

The growing interest in the microfoundations of institutions is also reflected in the overall interest in the present double volume of *Research in the Sociology of Organizations*. We contacted scholars working (or, interested in working) in the space of microfoundations and invited them to submit proposals on the topic of microfoundations of institutions. While corresponding with these scholars, we also shared an extended abstract of this introductory chapter. We hoped for significant interest in the topic of microfoundations, but even we as editors were surprised by the resonance, enthusiasm, and curiosity our call for chapters elicited. This double volume assembles a collection of 35 chapters, including conceptual, empirical, and methodological contributions to the emerging microfoundations agenda in institutional theory, as well as shorter "reflection" chapters that discuss past and current trends in microfoundational research. The double volume concludes with epilogues by John Meyer and Woody Powell, two of the "founding fathers" of institutional theory, as well as an epilogue by Teppo Felin and Nicolai Foss, two of the main advocates of the broader microfoundational research agenda in strategy and organization theory.

Across these contributions, the double volume reflects the state-of-the-art research on the microfoundations of institutions and, by pushing the research frontier, has the potential to give an important impetus to this exciting line of research. Research on microfoundations is certainly not new, as it is deeply rooted in the foundations of institutional theory, such as ethnomethodology

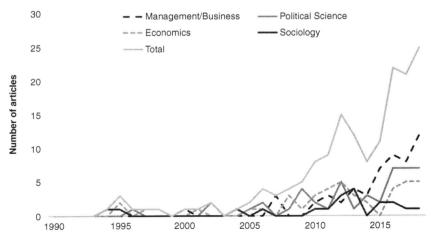

Fig. 1. Growing Popularity of Microfoundations of Institutions, 1990–2018.

(Zucker & Schilke, 2020, chapter 19B), symbolic interactionism (Furnari, 2020, chapter 10B), and Bourdieu's practice theory (Anesa, Chalkias, Jarzabkowski, & Spee, 2020, chapter 7B; Goldenstein & Walgenbach, 2020, chapter 6A). At the same time, however, there is ample opportunity to take advantage of some newer microfoundational lenses, such as inhabited institutionalism (Hallett & Hawbaker, 2020, chapter 16B) and Scandinavian institutionalism (Surachaikulwattana & Phillips, 2020, chapter 14B). The chapters in this double volume connect to and expand the theoretical roots while also further developing nascent research streams. Without doubt, these are exciting times for research on microfoundations of institutions, and the collective effort we see in these chapters may help to "rejuvenate" institutional theory after its supposed "mid-life crisis" (Alvesson & Spicer, 2019).

Taken as a whole, the chapters of the double volume reflect the scholarly excitement and fascination with a microfoundational research agenda. However, at the same time, they also reveal some skepticism, unease, and concern and an impression that the value a microfoundational research agenda can bring to our understanding of institutional processes and outcomes requires further clarification. Extending previous critiques of a microfoundational research program in institutional theory (Jepperson & Meyer, 2011), skeptics point to the potential pitfalls of reductionism (Meyer, 2020, chapter 21B) and warn against the analytical primacy of the micro-level at the expense of the development of a holistic multi-level perspective (Hwang & Colyvas, 2020, chapter 17B; Powell, 2020, chapter 22B; Steele, Toubiana, & Greenwood, 2020, chapter 18B). At the same time, contributors point out that a dedicated analysis of micro-level dynamics is lacking and suspect that the promise of a microfoundational research agenda has not yet been entirely fulfilled (Felin & Foss, 2020, chapter 20B).

Importantly, what emerges from the chapters is that there is a lack of consensus in the use of the term microfoundations. Scholars seem to hold different understandings of what microfoundations of institutions are and also disagree about why and how we should study them. Our introductory chapter seeks to address these issues. We attempt to develop an overview of where the emerging microfoundational agenda stands and in which direction it is moving. Building upon the prologue by Tolbert and Zucker (2020, Prologue) and other volume contributions, we discuss the question of what microfoundations of institutions are, what the "micro" in microfoundations represents, why we use the plural form (microfoundations vs microfoundation), why microfoundations of institutions are needed, and how microfoundations can be studied. Specifically, we highlight that there are several traditions of microfoundational research and outline a cognitive, communicative and behavioral perspective; we also explain that in each of these perspectives scholars tend to think of microfoundations in terms of an *agency*, *levels*, or *mechanisms* argument. The chapters of this double volume thus reflect a pluralist conception of microfoundations. Embracing such a pluralist conception and viewing microfoundations not as a full-fledged theory but rather as an auxiliary framework in the explanation of institutional processes acknowledges that the concept of "institution" itself has been informed by a diverse set of traditions and ontological-epistemological assumptions (Scott, 2008).

While embracing a pluralist conception, we also believe that a common meaning of microfoundations is possible and important. This introductory chapter therefore advocates a minimal view of microfoundations and suggests that microfoundations of institutions develop an *explanatory* account of institutional phenomena which typically (but not exclusively) involve micro-level processes. In addition, we delineate methodological implications and discuss important challenges (and thus opportunities) for future research. We explain why we believe that the debate on microfoundations will become a defining element in the further development of institutional theory, and we posit that microfoundational research will be empowered (rather than constrained) by the exchange with its supposed antithesis – that is, the "macrofoundations" of institutions. As we shall elaborate below, a constructive microfoundational research agenda in institutional theory is necessarily not in opposition to, but inclusive of, the analysis of "macrofoundations." While the metaphor of "foundations" implies the primacy or at least the *relevance* of the micro-level, advocates of microfoundations must not ignore the macro-level and its interrelationship with more micro-levels.

WHAT ARE MICROFOUNDATIONS OF INSTITUTIONS?

Microfoundations come in many forms, but scholarly understandings of microfoundations are often left implicit. As a result, there is a lack of consensus regarding what the microfoundations of institutions are (Hwang & Colyvas, 2020, chapter 17B). What do researchers study when they study the microfoundations of institutions, and what are the different research traditions that inform microfoundational research? In response to these questions, we identified three different *perspectives* on microfoundational research in institutional theory, which we also used to structure the double volume into different sections. The perspectives reflect the different research traditions that have informed research on different types of microfoundations. All three perspectives are embedded within an "ideational" paradigm (Suddaby, 2010a) and focus on the convergence over meanings by means of shared cognitions, utterances, or activities of social actors (individuals, groups, organizations, etc.). Specifically, scholars have emphasized a *cognitive* perspective exploring how institutional change and maintenance are shaped by thought structures and emotions; a *communicative* perspective highlighting the role of various communicative means in developing an understanding of appropriate behavior; and a *behavioral* perspective exploring how daily activities and routines structure and restructure institutional contexts. These perspectives are not incompatible, and many chapters incorporate elements from two or even three perspectives. Nonetheless, most chapters prioritize one over the other. In addition to the three perspectives, the chapters of this double volume also advance three *conceptions* of microfoundations of institutions, which partly overlap but are analytically distinct from the three perspectives. Conceptions reflect the common yet often implicit understandings that scholars hold about the microfoundations of institutions. Specifically, in the context of the structure-agency debate, researchers often think of microfoundations in terms of *agency*, whereas the microfoundations as *levels* argument reflects a focus on variations in the abstraction or the spatial size of social action. In turn, the conception of microfoundations as *mechanisms* emphasizes theoretical explanations of the antecedents and effects of social action. Mechanism-based conceptions often comprise arguments of agency and levels, but levels and agency conceptions sometimes lack an elaboration of mechanisms; thus, despite some overlap, a tripartite classification seems useful. Indeed, although perspectives and conceptions intersect, pulling them analytically apart helps bring clarity to the complex and often confusing landscape of microfoundational research in institutional theory.

Perspectives on Microfoundations

Cognitive Perspective

The cognitive perspective on microfoundations of institutions is reflected by the seminal works of Berger and Luckmann (1967) and Zucker (1977), as well as more recent contributions by scholars such as Thornton, Ocasio, and Lounsbury (2012). These works have characterized institutions as "cognitive structures" (Phillips & Malhotra, 2008, p. 702) or "taken-for-granted facts" (Barley & Tolbert, 1997, p. 94). with the term "cognition" referring to individual and collective thought structures and mental representations, such as frames, categories, schemas, and scripts, that prescribe legitimate ways of acting (Cornelissen, Durand, Fiss, Lammers, & Vaara, 2015; Sieweke, 2014; Thornton et al., 2012). Proponents of the cognitive perspective insist that cognition is a defining concept in institutional theory (DiMaggio, 1997; DiMaggio & Powell, 1991; Thornton et al., 2012) and go as far as to argue that "it is this cognitive focus that provides the distinctiveness of institutional theory" (Phillips & Malhotra, 2008, p. 702). While the specific approaches, concepts, and phenomena mobilized and studied under the cognitive perspective are diverse, contributors to this perspective share the view that "the psychology of mental structures provides a microfoundation to the sociology of institutions" (DiMaggio, 1997, p. 271). The cognitive perspective applies a broad understanding of cognition that also comprises values and the emotional underpinnings of institutions (Voronov, 2014; Voronov & Vince, 2012).

The majority of chapters of this double volume can be classified under the heading of the cognitive perspective, and some important themes emerge from the joint body of these works. The "foundational" character of cognition is perhaps most clearly epitomized by the construct of identity, which has long been central to the cognitive perspective and which constitutes a defining theme in several chapters. Roberts (2020, chapter 11A) maps the trajectory of research on identity within the microfoundations literature in institutional theory; she identifies a significant shift from top-down, psychology-based approaches to more social constructionist and pluralist conceptions, with the latter viewing identity both as an antecedent to and outcome of institutions. Glynn and Innis (2020, chapter 5A) elucidate the bottom-up and transformational role of collective identity in the creation of institutions, while Hazan and Zilber (2020, chapter 7A) focus on the top-down influence of institutions on identity formation and the role of identity work in the gradual internalization of institutionalized beliefs and worldviews. Boulongne, Cudennec, and Durand (2020, chapter 2A) theorize that identity maintenance, understood as the need to preserve a clear identity, attenuates market experts' favorable evaluations of categorical deviance. Cholakova and Ravasi (2020, chapter 4A) draw on the concept of role identity to predict variation in individuals' responses to institutional complexity.

Sensemaking stands out as another important topic in the cognitive perspective. Drawing on the context of animal rights, Hu and Rerup (2020, chapter 8A) examine how sensegiving through YouTube videos can stimulate sensemaking and positive engagement of audiences. The authors find that sensegiving accounts only stimulate positive engaged sensemaking when these accounts resonate with the audience's existing values and sentiments. Their work identifies the micro-level dynamics that may help social activists to transform a taken-for-granted yet deeply flawed institutional order. Drawing on the phenomenological concept of the life world (Schutz & Luckmann, 1973), Brandl, Dreher, and Schneider (2020, chapter 3A) elucidate how decoupling prompts a sensemaking process about the tension between an individual's principles and the priorities of organizational decision makers. Their study complements previous research which has shown that organizational members are motivated to resolve tensions and actively work against decoupling (Hallett, 2010; Tolbert & Zucker, 1996).

Focusing on the topic of practice variation, Tolbert and Darabi (2020, chapter 13A) suggest that different types of institutional pressure (normative vs informational) explain heterogeneity in adoption motivation, which in turn explains post-adoption outcomes. Conceptualizing institutions as heterogeneously distributed forms of knowledge that are consensually agreed upon within interconnected yet varying micro-contexts, Keller (2020, chapter 9A) examines the critical role of individuals' perceived congruence with the consensus of sub-cultures to explain heterogeneity in the institutionalization of corporate ethics practices.

Finally, several chapters study institutional change and institutionalization. Lizardo (2020, chapter 10A) specifies the set of "objects" that get institutionalized and thus sheds light on the "building blocks" of institutions. He argues that the most fundamental object that gets institutionalized is culture, which exists both in people (through internalization and learning) and in the world (through individuals' meaning-construction and objectification processes). In both cases, people are necessary to "keep institutions going" (Lizardo, 2020, chapter 10A, p. 224), which is why it is crucial for institutional theorists to develop microfoundations of institutions. Goldenstein and Walgenbach (2020, chapter 6A) argue that discursive and practical consciousness constitute two different kinds of taken-for-grantedness. Mapping the two kinds of taken-for-grantedness onto two kinds of institutional infrastructure (low vs high) yields four types of institutional changes. Goldenstein and Walgenbach point out that two of the four types (i.e., the types associated with practical consciousness) have remained largely unexplored and require increased attention. Roulet, Paollela, Gabbioneta, and Muzio (2020, chapter 12A) show how the aggregated characteristics of organizational members explain why organizations deviate from institutionalized practices. Bitektine and Nason (2020, chapter 1A) advance the idea that public, administrative, and legal domains of institutional action constitute a critical meso-level of analysis, which mediates the influence of the micro on the macro-level of legitimacy, a point that resonates with the work of Hallett and Hawbaker (2020, chapter 16B), who advocate social interaction as a meso-level of analysis.

In sum, while cognitive approaches to microfoundations have been criticized for being too atomistic and reducing "social reality to individual and collective cognitive categories" (Cornelissen et al., 2015, p. 11), the chapters of the present double volume demonstrate that cognition can serve as a critical window into the recursive relationships between the macro- and micro-levels of institutions.

Communicative Perspective
Several institutional scholars have highlighted the significance of communication for creating, shaping, and disrupting institutions, emphasizing that at "its core, institutional theory is a theory of communication" (Suddaby, 2011, p. 188). By "communication," this perspective refers to social interaction that draws on discourse (Phillips, Lawrence, & Hardy, 2004; Vaara & Monin, 2010), framing (Lefsrud & Meyer, 2012; Meyer & Höllerer, 2010), rhetoric (Green, 2004; Suddaby & Greenwood, 2005), narratives (Haack, Schoeneborn, & Wickert, 2012; Hardy & Maguire, 2010), tropes (Sillince & Barker, 2012), and other communicative means. The communicative perspective is influenced by social constructionism, ethnomethodology, and structuration theory, as well as linguistic philosophy, ranging from Wittgenstein's (1953) "language games" to Searle's (1969) "speech acts." Ontologically, communication is said to amount to a relational construct, which is defined as "a process of interaction within which actors exchange views and build up mutual understanding" (Cornelissen et al., 2015, p. 16). A central insight of the communicative perspective is that communication *constitutes* institutions, rather than simply transmitting them in the sense of sending and receiving messages as conceptualized in the "conduit metaphor" (Reddy, 1979). At the same time, the communicative perspective acknowledges that institutions that emerge from communication are unlikely to fully resemble the intentions of involved actors, given the nonlinear and contingent properties of language use (Suddaby, 2011).

An important theme that emerges from the double volume is that communication offers a means to analyze and make visible the taken-for-grantedness of institutions. For instance, Lok, Creed, and DeJordy (2020, chapter 4B) advance the point that the capacity for agency is not fully autonomous from the institutions toward which it is directed but rather emerges endogenously through a process of self-identity construction that responds to specific conventions of narrative necessity. Their research thus highlights that agency can be considered to constitute a socially constructed outcome of the narrative enactment of institutional constraints. In a similar vein, Harmon (2020, chapter 1B) elaborates that argument structure reflects the latent and taken-for-granted structure of institutions. Analyzing argument structure thus allows for mapping processes of institutionalization, and Harmon derives important methodological implications from this insight. Tchalian (2020, chapter 6B) draws on newly developed computational methods to develop a mixed-methods framework for discourse analysis, which allows him to align small-scale and large-scale textual analysis to detect theoretically relevant (but often latent) associations. Tchalian proposes that these associations demarcate the boundary between micro- and macro-levels and thus help researchers identify the mechanisms linking levels. Islam, Rüling, and Schüßler (2020, chapter 2B) show that critique made by various actors at climate change conferences is embedded in rituals of legitimate communication, constraining critics' influence on global governance and public policy. Both Harmon (2020, chapter 1B) and Islam and colleagues (2020, chapter 2B) allude to the role of taken-for-grantedness for maintaining the status quo and existing power relationships, reminding us that research on the microfoundations of institutions may have important normative implications (e.g., Amis, Munir, & Mair, 2017). Soppe and Pershina (2020, chapter 5B) elucidate how organizational storytelling allows actors to mitigate the tensions between conflicting institutional demands in the context of wildlife documentaries. The authors identify specific narrative strategies and also highlight the crucial role of emotion in balancing institutional demands. Lefsrud and Vaara (2020, chapter 3B) explore the formation of moral legitimacy over time by examining the change in prevalent frames that regulatory actors and the media use to construct fairness. Their chapter exemplifies not only the fact that legitimacy judgments are subject to contestation and social construction but also the individual and collective criteria that actors use to make such judgments.

Taken as the whole, the "communicative" chapters of this double volume shed light on the links between communication and the cognitive aspects of institutions, reminding us that cognition, communication, and institutions are inherently intertwined (Cornelissen et al., 2015). The chapters also raise important questions regarding the constraining influence of institutions and the level of agency actors command once these institutions give rise to the formation of legitimate genres of communication.

Behavioral Perspective
The behavioral perspective focuses on how practices, understood as clusters of recurrent human activity informed by shared institutional meanings (Schatzki, 1996), shape and are shaped by institutions (Barley & Tolbert, 1997). Hence, this perspective highlights that institutions "are not fixed in some structural order but are continuously and flexibly instantiated in the momentary processes by which individuals adjust to any given situation" (Smets, Jarzabkowski, Burke, & Spee, 2015, p. 937). The behavioral perspective has its roots in social constructionism (Berger & Luckmann, 1967), symbolic interactionism (Goffman, 1959),

and practice theories (Giddens, 1984). It draws on a process ontology whereby practices, while being institutionally embedded, also have the potential to (de-) stabilize institutions (Barley & Tolbert, 1997; Lawrence & Suddaby, 2006). Hence, this perspective takes a moderating stance between voluntarism and determinism by emphasizing how competent actors continuously (re)produce the institutions in which they are embedded (Smets et al., 2015; Zilber, 2002). Similar to the communicative perspective, the focal unit of analysis of the behavioral perspective is not the individual but rather the actions of and between individuals. The idea that individuals matter for institutions seems to be uncontroversial and constitute an ontological truism (Jepperson & Meyer, 2011). However, it is through the day-to-day practices and interactions of individuals (and collectives of individual actors, such as groups and organizations) that institutions exert their influence. For example, the studies by Smets and Jarzabkowski (2013) and Smets, Morris, and Greenwood (2012) underscore the criticality of studying interactions in order to advance microfoundational theorizing.

The contributions to this double volume draw on and extend the behavioral perspective in several ways. On the one hand, several chapters can be seen as consistent with "practice-driven institutionalism," whose agenda is to strengthen the ties between practice studies and institutional theory (Smets, Aristidou, & Whittington, 2017). Anesa et al. (2020, chapter 7B) draw on Bourdieu's theory of practice to explore how action can be oriented toward contradictory practices that are enacted simultaneously by the same actor across fields, and Eliasoph, Lo, and Glaser (2020, chapter 8B) explore how interaction orders come into being in settings of institutional complexity. These works offer important intellectual stimuli in that they explore links between practices, fields, logics, and institutions in ways that emphasize the importance of social interactions. Similarly, Furnari (2020, chapter 10B) attends to the importance of social situations and their potential for bolstering the transformational potential of social interactions. According to Furnari, institutional logics pattern "situational frames" that help individuals to comprehend specific situations and the institutionalized expectations that come with them. However, whether what he calls "situated actions" correspond with these frames is not fully predetermined by logics. Instead, interactions "on the ground" can lead to novel and unanticipated events and outcomes (see also Powell, 2020, chapter 22B). Jones, Lee, and Lee (2020, chapter 11B) focus on material practices and discuss institutional theorizing in relationship to social studies of technology and investigate how meaning, location, and material interact in the institutionalization and deinstitutionalization of place.

In addition to studies that advance linkages between practices and institutions, several chapters mobilize the concept of power to better understand how and under what circumstances, practices can be carried out. Studying hybrid professional organizations, Malhotra and Reay (2020, chapter 12B) bring to the fore the idea that the practice-institution nexus should be studied with an eye toward the role of different forms of power in managing tensions among competing logics in everyday work practices. Power is also central to Ruotsalainen (2020, chapter

13B) who advances our understanding of how actors with limited power can drive change and acquire the capacity to take institutional actions. In returning to some of the fundamental questions that matter for the behavioral perspective, Surachaikulwattana and Phillips (2020, chapter 14B) and Fohim (2020, chapter 9B) conceptualize micro–macro links in relation to practices and actions. Surachaikulwattana and Phillips leverage the "garbage can" model to explain the translation of an organizational form into a novel institutional context. Fohim contributes to the "institutional entrepreneurship" concept by identifying relevant skills of entrepreneurs. He stresses that skills do not merely reflect psychological traits but are the outcome of higher- and lower-level influences.

Cumulatively, the "behavioral" chapters in this double volume offer fruitful ways to advance microfoundational theorizing with a focus on actions and interactions. On the one hand, topics such as situations and materiality directly correspond with the research agenda that practice-driven institutionalism has initiated. On the other hand, there are important new ideas to be added to work that is focused on exploring the link between actions and institutions, including, but not limited to, power, translation, and skills.

Conceptions of Microfoundations

In addition to the aforementioned three perspectives, the chapters of this double volume also advance three common understandings, or *conceptions*, of the microfoundations of institutions. These conceptions form the background in scholars' theorizing but are rarely made explicit. Although the three conceptions overlap, they are analytically distinct and thus should be discussed separately.

Microfoundations as Agency

A first prominent conception of microfoundations of institutions is reflected in the "microfoundations as agency" argument. Proponents of this understanding see the microfoundations of institutions as tightly linked to agency and the capacity for purposeful action. As different forms of agency are reflected in the influential concepts of "institutional work" (Lawrence & Suddaby, 2006), "institutional entrepreneurship"(Battilana, Leca, & Boxenbaum, 2009), and, more recently, "institutional logics" (Smets et al., 2015), there has been almost a natural tendency in institutional theory to explain stability and change at aggregate levels through actors' agency. Considering that actors are said to be "embedded" within institutions, to be "constrained" or "empowered" by institutions, or otherwise to "inhabit" institutions (Hallett & Hawbaker, 2020, chapter 16B), scholars have sought to understand how the tension between agency and structure can conceptually and practically be solved. Indeed, microfoundations not only are equated with agency but also are often construed as a conceptual means to solve the tensions between agency and structure and tackle the "paradox of embedded agency" (Battilana et al., 2009). For instance, by suggesting that structure "orients" action toward certain possibilities and that agency is not only strategic but also pre-reflective in nature, Cardinale (2018, p. 148) suggests that he has developed "new microfoundations of institutions" that help "reconcile insights that have long been seen as conflicting in institutional theory."

An understanding of microfoundations as agency serves as the background for many of the chapters of this double volume. Not surprisingly, microfoundations as an agency constitutes the dominant understanding in the behavioral perspective; however, we also see this understanding reflected in the cognitive perspective (Goldenstein & Walgenbach, 2020, chapter 6A) and the communicative perspective (Lok et al., 2020, chapter 4B).

Microfoundations as Levels

Harmon, Haack, and Roulet (2019) highlight that "agency" and "structure" do not map consistently onto "micro" and "macro," respectively; rather, there are macro-instances of agency (e.g., social movements and collective action) as well as micro-instances of structure (e.g., habitus and routines). It follows that levels can be said to be analytically orthogonal to the agency-structure dichotomy. The "microfoundations as levels" argument thus constitutes a second prominent understanding of the microfoundations of institutions. It is informed by a "layered" ontology which conceives of institutions as nested systems that are hierarchically structured along different levels of analysis (Holm, 1995). "Levels of analysis" are often understood in spatial terms, in the sense that lower, "micro" levels comprise entities of smaller spatial size (e.g., an organization), whereas higher, "macro" levels represent a larger scale or "collection" of lower-level entities (e.g., an institutional field in which the organization is nested). Levels of analysis may also refer to degrees of causal complexity or abstraction, a question that is distinct from the question of scale (Jepperson & Meyer, 2011). While individuals play a contested role in the intellectual history of institutional theory (Boxenbaum, 2020, chapter 15B), they represent a special case of the microfoundations as levels argument (Felin et al., 2015). Indeed, "micro" and "macro" are relative terms given that any actor or entity is "micro" in relation to something and "macro" in relation to something else. Thus, it is important to make explicit one's understanding of "micro" and "macro" and explain why a given level should (or should not) be granted analytical primacy (Harmon et al., 2019). Finally, levels tend to be associated with certain disciplines, such as psychology and sociology. In these contexts, the microfoundations as levels argument is applied rather loosely to emphasize the merit of an interdisciplinary approach (e.g., when integrating psychological research into institutional theory, see Lefsrud & Vaara, 2020, chapter 3B).

Several chapters of this double volume draw on the microfoundations as levels argument in developing their contributions. While some authors make their understanding of institutions as layered and nested systems explicit, such as by conceptually distinguishing levels and modeling them as such (Keller, 2020, chapter 9A; Roulet et al., 2020, chapter 12A), in other contributions the reference to levels is less explicit but nevertheless forms the background of the researchers' theorizing (Harmon, 2020, chapter 1B; Lefsrud & Vaara, 2020, chapter 3B). In addition, the levels argument is not equally popular across the three microfoundations perspectives. For instance, while the "behavioral" chapter of Surachaikulwattana and Phillips (2020, chapter 14B) develop a levels argument to explain the translation of an organizational form, most contributors to the behavioral perspective abstain from level-based theorizing. This is perhaps not surprising, given that practice scholars have advocated a flat ontology, suggesting that the notion of levels is analytically at odds with an understanding of social action as inherently relational and reciprocal (Seidl & Whittington, 2014). In some chapters, we also noticed a concern with the term "microfoundations" as such, on the grounds that the notion of "foundations" implies a layered ontology, while the "micro" in microfoundations signals the primacy of lower levels of analysis, which some may consider to be inconsistent with what they perceive to be the onto-epistemological assumptions in institutional theory (Boxenbaum, 2020, chapter 15B; Hwang & Colyvas, 2020, chapter 17B).

Microfoundations as Mechanisms

Microfoundations are sometimes treated as quasi-synonymous with causal mechanisms. "Mechanisms" can be defined as "theoretical explanations of why focal phenomena or effects occur" (Davis & Marquis, 2005, p. 336). Mechanisms offer analytical tools above pure description and below universal law that contribute to make a theory "more supple, more accurate, or more general" (Stinchcombe, 1991, p. 367). While there are mechanisms that do not operate across different levels (e.g., action formation mechanisms; see below), the understanding of microfoundations as mechanisms is often combined with a levels argument. The reverse does not necessarily apply, as works drawing on the microfoundations as levels argument often fail to unambiguously identify relevant mechanisms.

When discussing cross- and within-level mechanisms, institutional theorists follow the broader microfoundations literature in strategy (Felin et al., 2015) and sociology (Hedström & Swedberg, 1998) and draw on the Coleman ("bathtub") model as depicted in Fig. 2.

Research has typically focused on three types of mechanisms (Hwang & Colyvas, 2020, chapter 17B; Weber & Glynn, 2006): a *situational* mechanism, through which the macro-level institutional context feeds into, triggers, or modifies the cognitions, judgments, and interpretations of actors at the micro-level

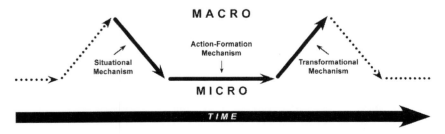

Fig. 2. "Bathtub" Model.

(macro–micro or "top-down" transition); an *action formation* mechanism, which explains how the aforementioned cognitions, judgments, and interpretations generate action at the micro-level (micro–micro transition); and a *transformational* mechanism, through which actions and interactions "scale-up" and coalesce into shifts in the taken-for-granted beliefs and expectations at the macro-level (micro–macro, or "bottom-up," transition). In this mechanism-based view of microfoundations, institutional maintenance and change are the outcome of a reciprocal and bi-directional relationship between inter-subjective processes among individual or collective actors and the extra-subjective realm of the institutional context (Bitektine & Haack, 2015; Gray, Purdy, & Ansari, 2015; Weber & Glynn, 2006). Fig. 2 also recognizes that microfoundations, if understood as mechanisms, imply a temporal dimension in which a macro-level explanans causes a macro-level explanandum over time, through situational, action-formation, and transformational mechanisms. Importantly, similar to a struturationist "flow model" of social action (Barley & Tolbert, 1997; Phillips, Lawrence, & Hardy, 2004), the explanandum of a first bathtub may constitute the explanans of a second bathtub, which through situational, action-formation, and transformational mechanisms generates the explanandum of the second bathtub, which in turn constitutes the explanans of a third bathtub, and so forth.

Fig. 2 depicts a parsimonious model of mechanism-based theorizing. One could easily develop a more complex model which acknowledges that institutions are nested systems that comprise more than two levels of analysis (Jepperson & Meyer, 2011). In this nested view, a specific level can be "macro" for one entity but "micro" for another, constituting a critical "meso" level of analysis. The number of these intermediate meso-levels can be fairly large. Each level (or layer), in such a model, can be assumed to be connected through situational, action-formation, or transformational mechanisms. The mechanisms can be assumed to affect the micro-level (the "bottom" of the bathtub) either indirectly through the facilitation of intermediate levels or directly without the facilitation of intermediate levels.

When advancing the microfoundations as mechanism argument, all three mechanisms fall under the microfoundations umbrella. Naturally, contributions to this double volume differ in terms of which of the "edges" of the bathtub they prioritize. Most chapters applying the microfoundations as mechanism view focus on situational mechanisms ("macrofoundations"). This is perhaps not surprising given that a huge body of literature has conceived of institutions as a context and explanans for other phenomena, while focusing less on the *process* of institutionalization (Meyer, Jancsary, Höllerer, & Boxenbaum, 2018; Tolbert & Zucker, 1996). Within the subset of volume chapters, only a few chapters examine instances of the action-formation mechanism, such as Hu and Rerup (2020, chapter 8A), who elaborate on why audience members become engaged and willing to take action. Moreover, only a few chapters discuss transformational mechanisms or hint at the transformational potential of transitions and/or interactions at lower levels (Bitektine & Nason, 2020, chapter 1A; Glynn & Innis, 2020, chapter 5A; Jones et al., 2020, chapter 11B).

Configurations of Microfoundational Research

Naturally, there is some overlap in our taxonomy of perspectives and conceptions. For example, the works under the communicative perspective also invoke cognition (Harmon, 2020, chapter 1B) and vice versa (Lizardo, 2020, chapter 10A), and works that construe microfoundations primarily in terms of agency are also concerned with the analysis of multiple levels (Surachaikulwattana & Phillips, 2020, chapter 14B). When editing the chapters, we also noticed that certain perspectives tend to be combined with certain conceptions of microfoundations, leading to specific *configurations*. Mapping perspectives onto conceptions to create a 3 × 3 matrix and then reviewing how much research has been conducted in each of the nine cells (or, in clusters comprising more than one cell) would allow researchers to identify common configurations in microfoundational research. Note that the cells of this matrix are not mutually exclusive in a typological sense but rather represent distinct but overlapping analytical devices. While it is not our intention to provide conclusive quantitative evidence, the present double volume nevertheless seems to reflect at least three common configurations: 1) a configuration combining the microfoundations as agency argument with the behavioral perspective, 2) a configuration combining the microfoundations as agency argument with the communicative perspective, and 3) a configuration combining the levels and mechanism arguments with the cognitive perspective. It is evident that significant research opportunities exist in the development of hitherto largely unexplored configurations, such as research combining the cognitive perspective with a conception of microfoundations as agency, as Goldenstein and Walgenbach (2020, chapter 6A) advocate. Future research may also want to examine whether the assumptions of both the three perspectives and the three conceptions are proximate enough to justify theoretical integration and form a coherent microfoundational theory of institutions.

SHOULD WE FOREGROUND LEVELS OF ANALYSIS?

An important insight that has emerged from the editorial process is that it is helpful for scholars to unambiguously reveal and make explicit their understanding(s) of microfoundations and the perspective(s) from which they address microfoundations. If they do not do so, the members of the nascent microfoundations community are at risk of talking past each other, making the accumulation of knowledge difficult and time-consuming (Harmon et al., 2019). While we are excited by the literature's depth and diversity, we contend that construct clarity is essential for the accumulation of scientific knowledge, especially for institutional theorists as scholars drawing on a social-constructionist epistemology (Suddaby, 2010b). Hence, we take up the suggestion of Felin and Foss (2020, chapter 20B) and propose a "minimal" view of the microfoundations of institutions to help reach a consensus on the "essence" of this line of inquiry. This minimal view is informed by our contention that microfoundational research in institutional theory can be significantly advanced by foregrounding the analysis of levels and mechanisms (Weber, 2006; Weber & Glynn, 2006). While conceptualizing microfoundations as "level-free" and as grounded in a flat or relational ontology has gained some currency, some important analytical benefits come with embracing a layered ontology, specifically with respect to the identification of causal mechanisms. A layered ontology offers an important analytical heuristic to account for how institutional phenomena play out in micro-contexts and how these dynamics and interactions coalesce into social structures at the macro-level (Jones et al., 2020, chapter 11B). If researchers do not take cross-level interactions into account, they risk looking at micro-level practice with little significance beyond the immediate context. In addition, theorizing multiple layers makes otherwise complex and abstract macro-level constructs such as institutional logics more tangible and assessable. Hence, following the "bathtub" model (Fig. 2), the minimal view of microfoundations of institutions entails that microfoundations comprise multiple, interconnected levels of analysis. In this view, a "full-cycle" microfoundational explanation comprises an analysis of multiple levels and of the interaction across these levels.

Importantly, microfoundations, in their minimal view, require an *explanatory* account of the interdependence of multiple levels of analysis and thus a consideration of mechanisms. Within a microfoundational perspective, this explanatory account involves *typically* more micro-levels (including the "meso" level, which, relative to higher levels, is a "micro" level). While not ruling out the existence of "pure" macro-level mechanisms, microfoundational research acknowledges the *relevance* of the micro-level and draws on micro-level theorizing to explain changes and/or heterogeneity at more macro-levels. Naturally, the choice for prioritizing more micro levels and micro mechanisms needs to be guided by theory rather than by taste, ideology, or the conventional research approaches in a given community. Treatises of microfoundations in institutional theory tend to argue that institutions are enacted, though not necessarily created or changed, by individual actors that may "carry" institutions (Scott, 2008). However, while institutional theorists have emphasized that micro-level units (including individual actors) are institutional constructions that are informed or even determined by roles, responsibilities, behavioral scripts, and models of actorhood (Barley & Tolbert, 1997; Meyer & Jepperson, 2000), institutional theory's "macrofoundations" should not be treated as a given. Rather, we need to acknowledge that "macrofoundations" and the status of social facticity and exteriority that is inherent to institutions come from *somewhere*. Applying a microfoundational perspective clarifies that the institutional context is the outcome of, and is molded by, a social construction process that involves local interactions "on the ground." These interactions and the unanticipated outcomes they generate at more aggregated levels constitute an important explanandum in their own right (Furnari, 2020, chapter 10B; Hallett & Hawbaker, 2020, chapter 16B). Thus, while the macro definitely affects the micro, the micro also helps illuminate the origin and effects of the macro (Lizardo, 2020, chapter 10A).

Acknowledging this insight, some of the seminal concepts in institutional theory have been recently "remodeled" as multi-level and inherently reciprocal constructs. Such remodeling has been accomplished for institutional logics (Thornton et al., 2012), legitimacy (Bitektine & Haack, 2015), institutional change (Smets et al., 2012), and the construct of "institution" itself (Gray et al., 2015; Weber & Glynn,

2006). Some of the chapters of this double volume hint at the possibility that such a multi-level view can be fruitfully extended to other not yet "remodeled" concepts in institutional theory. For instance, advancing a multi-level perspective of decoupling would require acknowledging that the decoupling concept focuses simultaneously on the societal pervasiveness of rational myths and the interpretative work individual actors invest to "pull down" and translate these myths to the everyday practicalities of local contexts (Steele et al., 2020, chapter 18B). Such a multi-level perspective of decoupling would place emphasis on the sensemaking activities of organizational members, showing that they are able and willing to attribute meaning to the anomalies and contradictions in decoupled settings, problematize these conflicts, and develop solutions for them, thereby generating and reproducing new understandings and practices that become institutionalized (e.g., Hallett, 2010). Seminal institutional theory constructs such as legitimacy and decoupling thus essentially operate at multiple levels, and there are huge gains to be had from modeling them as such. The need to make these multiple levels explicit and subject to theorizing and empirical testing logically follows from this insight.

WHY DO WE NEED MICROFOUNDATIONS OF INSTITUTIONS?

Microfoundational research is important because the knowledge of how cognition, communication, and behavior at micro-levels affect and are affected by higher-level structures allows scholars to develop an improved understanding of heterogeneity in institutional outcomes, as well as of the circumstances under which institutions persist or change (Powell, 2020, chapter 22B; Zucker & Schilke, 2020, chapter 19B). In this view, microfoundations are indeed "foundational" for institutional theory, as they facilitate the development of better theory. Microfoundations if understood as a foregrounding of levels of analysis and micro-mechanisms, can improve the robustness and explanatory power of institutional research. This point is eminently summarized by Lynne Zucker in the postscript of her 1991 "orange" book chapter (Zucker, 1991, pp. 105–106).

> Without a solid cognitive, micro-level foundation, we risk treating institutionalization as a black box at the organizational level, focusing on content at the exclusion of developing a systematic explanatory theory of process, conflating institutionalization with resource dependency, and neglecting institutional variation and persistence. Although important insights can be gained by examining the content of institutions, there is an ever-present danger of making the institutionalist enterprise a taxonomic rather than an explanatory, theory-building exercise. Institutional theory is always in danger of forgetting that labeling a process or structure does not explain it.

The quest for (cognitive, communicative, and behavioral) microfoundations must also be seen as a critique of the existing focus on single-level explanations that fail to incorporate situational and transformational mechanisms. Indeed, there seems to be a growing concern that a

> "taxonomic" approach has come to dominate institutional theory while there has been little attention paid to developing an explanation for the process of production of institutions in the first place. (Phillips & Malhotra, 2008, p. 393)

Tolbert and Zucker (2020, Prologue, p. 4) see a lack of "causal specificity" in research on institutional logics, asserting that scholarship has focused "on different organizational types that behave differently, rather than on the roots of these differences." Zucker and Schilke (2020, chapter 19B, p. 381) likewise encourage scholars to "avoid imprecise concepts such as diffusion that encompass a wide range of quite different underlying mechanisms causing practices to remain stable or new practices to be adopted."

In private conversations with contributors to this double volume, we sensed a general dissatisfaction with the explanatory power of mainstream institutional theory. Scholars are not content with the vague and inconsistent definitions of institutional theory's core concepts and are worried that the theory's interpretative capacity is fading. It may be the case that the "big tent" of institutional theory has become too voluminous, with institutional theory moving from an explanatory theory to an identity movement or "brand" (Alvesson, Hallett, & Spicer, 2019). Indeed, there tends to be a substantial amount of "evangelism" in institutional theory, and "institutional terminology seems to have become a prefix used to signal desired membership in a certain research community, rather than indicating the actual study of institutions" (Meyer & Höllerer, 2014, p. 1230). Astley (1985, p. 505) commented on the evangelistic character of scientific fields, noting that "the theories that gain dominance are those that are able to win the most converts; they need not necessarily have greater explanatory power to emerge victorious." In this context, it seems evident that advancing a microfoundational research agenda can enhance the empirical validation, rigor, and explanatory power of institutional theory.

It is our contention that side-stepping the issue of multi-level complexity on the grounds that it would bedevil empirical research or conceptual development, or assuming homogeneity at micro levels instead of studying it, unduly replaces the process of scientific inquiry with intellectual fatalism. However, Meyer (2020, chapter 21B) and Jepperson and Meyer (2011) remind us that explanation does not *automatically* require a micro-level account, and these scholars bring to the fore macro-mechanisms, which they see as foundational to institutions. While the minimal view posits that microfoundations of institutions *typically* involve an explanatory account at the micro-level, the "criterion for whether it is worthwhile to theorize at lower levels is whether it makes the theory at the higher levels better, not whether lower-level theorizing is philosophically necessary" (Stinchcombe, 1991, p. 367). Thus, the relevant question is not *whether* microfoundations are needed, but *when*. It is our conviction that microfoundations are needed rather often and that a microfoundational research agenda, if understood as a holistic, comprehensive, and integrative effort of multi-level theorizing, can bring profound insights and huge benefits to institutional theory (Steele et al., 2020, chapter 18B). Indeed, a full microfoundational explanation comprises situational mechanisms and thus covers what advocates of the term "macrofoundations" seem to have in mind. We suspect that the term "macrofoundations" reflects an unarticulated fear of a "positivist capture" and a fear that microfoundations scholars will "psychologize" institutional theory, removing it from its intellectual roots in social constructionism and phenomenology. We hope that this double volume demonstrates the opposite: that is, that microfoundations, if embedded in the larger conversation on multi-level research, enable scholars to re-connect to the intellectual origins of institutional theory and develop richer and more powerful theory (Zucker & Schilke, 2020, chapter 19B).

Several of the chapters in this double volume open the "black box" of institutions and illustrate the benefits and explanatory power that emerge from doing so. For instance, Tolbert and Darabi (2020, chapter 13A) highlight the distinction between normative and informational conformity, which reflect a desire for social approval and a desire for accuracy in making decisions. Different kinds of institutional pressures thus generate variations in motives for conformity – an insight that has been largely ignored by institutional theorists. Tolbert and Darabi show how the explicit recognition of different motives can improve our understanding of the heterogeneity in adoption decisions and post-adoption behavior, extending the work of Bitektine and Haack (2015), which highlighted that a seemingly stable and institutionalized macrostructure may mask significant heterogeneity in judgments and motives at the micro-level. Chapters in this double volume also highlight the crucial role of cognitive, communicative, and behavioral elements in explaining heterogeneity and change at more macro-levels. For instance, Cholakova and Ravasi (2020, chapter 4A) expand the works of Schilke (2018) and Raaijmakers et al. (2015) by suggesting that the complexity of individuals' cognitions of institutional logics and their role identities explain variations in individuals' perception of and response to institutional complexity. Meanwhile, Furnari (2020, chapter 10B) and Hallett and Hawbaker (2020, chapter 16B) elucidate the transformational potential of social interactions. The volume chapters offer valuable illustrations of when and why microfoundations of institutions are needed and how microfoundational research can help strengthen the explanatory power of institutional theory.

Ultimately, microfoundational research can also make institutional theory more "relevant" for developing practical implications. The presumed dichotomy between "rigor" and "relevance" seems nonsensical when considering real organizational and (grand) societal challenges. Most problems that managers and policy makers face imply phenomena at multiple levels, and the development of sound policy implications needs to consider these multiple levels. It follows that microfoundational research, with its explicit recognition of micro- and cross-level mechanisms, brings us closer to the reality and complexity of organizational practice and governance.

HOW CAN WE STUDY MICROFOUNDATIONS OF INSTITUTIONS?

Although the call for microfoundations of institutions has generated much positive response and yielded important conceptual contributions, thus far we have seen relatively little empirical research activity (Tchalian, 2020, chapter 6B). This is perhaps not surprising given that empirical research on microfoundations involves processes and variables at multiple levels of analysis and thus poses a challenge to model and test interactions and relationships within and across these levels. This challenge is echoed in the three perspectives to the extent that the methods that are typically used in the context of these perspectives are often rooted in capturing only one level of analysis.

Addressing the challenge of multi-level research thus requires that scholars update their methodological toolkit; develop novel research designs; and advance their sampling, data collection, and data analysis strategies. Scholars have suggested that a narrow set of measurement techniques and research approaches has constrained theory development on the microfoundations of institutions, such as when researchers employ proxies for institutions that are too distant from their ideational aspects and underlying meaning systems (Suddaby, 2010b; Zucker, 1989). The over-reliance on a narrow set of methods may thus have limited the ability of institutional theorists to address many pivotal questions on micro-level and multi-level institutional processes: "Standard research strategies are much more attuned to the covariance of factors than to the processes that underlie the production of institutional effects" (Schneiberg & Clemens, 2006, p. 200). Hence, while cross-sectional research designs provide snapshots of top-down influences and may help scholars to explore the impact of macro-level contexts on micro-level cognition, communication, and behavior, they seem less suited to examine the process dynamics and interactions that are constitutive of macro-level phenomena (Eckardt et al., 2019).

The study of the microfoundations of institutions and of the multi-level dynamics of institutional processes presupposes methodological diversity – or, more precisely, the elaboration and application of methodologies that are appropriate for the analysis of interactions across multiple levels and of the emergent properties of processes at the micro-level. The chapters in this double volume attest that there are plenty of opportunities for methodological innovation. Adding to these contributions, we would like to highlight three important avenues for future microfoundational research: mixed-methods approaches, multi-level analysis, and experimental research.

Mixed Methods

The term *mixed methods* refers to a combination of quantitative and qualitative approaches and it is presumed that a triangulation of different methods offers a better understanding of complex multi-level phenomena than either approach alone. Elsbach's (1994) study on legitimation exemplifies the merits of a mixed-methods approach. Her study qualitatively examined the verbal accounts used by organizational spokespersons to manage legitimacy in the California cattle industry and then assessed experimentally the effectiveness of these accounts, showing that accounts that combined acknowledgments with references to institutionalized characteristics resonated more strongly with the cognitions and expectations of relevant audiences. The chapters by Soppe and Pershina (2020, chapter 5B) and Tchalian (2020, chapter 6B) exemplify the value of mixed-methods approaches in advancing multi-level explanations in institutional theory. Certainly, a mixed-methods approach need not be present in every single article, but such an approach can be advanced within a larger "ecology" of research articles, while the integration of research findings can be accomplished with the help of systematic reviews and meta-analyses (Steele et al., 2020, chapter 18B).

As the use of mixed-methods approaches is far from institutionalized and deviates from established methodological approaches, such approaches pose opportunities and risks for researchers. On the one hand, given that researchers rarely use multiple methods that inform each other, mixed-methods research may become an important differentiator in publication decisions. On the other hand, mixed methods can be risky because there is a lack of standard procedures for using them, and submissions may attract reviewers with different disciplinary backgrounds and fundamentally different expectations regarding "good research" (Wright, Coff, & Moliterno, 2014). These strategic considerations notwithstanding, a good deal of risk-taking seems worthwhile, as the potential return on the investment is large.

Multi-level Analysis

Institutional scholars have long developed multi-level theory (e.g., institutional work or institutional logics) and used mostly qualitative methods to investigate situational, action-formation, and transformational mechanisms. To further advance our understanding of the microfoundations of institutions, we recommend the application of quantitative multi-level analysis. Multi-level analysis – or hierarchical linear modeling – considers the nestedness of units (e.g., individuals) within higher-level units (e.g., teams or organizations). Although multi-level analysis has become influential in management research (e.g., Hitt, Beamish, Jackson, & Mathieu, 2007; Paruchuri, Perry-Smith, Chattopadhyay, & Shaw, 2018), it is not yet established as a research approach in institutional theory. The present double volume includes two notable exceptions. First, Roulet et al. (2020, chapter 12A) use multi-level models with observations of employees nested within firms to explore how individual characteristics and organizational characteristics are related to the erosion and emergence of practices within the field of UK law firms. Keller (2020, chapter 9A) applies cultural consensus theory to link variance in individuals' micro-level conditions with cross-level variance in individuals' adoption of macro-level socially constructed knowledge.

These two works and the body of research upon which they draw can inspire future institutional research on situational and transformational mechanisms. With respect to situational mechanisms, we suggest that institutional theorists can learn much from research on organizational climate. Organizational climate refers to employees' shared perceptions of organizational policies and practices and their shared perception of behaviors that are supported and expected within an organization (Schneider, Ehrhart, & Macey, 2013). It follows that organizational climate may – at least to some extent – capture institutions within an organization; thus, organizational climate research is potentially relevant for institutional researchers from a method perspective, because climate researchers have gathered broad experience with regard to the analysis of macro–micro relationships within organizations (i.e., the situational mechanism) and with regard to whether and when researchers can aggregate individual-level beliefs and perceptions to form higher-level constructs. This knowledge is of value for institutional researchers who aim to analyze the recursive relationship between institutions (e.g., shared and taken-for-granted beliefs and behaviors of employees within an organization) and the beliefs and behavior of individuals (Zilber, 2012).

With respect to transformational mechanisms, we deem it important to analyze the emergence of institutions and the machinery through which taken-for-granted beliefs and behaviors coalesce into institutions. Analyzing transformational mechanisms and the process dynamics of emergent properties is important for institutional theory, as these mechanisms and dynamics may offer important insights into the origin of institutions. In these contexts, institutional researchers need to critically examine whether institutions represent *shared* or *configural* constructs (Klein & Kozlowski, 2000). That is, does the emergence of institutions from individual-level beliefs and behaviors require that all individuals – or at least a vast majority – share the beliefs and behaviors, or do institutions emerge from the complex conglomeration of the beliefs and behaviors of some (very influential) individuals? Qualitative comparative analysis (QCA) offers a promising methodological platform to explore this question (Misangyi et al., 2017) and may generate important insights into the bottom-up emergence of institutions.

Experiments

We also recommend greater use of experimental designs, such as laboratory and field experiments. Experiments can play a central role in advancing microfoundations and multi-level research in institutional theory (Bitektine, Lucas, & Schilke, 2018). For instance, in the context of legitimacy research, there is an opportunity to develop laboratory experiments that model and test legitimacy as a multi-level process (Bitektine & Haack, 2015). In addition, such experiments can help scholars to explore how institutional logics shape individual action (Glaser, Fast, Harmon, & Green Jr, 2016) and whether and how variations in institutionalization affect the decision and behavior of managers (Meyer & Rowan, 1977). However, it should be noted that adapting laboratory experimental designs from psychology or behavioral economics, which tend to focus on single-level outcomes and neglect the processual character of cross-level interaction, may often be inappropriate to advance a microfoundational research agenda in institutional theory. Future experimental designs thus need to pay attention to multiple levels and the social dynamics involved in institutional emergence.

Additionally, we see largely untapped potential in the use of natural experiments. Natural experiments represent situations in which an exogenous factor – such as new regulations and laws or natural disasters – creates a naturally occurring contrast that generates a treatment and a control condition to allow for plausible causal inferences. This assignment process is called an as-if randomization, meaning that the assignment is "plausibly as good as random" (Dunning, 2012, p. 10). The as-if random assignment is a major advantage of natural experiments because it rules out endogenous explanations for group differences (e.g., self-selection bias) and balances the treatment and control groups with regard to observable (e.g., demographic characteristics) and unobservable (e.g., beliefs) variables, so that any differences in the outcome variable can be plausibly attributed to the treatment. Natural experiments have received much attention in economics and political science, but they also have the potential to advance the microfoundational agenda in institutional theory. For example, institutional researchers may investigate the effect of exogenous shocks on dynamics related to institutional outcomes. In one instance, Rao and Greve (2018) used the exogenous shock of the influenza pandemic after World War I to explain why some communities were more resilient in the face of disaster than others. Haack and Sieweke (2018) analyzed the ramifications of the German reunification on the legitimacy of inequality in East Germany. Contrasting attitudinal data of East Germans (the treatment group) with data from West Germans (the control group) allowed for the identification of adaptation and replacement as two important mechanisms of inequality legitimation. Institutional scholars can also examine how exogenous shocks affect individuals' beliefs and behaviors, potentially leading to the emergence of new institutions and/or the modification or even deinstitutionalization of established institutions. Finally, researchers can exploit settings in which treatments are assigned based on a unit's score on an observed variable. Such regression discontinuity designs have been fruitfully applied in strategic management to analyze the causal relationship between corporate social responsibility and firm financial performance (Flammer, 2015) and in leadership research to analyze the effect of female leaders on female followers (Arvate, Galilea, & Todescat, 2018).

Time for Retooling

Why have we seen so little empirical research on the microfoundations of institutions? We see the past and current development of the microfoundations of institutions as the result of *theory-method co-evolution* (Greenwald, 2012), with the advancement of the field depending on a self-enforcing and continual cycle between theory development and empirical research aimed at testing and consolidating new theory. In this view, the development of methods is just as crucial for the advancement of the microfoundational research agenda as is theory development for the creation of new methodological approaches. Hence, methodology cannot advance in the absence of soundly developed theory; in other words, it is hampered by weakly defined concepts and an inadequate understanding of the relationships among different concepts. Conversely, a narrow set of measurement techniques and methodological tools may severely constrain theory development, such as when researchers employ proxies for their theoretical concepts that are too distant from the meaning systems and ideational aspects of institutions (Schneiberg & Clemens, 2006; Suddaby, 2010b).

Microfoundational research will benefit from collaborative teams of scholars with expertise in different methods and styles of theorizing. Engaging in more intense dialogue and interdisciplinary collaboration could prove highly fruitful, as it would help scholars integrate psychological and sociological perspectives on institutional phenomena (DiMaggio, 1997; DiMaggio & Markus, 2010). Institutional theorists need to overcome old habits, look beyond incentive structures, and make an effort to gain experience in and apply novel methods. Indeed, in order to advance a microfoundational research agenda, institutional scholars have to turn from "method specialists" (i.e., researchers who are constrained by a narrow set of methods) into "domain specialists"; that is, they need to learn to apply "more diverse, but sometimes less 'legitimate' (and therefore more 'risky') research methods to address research questions that cannot be explored through 'more legitimate' methods" (Bitektine, 2009, p. 219).

CONCLUSION

Today, microfoundational research in institutional theory constitutes a "fragmented adhocracy" (Whitley, 2000) that is impaired by a diffuse set of goals lacking coordination and a consistent terminology. It is evident that scholars in this field would benefit from developing a cohesive research community and a joint research agenda that integrates these fragmented discussions into a more coherent and comprehensive discourse on microfoundations and multi-level research on institutions. We believe that this discourse can be fruitfully bolstered by a dialogue between the two "camps" of micro-institutionalists and macro-institutionalists; such an exchange would help build bridges between scholars focusing either on the transformational force of micro-level mechanisms or the constraining influence of the macro-level context. The gap between micro-oriented or macro-oriented research is not only stabilized and perpetuated by identity concerns (Eckardt et al., 2019) but also reflects disciplinary divides and fundamental differences in the ontological and epistemological assumptions that come with such divides (Molloy, Chadwick, Ployhart, & Golden, 2011). However, integration and interaction between the two camps is highly needed, as scholars otherwise forego the opportunity to advance important questions of the microfoundational research agenda, such as how social interactions aggregate and coalesce into the taken-for-granted community beliefs that are characteristic of an institution. Hence, institutional scholars in each camp need to be cognizant of such divides and differences and would be well advised to develop tolerance and openness toward the insights generated by the other camp. The result will be a better and more powerful institutional theory.

It seems fair to say that institutional theory research has moved beyond questions of whether microfoundations are needed to an inquiry into when and what kind of microfoundations are needed. While building a "grand theory" of the microfoundations of institutions lies beyond the scope of the present double volume (and is perhaps neither possible nor desirable), we nevertheless hope that the chapters as a whole can help channel different micro-level conversations in institutional theory into key questions that can bring clarity and coherence to existing research. We hope that this double volume can act as a focal point, integrating disparate research streams and offering a unique contribution to the emerging microfoundational research agenda.

ACKNOWLEDGMENTS

We thank Vern Glaser, Derek Harmon, and Oliver Schilke for their comments on an earlier draft of this introduction. We also thank the German Research Foundation for funding the scientific research network "Microfoundations of Institutions."

NOTE

1. This introductory chapter focuses on neo-institutionalism in organizational theory (also referred to as organizational institutionalism), but we drop the prefix "neo" to make the chapter more readable.

REFERENCES

Alvesson, M., Hallett, T., & Spicer, A. (2019). Uninhibited institutionalisms. *Journal of Management Inquiry*, *28*(2), 119–127.
Alvesson, M., & Spicer, A. (2019). Neo-institutional theory and organization studies: A mid-life crisis? *Organization Studies*, *40*(2), 199–218.
Amis, J., Munir, K., & Mair, J. (2017). Institutions and economic inequality. In R. Greenwood, C. Oliver, T. B. Lawrence, & R. Meyer (Eds.), *The Sage handbook of organizational institutionalism*. Thousand Oaks, CA: Sage.
Anesa, M., Chalkias, K., Jarzabkowski, P., & Spee, A. P. (2020). Practicing capitals across fields: Extending Bourdieu to study inter-field dynamics. In P. Haack, J. Sieweke, & L. Wessel (Eds.), *Microfoundations of institutions* (RSO, Vol. *65B*, pp. 129–142). Bingley: Emerald Publishing Limited.
Arvate, P. R., Galilea, G. W., & Todescat, I. (2018). The queen bee: A myth? The effect of top-level female leadership on subordinate females. *The Leadership Quarterly*, *29*(5), 533–548.
Astley, W. G. (1985). Administrative science as socially constructed truth. *Administrative Science Quarterly*, *30*(4), 497–513.
Barley, S. R., & Tolbert, P. S. (1997). Institutionalization and structuration: Studying the links between action and institution. *Organization Studies*, *18*(1), 93–117.
Battilana, J., Leca, B., & Boxenbaum, E. (2009). How actors change institutions: Towards a theory of institutional change. *Academy of Management Annals*, *3*(1), 65–107.
Berger, P. L., & Luckmann, T. (1967). *The social construction of reality – A treatise in the sociology of knowledge*. New York, NY: Anchor Books.
Bitektine, A. (2009). What makes us faddish? Resource space constraints and the "garbage can" model of social science research. *Scandinavian Journal of Management*, *25*(2), 217–220.
Bitektine, A., & Haack, P. (2015). The macro and the micro of legitimacy: Towards a multi-level theory of the legitimacy process. *Academy of Management Review*, *40*(1), 49–75.
Bitektine, A., Lucas, J., & Schilke, O. (2018). Institutions under a microscope: Experimental methods in institutional theory. In A. Bryman & D. Buchanan (Eds.), *Unconventional methodology in organization and management research*. Oxford: Oxford University Press.
Bitektine, A., & Nason, R. S. (2020). Towards a multi-level theory of institutional contestation: Exploring category legitimation across domains of institutional action. In P. Haack,

J. Sieweke, & L. Wessel (Eds.), *Microfoundations of institutions* (RSO, Vol. *65A*, pp. 43–66). Bingley: Emerald Publishing Limited.

Boulongne, R., Cudennec, A., & Durand, R. (2020). When do market intermediaries sanction categorical deviation? The role of expertise, identity, and competition. In P. Haack, J. Sieweke, & L. Wessel (Eds.), *Microfoundations of institutions* (RSO, Vol. *65A*, pp. 67–84). Bingley: Emerald Publishing Limited.

Boxenbaum, E. (2020). Conceptual metaphors in microfoundations of institutional theory. In P. Haack, J. Sieweke, & L. Wessel (Eds.), *Microfoundations of institutions* (RSO, Vol. *65B*, pp. 299–316). Bingley: Emerald Publishing Limited.

Brandl, J., Dreher, J., & Schneider, A. (2020). "The HR generalist is dead": A phenomenological perspective on decoupling In P. Haack, J. Sieweke, & L. Wessel (Eds.), *Microfoundations of institutions* (RSO, VOl. 65A, pp. 85–98). Bingley: Emerald Publishing Limited.

Cardinale, I. (2018). Beyond constraining and enabling: Towards new microfoundations for institutional theory. *Academy of Management Review*, *43*(1), 132–155.

Chandler, D., & Hwang, H. (2015). Learning from learning theory: A model of organizational adoption strategies at the microfoundations of institutional theory. *Journal of Management*, *41*(5), 1446–1476.

Cholakova, M., & Ravasi, D. (2020). Why do individuals perceive and respond to the same institutional demands differently? On the cognitive structural underpinnings of institutional complexity. In P. Haack, J. Sieweke, & L. Wessel (Eds.), *Microfoundations of institutions* (RSO, Vol. *65A*, pp. 99–118). Bingley: Emerald Publishing Limited.

Cornelissen, J. P., Durand, R., Fiss, P. C., Lammers, J. C., & Vaara, E. (2015). Putting communication front and center in institutional theory and analysis. *Academy of Management Review*, *40*(1), 10–27.

Davis, G. F., & Marquis, C. (2005). Prospects for organization theory in the early twenty-first century: Institutional fields and mechanisms. *Organization Science*, *16*(4), 332–343.

DiMaggio, P. J. (1997). Culture and cognition. *Annual Review of Sociology*, *23*(1), 263–287.

DiMaggio, P. J., & Markus, H. R. (2010). Culture and social psychology: Converging perspectives. *Social Psychology Quarterly*, *73*(4), 347–352.

DiMaggio, P. J., & Powell, W. W. (1991). Introduction. In W. W. Powell & P. J. DiMaggio (Eds.), *The new institutionalism in organizational analysis* (pp. 1–38). Chicago, IL: University of Chicago Press.

Dunning, T. (2012). *Natural experiments in the social sciences*. Cambridge: Cambridge University Press.

Eckardt, R., Crocker, A., Ahn, Y., Floyd, S. W., Boyd, B. K., Hodgkinson, G. P., … Starbuck, W. H. (2019). Reflections on the micro–macro divide: Ideas from the trenches and moving forward. *Strategic Organization*, *17*(3), 385–402.

Eliasoph, N., Lo, J., & Glaser, V. L. (2020). "Navigation techniques": How ordinary participants orient themselves in scrambled institutions. In P. Haack, J. Sieweke, & L. Wessel (Eds.), *Microfoundations of institutions* (RSO, Vol. *65B*, pp. 143–166). Bingley: Emerald Publishing Limited.

Elsbach, K. D. (1994). Managing organizational legitimacy in the California cattle industry – The construction and effectiveness of verbal accounts. *Administrative Science Quarterly*, *39*(1), 57–88.

Felin, T., & Foss, N. (2020). Microfoundations for institutional theory? In P. Haack, J. Sieweke, & L. Wessel (Eds.), *Microfoundations of institutions* (RSO, Vol. *65B*, pp. 393–408). Bingley: Emerald Publishing Limited.

Felin, T., Foss, N. J., & Ployhart, R. E. (2015). The microfoundations movement in strategy and organization theory. *Academy of Management Annals*, *9*(1), 575–632.

Flammer, C. (2015). Does corporate social responsibility lead to superior financial performance? A regression discontinuity approach. *Management Science*, *61*(11), 2549–2568.

Fohim, E. (2020). Institutional entrepreneurs' skills: A multi-dimensional concept. In P. Haack, J. Sieweke, & L. Wessel (Eds.), *Microfoundations of institutions* (RSO, Vol. *65B* , pp. 169–192). Bingley: Emerald Publishing Limited.

Furnari, S. (2020). Situating frames and institutional logics: The social situation as a key institutional microfoundation. In P. Haack, J. Sieweke, & L. Wessel (Eds.), *Microfoundations of institutions* (RSO, Vol. *65B*, pp. 193–210). Bingley: Emerald Publishing Limited.

Giddens, A. (1984). *The constitution of society. Towards a theory of structuration*. Berkeley, CA: University of California Press.

Glaser, V. L., Fast, N. J., Harmon, D. J., & Green, S. E., Jr. (2016). Institutional frame switching: How institutional logics shape individual action. In J. Gehman, M. Lounsbury, & R. Greenwood (Eds.), *How institutions matter!* (Vol. *48A*, pp. 35–69). Bingley: Emerald Publishing Limited.

Glynn, M. A., & Innis, B. D. (2020). The generativity of collective identity: Identity movements as mechanisms for new institutions. In P. Haack, J. Sieweke, & L. Wessel (Eds.), *Microfoundations of institutions* (RSO, V65A, pp. 119–134). Bingley: Emerald Publishing Limited.

Goffman, E. (1959). *The presentation of self in everyday life*. New York, NY: Anchor Books.

Goldenstein, J., & Walgenbach, P. (2020). Embodied and reflexive agency in institutional fields: An integrative neo-institutional perspective of institutional change. In P. Haack, J. Sieweke, & L. Wessel (Eds.), *Microfoundations of institutions* (RSO, Vol. *65A*, pp. 135–152). Bingley: Emerald Publishing Limited.

Gray, B., Purdy, J. M., & Ansari, S. (2015). From interactions to institutions: Microprocesses of framing and mechanisms for the structuring of institutional fields. *Academy of Management Review*, *40*(1), 115–143.

Green, S. E. (2004). A rhetorical theory of diffusion. *Academy of Management Review*, *29*(4), 653–669.

Greenwald, A. G. (2012). There is nothing so theoretical as a good method. *Perspectives on Psychological Science*, *7*(2), 99–108.

Haack, P., Schoeneborn, D., & Wickert, C. (2012). Talking the talk, moral entrapment, creeping commitment? Exploring narrative dynamics in corporate responsibility standardization. *Organization Studies*, *33*(5–6), 815–845.

Haack, P., & Sieweke, J. (2018). The legitimacy of inequality: Integrating the perspectives of system justification and social judgment. *Journal of Management Studies*, *55*(3), 486–516.

Hallett, T. (2010). The myth incarnate: Recoupling processes, turmoil, and inhabited institutions in an urban elementary school. *American Sociological Review*, *75*(1), 52–74.

Hallett, T., & Hawbaker, A. (2020). Bringing society back in again: The importance of social interaction in an inhabited institutionalism. In P. Haack, J. Sieweke, & L. Wessel (Eds.), *Microfoundations of institutions* (RSO, Vol. *65B*, pp. 317–336). Bingley: Emerald Publishing Limited.

Hardy, C., & Maguire, S. (2010). Discourse, field-configuring events, and change in organizations and institutional fields: Narratives of DDT and the Stockholm convention. *Academy of Management Journal*, *53*(6), 1365–1392.

Harmon, D. (2019). When the Fed Speaks: Arguments, Emotions, and the Microfoundations of Institutions. *Administrative Science Quarterly*, *64*(3), 1–34.

Harmon, D. J. (2018). When the fed speaks: Arguments, emotions, and the Microfoundations of institutions. *Administrative Science Quarterly, forthcoming*.

Harmon, D. J. (2020). Arguments and institutions. In P. Haack, J. Sieweke, & L. Wessel (Eds.), *Microfoundations of institutions* (RSO, Vol. *65B*, pp. 3–22). Bingley: Emerald Publishing Limited.

Harmon, D. J., Haack, P., & Roulet, T. J. (2019). Microfoundations of institutions: A matter of structure versus agency or level of analysis? *Academy of Management Review*, *44*(2), 464–467.

Hazan, O., & Zilber, T. B. (2020). How do institutions take root at the individual level? In P. Haack, J. Sieweke, & L. Wessel (Eds.), *Microfoundations of institutions* (RSO, Vol. *65A*, 153–176). Bingley: Emerald Publishing Limited.

Hedström, P., & Swedberg, R. (Eds.). (1998). *Social mechanisms – An analytical approach*. Cambridge: Cambridge University Press.

Hitt, M. A., Beamish, P. W., Jackson, S. E., & Mathieu, J. E. (2007). Building theoretical and empirical bridges across levels: Multilevel research in management. *Academy of Management Journal*, *50*(6), 1385–1399.

Holm, P. (1995). The dynamics of institutionalization: Transformation processes in Norwegian fisheries. *Administrative Science Quarterly*, *40*(3), 398–422.

Hu, Y., & Rerup, C. (2020). Sensegiving and sensemaking of highly disruptive issues: Animal rights experienced through PETA youtube videos. In P. Haack, J. Sieweke, & L. Wessel (Eds.), *Microfoundations of institutions* (RSO, Vol. *65A*, pp. 177–196). Bingley: Emerald Publishing Limited.

Hwang, H., & Colyvas, J. A. (2020). What do we talk about when we talk about microfoundations? Conceptualizations of actor and multi-level accounts of the micro in institutional processes.

In P. Haack, J. Sieweke, & L. Wessel (Eds.), *Microfoundations of institutions* (RSO, Vol. *65B*, pp. 337–354). Bingley: Emerald Publishing Limited.

Islam, G., Rüling, C.-C., & Schüßler, E. (2020). Rituals of critique and institutional maintenance at the United Nations Climate Change Summits. In P. Haack, J. Sieweke, & L. Wessel (Eds.), *Microfoundations of institutions* (RSO, Vol. *65B*, pp. 23–40). Bingley: Emerald Publishing Limited.

Jepperson, R., & Meyer, J. W. (2011). Multiple levels of analysis and the limitations of methodological individualisms. *Sociological Theory*, *29*(1), 54–73.

Jones, C., Lee, J. Y., & Lee, T. (2020). Institutionalizing place: Materiality and meaning in Boston's north end. In P. Haack, J. Sieweke, & L. Wessel (Eds.), *Microfoundations of institutions* (RSO, Vol. *65B*, pp. 211–240). Bingley: Emerald Publishing Limited.

Keller, J. (2020). Connecting the tree to the rainforest: Examining the microfoundations of institutions with cultural consensus theory. In P. Haack, J. Sieweke, & L. Wessel (Eds.), *Microfoundations of institutions* (RSO, Vol. *65A*, pp. 197–216). Bingley: Emerald Publishing Limited.

Klein, K. J., & Kozlowski, S. W. J. (2000). From micro to meso: Critical steps in conceptualizing and conducting multilevel research. *Organizational Research Methods*, *3*(3), 211–236.

Lawrence, T. B., & Suddaby, R. (2006). Institutions and institutional work. In S. R. Clegg, C. Hardy, T. B. Lawrence, & W. R. Nord (Eds.), *The SAGE handbook of organization studies* (pp. 215–254). Los Angeles, CA: Sage.

Lefsrud, L. M., & Meyer, R. E. (2012). Science or science fiction? Professionals' discursive construction of climate change. *Organization Studies*, *33*(11), 1477–1506.

Lefsrud, L. M., & Vaara, E. (2020). Framing fairness: Microfoundations of the moral legitimacy of Alberta's oil sands. In P. Haack, J. Sieweke, & L. Wessel (Eds.), *Microfoundations of institutions* (RSO, Vol. *65B*, pp. 41–62). Bingley: Emerald Publishing Limited.

Lizardo, O. (2020). Specifying the "what" and separating the "how": Doings, sayings, codes, and artifacts as the building blocks of institutions. In P. Haack, J. Sieweke, & L. Wessel (Eds.), *Microfoundations of institutions* (RSO, Vol. *65A*, 217–234). Bingley: Emerald Publishing Limited.

Lok, J., Creed, W. E. D., & DeJordy, R. (2020). From cruise director to rabbi: Authoring the agentic self through conventions of narrative necessity. In P. Haack, J. Sieweke, & L. Wessel (Eds.), *Microfoundations of institutions* (RSO, Vol. *65B*, pp. 63–84). Bingley: Emerald Publishing Limited.

Malhotra, N., & Reay, T. (2020). Hybridity and power in the microfoundations of professional work. In P. Haack, J. Sieweke, & L. Wessel (Eds.), *Microfoundations of institutions* (RSO, Vol. *65B*, pp. 241–256). Bingley: Emerald Publishing Limited.

Meyer, J. W. (2020). The social construction of the "microsocial". In P. Haack, J. Sieweke, & L. Wessel (Eds.), *Microfoundations of institutions* (RSO, Vol. *65B*, pp. 409–418). Bingley: Emerald Publishing Limited.

Meyer, J. W., & Jepperson, R. L. (2000). The 'actors' of modern society: The cultural construction of social agency. *Sociological Theory*, *18*(1), 100–120.

Meyer, J. W., & Rowan, B. (1977). Institutionalized organizations: Formal structures as myth and ceremony. *American Journal of Sociology*, *83*(2), 340–363.

Meyer, R. E., & Höllerer, M. A. (2010). Meaning structures in a contested issue field: A topographic map of shareholder value in Austria. *Academy of Management Journal*, *53*(6), 1241–1262.

Meyer, R. E., & Höllerer, M. A. (2014). Does institutional theory need redirecting? *Journal of Management Studies*, *51*(7), 1221–1233.

Meyer, R. E., Jancsary, D., Höllerer, M. A., & Boxenbaum, E. (2018). The role of verbal and visual text in the process of institutionalization. *Academy of Management Review*, *43*(3), 392–418.

Misangyi, V. F., Greckhamer, T., Furnari, S., Fiss, P. C., Crilly, D., & Aguilera, R. (2017). Embracing causal complexity: The emergence of a neo-configurational perspective. *Journal of Management*, *43*(1), 255–282.

Molloy, J. C., Chadwick, C., Ployhart, R. E., & Golden, S. J. (2011). Making intangibles "tangible" in tests of resource-based theory: A multidisciplinary construct validation approach. *Journal of Management*, *37*(5), 1496–1518.

Nelson, R. R., & Winter, S. G. (1982). *An evolutionary theory of economic change*. Cambridge, MA: Harvard University Press.

Paruchuri, S., Perry-Smith, J. E., Chattopadhyay, P., & Shaw, J. D. (2018). New ways of seeing: Pitfalls and opportunities in multilevel research. *Academy of Management Journal, 61*(3), 797–801.

Phillips, N., Lawrence, T. B., & Hardy, C. (2004). Discourse and institutions. *Academy of Management Review, 29*(4), 635–652.

Phillips, N., & Malhotra, N. (2008). Taking social construction seriously: Extending the discursive approach in institutional theory. In R. Greenwood, C. Oliver, K. Sahlin, & R. Suddaby (Eds.), *The Sage handbook of organizational institutionalism* (pp. 702–720). Thousand Oaks, CA: Sage.

Powell, W. W. (2020). Institutions on the ground. In P. Haack, J. Sieweke, & L. Wessel (Eds.), *Microfoundations of institutions* (RSO, Vol. *65B*, pp. 419–428). Bingley: Emerald Publishing Limited.

Powell, W. W., & Rerup, C. (2017). Opening the black box: The microfoundations of institutions. In R. Greenwood, C. Oliver, T. B. Lawrence, & R. E. Meyer (Eds.), *The Sage handbook of organizational institutionalism* (2nd ed.). Thousand Oaks, CA: Sage.

Raaijmakers, A. G. M., Vermeulen, P. A. M., Meeus, M. T. H., & Zietsma, C. (2015). I need time! Exploring pathways to compliance under institutional complexity. *Academy of Management Journal, 58*(1), 85–110.

Rao, H., & Greve, H. R. (2018). Disasters and community resilience: Spanish flu and the formation of retail cooperatives in Norway. *Academy of Management Journal, 61*(1), 5–25.

Reddy, M. J. (1979). The conduit metaphor: A case of frame conflict in our language about language. In A. Ortony (Ed.), *Metaphor and thought* (pp. 284–324). Cambridge: Cambridge University Press.

Roberts, A. E. (2020). Identity within the microfoundations of institutions: A historical review. In P. Haack, J. Sieweke, & L. Wessel (Eds.), *Microfoundations of institutions* (RSO, Vol. *65A*, pp. 235–250). Bingley: Emerald Publishing Limited.

Roulet, T. J., Paolella, L., Gabbioneta, C., & Muzio, D. (2020). Microfoundations of institutional change in the career structure of UK elite law firms. In P. Haack, J. Sieweke, & L. Wessel (Eds.), *Microfoundations of institutions* (RSO, Vol. *65A*, pp. 251–268). Bingley: Emerald Publishing Limited.

Ruotsalainen, R. (2020). Outsourcing public services: A multilevel model of leadership-driven gradual institutional change of public services provision. In P. Haack, J. Sieweke, & L. Wessel (Eds.), *Microfoundations of institutions* (RSO, Vol. *65B*, pp. 257–272). Bingley: Emerald Publishing Limited.

Schatzki, T. R. (1996). *Social practices*. Cambridge: Cambridge University Press.

Schilke, O. (2018). A micro-institutional inquiry into resistance to environmental pressures. *Academy of Management Journal, 61*(4), 1431–1466.

Schneiberg, M., & Clemens, E. S. (2006). The typical tools for the job: Research strategies in institutional analysis. *Sociological Theory, 24*(3), 195–227.

Schneider, B., Ehrhart, M. G., & Macey, W. H. (2013). Organizational climate and culture. *Annual Review of Psychology, 64*(1), 361–388.

Schutz, A., & Luckmann, T. (1973). *The structures of the life-world*. Evanston, IL: Northwestern University Press.

Scott, W. R. (2008). *Institutions and organizations*. Thousand Oaks, CA: Sage.

Searle, J. (1969). *Speech acts*. Cambridge: Cambridge University Press.

Seidl, D., & Whittington, R. (2014). Enlarging the strategy-as-practice research agenda: Towards taller and flatter ontologies. *Organization Studies, 35*(10), 1407–1421.

Sieweke, J. (2014). Pierre Bourdieu in management and organization studies – A citation context analysis and discussion of contributions. *Scandinavian Journal of Management, 30*(4), 532–543.

Sillince, J. A. A., & Barker, J. R. (2012). A tropological theory of institutionalization. *Organization Studies, 33*(1), 7–38.

Smets, M., Aristidou, A., & Whittington, R. (2017). Towards a practice-driven institutionalism. In R. Greenwood, C. Oliver, T. B. Lawrence, & R. E. Meyer (Eds.), *The Sage handbook of organizational institutionalism* (pp. 365–390). Thousand Oaks, CA: Sage.

Smets, M., & Jarzabkowski, P. (2013). Reconstructing institutional complexity in practice: A relational model of institutional work and complexity. *Human Relations, 66*(10), 1279–1309.

Smets, M., Jarzabkowski, P., Burke, G. T., & Spee, P. (2015). Reinsurance trading in Lloyd's of London: Balancing conflicting-yet-complementary logics in practice. *Academy of Management Journal, 58*(3), 932–970.

Smets, M., Morris, T., & Greenwood, R. (2012). From practice to field: A multilevel model of practice-driven institutional change. *Academy of Management Journal, 55*(4), 877–904.

Soppe, B., & Pershina, R. (2020). Melting icebergs vs. spectacularization: Storytelling of conflicting institutional demands in wildlife documentaries. In P. Haack, J. Sieweke, & L. Wessel (Eds.), *Microfoundations of institutions* (RSO, Vol. *65B*, pp. 85–106). Bingley: Emerald Publishing Limited.

Steele, C., Toubiana, M., & Greenwood, R. (2020). Why worry? Celebrating and reformulating "integrative institutionalism". In P. Haack, J. Sieweke, & L. Wessel (Eds.), *Microfoundations of institutions* (RSO, Vol. *65B*, pp. 353–370). Bingley: Emerald Publishing Limited.

Stinchcombe, A. L. (1991). The conditions of fruitfulness of theorizing about mechanisms in social science. *Philosophy of the Social Sciences, 21*(3), 367–388.

Suddaby, R. (2010a). Challenges for institutional theory. *Journal of Management Inquiry, 19*(1), 14–20.

Suddaby, R. (2010b). Editor's comments: Construct clarity in theories of management and organization. *Academy of Management Review, 35*(3), 346–357.

Suddaby, R. (2011). How communication institutionalizes: A response to Lammers. *Management Communication Quarterly, 25*(1), 183–190.

Suddaby, R., & Greenwood, R. (2005). Rhetorical strategies of legitimacy. *Administrative Science Quarterly, 50*(1), 35–67.

Surachaikulwattana, P., & Phillips, N. (2020). Creating the British academic health science centres: Understanding the microfoundations of the translation of organizational forms. In P. Haack, J. Sieweke, & L. Wessel (Eds.), *Microfoundations of institutions* (RSO, Vol. *65B*, pp. 273–296). Bingley: Emerald Publishing Limited.

Tchalian, H. (2020). Microfoundations and recursive analysis: A mixed-methods framework for language-based research, computational methods, and theory development. In P. Haack, J. Sieweke, & L. Wessel (Eds.), *Microfoundations of institutions* (RSO, Vol. *65B*, pp. 107–125). Bingley: Emerald Publishing Limited.

Thornton, P. H., Ocasio, W., & Lounsbury, M. (2012). *The institutional logics perspective – A new approach to culture, structure, and process.* Oxford: Oxford University Press.

Tolbert, P. S., & Darabi, T. (2020). Bases of conformity and institutional theory: Understanding organizational decision-making. In P. Haack, J. Sieweke, & L. Wessel (Eds.), *Microfoundations of institutions* (RSO, Vol. *65A*, pp. 269–290). Bingley: Emerald Publishing Limited.

Tolbert, P. S., & Zucker, L. G. (1996). The institutionalization of institutional theory. In S. Clegg, C. Hardy, & W. R. Nord (Eds.), *Handbook of organization studies* (pp. 175–190). London: Sage.

Tolbert, P. S., & Zucker, L. G. (2020). Prologue: What are microfoundations and why study them? In P. Haack, J. Sieweke, & L. Wessel (Eds.), *Microfoundations of institutions* (RSO, Vol. *65A*, pp. 3–7). Bingley: Emerald Publishing Limited.

Tracey, P. (2016). Spreading the word: The microfoundations of institutional persuasion and conversion. *Organization Science, 27*(4), 989–1009.

Vaara, E., & Monin, P. (2010). A recursive perspective on discursive legitimation and organizational action in mergers and acquisitions. *Organization Science, 21*(1), 3–22.

Voronov, M. (2014). Towards a toolkit for emotionalizing institutional theory. In N. M. Ashkanasy, W. J. Zerbe, & C. E. J. Härtel (Eds.), *Emotions and the organizational fabric (Research on Emotion in Organizations)* (Vol. *10*, pp. 167–196). Bingley: Emerald Publishing Limited.

Voronov, M., & Vince, R. (2012). Integrating emotions into the analysis of institutional work. *Academy of Management Review, 37*(1), 58–81.

Weber, K. (2006). From nuts and bolts to toolkits: Theorizing with mechanisms. *Journal of Management Inquiry, 15*(2), 119–123.

Weber, K., & Glynn, M. A. (2006). Making sense with institutions: Context, thought and action in Karl Weick's theory. *Organization Studies, 27*(11), 1639–1660.

Whitley, R. (2000). *The intellectual and social organization of the sciences.* Oxford: Oxford University Press.

Wittgenstein, L. (1953). In G. E. M. Lanscombe (Trans.), *Philosophical investigations.* Oxford: Basil Blackwell.

Wright, P. M., Coff, R., & Moliterno, T. P. (2014). Strategic human capital: Crossing the great divide. *Journal of Management, 40*(3), 353–370.

Zilber, T. B. (2002). Institutionalization as an interplay between actions, meanings, and actors: The case of a rape crisis center in Israel. *Academy of Management Journal, 45*(1), 234–254.

Zilber, T. B. (2012). The relevance of institutional theory for the study of organizational culture. *Journal of Management Inquiry, 21*(1), 88–93.

Zucker, L. G. (1977). The role of institutionalization in cultural persistence. *American Sociological Review, 42*(5), 726–743.

Zucker, L. G. (1989). Combining institutional theory and population ecology: No legitimacy, no history. *American Sociological Review, 54*(4), 542–545.

Zucker, L. G. (1991). The role of institutionalization in cultural persistence. In W. W. Powell & P. J. DiMaggio (Eds.), *The new institutionalism in organizational analysis* (pp. 83–107). Chicago, IL: The University of Chicago Press.

Zucker, L. G., & Schilke, O. (2020). Towards a theory of micro-institutional processes: Forgotten roots, links to social-psychological research, and new ideas. In P. Haack, J. Sieweke, & L. Wessel (Eds.), *Microfoundations of institutions* (RSO, Vol. *65B*, pp. 371–390). Bingley: Emerald Publishing Limited.

SECTION 3

COGNITIVE PERSPECTIVE ON MICROFOUNDATIONS

CHAPTER 1

TOWARD A MULTI-LEVEL THEORY OF INSTITUTIONAL CONTESTATION: EXPLORING CATEGORY LEGITIMATION ACROSS DOMAINS OF INSTITUTIONAL ACTION

Alex Bitektine and Robert Nason

ABSTRACT

The authors explore how entrepreneurs with limited resources legitimated (or failed to legitimate) a new organizational category in different jurisdictions in Canada despite severe resistance. The authors identify three meso-level domains of institutional action (public, administrative, and legal), where actors intervene to change their macro-institutional environment. The findings suggest that these domains mediate the relationship between micro-level agency and macro-level institutions. The authors describe how macro-level consensus about the category legitimacy emerges through a competition between judgments embedded in different discourses and how a particular discourse attains validity, forcing other actors to change their initial unfavorable legitimacy judgments and recognize the category's legitimacy.

Keywords: Domains of institutional action; foundations of institutions; institutional competition; legitimacy; category emergence; contestation

Microfoundations of Institutions
Research in the Sociology of Organizations, Volume 65A, 43–65
Copyright © 2020 by Emerald Publishing Limited
All rights of reproduction in any form reserved
ISSN: 0733-558X/doi:10.1108/S0733-558X2019000065A008

INTRODUCTION

New category emergence entails major changes in the institutional environment (Durand & Khaire, 2017; Suchman, 1995). Despite the growing body of literature on social actors' agency with respect to institutions (DiMaggio, 1988; Lamin & Zaheer, 2012; Rao, 2004; Suddaby & Greenwood, 2005), the mechanisms through which social actors influence institutions to gain legitimacy, or prevent legitimation of an unwanted category of competitors, remain underexplored. The recent research in institutional theory has associated actors' efforts to effect institutional change with active use of rhetoric (David, Sine, & Haveman, 2013; Golant & Sillince, 2007; Haack, Schoeneborn, & Wickert, 2012) and framing (Gurses & Ozcan, 2015; Kaplan, 2008), political contestation (Aldrich & Fiol, 1994; Kaplan, 2008), and discursive problematization of existing practices (Maguire & Hardy, 2009). Nevertheless, it remains unclear *how these micro-level actions translate into macro-level institutional change* and *what social processes and strategies facilitate (or inhibit) this translation.*

By recognizing the multi-level nature of the process of institutional change, we respond to Lounsbury's (2007) call to "redirect the study of institutional diffusion toward finer-grained mechanisms, including the translation of symbolic systems of meaning and processes of practice creation ..." (p. 289) and empirically address one of the most challenging problems of multi-level theorizing in institutional theory – the translation of micro-level processes into macro-level institutional outcomes (Bitektine & Haack, 2015). In particular, we draw attention to what happens at the "meso" level – between micro-level actions and macro-level change in legitimacy – and introduce "domains of institutional action" as a meso-level concept to help facilitate understanding of micro-to-macro translation (Jepperson & Meyer, 2011). Through inductive analysis of a case study of emergence of a new organizational category of U-brews, or "ferment-on-premises" shops, we explore the microfoundations of institutions by describing how institutional change advances through the accumulation of contest wins in three meso-level domains – public, administrative, and legal. For competing interest groups, these domains represent distinct spaces for institutional action that mediate the effect of micro-level agency on macro-level institutions. The U-brews case reveals how a category's macro-level legitimacy was established through a competitive process that unfolded at the meso-level in public, administrative, and legal domains.

By exploring the social mechanisms that transform entrepreneurial action into a society-wide institutional change, we develop an analytical foundation for a multi-level approach to the emergence and legitimation of new categories of organizations. Since institutional action is centered on the issues of legitimacy (Suddaby & Greenwood, 2005; Vaara & Tienari, 2008), we also advance legitimacy theory by exploring the institutional strategies that actors use in the three domains to gain legitimacy for themselves or destroy the legitimacy of their opponents. Furthermore, our findings point to the diversity of means available to social actors and to the possibility of different paths to legitimation of a new organizational category or practice.

THEORETICAL BACKGROUND

What Is "Micro" in Organizational Research?

The concept of microfoundations is not meaningful, unless defined with relation to other levels within a theory – notably macro-level and, where applicable, meso-level(s). While levels in research can be defined in absolute terms, such as "individual – organization – organizational field," the relative specification of a particular level as "micro" highlights the relationship of this level to processes and outcomes at higher (meso- and/or macro-) levels, it draws attention to cross-level interactions within the system. Given our interest to cross-level processes around the legitimacy of a new category of entrepreneurial firms, we regard organizational legitimacy as a macro, field-level phenomenon and focus on microfoundations of legitimacy. We explore interactions at the level of individual and collective actors (U-brew entrepreneurs), including their efforts at collective mobilization, competition for social approval, and attempts to influence field-level institutions in different jurisdictions throughout Canada. We focus on how meso-level processes lead to contest resolution and judgment aggregation, mediating the translation of micro-level actions into macro-level institutional change.

Category Legitimacy

Organizational categories are cognitive structures shared among actors within the organizational field that allow identification of category members based on prototypical (i.e., central, distinctive, and enduring) attributes of the category (Albert & Whetten, 1985; Navis & Glynn, 2010; Rosch, 1978). Categories act as "disciplinary mechanisms that bring order to organizational interactions and existence" (Durand & Khaire, 2017, p. 88). Emergent organizational categories face a dual challenge. On the one hand, they are characteristically ambiguous (Navis & Glynn, 2010; Santos & Eisenhardt, 2005), and special effort is required to build category boundaries and define its domain of action (Santos & Eisenhardt, 2009). On the other hand, the very existence of the new category and its activity can be fundamentally questioned by the established actors (Aldrich & Fiol, 1994), further increasing risks and uncertainty to the new category members.

Since category members to a large extent share the same identity and hence the same fate (Dobrev & Gotsopoulos, 2010), they often have strong incentives to work together to build legitimacy of their category as an entity at the macro-level, that is, to create legitimacy – the generalized perception or assumption that the category is "desirable, proper, or appropriate within some socially constructed system of norms, values, beliefs, and definitions" (Suchman, 1995, p. 574). For an organization or a category, being legitimate implies a recognition of its "right to exist" (Maurer, 1971, p. 361) in the society. However, from a multi-level perspective (Bitektine & Haack, 2015), legitimacy is not only a perception or an attribute of an entity (organization or category), but a complex social process (Johnson, Dowd, & Ridgeway, 2006) of production, reproduction, and adjustment of evaluators' legitimacy judgments about it (Bitektine, 2011; Tost, 2011).

While "legitimacy ultimately exists in the eye of the beholder," (Zimmerman & Zeitz, 2002, p. 416) and thus can be construed as an individual's subjective perception, organizations and categories are said to have legitimacy "insofar as they have the moral approval of most members of society" (Barron, 1998, p. 207). This implies the collective, objectified nature of legitimacy. This dual, individual/collective nature of legitimacy suggests that the legitimacy judgment is formed with inputs that come from two different levels of analysis. The first input, termed *propriety* (Dornbusch & Scott, 1975; Tost, 2011), represents "an actor's belief that a social order's norms and procedures of conduct are desirable and appropriate patterns of action" (Johnson et al., 2006, p. 55). The second input, which is termed *validity beliefs*, consists of an actor's perceptions about how other actors in the society assess the legitimacy of that entity (Dornbusch & Scott, 1975; Johnson et al., 2006; Tost, 2011). Thus, propriety is an actor's own judgment of social acceptability, while validity beliefs represent the actor's perception of a collective assessment of legitimacy present at the level of organizational field or society. In other words, "the effect of validity <...> is driven by the presupposition of consensus" (Zelditch & Walker, 2000, p. 159). Thus, propriety and validity beliefs assessments require different kinds of information. The information for the assessment of propriety comes from observations of the organization, its features and behaviors, while the information about validity comes from observations of opinions and behaviors of other social actors.

Experimental research on legitimacy (Walker, Rogers, & Zelditch, 1988) suggests that validity has a significant direct effect on propriety assessments and that propriety, in turn, is an important factor in determining whether collective action is initiated to change a social structure. Nevertheless, the actual social processes and the contextual factors that drive changes in propriety and validity of a new category of actors remain underexplored. Thus, we address the outstanding research question: *what social mechanisms transform individuals' entrepreneurial action into a society-wide institutional change?*

DATA AND METHODS

Research Design

Since legitimation unfolds and evolves in time, a process study (Langley, 1999), based on a narrative history of category emergence (Chandler, 1962), was deemed most appropriate for the objectives of this research. The study was conducted using an embedded case study design (Yin, 2003), where the legitimation of a single organizational category (the primary unit of analysis) was traced through actions in public, administrative, and legal domains and across two interrelated jurisdictions – Ontario and British Columbia (BC).[1]

The organizational category selected for this study is often referred to as Ferment-on-Premise (FOP) shops. It consists of beer-brewing (U-brew) and winemaking (U-vint) shops, where clients can make their own beer or wine for home use at significant cost savings. *U-brew* shops usually offer all the ingredients (malt extract, barley grains and hops, etc.), equipment, and expertise needed to make batches of beer on their premises. A customer selects one of the brew recipes, gets assigned one of the kettles, and is shown how to measure ingredients and brew the beer. In a *U-vint*, a customer purchases a wine kit with ingredients (grape juice concentrate, yeast, etc.), pours the juice into a pail or carboy, and adds water and yeast. The shop operator then takes care of the racking, filtering, and storage of the customer's wine. In a few weeks, the customer returns to bottle the wine and take it home. The product is intended only for the client's personal use and not for sale. U-brews are in competition with other, well-established actors in the field of alcohol production and distribution: they arguably drew business away from commercial breweries, wineries, liquor stores, and brew pubs. This created economic conditions for competitive institutional challenges to U-brew activity.

Data Collection

Following Yin (2003), the exploration of category evolution was based on secondary data sources and interviews with shop owners, lobbyists, regulators, and other actors in the organizational field of alcohol production and distribution. The secondary data sources used in this study included media records retrieved from the ProQuest – Canadian NewsStand Database, Industry Canada's "Corporations Canada" database, parliamentary and Senate hearings (Parliamentary Information and Research Service [PIRS] transcripts from the Library of Parliament), industry reports (Kitching, 2006), trade association and individual company websites, as well as materials from trade associations and personal archives that some interview participants shared with the author. In total, over 500 documents were consulted and coded for this study.

The sampling of informants for the interviews was performed using theoretical sampling (Glaser & Strauss, 1967), where successive informants were chosen to complement information obtained from other interviews. Following the first set of interviews, the iterative process of sampling and interviewing continued until further interviews no longer added any additional insights (Eisenhardt, 1989; Glaser & Strauss, 1967). This approach captured perspectives of all major stakeholders – from store operators to brewing industry executives, lobbyists, and government officials.

Between 2008 and 2013, we performed three sets of audio-taped and transcribed interviews, in total – 29 interviews for a total time of 22 hours. Each 5–46-page transcript was analyzed and used as a basis to explore emerging themes in subsequent interviews. The first, exploratory set of interviews was used to develop a thorough understanding of the category and reconstruct its history (see below). We did a second set of interviews in 2010–2011, focusing on a more precise set of questions related to our emergent research framework. Finally, once case narratives were completed, a final set of validation interviews was conducted in 2013. The interviews which lasted for an average of 45 minutes, were open-ended but included some of the same general questions, such as "When did you become involved with U-brew business?," "What was the nature of your involvement?," "What interactions did you have with the U-brew trade association?," "Who supported U-brews?," and "Who resisted them, why and how?"

Data Analysis

The data analysis was performed in four stages. First, the events reflected in media coverage of the category were chronologically ordered to create an "event history database" (Van de Ven & Poole, 1990). The media records retrieved from the ProQuest-Canadian News Stand Database and the first exploratory interviews were the main data sources at this stage.

In the second stage of the analysis, the sequence of events reconstructed at the first stage was used to develop a narrative of U-brew history. The analysis conducted at this stage allowed the identification of the temporal scope of the case study, which extends from the founding of the first U-brew companies in Canada, to the formation and stabilization of the regulatory framework for U-brew activities in Ontario and to category diffusion into other provinces.

In the third stage, other data sources were introduced to validate and expand the history narratives. Interviews, archival materials, business reports, and trade association websites were used to "triangulate" and extend the findings from media reports. The interview transcriptions, as well as archival materials and documents that were available in electronic format, were also coded using Atlas.ti software. This *first-level* coding of raw data was performed in an iterative manner (Eisenhardt, 1989), circling back and forth between theory and data. The findings from the interviews and archival documents were then used to expand and triangulate (Leonard-Barton, 1990) the narrative histories of U-brew category development in each of the provinces.

In the fourth stage of the analysis, the narratives were coded to identify the effects of propriety and validity components of legitimacy and highlight similarities and differences in events, actions, and outcomes across provinces. These *second-level* codes initially emerged from the data and then were generalized into theoretical findings. Iteration between data and emergent theory (Miles, Huberman, & Saldana, 2014) helped further enrich the theory and allowed the identification of patterns in category legitimation across the provinces.

FINDINGS

Historical Background

The tradition of brewing in Canada dates back to the first settlers in the seventeenth century. Making beer was a "small cottage" industry until the first commercial brewery was founded in Quebec City in 1668. Since then, commercial brewing has expanded into a CAD$10 billion market. The return to small-scale brewing in North America in the 1980s and 1990s led to the emergence and dissemination of specialty microbreweries with distinct identities (Carroll & Swaminathan, 2000; Lamertz, Heugens, & Calmet, 2005). In this context, the revival of home brewing and emergence of U-brew stores constitute part of the small-scale brewing trend. However, since each Canadian province has its own alcohol policy, the social dynamics around this trend varied substantially across provinces.

U-brew Category Legitimation in Ontario

The first U-brew shop appeared in Ontario in 1986; there were three shops in 1989, but by 1993, the category grew to 250 shops, employing over 1,000 people (Cox, 1993) and generating CAD$40 million in revenues (Schreiner, 1996). The U-brews formed a trade association, the Brew on Premises Association of Ontario (BOPAO, later the Fermenters' Guild of Ontario) in 1990, when there were only six U-brews in the province. One of the founders commented:

> […] we realized that this concept was going to take off in an astronomical rate and in order for the industry to get a foothold and make sure that the industry survived was to form an association and make inroads into the government. The second reason was more of a "clean up factor." One of the operators had a fridge in the "back room" where samples were given out to "potential" customers. We realized that it was wrong and we wanted to set-up some sort of regulatory guidelines to make sure all operations were following the same rules.

Thus, during the first year of its existence, BOPAO created a voluntary code that defined the role of the operator in assisting U-brew customers and set rules for advertising.

Emergence of Opposition

The spread of knowledge about the new category through the media and its exponential growth did not lead directly to the legitimation of U-brews. Very soon after the association formation, the U-brews were singled out as a potential competitor to the existing actors in alcohol production and distribution. In 1991, only a year after the founding of the association, *The Globe and Mail*, a major Toronto newspaper, noted in its review of the beer market in the province:

> Brew-it-yourself shops are another threat. While still a relatively small industry – the Brew On Premises Association of Ontario has more than 40 members with annual sales of about $10-million – they enjoy a significant tax advantage that allows customers to make their own beer on the site for about half the price. (Heinzl, 1991)

Thus, as early as 1991, the category attracted media attention and was perceived as a potential threat to established players in alcohol production and distribution in Ontario. The diffusion of knowledge about U-brews alerted its competitors and triggered contestation of the category's right to exist.

Legitimation in the Legal Domain

One of the first moves of BOPAO was to approach the Liquor License Board of Ontario (LLBO) to confirm the legality of the U-brew business model under the provincial liquor laws, and in May, 1990, it obtained a memorandum from the LLBO stating that U-brews "posed no current problems, have taken initiative to regulate their own activities and have voluntarily consulted with the Board." Nevertheless, the "validation" of U-brews' legitimacy by one authority did not imply the automatic acceptance by others.

In early 1991, the Excise department of Revenue Canada, the Federal tax agency (hereafter, "Excise"), which had developed a long-standing relationship with commercial breweries, was very receptive to their complaints about market share losses to the emergent competitors. Excise took the position that U-brews were engaged in illegal manufacturing of liquor and threatened to lay charges against U-brew operators.

> [...] the government, typical government, right, "no, you can't do that" – well why – "well because we said." ... and that was the view of Excise .... (Interview with an industry consultant)

Furthermore, Excise refused even to meet with U-brew representatives as they were engaged in an "illegal activity." In order to prove its legitimacy and be heard, BOPAO obtained a legal opinion from a law firm McMillan Binch, which confirmed that in the U-brew model, the customer, not the operator, is the manufacturer of the beer for legal purposes (as long as it was the customer who added the yeast to the batch) and that the Excise Act "does not authorise the imposition of excise duties on beer on anyone other than the maker or the brewer of the beer" (Albrecht & Barnett, 1992, p. 10). Excise, however, still refused to meet with U-brew representatives, and, according to BOPAO informants, they had to go "over the head" of Excise to the office of the Deputy Minister of Finance to assert their right as taxpayers to meet with government officials. The validation of U-brews' legitimacy in the legal domain constrained the hostile regulator, while the intervention of higher levels of government forced Excise to recognize the legality of U-brews.

Legitimation in the Administrative Domain

As the breweries lost the contest in the legal domain, the focus of the institutional competition shifted to the administrative domain, specifically, to the provincial Ministry of Finance. Invoking the discourse of "fairness," Jan Westcott, Executive Director of the Brewers of Ontario, an association representing major breweries, complained of unfair tax treatment of brewers like Molson and Labatt:

> We pay this huge amount of tax and have all these restrictive rules and our members said, "Here's a group delivering beer into the market place almost free of all that." Jan Westcott, Brewers of Ontario, interview to the media. (Anonymous, 1993b)

This discourse was used both in the media and with public administrators across the country to induce heavy taxation of U-brews "to level the playing field" (Toomey, 1993).

In a context of economic crisis and declining tax revenue, the newly elected NDP (New Democratic Party) government was fairly receptive to the discourse promoting a new tax. Despite all the efforts of U-brews to be heard, the "cabinet" decision was made behind closed doors, without consultation with the industry:

> [...] we were walking into a meeting with the minister of finance, ... the breweries were walking out. And they had a big, smug, smile on their faces. I turned to the president <of BOPAO> at that time, and I said, Mark, huh, we're done... And sure enough that's when they announced the tax .... (Interview with former BOPAO executive)

Heeding the demands of commercial breweries, the Ontario government imposed a new 26 cents-a-liter tax on the province's 250 U-brews in May 1993.

While taxing signified the regulator's recognition of U-brews' right to exist, the economic consequences of this decision were severe. By early 1994, store revenues fell by as much as 75% and an estimated 40% of the province's U-brews went out of business (Cox, 1993).

Legitimation in the Public Domain

The success of the Brewers of Ontario in the administrative domain, however, was accompanied by a failure in the public domain: The "fairness" discourse was not very credible with the public (as evidenced by media records) and the tax was largely regarded as illegitimate. As a result, the government's policy itself was subjected to normative scrutiny. The Ontario U-brews also initiated legal action against the tax and a media campaign, invoking the "small business" rhetoric:

> The tax did not level the playing field .... What it did succeed in doing was flattening the small business sector of the Ontario economy. Mark Hamelin, BOPAO president. (Anonymous, 1993a)

Faced with legal action against the new tax, lack of public support, and declining tax revenues from U-brews due to declining sales, the government reduced the tax by half in April 1994. Thus, the administrative policy change induced by breweries' successful lobbying did not persist, as it faced resistance from the legal and public domains, which validated the legitimacy of U-brews. Another consequence of the tax controversy was that commercial breweries lost credibility with the regulators in Ontario. The adoption of the tax policy recommended by the breweries led to direct challenges to both the new policy and to the manner in which the government adopted it. As one of the informants put it, the government "had egg on its face, because it listened to the breweries."

In these circumstances, commercial breweries had to change their strategy against U-brews. As breweries could no longer have an effective direct influence on propriety judgments of public administrators through lobbying, they engaged in constituency building, or efforts to motivate other actors to political action (Hillman & Hitt, 1999; Keim & Zeithaml, 1986) and thus shape their environment "by using other types of organizations as tools" (Barley, 2010, p. 798). The discourse of the new public-domain attacks has changed from "fairness" to "social hazard." New attackers – alcohol abuse, health, and safety watchdog organizations with strong ties with commercial breweries, such as Mothers Against Drunk Driving (MADD), Bacchus Canada, and the Toronto Board of Health – presented U-brews as a contributor to public health and road safety problems. For example, Bacchus Canada, an alcohol education organization with significant sponsorship by the Brewers Association of Canada, Molson Inc., and The Association of Canadian Distillers, produced a report charging U-brews as a contributor to alcohol abuse by young people (but presented no data to support these charges).

Challenges of Collective Action

The successful legitimation of a vigorously contested organizational category could not be accomplished solely with rhetoric; it required member mobilization, coordinated action, as well as access to resources and expertise. As highly visible threats to a category's existence facilitate member mobilization for collective action (Barnett, 2006; Gurses & Ozcan, 2015), the resolution of the problem decreases members' commitment, especially in highly fragmented categories, such as the U-brew category. Accordingly, the first trade show organized by BOPAO in 1993, when it fought the 26 cents-a-liter tax, produced a very good turnout and the association membership stood at 60%. The second trade show in 1994 was less of a success, while the show in 1995 was regarded as a disaster. The association executives feared that this could be the death of the association and probably the death of the industry, as the attacks from alcohol manufacturers continued.

The situation was saved by the only ally U-brews could find at that time: suppliers of wine and beer kits. Although the wine kit manufacturers existed since the 1950s, supplying hobby winemakers, this small but very profitable industry did not form an association until 1993, when the French *Institut National des Appellations d'Origine* (INAO) challenged the use of trademarked names (such as Pinot, Cabernet, etc.) on Canadian wine kits. In 1995, when this issue was resolved and the newly formed Canadian Home Wine and Trade Association (CHWTA) created its own trademarks, CHWTA shifted its focus to market development and began to support U-brews as an important retail channel for its kits. Thus, BOPAO's void in resources due to declining membership was compensated by support from CHWTA.

Furthermore, in collaboration with CHWTA, BOPAO developed a voluntary Code and a business plan specifying how it could issue licenses and control the industry to ensure operators' conformance with the law. The Code was drafted in such a way that it could easily be converted into regulation by the government:

> You basically set the tone for a government that if they want to regulate, you've already done the regulations for them. (Interview with a consultant to BOPAO and CHWTA)

This codification of the industry's norms in a "regulator-friendly" format gave U-brews an important edge over their contestants. In 1998, when alcohol regulations in Ontario were opened for review, U-brews, equipped with the regulation-ready normative Code, were among the strongest advocates of more regulation. As a result, Regulation 58/00, which was adopted in 2000, was largely drafted from the industry's voluntary Code. The Breweries did not have a chance to influence this process, as "it was difficult for them to counter the momentum of a voluntary code and it being converted to regulations" (Interview with a consultant to BOPAO and CHWTA). The Regulation amended the province's Liquor License Act, defined the rules for U-brew operations, and introduced compulsory licensing. Thus, by 2000, all three domains – legal, public, and administrative – validated the legitimacy of U-brews in Ontario.

Discursive Competition
In the process of U-brew legitimation in Ontario, we have observed a competition between at least four different discourses: (1) the discourse of "fairness" promoted by large commercial breweries, (2) the discourse of "small business/entrepreneurs/

hobbyists" promoted by U-brews, (3) the discourse of "social hazard" promoted by quasi-independent constituencies with ties to the Breweries, and, finally, (4) the fiscal discourse of tax revenue maximization, which was advanced by administrators, such as the Ontario Finance minister (and by regulators in Nova Scotia – see discussion below). Table 1 provides illustrations of the four discourses.

Why did the U-brews' discourse eventually win in Ontario? The competition among different discourses evolves toward the institutionalization of one particular judgment as the most appropriate criterion. The more actors adopt a given discourse and hence make the legitimacy judgment that it conveys, the more institutionalized this judgment becomes and the greater influence it has on other actors' judgments. To illustrate this observation, Table 2 enumerates the "validations" that the four discourses received in public, administrative, and legal domains.

Table 1. Institutional Discourses around the U-brew Category.

Discourses	Examples
(1) The discourse of "fairness" (promoted by large commercial breweries)	"What you're seeing is a lot of people who are saying: 'Hey, why should I pay the taxes? The u-brews are taking advantage of a loophole in the law. … The u-brews aren't even obliged to keep track of what they produce" Daniel Gagnier, president of Brewers Association of Canada, interview to the media. (Casella, 1993, p. C.1) "We pay this huge amount of tax and have all these restrictive rules and our members said, 'Here's a group delivering beer into the market place almost free of all that.'" Jan Westcott, executive-director of the Brewers of Ontario, interview to the media. (Anonymous, 1993b) "From a public health standpoint, one may contend that taxation strategies for beer and wine should be applied uniformly regardless of whether the products are commercially manufactured or produced for personal use." (Toronto Board of Health Report, 1997, p.10)
(2) The discourse of "small business/ entrepreneurs/ hobbyists" (promoted by U-brews)	"What laundromats are to clothes, Canada's U-brews are to the thirsty and the heavily taxed." (Greenberg, 1993) "Labatt and Molson's were fighting tooth and nail to prevent us from, um, allowing this industry to grow … <…BOPAO> was a way to band together and <…> to voice the opinion as taxpayers and as citizens that, you know, here's an industry and it's here to stay and here's how the Ontario economy benefits." Interview with CCWA executive "The tax <…> flattened the small business sector of the Ontario economy" Mark Hamelin, BOPAO president. (Anonymous, 1993a)
(3) The "social hazard" discourse (promoted by constituents with ties to the breweries)	"In Ontario, u-brew and home produced beer and wine along with smuggled and illegally manufactured beverage alcohol, contribute to what is estimated to amount to a sizeable volume of unrecorded consumption." (Toronto Board of Health Report, 1997, p. 3) "… perhaps 70% of U-Brew products are not lawfully made (and presumably go untaxed). <…> 5-7% of Ontario's beer market is being served by the U-Brews and illegal production." (MackenzieInstitute, 1997)
(4) The fiscal discourse (adopted by administrators in Ontario and other provinces)	"… there was no tax there. I saw that as a loophole." Ontario Finance Minister Floyd Laughren, interview to the media. (Cox, 1993) "many concerns" about the U-brew industry: "inadequate taxation, lack of controls, and the possible creation of a black market" Natalie Lejeune, Regie des Permis d'Alcool (QC), interview to the media. (Toomey, 1993)

Table 2. Validations of Discourses in the U-brew Legitimacy Issue in Ontario.

	The Discourse of "Fairness"/"Level Playing Field"	"Small Business/Entrepreneurs/ Hobbyists" Discourse	The "Social Hazard" Discourse	The Fiscal Discourse
Public Domain	*Failed* due to lack of credibility of large corporations fighting small local businesses	*Validated* by the media and the public discourse	*Partially validated* through the presence in the media	*Failed* due to lack of public support for a growing tax burden
Administrative Domain	*Validated* by the Ontario Minister of Finance through the imposition of a tax (the judgment was later *reversed* by the reduction of the tax burden on U-brews)	- *Validated* by Liquor License Board of Ontario - *Validated* by the Ontario Minister of Finance (the imposition of a tax signified the recognition of U-brews' right to exist)	*Validated* by the Toronto Board of Health (a weak validation due to lack of credibility of constituents related to breweries)	*Validated* by the Ontario Minister of Finance (the judgment was later partially *reversed* by the reduction of the tax burden on U-brews)
Legal Domain	No action	- *Validated* by the legal opinion of McMillan Binch - *Rejected* by the Excise, the judgment was later *reversed*	No action	- *Failed* due to U-brews' legal action against the tax
Total Validations	1	4	1.5	1

The table shows that "small business/entrepreneurs/hobbyists" discourse received the greatest number of validations early on, and legitimacy judgments supported by the other discourses (i.e., that of Excise and the Minister of Finance in Ontario) were later reversed.

U-brew Category Legitimation in British Columbia (BC)

The number of U-brews in BC grew from one in 1991, to 20 in 1992, and to 51 in 1993. However, political developments around U-brews in BC lagged by at least 2 years behind similar developments in Ontario. Since U-brew opponents first sought to make the category illegal throughout Canada with their efforts in Ontario, they probably did not see the need to intervene in other provinces until their strategy of questioning legality of U-brews failed. As a result of this delay, all actors involved had a chance to observe the contestation process in that province and learn from its outcomes.

Legitimation in the Legal Domain

Since the breweries' attack through Excise occurred earlier and was fought by the Ontario U-brews, operators in BC were not challenged until 1993. In early 1993, however, through personal contacts in the provincial government, one of the storeowners found out that the breweries had lobbied legislators to ban U-brews, using the same "fairness" discourse as in Ontario and complaining of market share losses to U-brews. According to informants, U-brews' existence depended on a provincial law that allowed liquor to be transported from a place where it was made to clients' home. A change to that law could have made U-brews illegal.

In order to address this challenge, BC's U-brews created the Hobby Brewers and Vintners Association (HBVA, later the Fermenters' Guild of BC). BC U-brews responded to the breweries' challenge with the same "small business" discourse that was successful in Ontario.

> [...] and we just had a grassroots lobby where we just worked very hard to make our case known, so we met with the Liquor Control Board many times, <...> And we met with three different ministers and legislators, <...> we got the attention of the media. (a former HBVA executive)

The validity generated by grassroots lobbying in the regulative domain and positive media coverage in the public domain prompted the legislators to leave open the loophole that allowed the U-brews to exist.

Legitimation in the Public Domain

The legitimation of U-brews in Ontario in legal, public, and administrative domains was fairly consequential to the developments in other provinces: it increased the validity (Tost, 2011) of the new category. Reversing the institutionalization of the positive legitimacy judgment about the U-brew category required a mobilized and coordinated effort of the category's opponents. By 1995, the opposition to U-brews in BC developed a formal structure – the Hospitality Industry Coalition, led by the Western Brewers Association. It also included wineries, brewpub, and restaurant owners. Using private detectives with hidden cameras and an underage child posing as a customer, the coalition undertook a 4-month investigation to prove U-brews were not adequately taxed or regulated. As the coalition managed to uncover and publicize some troubling practices of U-brews, but the delegitimation momentum was lost as the public attention shifted to the coalition's use of an underage child to buy alcohol, which was deemed immoral. As the coalition lost its legitimacy, it could no longer pose a challenge to U-brews. Following these events, the negative coverage of U-brews in the media was in steady decline, and with introduction of regulations of the U-brew category in 2000, it practically disappeared, indicating the end of the contestation of U-brews' legitimacy in the public domain.

Legitimation in the Administrative Domain

One of the first actions taken by HBVA was to request BC's Attorney-General Colin Gabelmann to introduce regulation of U-brews. Throughout 1993–1996, the association had several meetings with the attorney general's office, but neither the liquor licensing board, nor the NDP government was sure what to do with the new category, and neither saw the need to intervene:

> In fact, I did have a meeting with a group of U-brew representatives on some of these issues after the matter was raised in the press. But beyond that, if there is any illegality in terms of the U-brew substance being utilized in an illicit fashion, then that becomes the responsibility of the police to investigate, as they do in all other cases. Hon. U. Dosanjh, Attorney-General, BC. (The Parliament of British Columbia, 1996)

Following the failed attack of the Hospitality Industry Coalition, the opposition to U-brews had difficulty securing a place at the table with the government and, according to an HBVA executive, since then the discussions on U-brews "were basically between ourselves and the Attorney General's Office and Liquor Control. I think it was basically an agreement there." The new Act adopted in 2000 defined rules for U-brew operators and introduced compulsory licensing with a license fee was set on a "cost recovery" basis, that is, to offset the costs of regulating U-brews.

Legitimation in Other Provinces

The legitimation of the U-brew category in two major Canadian provinces – Ontario and BC – presented an important validity cue for actors in other jurisdictions. As a result, there were no major public domain debates over U-brews' legitimacy in other provinces and the primary legitimation efforts of U-brews and their allies were focused on the legal domain. A consultant, who worked for CHWTA, summarized this change in the U-brew legitimation strategy as follows:

> [...] in Ontario it was 'entrepreneurship' <...> and a little bit out in BC, but in Quebec and New Brunswick, and Nova Scotia, it was the <wine kit> manufacturers that were instrumental. They took a shop and set it up as a U-Brew and then challenged the government to come and shut it down. So it was 'in your face' lobbying.

Thus, CHWTA, the association of wine kit manufacturers, took the lead in legitimizing U-brews outside Ontario and BC.

The fight for U-brew legitimation using this new strategy was successful in New Brunswick and Nova Scotia (although with a substantial delay caused by the government's resistance and attempts of prosecution), but ultimately failed in Alberta and Quebec. Alberta had a strong opposition from breweries and alcohol retailers, but it was also a relatively small market with sparse population, which made U-brew business in the province economically unattractive. There was also no motivated entrepreneur to champion the cause, which limited momentum for U-brew legitimation in the province.

Quebec was a larger potential market, but U-brews faced a strong opposition from the *Societé d'alcool du Quebec* (SAQ), a hybrid organization that combines the roles of a government-owned alcohol retailer monopoly and an actor engaged in formulation of alcohol policy in the province. Furthermore, as a mostly French-speaking province, Quebec has a culture that substantially differs from that of the English-speaking provinces in Canada. Given the strength of a separatist sentiment in the province, the validity cues generated by judgments and actions in English-speaking jurisdictions had little impact on legitimacy judgments made by actors in the Quebecois society. Faced with routine SAQ's complaints to the police and similarly routine criminal charges against U-brew operators, QC U-brews had to pool their resources for legal defense of individual stores. For a single operator, such litigation could have easily resulted in a bankruptcy. Although U-brews just as routinely were winning the legal cases, their legitimacy in the legal domain remains constantly contested, inhibiting the growth of U-brews in the province.

DISCUSSION AND THEORY DEVELOPMENT

The history of U-brew shops' struggle for legitimacy illustrates how a small category of organizations with limited resources has attained (or failed to attain) legitimacy in different Canadian provinces while facing resistance from powerful competitors and the reluctance of regulators to recognize it. This study reveals interesting insights on the process of a new category legitimation and on the social mechanisms through which social actors influence their institutional environment to gain legitimacy or to prevent legitimation of an unwanted category of competitors.

Domains of Institutional Action

The U-brew case study shows that there is no single source responsible for the "ultimate" legitimacy judgment in society. The U-brew case allowed us to identify three meso-level domains that play a pivotal role in "aggregating" legitimacy judgments of multiple actors in a collective, "validated" judgment and then providing validity cues to other evaluators. These three domains – public, administrative, and legal – also serve as "battlegrounds" where actors compete over which legitimacy judgment should be "validated" by the domain (Bitektine & Haack,

2015). In other words, this is where actors exercise their agency with respect to institutions. For this reason, we refer to these domains here as *domains of institutional action*. [The following] Table 3 summarizes some key observations about the actors, processes, and practices in the three domains and the influences they produce at the meso-level (i.e., on other domains) and on the macro-level. Table 3 also highlights the interrelated nature of the three domains and the way they mediate social actors' attempts to influence the macrofoundations of institutions.

Public Domain

The public domain encompasses communications, actions, and events accessible to broad audiences: media communications, press releases, advertising, mailing campaigns, as well as high-visibility actions like protests, speeches, demonstrations, strikes, etc. Mass media occupies a particularly important place in this domain. Media both *influence* (Hoffman & Ocasio, 2001; Pollock & Rindova, 2003) and *reflect* public perceptions of legitimacy (Baum & Powell, 1995; Deephouse, 1996; Elsbach, 1994). Media also perform a monitoring service and serve as the primary "battleground" for contests in the public domain. Since media provide the general public with a low-cost / low-effort access to information (Bonardi, Hillman, & Keim, 2005), they are a critical source of validity cues for evaluators' legitimacy judgments.

The Administrative Domain

The administrative domain is composed of government actors – elected officials and career bureaucrats – as well as of government bodies that are responsible for regulation in a given field, such as legislatures, ministries, agencies, etc. (Buchanan, 1999). Since these actors have authority and coercive power to ensure compliance, the legitimacy judgments they make are fairly consequential to organizations and categories (Russo, 1992). Apart from the direct effect associated with sanctions or authorizations, an administrator's legitimacy judgment also has an indirect effect: such a judgment is an important validity cue for other social actors who take it into account in their own legitimacy judgments. In effect, different interests compete for influence on regulators (Baysinger, 1984; Bonardi, 2004; Hillman, 2003; Hillman & Hitt, 1999). Bonardi et al. (2006) provide an evidence of differential outcomes of firms' efforts to influence public policy decisions in the presence and in the absence of active competition from other interest groups.

Legal Domain

The legal domain codifies institutionalized norms in statutes, acts, as well as in court rulings and opinions, which serve as precedents under the common law system. This body of legal texts, termed as "written law," is juxtaposed to "delivered law," or the actual pattern of outcomes that the legal system generates (LoPucki & Weyrauch, 2000). For individual evaluators, the *legality* of an entity (an organization or a category), that is, its conformance with the "written law," provides an important validity cue: the entity, its practices or outcomes are perceived as

Table 3. Public, Administrative, and Legal Domains.

Domain	Public Domain	Administrative Domain	Legal Domain
Key incumbent actors	Media (journalists, editors, media owners), experts, opinion leaders, and spokespeople	Legislators, career administrators, and government agencies	Judges, arbitrators, juries, lawyers, administrators, boards, and commissions
Interveners	PR professionals, spokespeople, activists, politicians, and experts	Professional lobbyists, representatives of interest groups, and experts	Parties and their legal teams, and experts
Judgment objects	Mostly individual actor examples; observations on prominent members generalized to categories	Usually apply to categories of actors, seldom to individual organizations	Mostly individual actors, seldom categories of organizations
Judgment validation texts	Media articles; validity is inferred from repetition (or share of voice) of a particular discourse	Regulations and legislative acts	Cases, judicial acts, and judicial opinions
Process	Public debate, mostly in mass media	Legislative process of law adoption, periodic regulation review, and public hearings	Court hearings, arbitration, consultations, and legal research
Competition	Competition for the share of voice in the media between the competing discourses	Competition for influence on public policy among lobbyists representing competing interest groups	Competition among lawyers for influence on legal outcomes
Outcome	Emergence of a dominant discourse and/or loss of interest in the issue	Adoption of a law or judgments regulation	Court ruling, legal opinion providing a normative justification of a judgment
Influence on other domains of institutional action	Creates validity (endorsement and authorization): Influences regulative domain through shaping public opinion; Some influence on judges and courts	Creates validity (authorization): Coercive influence on the media through censorship, licensing, financing, some political influence on courts and judges	Creates validity (authorization): Coercive influence on regulators through rulings, some ability to influence media through rulings and threats of litigation

"authorized" by the legal system and hence deserving to be supported or, at least, tolerated. This validity cue has a strong effect on propriety assessments by individual evaluators (Zelditch & Walker, 2000). While the practice of law is commonly described as an application of written law to facts of a case (Aldissert, 1997) and courts are seen as having a limited flexibility in application of the law (Rosen, 1999), a strategic view of the legal process holds that legal outcomes are socially constructed through a competitive process of argumentation, which involves normative arguments that lawyers advance to support the desired judgment. Furthermore, the outcomes of the legal process also suggest the primacy of social norms over the written law (LoPucki & Weyrauch, 2000, p. 1435).

Domain Interactions
The U-brew study shows how actors occupying key roles within each of the three domains (e.g., journalists, regulators, and judges) engaged in cognitive sensemaking to clarify the meaning of the U-brew category, rendered normative judgments about its social acceptability, and arrived to some form of a consensus- or authority-validated judgment, which they expressed in media articles, regulations, or judicial opinions and verdicts. This creates an opportunity for domains to influence each other. Thus, for example, Ozcan and Gurses (2018) suggest that firms may attempt to influence and play both regulators and the public off of each other.

In U-brew case, such influences were observed when some of the key actors – Excise, Finance ministries in Ontario and Nova Scotia – were pressured to reconsider their initial judgments. As the "validity" of the positive legitimacy judgment grew in the public domain (with the growing media consensus) and with the growing number of authoritative endorsements in regulative and legal domains (LLBO, McMillan Binch, Excise, Government of Ontario, Government of BC, etc.), its influence on other social actors increased, facilitating the U-brews' legitimation in other jurisdictions. These observations suggest that the interplay between the three domains at the meso-level occurs through the mechanism of validity, where domains whose judgment deviates from the validity established other domains is pressured to reconsider its judgment (or risk losing legitimacy).

It should be noted, however, that the diffusion of a new category, even after its validity has been established in some jurisdictions, is by no means an automatic. U-brew legitimation in the regulative domain was substantially delayed in Nova Scotia, and it took an open confrontation (provoked by the regulator) to force the government to recognize U-brews. In Quebec, the SAQ's avoidance of contacts with U-brews, coupled with routine litigation, stalled the U-brew legitimation process in the province, despite the public-domain support and validation of the category in many other jurisdictions. Finally, the U-brew category never emerged in Alberta, where both institutional and economic factors were unfavorable.

Cross-level Effects in the Legitimation Process
Despite extensive attention to the microfoundations of institutions, institutional theory still lacks an explanation of how a micro-level agency (i.e., actions of

individual and collective actors in an institutional contest) affects macro-level institutions. We argue here, that the effect of individual agency on macro-level institutions is not direct, but mediated by the domains of institutional action described above. The three domains of institutional action – public, administrative and legal – serve as intervention points through which actors exert influence on the legitimacy process. All three domains influence each other through validity that they create and all three domains shape the foundations of a category's legitimacy. The relationship between the three domains, propriety, validity, and aggregated legitimacy is outlined in Fig. 1.

Following the principles of exploration of emergence in microfoundations research (Felin, Foss, & Ployhart, 2015), Fig. 1 discerns three theoretically relevant levels – the level of actors competing for validation of their judgments (micro), the level of domains of institutional action that perform such a validation (meso), and the level of general institutional environment, where the consensus among the three domains is achieved and is integrated into a generalized legitimacy judgment. The process of legitimation of a new category proceeds from micro-level actions of individuals and interest groups (at the bottom of the figure) in public, administrative, and/or legal domains. Each domain has its own process of resolving disputes among actors and validating a judgment. But the degree of actors' engagement in a given domain, and hence the intensity of competition may vary depending on actors' perceptions of their chances for success in that domain and on the actions of their competitors. While successful validation of the desired judgment in a domain (white circles in Fig. 1) represents an important victory for the judgment proponents, the process of legitimation is not complete until

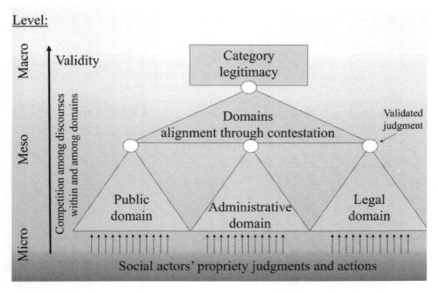

Fig. 1. Domains of Institutional Action and Category Legitimacy.

all three domains achieve the consensus and validate that same judgment about legitimacy of the category.

CONCLUSION

This chapter contributes to organizational theory and management practice by exploring the cross-level processes of legitimacy judgment formation and developing a conceptual framework of distinct domains of institutional action. In doing so, we open new lines of inquiry not only in the study of microfoundations of institutions but also in institutional entrepreneurship and new category formation. Future research in these directions will further explore how legitimacy judgments are aggregated and how public, administrative, and legal domains mediate the translation of micro-level actions into society-wide institutional change.

ACKNOWLEDGMENTS

We are very grateful to Steve Maguire, Jan Jorgensen, and Robert David (McGill University), Ann Langley (HEC Montreal), Michael Pratt (Boston College), and the members of the Montreal Organization Writing Workshop (MOWW) community in Montreal for their feedback on the earlier versions of this chapter. We are particularly grateful to John Kiedrowski (Compliance Strategy Group) for indispensable help and advice during the data collection for this project. This research was supported in part by a grant from the Research Office of HEC Montreal, Canada.

NOTE

1. While our data collection also captured developments in other provinces, the category legitimation outside of Ontario and BC was fundamentally qualitatively different and was accomplished using legitimation strategies that are more common among well-established and well-resourced interest groups. We have included a brief overview of these strategies in the section "Legitimation in Other Provinces" below.

REFERENCES

Albert, S., & Whetten, D. A. (1985). Organizational identity. In L. L. Cummings & B. Staw (Eds.), *Research in organizational behavior* (Vol. *14*, pp. 263–295). Greenwich, CT: JAI Press.

Albrecht, D. J., & Barnett, T. G. (1992). Memorandum of fact and law for BOPAO re. Excise Act – Draft Circular ED 212-10: McMillan Binch.

Aldissert, R. L. (1997). *Logic for lawyers: A guide to clear legal thinking* (3rd ed.). South Bend, IN: NITA.

Aldrich, H. E., & Fiol, C. M. 1994. Fools rush in? The institutional context of industry creation. *Academy of Management Review*, *19*(4), 645–670.

Anonymous. (1993a). Brew-your-own business drowning, association says. *The Hamilton Spectator*, p. C.8. Hamilton, Ontario. 23 Nov 1993..

Anonymous. (1993b). New tax batters brew-your-own. *Toronto Star*, p. 1. Toronto, Ontario. 25 Aug 1993.

Barley, S. R. (2010). Building an institutional field to corral a government: A case to set an agenda for organization studies. *Organization Studies, 31*(6), 777–805.

Barnett, M. L. (2006). Waves of collectivizing: A dynamic model of competition and cooperation over the life of an industry. *Corporate Reputation Review, 8*(4), 272–292.

Barron, D. N. (1998). Pathways to legitimacy among consumer loan providers in New York City, 1914–1934. *Organization Studies, 19*(2), 207–233.

Baum, J. A. C., & Powell, W. W. (1995). Cultivating an institutional ecology of organizations: Comment on Hannan, Carroll, Dundon, and Torres. *American Sociological Review, 60*(4), 529–538.

Baysinger, B. D. (1984). Domain maintenance as an objective of business political activity: An expanded typology. *Academy of Management Review, 9*(2), 248–258.

Bitektine, A. (2011). Towards a theory of social judgments of organizations: The case of legitimacy, reputation, and status. *Academy of Management Review, 36*(1), 151–179.

Bitektine, A., & Haack, P. (2015). The macro and the micro of legitimacy: Towards a multi-level theory of the legitimacy process. *Academy of Management Review, 40*(1), 49–75.

Bonardi, J.-P. (2004). Global and political strategies in deregulated industries: The asymmetric behaviors of former monopolies. *Strategic Management Journal, 25*(2), 101–120.

Bonardi, J.-P., Hillman, A. J., & Keim, G. D. (2005). The attractiveness of political markets: Implications for firm strategy. *Academy of Management Review, 30*(2), 397–413.

Buchanan, J. M. (1999). *The demand and supply of public goods.* Indianapolis, IN: Liberty Fund, Inc.

Carroll, G. R., & Swaminathan, A. (2000). Why the microbrewery movement? Organizational dynamics of resource partitioning in the U.S. brewing industry. *American Journal of Sociology, 106*(3), 715–762.

Casella, E. (1993). U-brew tax looms Big breweries are crying foul at tax loophole. In *The Hamilton Spectator*, p. C.1. 18 May 1993.

Chandler, A. D., Jr. (1962). In M. M. P. Cambridge (Ed.), *Strategy and structure: Chapters in the history of the American industrial enterprise* (p. 463). Cambridge, MA: MIT Press.

Cox, W. (1993). Tax "devastates" you-brew shops, *Kitchener Waterloo Record*, (p. B.6). 17 Nov 1993.

David, R. J., Sine, W. D., & Haveman, H. A. (2013). Seizing opportunity in emerging fields: How institutional entrepreneurs legitimated the professional form of management consulting. *Organization Science, 24*(2), 356–377.

Deephouse, D. L. (1996). Does isomorphism legitimate? *Academy of Management Journal, 39*(4), 1024–1039.

DiMaggio, P. (1988). Interest and agency in institutional theory. In L.G. Zucker (Ed.), *Institutional patterns and organizations: Culture and environment* (pp. 3–22). Cambridge, MA: Ballinger.

Dobrev, S. D., & Gotsopoulos, A. (2010). Legitimacy vacuum, structural imprinting, and the first mover disadvantage. *Academy of Management Journal, 53*(5), 1153.

Dornbusch, S. M., & Scott, W. R. (1975). *Evaluation and the exercise of authority.* San Francisco, CA: Jossey-Bass Publishers.

Durand, R., & Khaire, M. (2017). Where do market categories come from and how? Distinguishing category creation from category emergence. *Journal of Management, 43*(1), 87–110.

Eisenhardt, K. M. (1989). Building theories from case study research. *Academy of Management Review, 14*(4), 532–550.

Elsbach, K. D. (1994). Managing organizational legitimacy in the California cattle industry. *Administrative Science Quarterly, 39*(1), 57–88.

Felin, T., Foss, N. J., & Ployhart, R. E. (2015). The microfoundations movement in strategy and organization theory. *The Academy of Management Annals, 9*(1), 575–632.

Glaser, B., & Strauss, A. (1967). *The discovery of grounded theory: Strategies of qualitative research.* London: Wiedenfeld and Nicholson.

Golant, B. D., & Sillince, J. A. A. (2007). The constitution of organizational legitimacy: A narrative perspective. *Organization Studies, 28*(8), 1149–1167.

Greenberg, L. M. (1993). How to get ahead of high beer taxes: Visit a local U-brew — Shops where Canadians make their own have become popular gathering places. *Wall Street Journal*, Eastern ed., p. 1. 19 Aug 1993.

Gurses, K., & Ozcan, P. (2015). Entrepreneurship in regulated markets: Framing contests and collective action to introduce pay TV in the U.S. *Academy of Management Journal, 58*(6), 1709–1739.

Haack, P., Schoeneborn, D., & Wickert, C. (2012). Talking the talk, moral entrapment, creeping commitment? Exploring narrative dynamics in corporate responsibility standardization. *Organization Studies*, *33*(5–6), 815–845.

Heinzl, J. (1991). Smelly image gets cleanup. *The Globe and Mail*, p. B.1. Dec 9, 1991.

Hillman, A. J. (2003). Determinants of political strategies in U.S. multinationals. *Business and Society*, *42*(4), 455–484.

Hillman, A. J., & Hitt, M. A. (1999). Corporate political strategy formulation: A model of approach, participation, and strategy decisions. *Academy of Management Review*, *24*(4), 825–842.

Hoffman, A. J., & Ocasio, W. (2001). Not all events are attended equally: Toward a middle-range theory of industry attention to external events. *Organization Science*, *12*(4), 414.

Jepperson, R., & Meyer, J. W. (2011). Multiple levels of analysis and the limitations of methodological individualisms. *Sociological Theory*, *29*(1), 54–73.

Johnson, C., Dowd, T. J., & Ridgeway, C. L. (2006). Legitimacy as social process. *Annual Review of Sociology*, *32*, 53–78.

Kaplan, S. (2008). Framing contests: Strategy making under uncertainty. *Organization Science*, *19*(5), 729–752.

Keim, G. D., & Zeithaml, C. P. (1986). Corporate political strategy and legislative decision making: A review and contingency approach. *Academy of Management Review*, *11*(4), 828–843.

Kitching, A. (2006). Payday loan companies in Canada: Determining the public interest: 14. Ottawa, Canada: Library of Parliament – Parliamentary Information and Research Service.

Lamertz, K., Heugens, P. P. M. A. R., & Calmet, L. (2005). The configuration of organizational images among firms in the Canadian beer brewing industry. *Journal of Management Studies*, *42*(4), 817–843.

Lamin, A., & Zaheer, S. (2012). Wall Street vs. Main Street: Firm strategies for defending legitimacy and their impact on different stakeholders. *Organization Science*, *23*(1), 47–66.

Langley, A. (1999). Strategies for theorizing from process data. *Academy of Management Review*, *24*(4), 691–710.

Leonard-Barton, D. (1990). A dual methodology for case studies: Synergistic use of a longitudinal site with replicated multiple sites. *Organization Science*, *1*(3), 248–266.

LoPucki, L. M., & Weyrauch, W. O. (2000). A theory of legal strategy. *Duke Law Journal*, *49*(6), 1405–1486.

Lounsbury, M. (2007). A tale of two cities: Competing logics and practice variation in the professionalizing of mutual funds. *Academy of Management Journal*, *50*(2), 289–307.

MackenzieInstitute. (1997). Prohibition's hangover – Ontario's black market in alcohol. *Mackenzie briefing notes* (10th ed.). Toronto, Canada: Mackenzie Institute for the Study of Terrorism, Revolution and Propaganda.

Maguire, S., & Hardy, C. (2009). Discourse and deinstitutionalization: The decline of DDT. *Academy of Management Journal*, *52*(1), 148–178.

Maurer, J. G. (1971). *Readings in organizational theory: Open system approaches*. New York, NY: Random House.

Miles, M. B., Huberman, A. M., & Saldana, J. (2014). *Qualitative data analysis* (3rd ed.). Thousand Oaks, CA: Sage.

Navis, C., & Glynn, M. (2010). How new market categories emerge: Temporal dynamics of legitimacy, identity, and entrepreneurship in satellite radio, 1990–2005. *Administrative Science Quarterly*, *55*(3), 439–471.

Ozcan, P., & Gurses, K. (2018). Playing cat and mouse: Contests over regulatory categorization of dietary supplements in the U.S. *Academy of Management Journal*, *61*(5), 1789–1820.

Pollock, T. G., & Rindova, V. P. (2003). Media legitimation effects in the market for initial public offerings. *Academy of Management Journal*, *46*(5), 631–642.

Rao, H. (2004). Institutional activism in the early American automobile industry. *Journal of Business Venturing*, *19*(3), 359–384.

Rosch, E. (1978). Principles of categorization. In E. Rosch & B. Lloyd (Eds.), *Cognition and categorization* (pp. 27–48). Hillsdale, NJ: Lawrence Erlbaum.

Rosen, M. D. (1999). Nonformalistic law in time and space. *The University of Chicago Law Review*, *66*(3), 622–634.

Russo, M. V. (1992). Power plays: Regulation, diversification, and backward integration in the electric utility industry. *Strategic Management Journal, 13*(1), 13–27.

Santos, F. M., & Eisenhardt, K. M. (2005). Organizational boundaries and theories of organization. *Organization Science, 16*(5), 491–508.

Santos, F. M., & Eisenhardt, K. M. (2009). Constructing markets and shaping boundaries: Entrepreneurial power in nascent fields. *Academy of Management Journal, 52*(4), 643–671.

Schreiner, J. (1996). B.C. U-brews escape regulation: Consumers lap up cheaper alternative:, *Financial Post*, p. 15. Apr 18, 1996.

Suchman, M. C. (1995). Managing legitimacy: Strategic and institutional approaches. *Academy of Management Review, 20*(3), 571–610.

Suddaby, R., & Greenwood, R. (2005). Rhetorical strategies of legitimacy. *Administrative Science Quarterly, 50*(1), 35–67.

The Parliament of British Columbia. (1996). *1996 Legislative Session: 1st Session, 36th Parliament HANSARD*. Vancouver, BC: Library of Parliament.

Toomey, C. (1993). U-brew: Fight to allow people to make own beer on special sites heats up, *The Gazette*, p. D.1. Apr 17, 1993.

Tost, L. P. (2011). An integrative model of legitimacy judgments. *Academy of Management Review, 36*(4), 686–710.

Vaara, E., & Tienari, J. 2008. A discursive perspective on legitmation strategies in multinational corporations. *Academy of Management Review, 33*(4), 985–993.

Van de Ven, A. H., & Poole, M. S. 1990. Methods for studying innovation development in the Minnesota Innovation Research Program. *Organization Science, 1*, 313–335.

Walker, H. A., Rogers, L., & Zelditch, M. (1988). Legitimacy and collective action: A research note. *Social Forces, 67*(1), 216–228.

Yin, R. K. (2003). *Case study research: Design and methods* (3rd ed.). Thousand Oaks, CA: Sage Publications.

Zelditch, M., & Walker, H. (2000). The normative regulation of power. *Advances in Group Processes, 17*, 155–178.

Zimmerman, M. A., & Zeitz, G. J. (2002). Beyond survival: Achieving new venture growth by building legitimacy. *Academy of Management Review, 27*(3), 414–431.

CHAPTER 2

WHEN DO MARKET INTERMEDIARIES SANCTION CATEGORICAL DEVIATION? THE ROLE OF EXPERTISE, IDENTITY, AND COMPETITION

Romain Boulongne, Arnaud Cudennec and Rodolphe Durand

ABSTRACT

This chapter studies the conditions under which market intermediaries reward or sanction market actors who deviate from the prevailing categorical order. The authors first assess how the expertise of a market intermediary – an understudied determinant of their authority – can lead to a positive evaluation of categorical deviation. Then, the authors identify two inhibitors that are likely to temper such positive appraisal: identity preservation and competition among market intermediaries. Factoring in both micro-level and macro-level dimensions of market dynamics, this chapter contributes to research on market intermediaries, the evolution of category systems, and more broadly, to the microfoundations of institutional change.

Keywords: Microfoundations; categories; expertise; identity; competition; evaluation

Microfoundations of Institutions
Research in the Sociology of Organizations, Volume 65A, 67–83
Copyright © 2020 by Emerald Publishing Limited
All rights of reproduction in any form reserved
ISSN: 0733-558X/doi:10.1108/S0733-558X2019000065A009

Organizational scholars have long studied how institutional and cognitive forces shape market exchanges. In particular, research in institutional theory has underlined the need to extensively study the micro-level processes that instill institutional dynamics (Felin, Foss, & Ployhart, 2015; Greenwood, Oliver, Lawrence, & Meyer, 2017; Powell & Rerup, 2017). For example, in advancing research on the cognitive underpinnings of institutions (Powell & DiMaggio, 1991), studies have argued that categories play an important role in institutional change and preservation (Durand & Thornton, 2018; Rao, Monin, & Durand, 2003).

Categories in this context refer to schemas that enable market actors to make sense of the great flow of information they face (Durand & Paolella, 2013; Hannan, Pólos, & Carroll, 2007), acting as "the cognitive and normative interface among parties enabling market exchanges" (Durand & Khaire, 2017, p. 88). By organizing market actors and their offerings into categories, evaluators are able to compare and value them horizontally in terms of similarity and differences, and vertically in terms of quality. Far from eliciting a neutral commensuration, categories convey normative expectations both from and to market actors (Anteby, 2010; Phillips, Turco, & Zuckerman, 2013). Hence, categories serve a disciplinary role for producers, who must position both themselves and their offerings in the system of categories that govern market exchanges. But to what extent should producers conform to others' expectations? How far can they deviate from the norm? (Durand, Rao, & Monin, 2007; Paolella & Durand, 2016; Zhao, Fisher, Lounsbury, & Miller, 2017; Zuckerman, 2017).

This balancing act of conformism and deviance is sanctioned in most markets by market intermediaries, which are third parties that identify, assess, and order producers in their attempts to facilitate market exchanges between producers (i.e., sources of supply) and clients (i.e., sources of demand). Such intermediaries are ubiquitous and populate diverse marketplaces, from financial to cultural markets, systematically mediating the interactions between producers and consumers (Cattani, Porac, & Thomas, 2017).

Intermediaries play a dual role in market exchanges. First, they enforce categories in diverse contexts, including financial analysts (Zuckerman, 1999), rankers and raters (Chatterji, Durand, Levi, & Touboul, 2016; Sauder, 2008), critics (Becker, 1982; Durand et al., 2007; Hsu, Roberts, & Swaminathan, 2012), awarding academies (Anand & Jones, 2008), and accreditation agencies (Durand & McGuire, 2005), all of which maintain the structure and cohesion of the categorical system that rewards market actors.

Second, beyond rewards (in terms of ranks, stars, and price premiums), market intermediaries enable local meanings to connect to broader institutional meanings, notably by using and shaping classification structures (Glynn & Lounsbury, 2005; Koçak, Hannan, & Hsu, 2014; Ruef & Patterson, 2009). Through their discourses and justifications, they "play a major role in standardizing the components of a category, defining its boundaries, and publicizing models" (Blank, 2007, p. 13). As "meaning makers" (Glynn & Lounsbury, 2005), intermediaries deliver authoritative judgments and diffuse and legitimize evaluative schemas in their field (Durand & Khaire, 2017, p. 101; Hsu et al., 2012).

The dual role of market intermediaries – disciplining (rewarding) market actors and elaborating on the meaning and justification for categorization – rests on an understudied determinant of their authority: their expertise. In this chapter, we question the conditions that make market intermediaries value (or not) a market actor's deviation from expectations. More precisely, we focus on the experts' cognitive abilities that enable them to both make finer distinctions and derive meaning from novel associations between features. Both abilities lead us to expect that, compared with novice market intermediaries, on average, more expert market intermediaries will value greater categorical deviation. Furthermore, we identify two inhibitors, that is, factors that severely temper this propensity: identity preservation and competition. Thus, both an endangered self-image and a race to impose a greater influence inhibit the cognitive mechanisms that favor the acceptance of categorical deviation.

By connecting organizational studies to psychological studies on expertise and identity theory, this chapter contributes to a better understanding of market intermediaries' role and sanctioning behavior, which in return explain why and how these actors are central to the microfoundations of institutions. In this chapter, we understand microfoundations to be actions that occur concurrently at both the individual level (Powell & Colyvas, 2008, pp. 276–277) and the organizational level (e.g., Harmon, Haack, & Roulet 2019). By doing so, we follow the approach that defines microfoundations as being "about locating (theoretically and empirically) the proximate causes of a phenomenon (or explanations of an outcome) at a level of analysis lower than that of the phenomenon itself" (Felin et al., 2015, p. 586). Our analysis focuses on judgments by expert market intermediaries in connection with the processes of categorization and evaluation, which are themselves shaped by institutional forces. The micro-level actions contribute to creating, legitimating, and diffusing meanings on markets, which in turn foster macro-level institutional change (Koçak et al., 2014; Powell & Colyvas, 2008; Weber, Heinze, & DeSoucey, 2008).

MARKET INTERMEDIARIES AS EXPERTS

Market intermediaries play an important role in the exchanges and coordination between producers and buyers, and between suppliers of any kind of good and its consumers. Market intermediaries participate in the description, labeling, and ordering of producers and the goods they offer (Cattani et al., 2017; Rosa, Porac, Runser-Spanjol, & Saxon, 1999). In general, market intermediaries help lower uncertainty on quality (Biglaiser, 1993; Karpik, 2010). They are experts in their domain, and their judgments are trusted, which follows from the definition of *expertise* as "high levels of domain-specific knowledge" (Johnson, 2013, p. 331). For instance, stock market analysts are specialized in given industrial categories and rely on such categories to elaborate their evaluation of companies' stock (Zuckerman, 1999).

Experts are the key to laying the foundations that allow the transmission of early categorical meanings to audiences, leading to these meanings being recognized, counted, and accepted by audience members (Durand & Khaire, 2017; Kennedy, 2010; Khaire & Wadhwani, 2010). For instance, during the emergence of satellite radios, security analysts and specialized media played a key role in defining the relevant categorical boundaries (Navis & Glynn, 2010). Likewise, as a result of demand for the recognition of certain music genres and the institutional support of specialized media, from 1975, the Grammy Awards expanded its awards' classifications to include such categories as rock, metal, and rap (Anand & Watson, 2004). By including these new categories, market intermediaries sanctioned these categories, in the sense that they recognized them as legitimate genres in the field of mainstream music.

Hence, not only do market intermediaries create and diffuse meanings around producers and their offerings, they more fundamentally provide the regulative and normative bases of market evaluation (Ruef & Patterson, 2009). For example, in their study of the emergence of a national system of classification for creditworthiness, Ruef and Patterson (2009) explain how R.G. Dun & Company initiated and imposed its industrial classification of economic activities. This evaluative system's "regulative foundation" implied its recognition in law and jurisprudence, and its "normative foundation," its acceptance by field professionals. As industries mature, intermediaries occupy more legitimate and stable positions at the intersection of producers and clients (Pontikes & Kim, 2017). The intermediary's expertise is thus acknowledged by both transacting parties, which separate them from both less professional and more novice intermediaries (Blank, 2007; Hsu et al., 2012).

Expert and Novice Intermediaries

Compared with novice intermediaries, expert market intermediaries can more efficiently simplify vast amounts of information and meanings into straightforward and widely understandable categorical arrangements (Grodal, Gotsopoulos, & Suarez, 2015), and they do the necessary work of establishing categorical boundaries in a way that is more easily acceptable by others (Khaire & Wadhwani, 2010; Ruef & Patterson, 2009). Expert market intermediaries' greater legitimacy allows them not only to discriminate horizontally between categories but also to fill those categories with more or less standing, thus creating a vertical hierarchy that coincides with a quality scale. For instance, in the case of Indian modern art,

> major Western museums and galleries hired experts on modern Indian art and staged exhibitions that sanctified particular painters or movements, and sometimes the category as a whole .... The increasingly frequent exhibition of 20th-century Indian art in the world's major modern art museums validated the new ways of categorizing and assessing its aesthetic value and conveyed this value to the broader art world. (Khaire & Wadhwani, 2010, p. 1294)

Expert and novice market intermediaries differ in their knowledge base and their information processing. Due to their longer exposure to a particular domain, expert intermediaries have learned to use symbols, languages, and a system of meanings that are exclusive to their expertise sphere (Boudreau, Guinan, Lakhani, & Riedl, 2016; Johnson, 2013). As such, "experts in some domain of knowledge make use of attributes that are ignored by the average person" (Rosch,

Mervis, Gray, Johnson, &. Boyes-Braem, 1976, p. 430). Expert and novice market intermediaries do not focus their attention on the same categories' attributes, and thus cluster and process their knowledge differently. Hence, it is important for category-deviating producers and offerings to understand how market intermediaries assess them as a function of their expertise.

The More Expert the Intermediaries, the Finer Their Category Distinctions

Research in psychology has shown that, compared with novices, experts have a higher cognitive flexibility when categorizing, exhibited as a more flexible access to subordinate-level categories and the ability to make finer-grained distinctions (Johnson & Mervis, 1997; Tanaka & Taylor, 1991).

In markets, audience members negatively sanction categorical deviations because they generate a higher cognitive burden than categorical conformity. Indeed, audience members may struggle to process dissonant information that impedes both a clear identification of the entity and a thus clear expectation of its features and quality (Hannan, 2010; Zuckerman, 1999). However, the cognitive burden created by seemingly dissonant information is likely to be alleviated for experts. Experts' knowledge structures "are characterized by many links among elements and by the formation of abstract representations, all of which become unitized with frequent activation" (Peracchio & Tybout, 1996, p. 179).

Accumulated experience in a domain is likely to increase the frequency of the instantiation of the given categories, which attenuates the perception of dissonance (Barsalou, 1985; Loken, Barsalou & Joiner, 2008). Due to their accumulated experience and deeper knowledge, experts can draw links between seemingly unrelated elements and categories, and, compared with novices, can perceive such combinations as less uncommon and more acceptable. Expert intermediaries are more likely than novices to better comprehend and appreciate more those entities that deviate to a certain extent from pre-established categories because their expertise requires a lower cognitive effort to relate any deviation to their knowledge base (Gregan-Paxton & John, 1997; Meyers-Levy & Tybout, 1989; Moreau, Lehmann, & Markman, 2001). It follows from this first leg of argumentation that more expert intermediaries than novice intermediaries are more comfortable with producers' (categorical) deviation.

More Expert Intermediaries Make More Sense Out of Novelty

Recent works highlight the ability of market intermediaries' judgments to influence how audiences receive categorical deviation (Paolella & Durand, 2016; Zuckerman, 2017). For instance, in the context of corporate-legal services, following intermediaries' rankings, clients value more favorably those law firms that span categories. That is, Paolella and Durand (2016) find evidence for a mediation of intermediaries' rankings of corporate law firms' practices on the relationship between categorical spanning and performance. However, when faced with a producer's combination of features that fail to precisely match the existing categories, intermediaries vary in their ability to make sense out of the surprising assemblage. Prior literature indicates that, compared with novices, more expert agents are more able to find relevant analogies that are filled with meanings (Gregan-Paxton & John, 1997). For instance, the *Guide Gault et Millau* legitimized and diffused as high-status the category "nouvelle cuisine," an analogy to the French "nouveau roman" in literature or "nouvelle vague" in movies (Rao et al., 2003).

As expert evaluators forge meaning via analogies and associations, they tend to use their discretion more and refer less strictly to categories' definition than more novice intermediaries do. Research on cognition has shown that when categorizing entities, experts tend to focus more on functional attributes than on surface-level form attributes (Boster & Johnson, 1989; Shafto & Coley, 2003), preferring to evaluate entities based on their actual attributes rather than on their associated categories (Cowley & Mitchell, 2003; Proell, Koonce, & White, 2016). For instance, in the context of restaurants, Kovács and Hannan (2010) found that the inverted U-curve between category contrast and appeal is negatively moderated by more experienced restaurant-goers, who, in their evaluation, extend less importance to categorical boundaries (Kovács & Hannan, 2010).

Indeed, experts in general, and expert market intermediaries in particular, acknowledge more favorably the intentions and goals that new combinations of categorical features offer. They easily switch from assessing the congruence of an entity with existing prototypes to ad hoc categorization – that is, suggesting that entities coincide with special goals and functionalities (Barsalou, 1983, 1985; Durand & Paolella, 2013; Granqvist, Grodal, & Woolley, 2013). While novices tend to more stringently enforce categorical boundaries and therefore penalize deviant entities more systematically, experts are more likely to discern the rationale behind the proposed novelty, and thus to assess more positively category spanners and novel categorical combinations.

At the cognitive level, experts are more apt than novices at applying analogical reasoning and detecting conceptual combinations (Durand & Boulongne, 2017, chapter 24; Gregan-Paxton & John, 1997). Therefore, the second leg of the argumentation also leads to a more positive assessment of categorical deviation by expert intermediaries, relative to novice intermediaries. We propose, however, that these unique cognitive abilities are dwarfed and inhibited by two forces: identity (which is inward-focused) and competition (which is outward-focused). More specifically, identity and competition exert a major influence on how expert market intermediaries perceive and evaluate categorical deviation. On one hand, identity preservation pressures market intermediaries to conform to established categorical arrangements (Burke & Reitzes, 1991; Hsu, Hannan, & Koçak, 2009; Stryker & Burke, 2000). Competition, on the other hand, refocuses the attention of expert market intermediaries on commonly accepted categories and pushes them to focus on immediate and more intuitive categorical arrangements (Kahneman & Frederick, 2005; Pope & Schweitzer, 2011).

INHIBITOR 1: IDENTITY

Market intermediaries' two principal functions are to discipline (reward) market actors and develop meaning and justification for categorization. Expertise, as a foundational basis of their authority, enables market intermediaries to receive and assess categorical deviation more positively because experts (1) do not reject a priori unused prior combinations, as their deeper and broader knowledge base enables them to estimate the inherent value of novel entities, rather than their superficial correspondence with existing categorical systems; and (2) perceive the intentions and goals that novel entities entail, which leads them to ascribe associations, meanings, and valuable intentions to these deviations. In this section, we discuss the influence of market intermediaries' identity as an inhibitor of the main positive relationship between the extent of expertise and the positive evaluation of categorical deviation.

Drawing on identity theory (Stryker & Burke, 2000), we reason that in the presence of categorical deviation, market intermediaries' authority is put to a test, which engages their identity as intermediaries. For identity theorists, identity explains why people take actions. In general, actors both take into account what their audience reflects about their identity (their reflected appraisals) and "initiate behaviors that maintain or restore congruency between the identity and the reflected appraisals" (Burke & Reitzes, 1991, p. 242). As an illustration, critics on the Internet Movie Database (IMDb) tend to negatively sanction a specific combination of unforeseen film genres in the movie industry – for example, when a movie spans both the science fiction and western categories (Hsu et al., 2009). One explanation is that IMDb's contributors are not expert cinema critics and, compared with experts, tend to demote more harshly any previously unseen combinations. A complementary line of investigation relates to the tension that unseen combinations generate in critics' representation of their identity as market intermediaries.

Market intermediation is contingent on the existence and preservation of a category system. Welcoming any novel combination that unsettles the categorical system also undermines the position and legitimacy of market intermediaries. Given that identity is constructed by establishing boundaries between oneself and others (Abbott, 1995), a market intermediary's identity is associated with a specific market and its corresponding market categories. By extension, when a market intermediary systematically reacts favorably to producers' novel proposals in a market, it also discredits itself and, by extension, cast doubts on other intermediaries. As Goldberg, Hannan, and Kovács (2016) note, associating with atypical entities implies seeing oneself as atypical. Furthermore, building on the commitment to defend and maintain identity is a function of the extent and depth of the relationships in one's network (Stryker, 1968). Market intermediaries are thus highly constrained by the audiences with whom they connect – that is, producers and clients and their expectations about the market intermediaries' role. As market intermediaries are willing to – and need to – preserve a clear identity as being authoritative and relevant for market exchanges, identity maintenance will interfere with the two mechanisms that underlie expert intermediaries' positive appreciation of categorical deviation.

The wider the distance spanned between categories, the more intense the power of market participants' appraisals on the market intermediary's evaluation. As noted by Stryker and Burke (2000, p. 286), "Identities are internalized role expectations." Therefore, as the need to preserve their market identity increases, expert intermediaries will consciously (or not) temper their positive evaluation of deviations. Thus, when faced with categorical deviation, expert intermediaries will tend to access the inner structures of categorical combinations; however, in situations where they need to preserve their identity as intermediaries, they will respond less favorably and value more the superficial correspondence with existing categories than the originality of novel combinations. Likewise, when defending their identity, their ability to draw analogies and provide meaning to categorical deviation will be impaired. Indeed, identity is preserved when keeping the "impure" at distance from the "pure," and more generally, when delineating sharp boundaries that enable things to belong to their right category (Douglas, 1966).

Strongly associating with the market intermediary's identity, and thereby committing to that identity, tends to engender both close-mindedness (Dane, 2010; Ottati, Price, Wilson, & Sumaktoyo, 2015; Zerubavel, 1995) and actions closer to the expected roles of, in general, disciplining market actors and, more specifically, maintaining the instituted category systems. As a result, the efforts to preserve their identity as market intermediaries will also inhibit their capacity and propensity to value positively those producers and offerings that are categorically deviant.

INHIBITOR 2: COMPETITION

The second important influence that tempers why and how expert intermediaries assess categorical deviation positively relates to competition. Market intermediaries are influencers of market exchanges, and this position does not go without contestation, as market mediation attracts multiple actors that vie for exerting the most influence on market exchanges. Traditionally, comparable intermediaries rival and compete: multiple newspapers and media rank universities, culinary guides offer similar gastronomic advice, and security analysts represent similar financial institutions. More recently, with the digitization of our world, consumers and trendsetters have established themselves as market intermediaries and compete with professional intermediaries (Wang, Wezel, & Forgues, 2016).

Our analysis of the influence of competition among intermediaries on the relationship between the degree of a market intermediary's expertise and that intermediary's likelihood to value more or less positively categorical deviation is agnostic of the kind of competition borne by the focal intermediary. First, in a Foucauldian turn, we deem an intermediary to be an expert, as long as the market actors trust its judgments. Expertise is not an attribute declared by an intermediary but an attribute that market actors endow an intermediary with. Hence, some nonprofessional intermediaries (mostly in fields that offer experiential and hedonistic activities, such as in the film industry, the hospitality industry, and gastronomy) could, because of their expertise, be as trusted as professional intermediaries – if not more so. Second, at the level of a focal market intermediary, the mechanisms we identified and the two inhibitors (identity and competition) operate independently of whether the corresponding intermediary is nonprofessional, incumbent, or otherwise.

The question of whether competition moderates the main relationship between market intermediaries' expertise and the categorical deviation's assessment requires an understanding of how the risk of losing influence on market exchanges interferes with the two main mechanisms that lead experts to welcome novelty: higher acceptance of an unusual categorical combination and the capacity to make and diffuse sense regarding a categorical novelty. The main effect of increased competition on a focal intermediary is to reduce the opportunities of being heard by market actors. Indeed, when expert intermediaries promote a new categorical arrangement that is not widely accepted, they risk being cast in a minority position, hence creating an unbearable tension between their credibility as experts and the interests associated with their position in the market. As a result, market intermediaries facing increased competition tend to refocus their attention to those activities that make them valuable intermediaries – that is, enforcing the category systems' discipline and providing meaningful interpretations and analyses regarding market events. This effect of competition (i.e., the refocusing of attention) hinders the activation of the two mechanisms that lead expert intermediaries to value categorical deviation to a greater extent than novice intermediaries do (Gregan-Paxton & John, 1997; Peracchio & Tybout, 1996; Rosch et al., 1976).

First, when under competitive pressures, expert intermediaries pay more heed to the superficial correspondence of novel categorical combinations with existing prototypical features, thereby impeding their capacity to make finer distinctions and to perceive previously unheard associations of features as being coherent and valuable. Competition re-centers attention from the inner subtleties of categorical deviation to surface characteristics. Expert intermediaries thus pay less heed to novelty's delicacies and instead search for consensual judgments among market actors (and against rival intermediaries that could jeopardize market orders).

Second, when under competitive pressures, expert intermediaries have less room to draw on analogies, interpret producers' intentions and goals, and elaborate on refined discourses regarding categorical deviation. As competition increases the risk of loss aversion among expert market intermediaries (Pope & Schweitzer, 2011; Tversky & Kahneman, 1971), expert market intermediaries are more likely to rely on a more intuitive and immediate way of thinking (what Kahneman & Frederick, 2005, refer to as "system 1 thinking"), and subsequently are less likely to mobilize a more analytical and effortful way of thinking (what Kahneman & Frederick, 2005, refer to as "system 2 thinking"). Expert market intermediaries thus return to more effective and less costly communication to make their judgments accessible, recognizable, and trusted by market actors. Therefore, competition leads market intermediaries, and expert market intermediaries even more so, to refocus their attention and reinforce the segregating criteria that separate market categories, thereby leading to market actors trusting their judgments and discriminating among the various competitive offerings.

In summary, in a context of intense competition, experts are less prone both to make sense of attributes that are ignored by average evaluators and to draw parallels and comparisons across unseen categorical combinations. Pressures stemming from competition with other market intermediaries increase the probability that expert market intermediaries will rely less on an analytical and cognitively costly way of thinking, thereby reducing their ability to use analogical reasoning or conceptual combination, which consequently prevents them from either delineating a finer distinction among categories or making sense out of novelty (Durand & Boulongne, 2017, chapter 24; Gregan-Paxton & John, 1997). Competition hence leads expert intermediaries to rely on prototypes, which is an immediate and intuitive way of thinking, rather than the more effortful ideal of evaluating categorical deviation (Barsalou, 1985; Hannan et al., 2007). All in all, when competition increases among intermediaries, it dampens the positive effects of expertise in categorically assessing a market's deviant actors and offerings.

DISCUSSION

In this chapter, we investigated how market intermediaries engage in the evaluation of actors and offerings that deviate from established categories and analyzed the effects of expertise and the conditions under which expert market intermediaries sanction such categorical deviation. Taken together, expertise provides market intermediaries with the cognitive ability to make both finer judgments across categories and more sense of novel categorical combinations, leading to a positive evaluation of categorical deviation.

However, because market intermediaries' authority relates to a category system, categorical deviation challenges market intermediaries by engaging their identity as reliable intermediaries in posing judgments, which leads to their refraining from systematically accepting excessively large deviations. As expert intermediaries need to preserve their identity as reliable intermediaries, they engage less in terms of both the deep structure of categories' connections and elaborating on detailed meanings, which reduces the positive effect of expertise on categorical deviation. In addition, competition pushes market intermediaries to be more conservative in their claims. Thus, as market intermediaries (1) refocus their attention to align their judgments with widely shared expectations and (2) are more subject to bias, leading them to avoid the risk of supporting uncommon categorical combinations, the effect is to impair the two mechanisms associated with expertise that lead to expert intermediaries tolerating and assessing categorical deviation more positively.

Identity preservation and competition thus significantly attenuate the positive effect of market intermediaries' expertise on valuing categorical deviation and can even tilt it to negative. By providing a theoretical model that explains the conditions under which market intermediaries positively or negatively sanction categorical deviation, this chapter contributes to research on market intermediation, the evolution of category systems, and more broadly, institutional change.

Market Intermediaries as Ambiguous Gatekeepers

Our conceptualization of market intermediaries' engagement with categorical deviation leads to an apparent paradox: although expert market intermediaries may be at the vanguard of the formation of novel categories – due to their ability to make finer distinctions and derive meaning from novel categorical combinations – under the conditions of identity preservation and severe competition among market intermediaries, they are likely to endorse the role of "guardian of the temple." When their market intermediary's identity is put to the test and needs to be preserved, market intermediaries tend to curb their tendency as experts to welcome novelty: they adopt a behavior aligned with the expectations of other markets' actors in terms of what their role should be – that is, they discipline producers by enforcing a specific agreed-upon theory of value (Paolella & Durand, 2016; Zuckerman, 2017).

Our work thus calls for a closer look at conditions and settings, such as when and where market intermediaries' identity is or is not threatened, giving leeway to tolerating and encouraging finer distinctions across categories and novel categorical combinations. For instance, when market intermediaries benefit from the legitimacy conferred by their title, their identity is well preserved by an external source of legitimacy, and they are subsequently less vulnerable to the identity threat. As an illustration, we would expect that an official academic accreditation agency would be more likely to provide accreditation to a category-mixing university than for newspapers to include this hybrid university in its ranking of educational institutions.

Similarly, fierce competition among market intermediaries mechanically increases the probability that expert market intermediaries will refocus their attention to (1) established surface relationships between attributes and (2) expected core prototypical features, hence expanding the acceptance of widely shared prototypes across market actors (Hsu et al., 2009; Kennedy & Fiss, 2013). In this sense, our work aims to open the possibility of studying settings where competition among market intermediaries is more or less severe. When competition among market intermediaries is less intense, expert market intermediaries have an opportunity to use their distinctive cognitive abilities to positively sanction categorical deviation.

Expert Market Intermediaries, the Evolution of Category Systems, and Institutional Change

This chapter highlights the key factors that drive the influence of expertise on market intermediaries' appraisal of categorical deviation. In doing so, we bridge micro-level analyses to macro-level categorical dynamics in markets, thereby contributing to studies on the evolution of category systems (Durand & Khaire, 2017) and their effects on institutional change (Durand & Thornton, 2018).

Recent works in organization theory have called for scholars to better connect the evolution of category systems with the process of evaluation – that is, the cognitive mechanisms that audiences use at the moment of evaluation (Durand & Boulongne, 2017, chapter 24; Granqvist et al., 2013). We respond to this call by identifying the cognitive mechanisms and two critical factors that explain why and how market intermediaries – more expert intermediaries, specifically – welcome or reject categorical deviation. The process of evaluation, and the related cognitive mechanisms that market actors use to reach an evaluation, should not be disconnected from either the market actors' necessity to preserve their market identity or the competitive context in which they evolve. Hence, departing from analyzing intermediaries' *average* evaluating behaviors, it is necessary to contextualize the assessment of categorical deviation: identity preservation and competition alter how the expert market intermediaries perceive and evaluate categorical deviation, leading to a reduced acceptance of novelty (Durand & Khaire, 2017; Sharkey, 2014; Zuckerman, 2017).

This chapter also lays the groundwork to better understand the role of market intermediaries and their expertise on institutional change. As noted earlier, when identity threat and competition are weak, expert market intermediaries can actively promote new categorical combinations, using their expertise to grant legitimacy to category systems by sanctioning both the features that belong to categories and their associated rules of membership (Becker, 1982). Their position as intermediaries leads to other market actors using, diffusing, and routinely enforcing such categories, which then become the norm (Grodal et al., 2015; Vergne & Wry, 2014, p. 77).

While studies on institutional change have focused on the interface between producers and audiences (e.g., Fiss & Zajac, 2006; Thornton & Ocasio, 1999), recent research has shown that market intermediaries play a key role in institutional maintenance and change (see Anand & Jones, 2008; Durand et al., 2007; Kennedy, 2010; Lounsbury & Rao, 2004.). On a micro-level, scholars have also emphasized how the activation of specific cognitive mechanisms, such as analogical reasoning, plays a key role in promoting institutional change (Cornelissen, Holt, & Zundel, 2011; Etzion & Ferraro, 2010). We connect these streams of research by highlighting how and why expert market intermediaries are central to the promotion of institutional change. Their appreciation of novelty depends on the context of their evaluation: as they face less pressure to maintain their identity and less competition from rival intermediaries (professional or otherwise), they tend to sanction category deviation more positively, hence redefining current institutional arrangements.

Boundary Conditions and Extensions

First, our two-pronged proposition that positively correlates market intermediaries' level of expertise with evaluations of categorical deviation is not unconditional. This positive relationship stands as long as the magnitude of deviation is moderate to high, but will likely curb or even become negative for the highest degrees of deviation, such as misnaming (e.g., when a producer presents itself as being low cost when it is not) and undue category appropriation (e.g., when a product illegally assumes the attributes of a higher-quality label). We therefore focused our attention in this chapter to the largest pool of observable deviations, and not to outliers at the extremities of deviation.

Furthermore, although we developed our theory based on mature category systems, when categories and attributes are easily recognizable by market actors, we expect our model to also hold when categories and attributes are under construction. Indeed, expert market intermediaries make finer distinctions and more analogical associations than novices do (Grodal et al., 2015). Note, however, that in an emergent category system, the inhibitor role of identity would likely not be as strong, while that of competition would likely be reinforced. Also, intermediaries would be identified with categories whose membership and associated features are still ambiguous. As an example, Chatterji et al. (2016) found that in the emerging category of socially responsible investments, the lack of common theorization and commensurability impedes raters from being clearly identified (Chatterji et al., 2016, pp. 1608–1609). As such, this lack of identification reduces the risk of identity threat, which is likely to lower the inhibitor role played by identity.

For its part, in a context of category emergence, competition among intermediaries would likely dissuade expert market intermediaries from using their specific cognitive abilities to positively assess category deviance, as they would risk being marginalized, and hence lose the advantages associated with their status (Durand & Khaire, 2017; Suarez, Grodal, & Gotsopoulos, 2015). As such, when meanings converge toward a dominant category, expert market intermediaries risk losing their credibility by endorsing a category whose meaning is not sustained both over time and across market actors (i.e., producers, buyers, and other market intermediaries). As a result, expert market intermediaries would be less likely to mobilize their unique cognitive features that allow them to positively assess categorical deviation. Competition is thus consistently associated with pressures to conform, irrespective of the maturity of the category system in which the expert market intermediaries operate.

Finally, we theorized about the effects of competition on the ability of expert market intermediaries to use their unique cognitive abilities, net of the effects of their own status. High-status actors have more leeway to break with membership norms and to positively evaluate categorical deviation (Phillips et al., 2013; Phillips & Zuckerman, 2001). Further research should hence explore how status interacts with expertise, and how it can affect the ability of expert market intermediaries to pursue differentiation strategies by positively evaluating categorical deviation (Wry & Castor, 2017).

Overall, this chapter offers an approach for organizational scholars to better understand the paradoxical position of market intermediaries as "ambiguous gatekeepers" – that is, to understand the conditions under which they sanction, positively or negatively, categorical deviation. In doing so, we apply a micro-level lens to analyze the effects on markets' institutional dynamics as a result of the actions stemming from judgments.

This chapter underlines the need to articulate the cognitive dimensions of categorization by using contextual determinants of the appraisal of categorical deviation – namely identity preservation and competition. Thus, we encourage further research to develop empirical and methodological advancements to capture how market intermediaries' expertise, identity preservation, and competitive forces affect the process and outcome of evaluation. Market intermediaries, both individuals (e.g., cultural critics and financial analysts) and organizations (e.g., media, rankers, and rating agencies) are not isolated "heroic" actors of institutional change but contribute by disseminating their judgments to initiate and convey institutional change or preservation.

By analyzing the cognitive mechanisms implied by expertise and acknowledging the effects of identity and competition on those micro-mechanisms, we explain the conditions under which market intermediaries participate in the evolution of category systems, and more broadly, how they work to precipitate, or not, institutional change. Beyond addressing market intermediaries, we question the role of expertise, the contextual conditions of identification, and the evaluation of categorical deviation for any audience, including clients and regulators, in an effort to bring more nuances and relevance to studies on market categories.

ACKNOWLEDGEMENTS

The authors are grateful for the feedback of the editor, Jost Sieweke, and one anonymous reviewer.

REFERENCES

Abbott, A. (1995). Things of boundaries. *Social Research, 62*(4), 857–882.
Anand, N., & Jones, B. C. (2008). Tournament rituals, category dynamics, and field configuration: The case of the Booker Prize. *Journal of Management Studies, 45*(6), 1036–1060.
Anand, N., & Watson, M. R. (2004). Tournament rituals in the evolution of fields: The case of the Grammy Awards. *Academy of Management Journal, 47*(1), 59–80.
Anteby, M. (2010). Markets, morals, and practices of trade: Jurisdictional disputes in the U.S. commerce in cadavers. *Administrative Science Quarterly, 55*(4), 606–638.
Barsalou, L. W. (1983). Ad hoc categories. *Memory & Cognition, 11*(3), 211–227.
Barsalou, L. W. (1985). Ideals, central tendency, and frequency of instantiation as determinants of graded structure in categories. *Journal of Experimental Psychology – Learning Memory and Cognition, 11*(4), 629–654.
Becker, H. S. (1982). *Art worlds*. Berkeley, CA: University of California Press.
Biglaiser, G. (1993). Middlemen as experts. *The RAND Journal of Economics, 24*(2), 212–223.
Blank, G. (2007). *Critics, ratings, and society*. New York, NY: Rowman & Littlefield.
Boster, J. S., & Johnson, J. C. (1989). Form or function: A comparison of expert and novice judgments of similarity among fish. *American Anthropologist, 91*(4), 866–889.
Boudreau, K. J., Guinan, E. C., Lakhani, K. R., & Riedl, C. (2016). Looking across and looking beyond the knowledge frontier: Intellectual distance, novelty, and resource allocation in science. *Management Science, 62*(10), 2765–2783.
Burke, P. J., & Reitzes, D. C. (1991). An identity theory approach to commitment. *Social Psychology Quarterly, 54*(3), 239–251.
Cattani, G., Porac, J. F., & Thomas, H. (2017). Categories and competition. *Strategic Management Journal, 38*(1), 64–92.
Chatterji, A. K., Durand. R., Levine D. I., & Touboul, S. (2016). Do ratings of firms converge? Implications for managers, investors and strategy researchers. *Strategic Management Journal, 37*(8), 1597–1614.
Cornelissen, J. P., Holt, R., & Zundel, M. (2011). The role of analogy and metaphor in the framing and legitimization of strategic change. *Organization Studies, 32*(12), 1701–1716.

Cowley, E., & Mitchell, A. A. (2003). The moderating effect of product knowledge on the learning and organization of product information. *Journal of Consumer Research, 30*(3), 443–454.

Dane, E. (2010). Reconsidering the trade-off between expertise and flexibility: A cognitive entrenchment perspective. *Academy of Management Review, 35*(4), 579–603.

Douglas, M. (1966). *Purity and danger. An analysis of the concepts of pollution and taboo.* New York, NY: Routledge and Kegan Paul.

Durand, R., & Boulongne, R. (2017). Advancing research on categories for institutional approaches of organizations. In R. Greenwood, C. Oliver, T. B. Lawrence, & R. E. Meyer (Eds.), *The SAGE handbook of organizational institutionalism* (pp. 647–668). London: SAGE.

Durand, R., & Khaire, M. (2017). Where do market categories come from and how? Distinguishing category creation from category emergence. *Journal of Management, 43*(1), 87–110.

Durand, R., & McGuire, J. (2005). Legitimating agencies in the face of selection: The case of AACSB. *Organization Studies, 26*(2), 165–196.

Durand, R., & Paolella L. (2013). Category stretching: Reorienting research on categories in strategy, entrepreneurship, and organization theory. *Journal of Management Studies, 50*(6), 1100–1123

Durand, R., Rao, H., & Monin, P. (2007). Code and conduct in French cuisine: Impact of code changes on external evaluations. *Strategic Management Journal, 28*, 455–472.

Durand, R., & Thornton P. (2018). Categorizing institutional logics, institutionalizing categories: A review of two literatures. *Academy of Management Annals, 12*(2), 631–658.

Etzion, D., & Ferraro, F. (2010). The role of analogy in the institutionalization of sustainability reporting. *Organization Science, 21*(5), 1092–1110.

Felin, T., Foss, N. J., & Ployhart, R. E. (2015). The microfoundations movement in strategy and organization theory. *The Academy of Management Annals, 9*(1), 575–632.

Fiss, P. C., & Zajac, E. C. (2006). The symbolic management of strategic change: Sensegiving via framing and decoupling. *Academy of Management Journal, 49*(6), 1173–1193.

Glynn, M. A., & Lounsbury, M. (2005). From the critics' corner: Logic bending, discursive change and authenticity in a cultural production system. *Journal of Management Studies, 42*(5), 1031–1055.

Goldberg, A., Hannan, M. T., & Kovács, B. (2016). What does it mean to span cultural boundaries? Variety and a typicality in cultural consumption. *American Sociological Review, 81*(2), 215–241.

Granqvist, N., Grodal, S., & Woolley, J. L. (2013). Hedging your bets: Explaining executives' market labeling strategies in nanotechnology. *Organization Science, 24*(2), 395–413.

Gregan-Paxton, J., & John, D. R. (1997). Consumer learning by analogy: A model of internal knowledge transfer. *Journal of Consumer Research, 24*(3), 266–284.

Greenwood, R., Oliver, C., Lawrence, T. B., & Meyer, R. (2017). Introduction: Into the fourth decade. In *The SAGE handbook of organizational institutionalism* (2nd ed., pp. 1–23). London: SAGE.

Grodal, S., Gotsopoulos, A., & Suarez, F. F. (2015). The coevolution of technologies and categories during industry emergence. *Academy of Management Review, 40*(3), 423–445.

Hannan, M. T. (2010). Partiality of memberships in categories and audiences. *Annual Review of Sociology, 36*, 159–180.

Hannan, M. T., Pólos, L., & Carroll, G. R. (2007). *Logics of organization theory.* New York, NY: Princeton University Press.

Harmon, D., Haack, P., & Roulet, T. J. (2019). Microfoundations of institutions: A matter of structure vs. agency or level of analysis? *Academy of Management Review, 44*(2), 464–466.

Hsu, G., Hannan, M. T., & Koçak, Ö. (2009). Multiple category memberships in markets: An integrative theory and two empirical tests. *American Sociological Review, 74*(1), 150–169.

Hsu, G., Roberts, P. W., & Swaminathan, A. (2012). Evaluative schemas and the mediating role of critics. *Organization Science, 23*(1), 83–97.

Johnson, K. E. (2013). Culture, expertise, and mental categories. In D. Reisberg (Ed.), *The Oxford handbook of cognitive psychology* (pp 330–345). Oxford: Oxford University Press.

Johnson, K. E., & Mervis, C. B. (1997). Effects of varying levels of expertise on the basic level of categorization. *Journal of Experimental Psychology: General, 126*(3), 248–277.

Kahneman, D., & Frederick, S. (2005). A model of heuristic judgment. In K. J. Holyoak & R. G. Morrison (Eds.), *The Cambridge handbook of thinking and reasoning* (pp. 267–293). New York, NY: Cambridge University Press.

Karpik, L. (2010). *Valuing the unique.* New York, NY: Princeton University Press.

Kennedy, M. T. (2010). Getting counted: Markets, media, and reality. *American Sociological Review*, *73*, 270–295.

Kennedy, M. T., & Fiss, P. C. (2013). An ontological turn in categories research: From standards of legitimacy to evidence of actuality. *Journal of Management Studies*, *50*(6), 1138–1154.

Khaire, M., & Wadhwani, R. D. (2010). Changing landscapes: The construction of meaning and value in a new market category – Modern Indian art. *Academy of Management Journal*, *53*(6), 1281–1304.

Koçak, Ö., Hannan, M. T., & Hsu, G. (2014). Emergence of market orders: Audience interaction and vanguard influence. *Organization Studies*, *35*(5), 765–790.

Kovács, B., & Hannan, M. T. (2010). The consequences of category spanning depend on contrast. In *From categories to categorization: Studies in sociology, organizations and strategy at the crossroads. Research in the sociology of organizations* (pp. 175–201). Bingley: Emerald Publishing Limited.

Loken, B., Barsalou, L. W., & Joiner, C. (2008). Categorization theory and research in consumer psychology: Category representation and category-based inference. In C. P. Haugtvedt, P. M. Herr, & F. R. Kardes (Eds.), *Handbook of consumer psychology. Series: Marketing and consumer psychology series* (pp. 133–163). New York, NY: Psychology Press.

Lounsbury, M., & Rao, H. (2004). Sources of durability and change in market classifications: A study of the reconstitution of product categories in the American mutual fund industry, 1944–1985. *Social Forces*, *82*(3), 969–999.

Meyers-Levy, J., & Tybout, A. M. (1989). Schema congruity as a basis for product evaluation. *Journal of Consumer Research*, *16*(1), 39–54.

Moreau, C. P., Lehmann, D. R., & Markman, A. B. (2001). Entrenched knowledge structures and consumer response to new products. *Journal of Marketing*, *38*(1), 14–29.

Navis, C., & Glynn, M. A. (2010). How new market categories emerge: Temporal dynamics of legitimacy, identity, and entrepreneurship in satellite radio (1990–2005). *Administrative Science Quarterly*, *55*(3), 439–471.

Ottati, V., Price, E. D., Wilson, C., & Sumaktoyo, N. (2015). When self-perceptions of expertise increase closed-minded cognition: The earned dogmatism effect. *Journal of Experimental Social Psychology*, *61*(C), 131–138.

Paolella, L., & Durand, R., (2016). Category spanning, evaluation, and performance: Revised theory and test on the corporate law market. *Academy of Management Journal*, *59*(1), 330–351.

Peracchio, L. A., & Tybout, A. M. (1996). The moderating role of prior knowledge in schema-based product evaluation. *Journal of Consumer Research*, *23*(3), 177–192.

Phillips, D. J., & Zuckerman, E. W. (2001). Middle-status conformity: Theoretical restatement and empirical demonstration in two markets. *American Journal of Sociology*, *107*, 379–429.

Phillips, D. J., Turco, C. J., & Zuckerman, E. W. (2013). Betrayal as market barrier: Identity-based limits to diversification among high-status corporate law firms. *American Journal of Sociology*, *118*(4), 1023–1054.

Pontikes, E. G., & Kim, R. (2017). Strategic categorization. In *From categories to categorization: Studies in sociology, organizations and strategy at the crossroads*. Research in the Sociology of Organizations (pp. 71–111). Bingley: Emerald Publishing Limited.

Pope, D. G., & Schweitzer, M. E. (2011). Is Tiger Woods loss averse? Persistent bias in the face of experience, competition, and high stakes. *American Economic Review*, *101*(1), 129–157.

Powell, W. W., & Colyvas, J. A. (2008). The microfoundations of institutions. In R. Greenwood, C. Oliver, T. B. Lawrence, & R. E. Meyer (Eds.), *The SAGE handbook of organizational institutionalism* (pp. 276–298). London: Sage Publications.

Powell, W. W., & DiMaggio, P. J. (1991). *The new institutionalism in organizational analysis*. Chicago, IL: The University of Chicago Press.

Powell, W. W., & Rerup, C. (2017). Opening the black box: The Microfoundations of institutions. In R. Greenwood, C. Oliver, T. B. Lawrence, & R. E. Meyer (Eds.), *The SAGE handbook of organizational institutionalism* (2nd ed., pp 311–337). London: Sage Publications.

Proell, S. C., Koonce, L., & White, B. (2016). How do experienced users evaluate hybrid financial instruments? *Journal of Accounting Research*, *54*(5), 1267–1296.

Rao, H., Monin, P., & Durand, R. (2003). Institutional change in Toque Ville: Nouvelle cuisine as an identity movement in French gastronomy. *American Journal of Sociology, 108*(4), 795–843.

Rosa, J. A., Porac, J. F., Runser-Spanjol, J., & Saxon, M. S. (1996). Sociocognitive dynamics in a product market. *Journal of Marketing, 63*(4), 64–77.

Rosch, E., Mervis, C. B., Gray, W. D., Johnson, D. M., & Boyes-Braem, P. (1976). Basic objects in natural categories. *Cognitive Psychology, 8*(3), 382–439.

Ruef, M., & Patterson, K. (2009). Credit and classification: The impact of industry boundaries in nineteenth-century America. *Administrative Science Quarterly, 54*(3), 486–520.

Sauder, M. (2008). Interlopers and field change: The entry of US news into the field of legal education. *Administrative Science Quarterly, 53*(2), 209–234.

Shafto, P., & Coley, J. D. (2003). Development of categorization and reasoning in the natural world: Novices to experts, naive similarity to ecological knowledge. *Journal of Experimental Psychology: Learning, Memory, and Cognition, 29*(4), 641–649.

Sharkey, A. J. (2014). Categories and organizational status: The role of industry status in the response to organizational deviance. *American Journal of Sociology, 119*(5), 1380–1433.

Stryker, S. (1968). Identity salience and role performance: The relevance of symbolic interaction theory for family research. *Journal of Marriage and the Family, 30*(4), 558.

Stryker, S., & Burke, P. J. (2000). The past, present, and future of an identity theory. *Social Psychology Quarterly, 63*(4), 284–297.

Suarez, F. S., Grodal, S., & Gotsopoulos, A. (2015). Perfect timing? Dominant category, dominant design and the window of opportunity for firm entry. *Strategic Management Journal, 36*(3), 437–448.

Tanaka, J. W., & Taylor, M. (1991). Object categories and expertise: Is the basic level in the eye of the beholder? *Cognitive Psychology, 23*(3), 457–482.

Thornton, P. H., & Ocasio, W. (1999). Institutional logics and the historical contingency of power in organizations: Executive succession in the higher education publishing industry, 1958–1990. *American Journal of Sociology, 105*(3), 801–843.

Tversky, A., & Kahneman, D. (1971). Belief in the law of small numbers. *Psychological Bulletin, 76*, 105–110.

Vergne, J. P., & Wry, T. (2014). Categorizing categorization research: Review, integration, and future directions. *Journal of Management Studies, 51*(1), 56–94.

Wang, T., Wezel, F. C., & Forgues. B. (2016). Protecting market identity: When and how do organizations respond to consumers' devaluations? *Academy of Management Journal, 59*(1), 135–162.

Weber, K., Heinze, K., & DeSoucey, M. (2008). Forage for thought: Mobilizing codes in the movement for grass-fed meat and dairy products. *Administrative Science Quarterly, 53*, 529–567.

Wry, T., & Castor, A. R. (2017). Opportunity, status, and similarity: Exploring the varied antecedents and outcomes of category spanning innovation. In *From categories to categorization: Studies in sociology, organizations and strategy at the crossroads.* Research in the Sociology of Organizations (pp. 355–389). Bingley: Emerald Publishing Limited.

Zerubavel, E. (1995). The rigid, the fuzzy, and the flexible: Notes on the mental sculpting of academic identity. *Social Research, 62*(4), 1093–1106.

Zhao, E. Y., Fisher, G., Lounsbury, M., & Miller, D. (2017). Optimal distinctiveness: Broadening the interface between institutional theory and strategic management. *Strategic Management Journal, 38*(1), 93–113.

Zuckerman, E. W. (1999). The categorical imperative: Securities analysts and the illegitimacy discount. *American Journal of Sociology, 104*(5), 1398–1438.

Zuckerman, E. W. (2017). The categorical imperative revisited: Implications of categorization as a theoretical tool. In *From categories to categorization: Studies in sociology, organizations and strategy at the crossroads. Research in the sociology of organizations* (pp. 31–68). Bingley: Emerald Publishing Limited.

CHAPTER 3

"THE HR GENERALIST IS DEAD": A PHENOMENOLOGICAL PERSPECTIVE ON DECOUPLING

Julia Brandl, Jochen Dreher and Anna Schneider

ABSTRACT

According to neo-institutional scholars, experts need to support decoupling, yet doing so may be more or less subjectively understandable for those who are employed as experts. The authors mobilize the phenomenological concept of the life-world as a lens for reconstructing how individuals give meaning to decoupling processes. Based on a hermeneutic analysis of a human resource management expert's reflections on his activities, the authors highlight the subjective experience of decoupling as a process of solving tensions between an individual's convictions and the relevances imposed by an organization. The authors conclude that a phenomenological lens enriches microfoundations debates by focusing on an individual's learning within the framework of an imposed organizational reality.

Keywords: Decoupling; experts; life-world; phenomenology; socio-scientific hermeneutics; human resource management profession

INTRODUCTION

An important notion in neo-institutional theory related to decoupling policy from practice is that experts support coordination behind the "facades" (Meyer & Rowan, 1977), meaning that experts are supposed to work collaboratively on

Microfoundations of Institutions
Research in the Sociology of Organizations, Volume 65A, 85–97
Copyright © 2020 by Emerald Publishing Limited
All rights of reproduction in any form reserved
ISSN: 0733-558X/doi:10.1108/S0733-558X2019000065A010

solutions that maintain faith in an organization even when these solutions deviate from formal rules. Considerable research on the consequences of employing experts suggests that they contribute to the implementation of formal rules in organizations (Dobbin, 2009; Edelman, Petterson, Chambliss, & Erlanger, 1991) and re-coupling processes (Boiral, Cayer, & Baron, 2009; Currie & Spyridonidis, 2016; Hallett, 2010). In contrast, not much attention has been paid to what it means for an individual to "function" as an expert in an organization that decouples policy from practice.

Addressing this question is important for institutional theory because (the functioning of) decoupling depends on the meaning it has for individuals as organization members. Recognizing that reality is socially constructed in processes of interaction between individuals, phenomenological theorists argue that individuals experience this reality as part of their life-world (Schutz & Luckmann, 1973). The life-world is our subjectively experienced world that involves the social world and everyday transcending realities, including, specifically, organizational reality. "Relevance" here refers to the structuring of the knowledge of our life-world. By appreciating how relevances of individuals are affected by their interactions with other organizational members, a phenomenological lens can provide a helpful framework for understanding how individuals give meaning to their purpose as experts in organizational settings where decoupling operates.

Our phenomenological lens to research on decoupling depicts the subjective experience of decoupling as a process of solving tensions between one's intrinsic relevances and those imposed by an organization. We capture this process by drawing on the case of an expert who was initially motivated to establish formal rules when he started working for a semi-public organization, faced strong resistance from other managers against these rules, and ended up by concluding that his expert knowledge was a fiction with no practical relevance. Our focus on the problem solving of an individual with specific professional convictions enriches current perspectives in microfoundations research, such as identity control theory (Brandl & Bullinger, 2017), sensemaking, and practice theory (see Powell & Rerup, 2017, for an overview). On a more abstract level, our phenomenological lens offers ideas for addressing ambiguities inherent in the concept of decoupling (Tolbert & Zucker, 1996), which could open viable avenues for future empirical analyses.

The field of expertise that we focus on is human resource management (HRM). The considerable accumulated wisdom of contemporary scholarly and non-scholarly HRM knowledge stands in stark contrast to explanations provided by neo-institutional scholars as to how organizations survive. HRM scholars typically stress employee behavior as the primary determinant of organizational success and assume that desired employee behavior can be produced by introducing formal employment rules and ensuring that they are consistently applied. Scholars in this field recognize informal practices, but problematize deviations from rules violating employee fairness perceptions and commitment. The designated purpose of human resource experts is to design rules and ensure their implementation in cooperation with other managers.

Since much HRM literature tends to portray organizations as rational systems, HR experts are expected that they can resolve conflicts with other managers by using the right approach. In sum, HRM knowledge offers individuals working in this field an appealing way of understanding themselves as experts for organizational success, which can be achieved by managing employee behavior by formal employment rules and which provides a strong rationale for their interventions in other managers' activities. Thus, HRM is an ideal field of expertise for understanding how individuals give meaning to their purpose as experts in settings where decoupling operates. Before we turn to the case of an HR manager who was convinced of this knowledge, we briefly discuss the relation between experts and decoupling in the neo-institutional debate and introduce the concept of the life-world as a framework for analyzing how experts experience decoupling.

EXPERTS AND DECOUPLING

Neo-institutional theory suggests that organizations incorporate formal rules and standards that are institutionalized in society in order to increase their legitimacy (Meyer & Rowan, 1977). Since formal rules can conflict with efficient collaboration, organizations seek to reduce the impact that these institutionalized elements have on how work really gets done. Organizations seek to uphold the gaps between these elements and actual practices; in other words, they decouple (Bromley & Powell, 2012). Central to Meyer and Rowan's argument of decoupling is that experts employed by organizations not only create an aura of confidence that the organization operates according to rules but they also support decoupling by tolerating inconsistencies between institutionalized elements and practices using avoidance, discretion, and overlooking. Whether an organization is able to conceal inconsistencies depends on how well its experts' actions support decoupling.

The ideal situation described by Meyer and Rowan is one in which experts understand the purpose of their position in ways that they support decoupling. This understanding, however, may be more or less subjectively clear to the individuals who are employed as experts. Considering the ideas in neo-institutional theory about how experts should contribute to organizational legitimacy, their "functioning" is at least not trivial. First, using outside experts helps organizations to signal compliance, yet expert outsiders rarely know what they are actually expected to do (or not to do) in their interactions with organization members because organizations typically conceal decoupling processes to outsiders. Second, while employing individuals with extensive expertise and professional credentials helps organizations to increase confidence in its activities in this specific field, individuals with such desired expertise and credentials may also have their own professional convictions and intentions about how to use their expertise in practice, meaning that they seek to eliminate practices that contradict these convictions. If we cannot expect that experts will know and support decoupling automatically and if we want to understand how they may still contribute to decoupling, we need a perspective that captures how individuals recognize and understand decoupling and incorporate it into their activities.

Current neo-institutional research provides little guidance here. Scholars have pointed out that the notion of having gaps between institutionalized elements and practices is conceptually problematic (Tolbert & Zucker, 1996). Macro-studies demonstrate that employing experts goes hand in hand with the elaboration of formal rules in organizations (e.g., Dobbin, 2009; Edelman et al., 1991). This research suggests that experts do not limit themselves to representing the organization, yet it is far from capturing the orientation of individual actors in relation to decoupling. The small body of micro-research captures different aspects of decoupling. For instance, scholars have studied how decoupling processes operate (Hallett, 2010; Sandholtz & Burrows, 2016; Tilcsik, 2010), examined how experts' activities differ according to the nature of their expertise (Risi & Wickert, 2017), their action logics (Boiral et al., 2009) or social position (Currie & Spyridonidis, 2016), how individuals master situations in which inconsistencies between institutionalized elements and practices become public (Brandl & Bullinger, 2017), and explored how experts are emotionally affected by decoupling (Vo, Culié, & Mounoud, 2016). In sum, extant research is limited to portraying individuals either as being an integral part of decoupling practices or as being positioned to decoupling in different ways, rather than capturing how individuals recognize decoupling and incorporate it into their activities. A theoretical lens that depicts decoupling with respect to the actions of the individuals involved in organizations would enable us to explore the processes through which individuals recognize the meaning of decoupling from their subjective perspective.

LIFE-WORLD, REALITIES, AND RELEVANCES

Schutz's concept of the life-world (Schutz & Luckmann, 1973, Ch. 1–5) is part of his phenomenologically oriented sociology.[1] This perspective decidedly departs from Max Weber's "methodological individualism", in that it assumes that sociological theory always has to reflect social phenomena, with a focus on the individual actor. One cannot practice phenomenologically oriented sociology without taking the actor and his or her actions into consideration. If we use this perspective to analyze the phenomenon of "decoupling," this would mean that we always have to also refer to individual actors – executives, CSR managers, workers, etc. – who are involved in processes of "decoupling". In this context, interpretive research specifically allows us to reconstruct the meaning the involved actors give to their actions and also to understand how they themselves describe and interpret what they experience within an organizational reality.

The subjectively centered life-world is the world experienced by the individual subject. It consists of the world of the experiencing "I" as well as the social world that is characterized by intersubjectivity. Furthermore, it includes multiple realities, such as the paramount reality of everyday life in which we act and communicate. Other realities are worlds of religious experience, of politics, of science as well as our dreams and the play world of children (Schutz, 1962b). Organizations also establish specific worlds of meaning that can be considered as "everyday transcending" realities. Decoupling, then, can be seen as part of the organizational reality. As part of our life-world, the "social world" includes all other fellow human beings with whom we are associated. From a phenomenological standpoint, our shared knowledge of the social world and of organizational reality, more specifically, is always relative to the biographical situation of the individual. Since the concept of the social world includes all social phenomena – local and global – this phenomenological standpoint uses no micro–macro distinction. From the life-world perspective, such a distinction is unnecessary for analyzing social phenomena. If we are concentrating on phenomena such as decoupling (on the so-called organizational level), which is produced by human beings, it is always relevant to reconstruct the motivations of individual actors (considered to be the individual level) who work collaboratively on solutions that deviate from formal rules.

Schutz's (1970) concept of "relevance" is especially important here. It establishes a theoretical bridge between the knowledge and motivation of the individual and the imposed structural preconditions of the organization. By relevance, we refer to the knowledge and motivation involved in actions as they relate to decision making. Our actions depend on different relevances: some of them are determined by immediate pragmatic interests, others by the general situation in society (Berger & Luckmann, 1989, p. 45), or – with respect to our empirical focus – by those relevances in an organizational setting. The concept of relevance enables us to understand organizational phenomena at the interface of objective and subjective reality because it functions as a regulative principle of reality construction. The relevance concept coordinates the knowing and experiencing of the social world and it allows the individual to define the situation (Nasu, 2003, p. 91). The social world possesses a structure of meaning and relevance for all those who live, think, and act in it (Schutz, 1962a, p. 5f.).

The relevance concept enables us to investigate the subjective motivation of the individual entering into processes of action. The individual living in the world and participating as a member of an organization experiences himself or herself in a certain situation which – according to the Thomas theorem (Thomas & Thomas, 1928, p. 572) – has to be defined by himself or herself. The definition of the situation is characterized by two components: the first one is the result of the ontological structure of the pre-given world and the second one is defined by the actual biographical state of the individual. The first component cannot be changed by the individual and determines the "imposed relevances" that are not connected with his or her chosen interests; there is no possibility to change them. The second component determines our "intrinsic relevances" that are related to our chosen interests, established by our spontaneous decision to solve a problem by our thinking or by our attempt to attain a goal by our action, for instance (Schutz, 1964, p. 126f.; Schutz & Zaner, 1970, p. 26ff.).

The reference to imposed and intrinsic relevances is especially useful for analyzing decoupling, since it establishes the bridge between structure (in our case decoupling) and action. It emphasizes that an individual organization member's actions cannot be completely determined by the structural preconditions related to the imposed relevances; individuals also act according to their specific motivations and interests related to their personal biography – in other words, they follow their intrinsic relevances. Building on their intrinsic relevances, experts may reject the pre-given structural condition (of decoupling policy from practice) and act according to their professional or other convictions, which might not be in accordance with the structural condition. On the other hand, as individuals fail in their attempts to realize their intrinsic relevances, upholding their reality becomes more difficult and they start a process of making meaning with the "raw material" offered by the imposed relevances. This dynamic process opens up possibilities for analyzing how individuals reconstruct decoupling as part of the reality of organizations. Our research, therefore, focuses on the change of relevances of an individual who was employed as an expert.

METHODOLOGY

Our study of decoupling is based on the reflections of an expert in the field of HRM, whom we call Peter (fictional name). Peter became the chief human resource officer (CHRO) of a large semi-public organization that had recently started a privatization process. High fixed personnel costs and a performance-adverse mentality were defined as important obstacles for the organization's competitiveness and the organization was looking for a CHRO with experience in the private sector. Peter had a background in business and management, had worked in senior HR positions for over 20 years, and had been employed by several reputable companies, all of which gave him substantial experience as an HR expert who could help to make the organization competitive. Shortly after Peter had been appointed to the CHRO position, he contacted one of the authors and asked to run a workshop on performance-based pay systems for the members of the organization's HRM department. Given this author's research interest in HR, the workshop was followed by a one-and-a-half-hour interview with Peter that focused on his understanding of the purpose of his job as CHRO in this organization, particularly in supporting its privatization process and the challenges that he might face. Peter appeared to be highly committed to HRM knowledge and particularly convinced of the integrative function of formal employment rules for the organization. He described his understanding of the interaction between himself and other managers as following:

> For me, I demand that I bring my position in the decision-making processes in a constructive, factual way. That's the role that I think is the right one, for the HR managers personalists of the future. Or the present, because we've been talking about that for ten years, that's the role.

> – Peter, CHRO

Four years later, this same author learned that the organization had dismissed Peter. Because this outcome appeared to be inconsistent with the reasoning expected by current HRM knowledge (briefly described in the introduction), the author invited Peter for another interview off-site. The second interview took place one year after his dismissal and lasted two hours. In this interview, Peter shared that the organization had abandoned various programs that had been adopted under his guidance, and that his successor as CHRO was a person whose background was in the public sector and who completely lacked private sector experience. Peter gave various examples of the reactions from other managers when he attempted to establish his understanding of the CHRO's purpose and reflected on the reasons for these reactions. He concluded in an unemotional way that any idea about the HR expert role that goes beyond administratively supporting other managers is unrealistic. Some months after this interview, Peter became CHRO in a different company where he remained employed until his retirement.

The methodology used for our analysis of decoupling is socio-scientific hermeneutics, which is a technique and capability for interpreting symbolic human expressions and products of action. It can be seen as a scientific method of analysis based on an elaborate writing system and texts transmitted in written form. Hermeneutics concentrates on carving out the typical and the distinctiveness of individual cases. Strictly speaking, it is about the reconstruction not only of the interaction and interaction products but also the reconstruction of pre-scientific, everyday accomplishments of comprehension (Soeffner, 2004, p. 119). Socio-scientific hermeneutics aims to hypothetically reconstruct an action or problem situation (Soeffner & Hitzler, 1994, p. 111).

Our analysis cannot provide findings that are representative for a specific social group or society. The study – an interpretation of a concrete case – is based on the reconstruction of "the particular" that allows for an understanding of "the general" (Soeffner & Hitzler, 1994, p. 111f.). The specific case of our HR manager, Peter, presented in the interviews, allows us to understand how the phenomenon of decoupling is generally *experienced* by individual subjects who operated as experts in organizations. The individual case can therefore be seen as a specific solution to an interaction problem that our interviewee experienced within the objective circumstances in the organization that he was subjected to.

The reconstructive method of socio-scientific hermeneutics is sequence analysis, which is used to interpret textualizations of interviews or conversations that are protocols of former irreversible interactions. Sequence analysis departs from the idea that each utterance in a sentence – with respect to its meaning – is connected to the utterances that follow it. The procedural development of the formulated sentence – the sequence of the utterances – is taken into consideration in the interpretation. This quasi word-by-word interpretation of key passages of a text allows the interpreter to reconstruct the meaning of the text in the line of the occurrence (of the interaction) (Soeffner & Hitzler, 1994, p. 117). While the interpretation focuses on the concrete text itself, the aim of the interpreter is to establish a structure hypothesis on the circumstances that gave rise to this text. Structure hypotheses can partly consist of non-directly observable phenomena, such as decoupling, if the interpreters are interested in these phenomena. We use this method here to reconstruct the subjective meaning given by Peter for his situation as an expert confronted with processes of decoupling that he had been formerly unaware of.

"THE HR GENERALIST IS DEAD"

The following interpretation of a key passage of the second interview with Peter presents a structure hypothesis related to interaction, problem solving, and legitimization in a specific organizational reality. The structure hypothesis was developed based on a hermeneutic word-by-word interpretation of the following key passage:[2]

> For me the résumé is, the HR generalist is dead, yes [...]. But the HR manager as coequal partner, as business partner, as strategic partner is dead. In case he was ever alive, I don't know.
>
> – Peter, ex-CHRO

First, Peter introduces the concept of the HR generalist, who is an executive who is responsible for relying on and bringing together the interests of different groups or stakeholders. The HR generalist is able to deal with contradictory interests and role requirements of the respective interest groups. The HR generalist is entitled to involve him- or herself proactively in decision-making processes and influence other managers based on his or her superior knowledge of how to effectively manage an organization's most important success factor: employees. A decisive argument of Peter's is that the HR generalist is dead, which means that he is first of all convinced that the HR generalist used to live and did exist in the past. Now, he argues, this specific executive has become ineffective and is now irrevocably gone. According to Peter, the HR generalist could have established an overarching conceptual picture through HRM, somehow uniting the differing interests of the cooperating parties within the organization. The crucial capacity of the HR generalist in this sense would be his or her expertise in different business sectors.

What Peter expresses is that the function of the HR generalist was invented by a currently popular version of HRM. The HR manager as executive incorporates a role model that only makes sense within this particular version, in which the competencies and motivation of employees have priority over material resources. On the one hand, the utterance of Peter signifies that the HR generalist has "resigned" or ceased to make sense for a semi-public organization. There is also the signification that the HR generalist principally has said "goodbye" and given up his or her existence. "The HR generalist dead" also contains the meaning expressions that he or she is in fact physically present, but is completely ineffective. When Peter presents the concept HR generalist, he opens up an opposition to service law and administration HR managers.

The role of Peter as HR generalist was not accepted by the other executives. This was specifically deduced in the first interview, where he uttered that these executives were not interested in his advice or in implementing any policies that he might propose. In other instances, the executives signaled their willingness to support him, yet their actions were in complete opposition. He explained to other executives that employees accept decisions better if those decisions are rule-based and he developed formal agreements for topics such as salary increases and early retirement, but the executives violated these rules and the CEO did nothing to support him in reinforcing them. In this sense, the HR generalist is ineffective and "dead" because cooperation with executive colleagues resulted to be impossible.

Based on this argument, Peter provides evidence that the HR generalist has ceased to exist, has said goodbye, is "dead," and that many other HR executives can confirm this. Since "the HR manager as coequal partner, as business partner, as strategic partner is dead," any partnership for Peter as HR generalist becomes in many regards impossible. His colleagues neither acknowledge his respective expertise, nor do they respect him as far as their own activities in managing employees are concerned. The questions Peter still asks himself are whether his partners in the organization ever had the same interest as he did and whose responsibility it was to stick to the agreements that were decided upon. Peter remains unsure if the HR generalist "ever was alive," which can be interpreted as a serious doubt concerning the role and the function of this executive position. Peter questions the "figure" of the HR generalist and suggests that there possibly has never been an HR generalist. The HR generalist as invented and proposed by popular HRM literature could therefore be a fictional reality, or myth, that actually has never existed. These fictional figures are continuously presented by those who tell the narratives about them (e.g., the scholarly community); in this way, figures like the HR generalist are communicatively updated all the time. Peter does not know if these figures – as part of mythical social construction – have ever existed; based on his own experiences, the existence of the HR generalist cannot be supported.

If we bring the interpretation to a further level, it becomes obvious that Peter is reflecting on his own situation as a failed HR generalist, as he was five years before he had to leave the organization and the interview took place. With this timely distance on his fate in this organization, he could reflect on an inscrutable work situation that did not make sense to him at the time. Saying "goodbye" to the HR generalist and recognizing this figure as standing outside the paramount reality can be interpreted as liberation for Peter. He has been able to identify that this figure was not practically helpful for building relationships with other organization members and understands that his conviction that this figure did exist may have contributed to his fate in the former organization.

The "figure" of the HR generalist as proposed by HRM literature, in his opinion, never had a chance to survive in this particular organization, and may not have a chance in other organizations either. Peter could not be successful with his projects and activities because they contradicted the functional processes of the organization. The reason why he could not succeed in this organization in the past is not related to his (potentially) inappropriate decision-making that resulted from following his intrinsic relevances. Rather, it was the evolved and established organizational reality that did not provide a possibility for including him as the respective HR generalist. HRM and the "figure" of the HR generalist were installed in the organization as "symbol politics" to demonstrate that a traditional organization adopts management concepts that enable its survival in a private sector environment. But indeed, as suggested by Peter, there was no need for HRM or the HR generalist at all. Therefore, cooperation with the other executives and with his CEO resulted to be impossible – it could not have been included in the functional processes of the organization. This is exactly why the "HR generalist is dead," and maybe has never even existed in past, because this person is just an invention of the HRM literature. Since Peter gave up the HR generalist as a guidline for his interactions with other individuals in organizations and shifted it to the world of fiction, he is now open to other figures that could help establish relationships when working as an HR expert in the future.

CONCLUDING DISCUSSION

In concluding the above analysis and reflecting on what Peter's thoughts tell us about how individual actors give meaning to decoupling, we highlight two contributions a phenomenology lens can offer for current and future research on decoupling.

First, Peter's case teaches us that attempting to enact professional convictions about formal rules in organizations has an impact on the location of such rules in the individual actor's life-world. We describe this process in terms of the individual's bodily experiences of organizational reality, discrepancies with intrinsic relevances, and a subsequent change of relevance structures. It starts when individuals recognize the discrepancy between their explicitly articulated expectations of experts and their actual expectations via their actions to enact explicitly articulated expectations. Discrepancies "weigh" on acting individuals and offer a momentum of insight and opportunity for a revision of convictions about the meaning of being an expert. Eventually, we see that an individual actor's capacities for sustaining intrinsic relevances that operate in opposition to imposed relevances prevailing in organizations are limited. While the professional convictions can no longer be used as a meaningful source for relevant responsibilities and relationships with other significant organization members, an individual actor can continue to reflect on them as part of a different, fantastic reality.

Such a phenomenological lens with a focus on the concept of the life-world enriches current perspectives on microfoundations of institutions (Powell & Rerup, 2017; Smets, Aristidou, & Whittington, 2017). Phenomenology, even more explicitly than practice theory, emphasizes the intentionality and motivation of individuals for taking particular courses of action; therefore, decoupling cannot be seen as a "pure" structural phenomenon independent of the acting individual. With sensemaking, a phenomenological lens shares the interest in an individual actor's lived experience of institutions and how they trigger sensemaking (Weber & Glynn, 2006). But phenomenology is more interested in the dynamics in experience and focuses on the interplay of decision-making and sensemaking. Along with identity control theory (e.g., Brandl & Bullinger, 2017), phenomenology shares the assumption that individuals organize multiple intrinsic relevances that dynamically evolve. While identity control theory claims that transcending experiences involve arousal and alienation, the emphasis of phenomenology is on the individual's enlightenment and satisfaction that are associated with regarding themselves as "insiders" who can predict what does work and what does not work (Meyer, 1986). Also, phenomenology is less concerned with the assertion made by identity control theory that intrinsic relevances generally need to be confirmed in interactions with others.

Second, our analysis provides an empirically based understanding of the relationship between institutionalized rules and the activities of individual actors in organizations. This understanding is potentially useful for addressing concerns about the suitability of the concept of decoupling as a part of a phenomenological version of neo-institutional theory. Tolbert and Zucker argue that the institutionalization of rules contradicts the claim that rules are apt to be decoupled from action: "To *be* institutional, structure must generate action" (Tolbert & Zucker, 1996, p. 179; emphasis in original). The case of Peter suggests that rules, in the form of widely accepted professional knowledge, indeed can generate an individual actor's courses of action in organizational contexts. This observation, though, needs to be complemented by considering that individual actors in the paramount reality of everyday life solve problems based on pragmatic motives. If actors recognize discrepancies between professional convictions and organizational reality, their relevances may change. A phenomenological lens is particularly helpful for considering two aspects of this change, which we have not directly addressed in our empirical analysis but which are implied by the concept of the life-world. The first aspect concerns the "location" of institutionalized rules in the subjective life-world. We argue that using professional knowledge for "representational purposes" (e.g., in a job interviews) is no less a sign of intentional use of this knowledge than using it in the functional processes of the organization. The life-world concept allows us to acknowledge how individual actors organize different intentions within a phenomenological perspective instead of privileging one particular reality over others. The second aspect concerns the characteristics of organizational reality. If we accept that organizations are institutions themselves and that individuals take their characteristics for granted (Zucker, 1977), we need to be open to note that phenomena such as decoupling may be one of these characteristics, instead of assuming that only bureaucratic characteristics of organizations are taken for granted. In other words, we should be interested examining if individuals "automatically" support decoupling if they consider themselves in an organizational context.

Our lens opens up possibilities for doing empirical research on decoupling. One way forward is to examine the patterns of individuals' actions as they regard themselves in an organizational setting in order to reveal whether they take into consideration decoupling processes. From a phenomenological lens, empirical research must consider the interrelationship of individual action and structure in order to understand decoupling processes. Although it is a social phenomenon, decoupling does not exist independent of individual actors and cannot be analyzed in the absence of individual actors. In order to address issues such as whether and where decoupling is a temporary phenomenon in organizations or in studying the dynamics of decoupling (Haack & Schoeneborn, 2015, p. 308), empirical research needs to refer to the meaning individual actors involved in the process of organizing within bureaucratic organizations give to their actions. To this end, socio-scientific hermeneutics, the methodology that we introduced in this chapter is a way forward.

NOTES

1. This theoretical position is related to what John W. Meyer considers a "phenomenological perspective of sociological institutionalism" (Meyer, 2017).

2. The hermeneutic interpretation was based on the original interview transcription in German; what follows here is an English translation of the text.

REFERENCES

Berger, P. L., & Luckmann, T. (1989). *The social construction of reality. A treatise in the sociology of knowledge*. New York, NY: Anchor Books.

Boiral, O., Cayer, M., & Baron, C. M. (2009). The action logics of environmental leadership: A developmental perspective. *Journal of Business Ethics, 85*(4), 479–499. doi:10.1007/s10551-008-9784-2

Brandl, J., & Bullinger, B. (2017). Individuals' considerations when responding to competing logics: Insights from identity control theory. *Journal of Management Inquiry, 26*(2), 181–192. doi:10.1177/1056492616677297

Bromley, P., & Powell, W. W. (2012). From smoke and mirrors to walking the talk: Decoupling in the contemporary world. *The Academy of Management Annals, 6*(1), 483–530.

Currie, G., & Spyridonidis, D. (2016). Interpretation of multiple institutional logics on the ground: Actors' position, their agency and situational constraints in professionalized contexts. *Organization Studies, 37*(1), 77–97.

Dobbin, F. (2009). *Inventing equal opportunity*. New York, NY: Princeton University Press.

Edelman, L. B., Petterson, S., Chambliss, E., & Erlanger, H. S. (1991). Legal ambiguity and the politics of compliance: Affirmative action officers' dilemma. *Law & Policy, 13*(1), 73–97. doi:10.1111/j.1467-9930.1991.tb00058.x

Haack, P., & Schoeneborn, D. (2015). Is decoupling becoming decoupled from institutional theory? A commentary on Wijen. *Academy of Management Review, 40*(2), 307–310.

Hallett, T. (2010). The myth incarnate recoupling processes, turmoil, and inhabited institutions in an urban elementary school. *American Sociological Review, 75*(1), 52–74.

Meyer, J. W. (1986). The self and the life course: Institutionalization and its effects. In A. B. Sørensen, F. E. Weinert, & L. R. Sherrod (Eds.), *Human development and the life course: Multidisciplinary perspectives* (pp. 199–216). Hillsdale, NJ: Lawrence Erlbaum Associates.

Meyer, J. W. (2017). Reflections on institutional theories of organizations. In R. Greenwood, C. Oliver, T. B. Lawrence, & R. E. Meyer (Eds.), *The Sage handbook of organizational institutionalism* (2nd ed., pp. 831–852). London: Sage.

Meyer, J. W., & Rowan, B. (1977). Institutionalized organizations: Formal structure as myth and ceremony. *American Journal of Sociology, 83*(2), 340–363.

Nasu, H. (2003). A Schutzian approach to the problem of equality–inequality. Retrieved from http://ipjp.org/images/e-books/OPO%20Essay%2042%20-%20A%20Schutzian%20Approach%20to%20the%20Problem%20of%20Equality-Inequality%20-%20By%20Hisashi%20Nasu.pdf

Powell, W. W., & Rerup, C. (2017). Opening the black box: The microfoundations of institutions. In R. Greenwood, C. Oliver, T. B. Lawrence, & R. E. Meyer (Eds.), *The Sage handbook of organizational institutionalism* (Vol. 2, pp. 311–337). Thousand Oaks, CA: Sage.

Risi, D., & Wickert, C. (2017). Reconsidering the 'symmetry' between institutionalization and professionalization: The case of corporate social responsibility managers. *Journal of Management Studies, 54*(5), 613–646.

Sandholtz, K. W., & Burrows, T. N. (2016). Compliance police or business partner? Institutional complexity and occupational tensions in human resource management. In L. E. Cohen, D. M. Burton, & M. Lounsbury (Eds.), *The structuring of work in organizations. Research in the sociology of organizations*. (Vol. 47, pp. 161–191). Bingley: Emerald Publishing Limited.

Schutz, A. (1962a). Common-sense and scientific interpretation of the social world. In M. Natanson (Ed.), *Collected papers, Vol. I: The problem of social reality* (pp. 3–47). The Hague, Netherlands: Nijhoff (Reprinted from 1953).

Schutz, A. (1962b). Symbol, reality and society. In M. Natanson (Ed.), *Collected papers, Vol. I: The problem of social reality* (pp. 287–356). The Hague, Netherlands: Nijhoff (Reprinted from: 1955).

Schutz, A. (1964). The well-informed citizen: An essay on the social distribution of knowledge. In A. Brodersen (Ed.), *Collected papers, Vol. II. Studies in social theory* (pp. 120–134). The Hague, Netherlands: Nijhoff (Reprinted from 1946).

Schutz, A., & Luckmann, T. (1973). *The structures of the life-world (Vol. 1)*. Evanston, IL: Northwestern University Press.

Schutz, A., & Zaner, R. M. (1970). *Reflections on the problem of relevance*. New Haven, CT: Yale University Press.

Smets, M., Aristidou, A., & Whittington, R. (2017). Towards a practice-driven institutionalism. In R. Greenwood, C. Oliver, T. B. Lawrence, & R. E. Meyer (Eds.), *The Sage handbook of organizational institutionalism* (2nd ed., pp. 365–391). London: Sage Publications.

Soeffner, H.-G. (2004). Hermeneutik. Zur Genese einer wissenschaftlichen Einstellung durch die Praxis der Auslegung [Hermeneutics. The Genesis of the Scientific Attitude through Interpretation]. In H.-G. Soeffner (Ed.), *Auslegung des Alltags – Der Alltag der Auslegung. Zur wissenssoziologischen Konzeption einer sozialwissenschaftlichen Hermeneutik [Interpretation of Everyday Life - The Everyday Life of Interpretation. The Sociology of Knowledge Conception of Social Scientific Hermeneutics]* (pp. 114–159). Konstanz, Germany: UVK.

Soeffner, H.-G., & Hitzler, R. (1994). Qualitatives Vorgehen – Interpretation. 3. Kapitel. In T. Herrmann (Ed.), *Enzyklopädie der psychologie [Qualitative Research - Interpretation. Chapter 3]* (Vol. 1, pp. 98–136). Göttingen, Germany: Hogrefe.

Thomas, W. I., & Thomas, D. S. (1928). The methodology of behavior study. In *The child in America: Behavior problems and programs* (pp. 553–576). New York, NY: Alfred A. Knopf.

Tilcsik, A. (2010). From ritual to reality: Demography, ideology, and decoupling in a post-communist government agency. *Academy of Management Journal, 53*(6), 1474–1498.

Tolbert, P. S., & Zucker, L. G. (1996). The institutionalization of institutional theory. In S. R. Clegg, C. Hardy, & W. R. Nord (Eds.), *Handbook of organizational studies* (pp. 175–190). London: Sage.

Vo, L.-C., Culié, J.-D., & Mounoud, E. (2016). Microfoundations of decoupling: From a coping theory perspective. *M@n@gement, 19*(4), 248–276.

Weber, K., & Glynn, M. A. (2006). Making sense with institutions: Context, thought and action in Karl Weick's theory. *Organization Studies, 27*, 1639–1660.

Zucker, L. G. (1977). The role of institutionalization in cultural persistence. *American Sociological Review, 42*, 726–743.

CHAPTER 4

WHY DO INDIVIDUALS PERCEIVE AND RESPOND TO THE SAME INSTITUTIONAL DEMANDS DIFFERENTLY? ON THE COGNITIVE STRUCTURAL UNDERPINNINGS OF INSTITUTIONAL COMPLEXITY

Magdalena Cholakova and Davide Ravasi

ABSTRACT

Research has begun to explore how individuals perceive and respond to institutional complexity differently. The authors extend such efforts and theorize how the complexity of individuals' cognitive representations of the institutional logics (based on their perceived differentiation *and* integration *of the external environment) and of their role identities (based on the* pluralism *and* unity *of their self-representations) can predict such variation. The authors argue that the former explains whether individuals are capable of enacting norms and beliefs from different logics and of envisioning possibilities to reconcile their contradictory demands, whereas the latter explains whether they are* moti-vated *to implement a given response.*

Keywords: Cognitive complexity; self-unity; self-pluralism; cognitive differentiation and integration; novel institutional complexity; microfoundations

Microfoundations of Institutions
Research in the Sociology of Organizations, Volume 65A, 99–118
Copyright © 2020 by Emerald Publishing Limited
All rights of reproduction in any form reserved
ISSN: 0733-558X/doi:10.1108/S0733-558X2019000065A011

Institutional theorists introduced the notion of institutional complexity to refer to situations where actors "confront incompatible prescriptions from multiple institutional logics" (Greenwood, Raynard, Kodeih, Micelotta, & Lounsbury 2011, p. 318), manifesting in hard-to-reconcile pressures from constituents. Such circumstances represent "moments of flux and crisis, in which competing logics collide" (Jarzabkowski, Smets, Bednarek, Burke, & Spee, 2013), and create novel situations that actors have not been socialized into, and for which they may have no readily available response (cf., Battilana & Dorado, 2010; Reay & Hinings, 2009; Smets, Morris, & Greenwood, 2012).

Past research has observed that, confronted with institutional complexity, actors may respond differently (e.g., Bertels & Lawrence, 2016; Binder, 2007; Murray, 2010; Purdy & Gray, 2009; Raaijmakers, Vermeulen, Meeus, & Zietsma, 2015). Early theoretical work explained such differences in responses in terms of the relative compatibility between the sets of "assumptions, values, beliefs and rules" (Thornton & Ocasio, 1999, p. 804) that guide interpretation and prescribe action in the organization, referred to as institutional logics, and in terms of the degree to which logics are "represented" internally in organizations (Besharov & Smith, 2014; Pache & Santos, 2010). These theories assumed that people act as "carriers" of different logics, reflecting their professional training or work-group affiliation, and strive for their implementation in organizational structures and policies (Almandoz, 2012; Pache & Santos, 2010). Such assumptions allow to explain how organizations resolve internal tensions between groups, but they arguably restrict our capacity to account for possible variations in the way individuals themselves perceive the logics in play and commit to the role identities that they inform (Pache & Santos, 2013b), and how these perceptions can shape their responses.

Building on the idea that institutional logics "have a perceptual component that operates cognitively at the level of individuals" (George, Chattopadhyay, Sitkin, & Barden, 2006; Suddaby, 2010, p. 17) and that individuals within an organization may perceive different degrees of compatibility between the same two logics as they selectively "draw on, interpret and enact" them (Besharov & Smith, 2014, p. 368; see also Pache & Santos, 2013b), recent theoretical work has therefore begun to examine the role of individual-level characteristics on the capacity of individuals to perceive and combine different logics. These theories explain individuals' responses to institutional complexity in terms of their level of "familiarity" with the relevant logics (Pache & Santos, 2013b), their apprehension of the malleability of the contradictions between the perceived logics (Voronov & Yorks, 2015) and, more recently, the alignment between role and personal identities reflecting different logics (Wry & York, 2017). Yet, existing work still assumes that an inner motivation to enact a logic – because of internal accountability or identification – will necessarily imply knowledge of its prescriptions, and that, as long as an individual is knowledgeable about and committed to the multiple logics in play in a situation, they will reconcile and integrate their prescriptions. Past research shows, however, that actors confronting situations of *novel* complexity, such as those associated with career transitions (e.g., Amiot, La Sablonnière, Terry, & Smith, 2007; Hwang & Powell, 2009; Meyer & Hammerschmid, 2006;

Pratt, Rockmann, & Kaufmann, 2006) or operating at the intersection of fields governed by different logics (e.g., Jain, George, & Maltarich, 2009), often have trouble reconciling different commitments and prescriptions. In adapting to such novel complexity, some individuals may rely on "provisional selves" as "to bridge the gap between their current capacities and self-conceptions" and their representations of what is expected in their new environment (Ibarra, 1999, p. 765).

Therefore, we argue that in order to understand how individuals perceive the new demands, and envision ways to respond to them, we have to consider *simultaneously* individuals' representations of the logics in play, as well as their representations of the role identities, associated with these demands, which are internalized in their self-concept. Drawing on research from cognitive and social psychology, we theorize the former, using the complexity of an individual's representation of the external environment (Scott, 1969; Suedfeld, Tetlock, & Streufert, 1992), and the latter using the complexity of her self-representations (Linville, 1985; Campbell, Assanand, & Di Paula, 2003). The complexity of one's representations of the external environment reflects one's knowledge of a given domain and is based on the number of constructs that she perceives when defining it, and the links that she can build among them, whereas the complexity of one's self-representations reflects one's self-knowledge and is based on the number of role identities that she has developed and the extent to which they are integrated within a coherent core self. We argue that the former will influence the extent to which an individual is capable of perceiving and enacting norms and beliefs from different logics (as opposed to only one of them), and of envisioning possibilities to reconcile apparently contradictory logics while doing so (as opposed to clearly demarcating their enactment). On the other hand, the complexity of one's self-representations will influence their willingness and emotional capacity to implement a selected response. Considering both of these aspects simultaneously allows us to theorize more comprehensively how and why individuals may respond differently to institutional complexity, by accounting not only for their *ability* to comprehend and enact different logics, but also for their *motivation* to act in accordance with their various prescriptions and cope emotionally with the responses they have chosen.

A COGNITIVE STRUCTURAL PERSPECTIVE ON INSTITUTIONAL COMPLEXITY

Research on cognitive structure and cognitive complexity originated from an interest in understanding how individuals perceive their social world and respond to changes within it (Bieri, 1955). Some of the early works, starting with Kurt Lewin's field theory (1936), considered the individual's situation (or "life space") as a function of both the person and his/her environment, and emphasized the role of perception in explaining how an individual moves toward desired or away from undesired states. These studies focused on identifying the constructs that individuals use to differentiate or unite objects in their environment (Scott, 1963; Zajonc, 1960), and defined a cognitively complex individual as someone whose system of cognitive constructs differentiates highly among events, people, or objects (Bieri, 1955, 1966). Later work enriched this perspective by arguing that one should focus not only on how well an individual differentiates among objects in their environment but also on how integrated these differentiated representations are (Harvey, Hunt, & Schroder, 1961; Scott, 1969; Wyer, 1964). Having high differentiation and high integration of a given domain was considered beneficial, as it equipped the individual with a richer and more nuanced understanding of the domain, and enhanced their behavioral repertoire and capacity to adapt to changes in their environment.

In addition to addressing the complexity of one's cognitive representation of the *external environment*, based on the number of construct dimensions with which one can perceive and describe the people, events and objects in their environment, and the relationships among them (Bieri, 1955; Scott, 1969; Suedfeld et al., 1992), subsequent research in this field extended its focus to the complexity of one's representations of their *own self*, by exploring the number of role identities they have and the extent to which they are united within one's core self (Block, 1961; Campbell, Assanand, & Di Paula, 2003; Donahue, Robins, Roberts, & John, 1993; Linville, 1985; Rogers, 1959). Research in this domain has emphasized that greater self-complexity can support an individual's well-being by helping them cope better with stressors and change events.

In the following section, we outline each of these two aspects and begin to illustrate the way they can jointly influence individuals' perceptions of and responses to novel institutional complexity.

Representations of the External Environment: Differentiation and Integration

Cognitive differentiation has been defined as the extent to which a given cognitive domain – understood as a cognitive representation of a "particular class of objects" (Scott, 1969, p. 261) – is "broken up into clearly defined and articulated parts" (Wyer, 1964, p. 496), and as the granularity of one's perception of each object in terms of constitutive *attributes* that characterize this object and distinguish it from others (Scott, 1969). Cognitive differentiation, however, does not necessarily imply an integrated organization of this knowledge: an individual characterized by high differentiation may be able to "entertain multiple alternatives," see "both poles of a conflict," and give "equal plausibility of both sides"; however, she may still be unable to "encompass these possibilities into a meaningful integrative framework" (Harvey & Schroder, 1963, p. 148). Cognitive integration, on the other hand, has been considered as the extent to which an individual traces connections among the various attributes of objects within a given cognitive domain (Harvey et al., 1961; Tetlock, 1986). Differentiation and integration are thus seen as the fundamental cognitive structural properties that define how our perceptions of the environment are organized (Scott, Osgood, & Peterson, 1979), where differentiation is considered to be a necessary but not a sufficient condition for integration (Tetlock, 1986).

To apply this cognitive structural lens to our study of how individuals *perceive* institutional complexity, we can conceive of the particular *situation* an individual confronts as a cognitive *domain*, the different *logics* that may apply to the situation and guide action as the *objects* of this domain, and the *elements* of each logic as the *attributes* of each object. Following Thornton, Ocasio, and Lounsbury (2012), we assume here that, at the individual level, logics can be understood as "learned knowledge structures" that direct attention and guide interpretation (pp. 83–84; see also DiMaggio, 1997), and that "individuals learn multiple contrasting and often contradictory institutional logics through social interaction and socialization" (Thornton et al., 2012, p. 83). Depending on their life experiences, then, individuals differ in the number of logics they are aware of (McPherson & Sauder, 2013) – or, in other words, that are "available" for them to use in social interaction (Thornton et al., 2012) – and in the sophistication of their understanding of these logics (Pache & Santos, 2013b). This assumption is consistent with the more general idea that individuals tend to behave according to cultural norms and beliefs that operate under the threshold of their consciousness, with some displaying a heightened awareness of these norms and beliefs, characteristic of their own culture or other ones (Berry, 1997).

Differentiation then, understood as the granularity of one's representation of a cognitive domain, is considered to refer to one's capacity to make fine-grained distinctions between the different logics in play.[1] An individual characterized by high differentiation will be familiar with the different logics, and able to distinguish them along multiple elements[2] (e.g., sources of legitimacy, authority, identity, etc.). For instance, she will associate a family logic with the promotion of the well-being of the family, unconditional loyalty, patriarchal authority, etc., and business logic with profit seeking, market competition, hierarchical authority, etc. High differentiation, we argue, affects an individual's capacity to respond to institutional complexity, by helping her grasp the more general norms and values informing the demands of her constituents.

Integration, instead, represents the amount of connections that an individual can draw across logics – or in other words, the extent to which she perceives two or more elements from different logics to be relatively compatible. If an individual has highly differentiated perceptions of the logics of family and business, low integration will be manifested in her perception of the two logics as largely incompatible. For instance, she may be uncomfortable at – or even unable to imagine – the idea to be unconditionally loyal to her employer, or to use economic rewards to direct her children's behavior. Instead, high integration may be manifested in seeing unconditional loyalty to the organization (family logic) as a way to enhance competitiveness and profitability (business logic).

The different combinations of differentiation and integration therefore are: low differentiation and low integration, which we refer to as *struggling* with complexity; high differentiation and low integration, which we refer to as *buffering* complexity; and high differentiation and high integration, which we refer to as *embracing* complexity. We exclude conceptually one of the four combinations, namely low differentiation and high integration, because, as discussed by Scott (1969), it is not possible to draw many connections (hence integrate) across what is otherwise largely a unidimensional cognitive domain (low differentiation). As Streufert and Swezey (1986) also remark, "integration without differentiation is impossible" (p. 63). The three combinations that we have outlined are presented in Table 1.

Table 1. Cognitive Structural Representations of the External Environment: The Ability to Respond to Institutional Demands.

	Low Differentiation and Low Integration	High Differentiation and Low Integration	High Differentiation and High Integration
Definition from psychology	Views an issue through a one-dimensional lens and would tend to discount alternative perspectives	Can consider two (or more) distinct ways in which to view an issue/ situation, yet does not have the capacity to draw connections between different perspectives on an issue	Can apply different perspectives when interpreting an issue and can consider their "mutual influence and interdependence"
Application to institutional logics	Granular understanding of one logic. No awareness or only coarse-grained understanding of the second. If aware of a second logic, it is classified as incompatible with the first	Can discern and distinguish both logics in play, yet attends to their demands sequentially or in a structurally demarcated manner only	Granular understanding of both logics and ability to discern opportunities to integrate between their demands

Representations of Self: Self-Pluralism and Self-Unity

When addressing the internal structure of one's *self*-representations, research in cognitive complexity has focused on two aspects – namely, the *pluralism* and the *unity* of one's self-concept (Campbell et al., 2003; Linville, 1985; Rafaeli-Mor, Gotlib, & Revelle, 1999; Rafaeli-Mor & Steinberg, 2002). People who have a high level of self-pluralism are characterized by having multiple, yet distinct and non-overlapping self-aspects within their core self-definitions (Linville, 1985). In the symbolic interactionist perspective we adopt in this chapter (Cooley, 1902; Mead, 1934), these self-aspects correspond to the role identities that, at any point in time, rank highly in one's salience hierarchy and are central to one's self-definition. Having high self-pluralism, however, does not, in and of itself, suggest that individuals would also have developed a fine-grained understanding of when and how each of the roles within their self should be enacted, and how they fit within their overall core self. Even though some authors have emphasized the benefit of having multiple, non-overlapping role identities, other researchers have argued that such plural-ism may also cause self-fragmentation, a condition associated with emotional distress and/or reacting haphazardly to situations (Block, 1961; Lutz & Ross, 2003; Rafaeli-Mor & Steinberg, 2002). This condition, scholars argue, is due to the absence of an "internal reference which can affirm his continuity and self-integrity" (Block, 1961, p. 392; see also Lutz & Ross, 2003) and the dif-ficulty to reconcile multiple identities within a core sense of self (Amiot et al., 2007). In order to understand how individuals respond to and cope with this, prior research has focused on "how different identities become integrated in the self" (Amiot et al., 2007, p. 370) and whether or not individuals have the capacity to establish "higher-order superordinate self-abstractions" that can facilitate the integration of different self-representations and thus help them better address any contradictions among them in response to change events (Amiot et al., 2007, p. 370; see also Mascolo & Fisher, 1998). *Self-unity*, therefore, has been argued to be an important complement of self-pluralism, serving to prevent feelings of self-fragmentation (Block, 1961; Campbell et al., 2003). The presence of self-unity allows individuals to effectively integrate multiple identities within a consistent, coherent core self, thus minimizing the experience of cognitive dissonance or self-incongruence (Lecky, 1945). Having self-unity provides guidance about when to enact different roles, and how each of them can be accommodated within a core sense of self. In the absence of unity, individuals' response to multiple demands, even if ultimately synergistic, may be short-lived because of the stress and burnout the perceived self-incongruence generates for them (see also Brandl & Bullinger, 2017, on the influence of self-verification tensions).

Self-pluralism affects an individual's response to institutional complexity because it influences the sets of expectations (social roles), associated with the multiple logics in play that she perceives as motivating and to which she feels compelled and accountable to attend. In theorizing the impact of self-pluralism on an individual's response to institutional complexity, we adopt the simplifying assumption of circumscribing our analysis to role identities that are relevant to the logics in play. Based on this assumption, we consider an individual characterized by low self-pluralism when only one of the logics in play is represented among the identities that constitute her core self.

We again outline three possible combinations of self-pluralism and self-unity. The first one is based on low self-pluralism and high self-unity, which we refer to as a *rigid core self*. Such self-representations are dominated by a single identity that shapes individuals' responses across different situations (Amiot et al., 2007; Linville, 1985; Roccas & Brewer, 2002), thereby reinforcing a strong sense of self-consistency and congruence (Lecky, 1945). The second one is based on high self-pluralism and low self-unity, which we refer to as a *fragmented core self*. Even though those individuals would have developed multiple identities that they consider important and relevant for their self-definition, it would be difficult for them to draw connections among each of them (Block, 1961; Lutz & Ross, 2003), and they will tend to behave differently across situations, often lacking oversight as to whether and how their different identities fit together. The last one is based on high self-pluralism and high self-unity, which we refer to as an *agile core self*. Such individuals are able to create connections among their various identities, and thus find "meaningful higher order self-representations … which bind the different self-components" (Amiot et al., 2007, p. 370). Such higher-order self-representations are the key to responding successfully to conflicting demands as otherwise individuals have been found to experience a mismatch between their identities and their expected behavior (see Brandl & Bullinger, 2017). Finally, we exclude conceptually the combination of low self-pluralism and low self-unity since if the individual has a low level of self-pluralism, she would have one core identity, in which case it would not be meaningful to have low self-unity as well (Campbell et al., 2003). The three combinations are summarized in Table 2.

Table 2.   Cognitive Structural Representation of the Self: The Motivation to
Enact a Given Response.

	Low Self-pluralism and High Self-unity	High Self-pluralism and Low Self-unity	High Self-pluralism and High Self-unity
Definition from psychology	Has a single dominant role identity	Has both (multiple) role identities present in her self-concept, however, lacks a clear sense of where and how to enact them consistently	Has both (multiple) role identities and is able to integrate them within a coherent core self
Application to institutional logics	Tends to act in accordance with a single (dominant) role identity and behaves similarly across situations, in accord with the prescriptions of the dominant role	Experiences tension and anxiety associated with self-fragmentation, as she is unable to internalize the roles' prescriptions and responds by attending to their demands separately or fitfully	Experiences a stable emotional pattern, as she is motivated to act upon the prescriptions of both identities and is aware how to jointly address their demands

COGNITIVE COMPLEXITY AND RESPONSES TO MULTIPLE LOGICS

In the previous section, we have theorized how the complexity of an individual's representations of the external environment and her own self influence how she experiences institutional complexity. In this section, we use these theoretical arguments to examine how different combinations of these four structural properties of cognition may influence the responses individuals are more likely to enact when addressing institutional complexity. We focus on situations of novel complexity, where individuals do not rely on automatic or routine responses but rather attend effortfully to the situation, triggering "bottom-up attention processes" (Thornton et al., 2012, p. 84). We organize our arguments by grouping individuals according to the complexity of their representations of the external environment (logics) and theorize the implications of having a rigid, fragmented, or an agile core self on the type of response that they would be motivated to enact to the perceived institutional complexity. The response types that individuals are likely to exhibit, based on our classification, are summarized in Fig. 1.

Our arguments are based on the assumption that, in a given situation, an individual's actions will reflect her current level of understanding of the logics that she perceives to be relevant to the situation. However, neither the complexity of one's representation of the external environment, nor of her self, represent static structural properties of an individual's cognitive system (Rafaeli-Mor & Steinberg, 2002; Scott et al., 1979). Albeit slow to change, they are subject to gradual development, given certain stimulations in the external environment – possibly based on the very tentative engagement with multiple logics (Creed, DeJordy, & Lok, 2010). In this respect, cognitive complexity can be understood

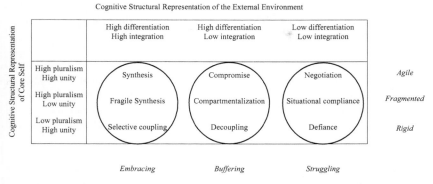

Fig. 1. Cognitive Complexity and Responses to Institutional Complexity.

as both shaping and being shaped dynamically by one's experiences across existing institutional settings.

High Differentiation and High Integration: Embracing Complexity

As discussed in the previous section, decision-makers characterized by high differentiation and high integration are more likely to *embrace* complexity as an opportunity for novel action. Yet, the specific form that the *response* of these individuals will take – we argue – depends further on the complexity of their representation of self, based on their level of self-pluralism and self-unity, which we outline below.

High Self-pluralism and High Self-unity (Agile Core): Synthesis

When characterized by high self-pluralism and high self-unity, an individual will feel compelled to enact all the logics in play, because she perceives role identities associated with these logics as core to her sense of self. When characterized also by high differentiation and integration, she will not only be motivated but also able to respond to institutional complexity by engaging in activities or designing structures that *synthesize* elements from different logics, and by attempting to simultaneously enact the related role identities into new hybrid structures and practices (see, for instance, Dalpiaz, Rindova, & Ravasi, 2016; Jay, 2013). She will implement this response in a confident, consistent way, her high degree of self-unity enabling her to attend to different expectations comfortably, and to reconcile possible tensions within her core sense of self.

An example of this type of response can be found in Binder's (2007) study of how three departments within a transitional housing organization respond differently to institutional complexity. Anna, the leader of one these departments, "rather than seeing the two aspects of her environment as being at cross-purposes with one another, and as fundamentally uncoupled," creatively blended elements of the bureaucratic logic behind funding regulations and the professional logic of childhood education "to ensure the smooth flow of resources into her department," and "to stay true to … her commitment to her professional ideology: children's health and wellbeing" (Binder, 2007, pp. 556–559).

A second example can be found in the case of Alberto Alessi, who integrated the logics of industry and the arts to produce new hybrid practices to design and commercialize kitchenware that target simultaneously cultural institutions and affluent customers (Dalpiaz et al., 2016). The development of these practices reflected the gradual complexification of Alberto Alessi's understanding of his self as performing simultaneously the role of an industrial manufacturer and an "artistic mediator."

High Self-pluralism and Low Self-unity (Fragmented Core): Fragile Synthesis
In the presence of high self-pluralism, but low self-unity, an individual characterized by high differentiation and integration may be able to envision ways to simultaneously enact the prescriptions from different logics, but her "embracement" of complexity may be troubled and short-lived, which we label as "fragile." By lacking clarity as to how the different role identities fit within their core self, and how potential role conflicts can be addressed (Block, 1961; Campbell et al., 2003), the individual will lack the confidence, direction, and deliberation to pursue hybrid strategies (despite being committed to enact the relevant role identities), and may be induced to give up her efforts because she experiences the situation as excessively taxing (cognitively and emotionally).

Finding examples of fragile synthesis in previous literature is not easy, as this response has not been described as such before, however, it could be represented in Battilana and Dorado's (2010) work on microfinance ventures, where they explained the failure of one of the ventures with the inability of leaders to instill in their employees an overall sense of self that could direct and justify implementing simultaneously a commercial and a social welfare logic.

Low Self-pluralism and High Self-unity (Rigid Core): Selective Coupling
Finally, when characterized by a rigid sense of self, the individual would have one role identity dominating the salience hierarchy and would thus tend to behave similarly across different contexts. Coupled with high differentiation and integration, this combination of factors is likely to result in the *selective coupling* response described by Pache and Santos (2013a). This individual will be aware of logic-specific expectations associated with different social roles (high differentiation) and will see opportunities to attend to these expectations (high integration). Low self-pluralism, however, will induce her to focus only on the core role identity, and to enact prescriptions of other logics only to the extent that those are compatible with this identity.

We can find an example of this response in some of the traders interviewed by Lok (2010) who, while being familiar with both the traditional "shareholder value maximization" logic and the rising "enlightened shareholder" logic, were committed to the maximization of the value of their clients' portfolios, and "selectively" appropriated practices from the other logic to legitimate themselves with some constituents, only "in the service of their pre-existing trader identity" (pp. 323–324).

High Differentiation and Low Integration: Buffering Complexity

When decision-makers possess a nuanced understanding of different logics (high differentiation), but see their prescriptions as incompatible (low integration), they will instead *buffer* complexity, by selecting responses that allow them to attend to these prescriptions separately or symbolically in order to minimize interference between activities enacting either logic. Their exact response will again depend on the manner in which the pertaining role identities are represented and united within their core self.

High Self-pluralism and High Self-unity: Compromise

Having an agile core induces an individual to perform multiple roles, associated with the logics in play and to do so with ease, as the high self-unity provides direction to the manner in which her roles fit within her core self. The relatively low degree of compatibility that she sees in the different logics she considers (low integration), however, will make it difficult for her to enact elements of both synergistically or in novel ways. Instead, we argue, this individual will search for *compromise* (Oliver, 1991), or, in other words, will try to enact each logic – which, because of her high differentiation, she understands well – to a limited degree, and only to the extent that doing so does not hinder attendance to the competing set of prescriptions and expectations.

In our framework, we consider "compromise" as an attempt to conform to a minimum set of prescriptions from one logic in a way that does not undermine the enactment of the other logic. For example, in their study of community mental health centers diversifying into drug abuse treatment, D'Aunno, Sutton, and Price (1991) have shown the challenge of reaching a compromise: centers that attempted to legitimize themselves in both the mental health sector and the field of drug abuse ended up adopting contradictory practices that reduced the support from their traditional constituents.

High Self-pluralism and Low Self-unity: Compartmentalization

This combination refers to an individual characterized by a fragmented self, who tends to act differently across contexts, lacking a clear, coherent and stable core self that ties her different roles together (Block, 1961). Coupled with a high differentiation and a low integration, we expect this combination to result in a *compartmentalized* response to multiple logics (Greenwood et al., 2011). This individual, we argue, will recognize different logics (because of self-pluralism) and feel compelled to attend to the related sets of role expectations. Low self-unity, however, will cause tension because of her inability to reconcile different role identities into a coherent sense of self. Under these conditions, we expect that she may attempt to enact different logics in a sequential and clearly demarcated manner, without attempting to build any linkages among them.

An excellent example of compartmentalization as a response to institutional complexity can be found in the experience of homosexual ministers in main-line Protestant denominations, described by Creed and colleagues (2010). For these ministers, the inability to reconcile their religious, family, and sexual identities (low self-unity) initially manifested in the "compartmentalization" of the personal and the religious spheres of their lives; only after "theologizing the personal" – that is, revising their understanding of Christian teachings and church practices "to make institutional premises of incompatibility disappear" (Creed et al., 2010, p. 1350) (moving from low to high integration and self-unity) – did they shift their response from buffering to embracing and reconciling contradictions.

Low Self-pluralism and High Self-unity: Decoupling

This individual could be relatively inflexible in accommodating prescriptions and expectations that do not fit within her core self (self-unity). While aware of different logics in play in a situation (high differentiation), she not only sees little opportunity to reconcile them and enact principles of both in her responses (low integration) but also displays only minimal commitment to all but the role identity shaping her core self-definition.

We expect that such individuals would engage in *decoupling* symbolic conformity to prescriptions from one logic from the substantial implementation of behaviors prescribed by another (Boxenbaum & Jonsson, 2008). They will enact the prescriptions of the logic that more closely matches their core role identity, and conform only "ceremonially" to constituents' demands reflecting a different logic (Meyer & Rowan, 1977) – at least to the extent that they can avoid the close scrutiny of these constituents.

Low Differentiation and Low Integration: Struggling with Complexity

Lastly, individuals with low differentiation and low integration would tend to interpret events and situations only through a single perspective, and have little understanding or awareness of any alternative ones.

Such individuals would be familiar with only one of the logics in play, and remain unable to appreciate the fundamentally different beliefs, goals, and values (logics) that inform some of the demands they confront. When facing novel complexity, they will *struggle* to understand the principles behind some of the demands they face, and – because of their poor understanding of these principles – they will have difficulties envisioning ways of addressing these demands outside of the particular terms in which they are expressed.

High Self-pluralism and High Self-unity: Negotiation

Individuals with agile cores will have internalized multiple social roles and accommodated them within a coherent sense of self. In the presence of low differentiation and low integration, however, they will have only a limited understanding of the expectations associated with the role identities embedded in logics with which they are not familiar. As discussed previously, this could be the case of individuals transitioning to a new career at the intersection of different fields (e.g., Jain et al., 2009) or exposed to shifting expectations due to institutional change (e.g., Sanders & McClellan, 2014).

When confronted with role expectations and demands that appear inexplicable and/or incompatible with their dominant logic, such individuals – because of their high self-pluralism – will feel compelled to attend to these expectations (rather than defying some of them, as discussed later), but will find it difficult to do so because of their limited understanding of them, or because of the discrepancy between these demands and how they would behave based on their own dominant logic. Under these circumstances, individuals will engage in a *negotiation* with their constituents in order to work out a form of compliance that will enable them to enact their role identities, while remaining consistent with the general principles they operate upon, based on the logic associated with their core self (rather than searching for a compromise between different logics). These arguments are consistent with the observation that transitions to new roles are characterized by the attempt to "negotiate" role definitions and expectations to preserve valued aspects of self, associated with one's other role identities (Ibarra, 1999; Nicholson, 1984).

We can find a good example of this response in an experimental study of how childcare managers respond to conflicting pressures to implement new pedagogical methods (Raaijmakers et al., 2015). These managers, when aligned with the request (i.e., subscribing to its logic), handled conflicting pressures for and against the proposed method by engaging in "accommodative" tactics and negotiated limited, experimental implementation of the new methods.

High Self-pluralism and Low Self-unity: Situational Compliance
A fragmented self, combined with a narrow and coarse-grained understanding of the logics in play, will push individuals to enact multiple role identities (high self-pluralism), without having a clear understanding of how to address complexity. Compared to individuals with an agile core, their lack of a clear sense of self decreases their confidence, deliberation, and consistency to effectively engage in negotiation. Absence of clear understanding of when to enact their different role identities (low self-unity) may then induce them to mimic behaviors that they observe around them, without necessarily being able to connect how these behaviors relate to different logics (due to low differentiation) or how to accommodate them within their core self.

This idea is aligned with Pache and Santos's observation that compliance involves "different degrees of consciousness, ranging from taken-for-granted habit, unconscious imitation, and voluntary compliance" (2013b, p. 13). Finding specific examples of such situational compliance in past studies of institutional complexity, however, is not easy because of the tendency of researchers to focus on consistent patterns (e.g., Purdy & Gray, 2009; Reay & Hinings, 2009), rather than erratic behavior.

Low Self-pluralism and High Self-unity: Defiance

Finally, individuals characterized by a rigid core, combined with a narrow and coarse-grained understanding of their environment (low differentiation and integration), will act inflexibly across different situations. These individuals will thus tend to respond to institutional complexity by *defying* demands that they see as incompatible with the general principles that they feel apply to the situation and/ or are incoherent with their sense of self. Pache and Santos consider defiance as the "explicit rejection of at least one of the institutional demands in an attempt to actively remove the source of contradiction" (2010, p. 463). This can be exemplified by Murray's account of scientists' resistance to DuPont's patenting of genetically modified mice for oncology research, where only coercive pressure will induce these individuals to conform reluctantly to their prescriptions (Murray, 2010). A similar example could be found in the struggle that East Germans may have experienced after the reunification, when they were confronted with the need to engage with the new "capitalist" logic, severely conflicting with their dominant "socialist" logic (Haack & Sieweke, 2018).

DISCUSSION AND CONCLUSION

In this chapter, we have theorized how structural components of cognition influence how individuals experience and respond to institutional complexity. Our ideas offer a comprehensive theoretical account of the observed, but still largely unexplained, variation in individual responses to "novel" institutional complexity caused, for instance, by institutional change (e.g., Reay & Hinings, 2009), new field formation (e.g., Purdy & Gray, 2009), or cross-field interactions (e.g., Murray, 2010). While past research has consistently shown that different actors may respond differently to these unsettled institutional circumstances, current theories of how actors engage with and respond to the same conditions of complexity, has offered only a partial explanation of the factors involved.

Existing research documenting individuals' responses to institutional complexity has so far focused either on *what* individuals *know* about the logics (knowledge component) and/or the identities that they inform (Wry & York, 2017), or has addressed how they *feel* about them (affect component) (see also Pache & Santos, 2013b; Toubiana & Ziestma, 2017; Voronov & Yorks, 2015; Wry & York, 2017). These studies lay critical foundations for future research on how individuals address institutional complexity, as they begin to theorize the relevance of both one's understanding of the logics and of the role identities in play. However, given our focus on *novel* institutional complexity, we propose that there is another aspect that is particularly important, yet has received much less research attention in the institutional literature so far, namely *how* this knowledge *is organized* and *represented* internally within the individual's cognitive *structure* (Amiot et al., 2007; Block, 1961; Scott, 1969). In order to theorize the influence of cognitive structure on how individuals experience and respond to institutional complexity, we have drawn on research within social and personality psychology that has addressed how individuals structure their perceptions of the external environment and of their own selves. We have argued that the *differentiation* and *integration* of their perceptions of the external environment will influence whether they see institutional complexity as an opportunity to generate novel action that they can *embrace*; as a set of fundamentally incompatible prescriptions that need to be *buffered* somehow; or as a tension between bothersome and, to some extent, inexplicable demands, which they *struggle* to accommodate. Within these three general categories, we have further argued that different combinations of self-*pluralism* and self-*unity* (namely *agile, fragmented,* or *rigid* core) will contribute to shape individuals' specific responses to complexity, depending on their motivation to enact multiple roles (in response to the prescriptions and expectations associated with these logics), and to preserve a coherent sense of self while doing so. The proposed framework aims to extend our understanding of why individuals confronted with the same institutional complexity can perceive and respond to it very differently.

We believe that our conceptual framework opens up an important research agenda as it offers us a much more nuanced understanding of the factors that can explain whether and how individuals grappling with multiple conflicting logics may be able and motivated to enact and sustain a certain response to them. This enriches McPherson and Sauder's (2013) notion of logics as "tools" and "implements that can be used by whoever picks them up" and "in ways that suit the purpose at hand" (p. 14), as it helps us understand why certain individuals may have a significantly easier or harder time of doing so, as compared to others, and provides guidance as to the ways in which we could anticipate this. The proposed framework could for instance explain why only some of the professionals within their court negotiations study could flexibly engage with logics from other court actors, whereas others could not. As McPherson and Sauder (2013) have shown, the probation officers had the greatest flexibility in shifting among different logics in the court, whereas the clinicians predominantly stayed within one logic (rehabilitation), yet with a few exceptions. We argue that by studying how individuals negotiate the way they connect elements across different logics, as opposed to shifting among logics, and how they unite their role identities under a coherent core self, we can better understand and predict when and why some individuals may be better equipped to cope with and respond to conflicting institutional demands as compared to others.

Implications for Future Research

Extending the Notion of Self-Pluralism

Building directly on the previous point, future research could explore how individuals may benefit from the complexity of their self-structure beyond the identities directly informed by the logics at play. Even though in this chapter, we have used the simplifying assumption of focusing only on role identities informed by the logics in play, it is theoretically possible that individuals may be committed to a greater number of role identities, not all of which associated with the logics in a given situation (Thornton et al., 2012). These identities may be based on prior life experiences, as well as vicarious observation and/or interaction with family, friends, or individuals with very different backgrounds and institutional biographies (Bertels & Lawrence, 2016; Pache & Santos, 2013b). Having such broader sets of role identities in general may increase individuals' overall capacity for flexible adaptation to any new (role) demands, allowing them to more fluidly integrate a new role identity into their already existing core self. Future research could therefore explore whether individuals characterized by multiple non-overlapping role identities, which are united in a core sense of self, can be better equipped to cope in situations of novel institutional complexity, as they could flexibly draw on elements from their existing role set to construct and negotiate the integration of a new role identity, thus increasing their capacity to respond to the demands of conflicting logics.

Experimental Investigation of Micro-level Institutional Processes
In recent years, there have been repeated calls for the use of micro-research methods in institutional theory (Powell & Colyvas, 2008; Thornton & Ocasio, 2008). The grounding of our ideas in research on cognitive psychology makes our framework particularly suitable to support experimental studies, which are seen as an important direction for future research in institutional complexity (see Schilke, Levine, Kacperczyk, & Zucker, 2019; Smith & Rand, 2018). In particular, the influence of the different types and combinations of complexity of self and the environment can be manipulated (based on vignettes) in order to evaluate their exact impact on how individuals interpret and respond to institutional complexity.

Past research on cognitive psychology has developed sophisticated methods to capture the complexity of external representations (e.g., Scott et al., 1979; Streufert & Swezey, 1986; Suedfeld et al., 1992) and the complexity of self (e.g., Campbell et al., 2003; Linville, 1985; Rafaeli-Mor et al., 1999). These methods could be adapted to the specific case of institutional complexity to explore empirically the impact of cognitive complexity on individuals' response to logic multiplicity.

The Interplay Between Cognition and Emotions
While we chose to focus on cognition, emotions play an important role in the process we examined as well. As Creed et al. (2010, p. 1356) argue, the experience of incompatibility of institutional logics is "often highly emotionally charged," as these contradictions are not only cognitively perceived but also fully experienced. By focusing on the complexity of self-representations, we do touch upon individuals' coping with negative emotions to the extent that high self-unity helps manage the stress associated with conflicting role identities. Future research may want to examine the interplay between cognition and emotion further by mapping how one's feelings toward given logics can influence her perceptions and responses to them.

Consistent with earlier work on institutional complexity, in this chapter, we have assumed that individuals differ mainly in terms of their relative understanding of different logics (see McPherson & Sauder, 2013; Pache & Santos, 2013b). However, individuals may differ also in terms of the extent to which they like or dislike principles associated with a particular logic. As Lewin (1935) has argued early on, when strong emotions characterize a specific aspect of an individual's "life space," the differentiation between the attributes that describe specific objects within it decreases, hence resulting in a more coarse integration within their cognitive domain. Future research, may therefore explore whether the affective properties ascribed to the different logics within one's cognitive domain can interact with individuals' ability to effectively integrate across their elements, and contribute more effectively to building a well-rounded representation of the individual decision-maker within institutional theory research (see also Creed, Hudson, Okhuysen, & Smith-Crowe, 2014; Voronov & Vince, 2012).

Exploring the Antecedents and Development of Cognitive Complexity
Finally, future field-based research may investigate how the very engagement with institutional complexity may influence the evolving complexity of one's representation of logics and self. In this chapter, for the sake of simplicity, we have examined how, at a given point in time, the cognitive complexity of an individual will influence her response. Past research, however, shows that while some actors are relatively stable in their response, possibly to the point of jeopardizing their survival (Purdy & Gray, 2009), others may alter their response over time, likely based on a modified understanding of the different logics at play (Murray, 2010) as well as of their own self (Creed et al. 2010).

ACKNOWLEDGMENTS

We are grateful for the helpful comments from the OTREG community, and the participants of the sub-theme "Rethinking Responses to Institutional Complexity" at the European Group of Organization Studies meeting in 2014. We also wish to extend our deep gratitude to Royston Greenwood and Ivano Cardinale for their feedback, advice and engagement with earlier versions of our work.

NOTES

1. Following earlier work (e.g., Besharov & Smith, 2014; Pache & Santos, 2010, 2013b), when theorizing the impact of structural components of cognition on individuals' perceptions of and responses to institutional complexity, we will consider the simplified case of individuals potentially handling two different logics – as opposed to three, or more. This simplification does not appear problematic, because past research shows that in most circumstances individuals really confront two logics (Greenwood et al., 2011) – either because they have to resolve their conflicting demands, or because they are considering their possible hybridization.

2. By elements of logic, we refer to the fundamental assumptions and beliefs that, according to Thornton et al. (2012), distinguish between logics along certain analytical categories.

REFERENCES

Almandoz, J. (2012). Arriving at the starting line: The impact of community and financial logics on new banking ventures. *Academy of Management Journal*, *55*(6), 1381–1406.

Amiot, C. E., La Sablonnière, R. de, Terry, D. J., & Smith, J. R. (2007). Integration of social identities in the self: Toward a cognitive-developmental model. *Personality and Social Psychology Review*, *11*(4), 364–388.

Battilana, J., & Dorado, S. (2010). Building sustainable hybrid organizations: The case of commercial microfinance organizations. *Academy of Management Journal*, *53*(6), 1419–1440.

Berry, J. W. (1997). Immigration, acculturation, and adaptation. *Applied Psychology*, *46*(1), 5–34.

Bertels, S., & Lawrence, T. B. (2016). Organizational responses to institutional complexity stemming from emerging logics: The role of individuals. *Strategic Organization*, *14*(4), 336–372.

Besharov, M. L., & Smith, W. K. (2014). Multiple institutional logics in organizations: Explaining their varied nature and implications. *Academy of Management Review*, *39*(3), 364–381.

Bieri, J. (1955). Cognitive complexity–simplicity and predictive behavior. *The Journal of Abnormal and Social Psychology*, *51*(2), 263–268.

Bieri, J. (1966). Cognitive complexity and personality development. In O. Harvey (Ed.), *Experience, structure, and adaptability* (pp. 13–38). New York, NY: Springer.

Binder, A. (2007). For love and money: Organizations' creative responses to multiple environmental logics. *Theory and Society*, *36*(6), 547–571.

Block, J. (1961). Ego identity, role variability, and adjustment. *Journal of Consulting Psychology*, *25*(5), 392–397.

Boxenbaum, E., & Jonsson, S. (2008). Isomorphism, diffusion and decoupling. In R. Greenwood, C. Oliver, K. Sahlin-Andersson, & R. Suddaby (Eds.), *The Sage handbook of organizational institutionalism* (pp. 78–98). London: Sage.

Brandl, J., & Bullinger, B. (2017). Individuals' considerations when responding to competing logics: Insights from identity control theory. *Journal of Management Inquiry*, *26*(2), 181–192.

Campbell, J. D., Assanand, S., & Di Paula, A. (2003). The structure of the self-concept and its relation to psychological adjustment. *Journal of Personality*, *71*(1), 115–140.

Cooley, H. (1902). *Human nature and the social order*. New York, NY: Scribner.

Creed, W. E., DeJordy, R., & Lok, J. (2010). Being the change: Resolving institutional contradiction through identity work. *Academy of Management Journal*, *53*(6), 1336–1364.

Creed, W. D., Hudson, B. A., Okhuysen, G. A., & Smith-Crowe, K. (2014). Swimming in a sea of shame: Incorporating emotion into explanations of institutional reproduction and change. *Academy of Management Review*, *39*, 275–301.

D'Aunno, T., Sutton, R., & Price, R. (1991). Organizational isomorphism and external support in conflicting institutional environments: The case of drug abuse treatment units. *Academy of Management Journal*, *34*, 636–661.

Dalpiaz, E., Rindova, V., & Ravasi, D. (2016). The making of a design factory. Combining institutional logics strategically to create and pursue new market opportunities. *Academy of Science Quarterly*, *61*(3), 347–392.

DiMaggio, P. (1997). Culture and cognition. *Annual Review of Sociology*, *23*(1), 263–287.

Donahue, E., Robins, R., Roberts, B., & John, O. (1993). The divided self: Concurrent and longitudinal effects of psychological adjustment and social roles on self-concept differentiation. *Journal of Personality and Social Psychology*, *64*, 834–846.

George, E., Chattopadhyay, P., Sitkin, S. B., & Barden, J. (2006). Cognitive underpinnings of institutional persistence and change: A framing perspective. *Academy of Management Review*, *31*(2), 347–365.

Greenwood, R., Raynard, M., Kodeih, F., Micelotta, E. R., & Lounsbury, M. (2011). Institutional complexity and organizational responses. *The Academy of Management Annals*, *5*(1), 317–371.

Haack, P., & Sieweke, J. (2018). The legitimacy of inequality: Integrating the perspectives of system justification and social judgment. *Journal of Management Studies*, *55*(3), 486–516.

Harvey, O. J., Hunt, D., & Schroder, H. (1961). *Conceptual systems and personality organization*. New York, NY: John Wiley & Sons.

Harvey, O., & Schroder, H. (1963). Cognitive aspects of self and motivation. In O. J. Harvey (Ed.), *Motivation and social interaction: Cognitive determinants* (pp. 95–133). New York, NY: The Ronald Press Company.

Hwang, H., & Powell, W. W. (2009). The rationalization of charity: The influences of professionalism in the nonprofit sector. *Administrative Science Quarterly, 54*(2), 268–298.

Ibarra, H. (1999). Provisional selves: Experimenting with image and identity in professional adaptation. *Administrative Science Quarterly, 44*(4), 764–791.

Jain, S., George, G., & Maltarich, M. (2009) Academic or entrepreneurs? Investigating role identity modification of university scientists involved in commercialization activity. *Research Policy, 38*, 922–935.

Jarzabkowski, P., Smets, M., Bednarek, R., Burke, G., & Spee, P. (2013). Institutional ambidexterity: Leveraging institutional complexity in practice. In *Institutional logics in action, part B* (pp. 37–61). Bingley: Emerald Publishing Limited.

Jay, J. (2013). Navigating paradox as a mechanism of change and innovation in hybrid organizations. *Academy of Management Journal, 56*, 137–159.

Lecky, P. (1945). *Self-consistency: A theory of personality*. New York, NY: Island Press.

Lewin, K. (1935). *A dynamic theory of personality*. New York, NY: McGraw-Hill.

Lewin, K. (1936). *Principles of topological psychology*. New York, NY: McGraw-Hill.

Linville, P. (1985). Self-complexity and affective extremity: Don't put all of your eggs in one cognitive basket. *Social Cognition, 3*, 94–120.

Lok, J. (2010). Institutional logics as identity projects. *Academy of Management Journal, 53*(6), 1305–1335.

Lutz, C. J., & Ross, S. R. (2003). Elaboration versus fragmentation: Distinguishing between self-complexity and self-concept differentiation. *Journal of Social and Clinical Psychology, 22*(5), 537–559.

Mascolo, M. F., & Fischer, K. W. (1998). The development of self through the coordination of component systems. In M. Ferrari, & R. Sternberg (Eds.), *Self-awareness: Its nature and development* (pp. 332–384). New York, NY: Guilford Press.

McPherson, C. M., & Sauder, M. (2013). Logics in action. *Administrative Science Quarterly, 58*(2), 165–196.

Mead, G. (1934). *Mind, self, and society from the standpoint of a social behaviorist*. Chicago, IL: University of Chicago Press.

Meyer, R. E., & Hammerschmid, G. (2006). Changing institutional logics and executive identities. *American Behavioral Scientist, 49*(7), 1000–1014.

Meyer, J. W., & Rowan, B. (1977). Institutionalized organizations: Formal structure as myth and ceremony. *American Journal of Sociology, 83*, 340–363.

Murray, F. (2010). The oncomouse that roared: Hybrid exchange strategies as a source of distinction at the boundary of overlapping institutions. *American Journal of Sociology, 116*, 341–388.

Nicholson, N. (1984). A theory of work role transitions. *Administrative Science Quarterly, 29*(2), 172–191.

Oliver, C. (1991). Strategic responses to institutional processes. *The Academy of Management Review, 16*(1), 145–179.

Pache, A., & Santos, F. (2010). When worlds collide: The internal dynamics of organizational responses to conflicting institutional demands. *Academy of Management Review, 35*, 455–476.

Pache, A., & Santos, F. (2013a). Inside the hybrid organization: Selective coupling as a response to competing institutional logics. *Academy of Management Journal, 56*(4), 972–1001.

Pache, A., & Santos, F. (2013b). Embedded in hybrid contexts: How individuals in organizations respond to competing institutional logics. *Research in the Sociology of Organizations, 39*, 3–35.

Powell, W., & Colyvas, J. A. (2008). Microfoundations of institutional theory. In R. Greenwood, C. Oliver, K. Sahlin, & R. Suddaby (Eds.), *The Sage handbook of organizational institutionalism* (pp. 276–298). London: Sage.

Pratt, M. G., Rockmann, K. W., & Kaufmann, J. B. (2006). Constructing professional identity: The role of work and identity learning cycles in the customization of identity among medical residents. *Academy of Management Journal, 49*(2), 235–262.

Purdy, J. M., & Gray, B. (2009). Conflicting logics, mechanisms of diffusion, and multilevel dynamics in emerging institutional fields. *Academy of Management Journal, 52*(2), 355–380.

Raaijmakers, A. G. M., Vermeulen, P. A. M., Meeus, M. T. H., & Zietsma, C. (2015). I need time! Exploring pathways to compliance under institutional complexity. *Academy of Management Journal, 58*(1), 85–110.

Rafaeli-Mor, E., Gotlib, I., & Revelle, W. (1999). The meaning and measurement of self-complexity. *Personality and Individual Differences, 27*, 341–356.

Rafaeli-Mor, E., & Steinberg, J. (2002). Self-complexity and well-being: A review and research synthesis. *Personality and Social Psychology Review, 6*(1), 31–58.

Reay, T., & Hinings, C. R. (2009). Managing the rivalry of competing institutional logics. *Organization Studies, 30*(6), 629–652.

Roccas, S., & Brewer, M. B. (2002). Social identity complexity. *Personality and Social Psychology Review, 6*(2), 88–106.

Rogers, C. (1959). A theory of therapy, personality and interpersonal relationships as developed in the client-centered framework. In S. Koch (Ed.), *Psychology: A study of a science. Vol. 3: Formulations of the person and the social context.* New York, NY: McGraw-Hill.

Sanders, M. L., & McClellan, L. G. (2014). Being business-like while pursuing a social mission: Acknowledging the inherent tensions in US nonprofit organizing. *Organization, 21*, 68–89.

Schilke, O., Levine, S. S., Kacperczyk, O., & Zucker, L. G. (Eds.). (2019). Call for Papers-Special Issue on Experiments in Organizational Theory. *Organization Science, 30*(1), 232–234.

Scott, W. (1963). Conceptualizing and measuring structural properties of cognition. In O. Harvey (Ed.), *Motivation and social interaction* (pp. 266–288). New York, NY: The Ronald Press Company.

Scott, W. A. (1969). Structure of natural cognitions. *Journal of Personality and Social Psychology, 12*(4), 261–278.

Scott, W., Osgood, D., & Peterson, C. (1979). *Cognitive structure: Theory and measurement of individual differences.* New York, NY: John Wiley & Sons.

Smets, M., Morris, T., & Greenwood, R. (2012). From practice to field: A multilevel model of practice-driven institutional change. *Academy of Management Journal, 55*(4), 877–904.

Streufert, S., & Swezey, R. W. (1986). *Complexity, managers, and organizations.* London: Academic Press.

Suddaby, R. (2010). Challenges for institutional theory. *Journal of Management Inquiry, 19*, 14–20.

Suedfeld, P., Tetlock, P., & Streufert, S. (1992). Conceptual/integrative complexity. In C. Smith, J. Atkinson, D. McClelland, & J. Veroff (Eds.), *Motivation and personality: Handbook of thematic content analysis* (pp. 393–400). New York, NY: Cambridge University Press.

Tetlock, P. E. (1986). A value pluralism model of ideological reasoning. *Journal of Personality and Social Psychology, 50*(4), 819–827.

Thornton, P. H., & Ocasio, W. (1999). Institutional logics and the historical contingency of power in organizations: Executive succession in the higher education publishing industry, 1958–1990. *American Journal of Sociology, 105*, 801–843.

Thornton, P., & Ocasio, W. (2008). Institutional logics. In R. Greenwood, C. Oliver, K. Sahlin, & R. Suddaby (Eds.), *Handbook of organizational institutionalism* (pp. 99–129). Thousand Oaks, CA: Sage.

Thornton, P., Ocasio, W., & Lounsbury, M. (2012). *The institutional logics perspective.* Oxford: Oxford University Press.

Toubiana, M., & Zietsma, C. (2017). The message is on the wall? Emotions, social media and the dynamics of institutional complexity. *Academy of Management Journal, 60*(3), 922–953.

Voronov, M., & Vince, R. (2012) Integrating emotions into the analysis of institutional work. *Academy of Management Review, 37*, 58–81.

Voronov, M., & Yorks, L. (2015). "Did you notice that?" Theorizing differences in the capacity to apprehend institutional contradictions. *Academy of Management Review, 40*(4), 563–586.

Wry, T., & York, J. G. (2017). An identity-based approach to social enterprise. *Academy of Management Review, 42*(3), 437–460.

Wyer, R. (1964). Assessment and correlates of cognitive differentiation and integration. *Journal of Personality, 32*, 495–509.

Zajonc, R. (1960). The process of cognitive tuning in communication. *Journal of Abnormal and Social Psychology, 61*, 159–167.

CHAPTER 5

THE GENERATIVITY OF COLLECTIVE IDENTITY: IDENTITY MOVEMENTS AS MECHANISMS FOR NEW INSTITUTIONS

Mary Ann Glynn and Benjamin D. Innis*

ABSTRACT

The authors theorize the role that identity, and especially collective identity, plays in the creation of new institutions. The authors begin by reviewing the literature on social movements, focusing on identity movements; from this, the authors extract and explore the role of identity in collective action and institutional formation. The authors propose that identity and lifestyle movements create institutions that furnish the necessary cultural tools to support and enact a given identity. As an example of this process, the authors examine Martha Stewart's cultivation of a lifestyle-driven brand. The authors discuss the implications of their work on social movement theory and institutional theory.

Keywords: Identity; social movements; lifestyles; collective action; transformational mechanism; institutionalization

Institutions shape identities and enable processes of identity construction (Glynn, 2008), yet the reverse is also true: the development and maintenance of identities can lead to the creation of novel institutions. Institutions furnish actors with sets of "possible legitimate identity elements with which to construct,

---

*The authors contributed equally and are listed alphabetically.

Microfoundations of Institutions
Research in the Sociology of Organizations, Volume 65A, 119–134
ISSN: 0733-558X/doi:10.1108/S0733-558X2019000065A014

give meaning to, and legitimize firm identities and symbolization" (Glynn, 2008, p. 358), yet actors can create novel identity elements, or modify existing ones, that can become the microfoundations for new or changed institutions. Here, we examine the latter, exploring how identities can furnish the necessary building blocks for institutional formation. We adopt Scott's (2008, p. 48) definition of institutions as durable "social structures...composed of cultural-cognitive, normative, and regulative elements that...provide stability and meaning to social life" because it incorporates a number of the core microfoundational elements – cognitive, communicative, and behavioral (Haack, Sieweke, & Wessel, this volume) – that allow us to forge linkages between identity and institutions. Essentially, we argue that identity provides a potent foundation upon which new institutions are developed, and in this way represents a powerful microfoundation of institutions.

Microfoundational research refocuses our attention from purely structural institutional accounts of organizations and society, to articulate a "richer understanding of how individuals locate themselves in social relations and interpret their context" (Powell & Colyvas, 2008, p. 276). Given the explosion of interest in the topic, microfoundational research embraces a variety of approaches, which Haack et al. (this volume) usefully categorize as: the *cognitive* perspective, the *communicative* perspective, and the *behavioral* perspective. Each perspective offers a unique lens on the microfoundations of institutions, and together they provide a comprehensive view of the manner in which individuals and other micro-level actors can create, transform, threaten, support, or maintain existing institutions. And yet, as we see it, research on microfoundations can address several challenges. Prominent among these, we propose, is the development of a bridge between the micro- and macro-foundations of institutionalism. Explorations of how microfoundational processes "aggregate and coalesce into the taken-for-granted beliefs of a community that are characteristic of an institution" (Haack et al, this volume) are essential to explaining emergence of, and change in, institutions.

Powell and Colyvas (2008) describe two conceptualizations scholars have adopted with regard to microfoundations: the first is a bottom-up process, whereby "micro-level rituals and negotiations aggregate over time ... and threaten or replace macro-level coherence"; and the second is a top-down process whereby "macro-orders are 'pulled down,' and become imbricated in local or particular cases" (p. 278). The first is built around transformational mechanisms, which describe how "individuals, through their actions and interactions, generate macro-level outcomes" (Hedström & Swedberg, 1998, p. 22), while the second is built around situational mechanisms, which describe "how macro-level events or conditions affect the individual" (Hedström & Swedberg, 1998, p. 21). We view Powell and Colyvas's two conceptualizations as complementary to Haack, Sieweke, and Wessel's three perspectives, such that microfoundations operate at lower levels, via cognitive, communicative, or behavioral pathways, to affect the development or maintenance of institutions; complementing this, we see macrofoundations as supplying those meanings, roles, or other cultural apparatuses that can afford micro-level instantiations of macro-level institutions. We argue that identity is an important microfoundational element, critical to cognition, communication, and behavior. In this chapter, we seek to explore the processes that undergird how identity contributes to the development of new institutions, and, in particular, to illuminate the role identity plays in bringing people together to develop cohesive cultural understandings and durable patterns of action that come to constitute (or re-constitute) institutions.

A useful starting point for our exploration is the social movements literature. Identity is ubiquitous in the social movements literature, and is recognized as an important dynamic in "new social movements" (Laraña, Gusfield, & Johnston, 2009) and "identity movements" (Rao, Monin, & Durand, 2003) in particular. Identity movements involve a collective attempt to institutionalize a novel identity, often through the social mechanisms – for example, framing, bricolage, or translation (Campbell, 2005) – that drive more "traditional" social movements oriented toward righting civil injustice. However, in contrast to the "contentious politics" that can typify traditional social movements, which tend to arise in opposition to some perceived social injustice (Tarrow, 2011), identity movements "seek autonomy rather than justice, aspire to cultural change, and promote new institutional logics" (Rao et al., 2003, p. 796). Importantly, Rao et al. (2003) explain how "social movements are important motors of institution building, deinstitutionalization, and reinstitutionalization in organizational fields" (p. 796). In a related stream of research, Haenfler, Johnson, and Jones (2012, p. 2) emphasize the importance of the "intersections of private action and movement participation, personal change and social change" that culminate in articulating a particular identity or an associated lifestyle as a strategy for inducing social change; they conceptualize such movements as "lifestyle movements." Lifestyle movements rely on their constituents' identities to initiate cultural change and, through their accumulated and sustained efforts, create new institutions supporting those identities. Generally speaking, social movements – identity and lifestyle movements included – encompass all three microfoundational elements, that is, cognitive, behavioral, and communicative aspects, and thus permit a rich exploration of how these elements affect institution building and change.

Examining the bottom-up processes whereby identity shapes cognition, perceptions, beliefs, values, and norms, we focus on the transformational mechanisms that create enduring patterns of action which represent new institutions. Our work emphasizes the cognitive perspective in driving this process, and acknowledges the roles of behavioral and communicative elements. In our view, identities are constructed by piecing together "bits of meaning, symbols, or values" (Glynn, 2008) and thus are cognitive constructions; lifestyle movements, however, go beyond the cognitive to involve the communicative and behavioral enactment – in both symbolic and material terms – of a specific identity. Broadly, we pursue the following question: how do identity and lifestyle movements develop and establish institutions that support the focal identity? We begin by reviewing the social movements literature, highlighting the microfoundational power of identity for influencing the emergence and evolution of higher-level institutions. Then, we illustrate these dynamics by focusing on one particular lifestyle movement: Martha Stewart's cultivation of a lifestyle-driven brand. Finally, we discuss directions for future research at the intersection of identity, social movements, and the microfoundations of institutions.

SOCIAL MOVEMENTS AND IDENTITY

Social movement scholars have explored the role of identity – and especially collective identity – for decades. Wry, Lounsbury, and Glynn (2011, p. 449) observe that "scholars have defined collective identities as groups of actors that can be strategically constructed and fluid, organized around a shared purpose and similar outputs." Melucci (1995, pp. 43–44) argues that collective identity represents the mechanism through which social movements emerge as collectives and begin to engage in collective action, stating that

> the empirical unity of a social movement should be considered as a result rather than a starting point, a fact to be explained rather than evidence…I call collective identity this process of "constructing" an action system.

Melucci goes on to outline three cognitive underpinnings of collective identification (p. 46): (1) self-reflection; (2) sensemaking and attribution with regard to one's own influence; and (3) the perception of duration, and especially the temporal location of one's own actions within a given chain of events. Polletta and Jasper (2001, p. 285) define collective identity as "an individual's cognitive, moral, and emotional connection with a broader community, category, practice, or institution." Collective identity is theorized as a critical mechanism through which social movement organizations can mobilize movement constituents for collective action (Melucci, 1995). And yet, collective identity is typically seen only as a mobilizing mechanism; we seek to recognize the power of identity beyond mobilization, as a force of social stability and as one foundation upon which institutions are built.

Social movements tend to unfold in a relatively predictable manner. Early scholars of movements described four phases of social movements: social ferment, popular excitement, formalization, and institutionalization (Blumer, 1951; cited in Della Porta & Diani, 2006). During the initial social ferment stage, potential movement participants may feel as though a part of their identity or lifestyle is threatened or unfulfilled, potentially in cognitive, behavioral, or communicative terms. It is during this phase that "counter hegemonic ideas and oppositional identities" are formed (Polletta & Jasper, 2001, p. 288). Examples of such "oppositional identities" include "groups such as classical versus nouvelle cuisine chefs (Rao et al., 2003), Boston trustees versus New York money managers (Lounsbury, 2007), and industrial versus craft brewers (Carroll & Swaminathan, 2000)" (Wry et al., 2011, p. 449). During the second stage, popular excitement, movement participants begin to organize, grow in size, and engage in collective action. Movement organizers make considerable effort during this stage to frame collective identities so as to attract additional movement participants. One way movement organizers frame identities is by leveraging the nascent identity that defines the movement, developing what Wry et al. (2011, p. 450) describe as "a collective identity defining story that outlines their group's core purpose and practices, theorizing their meaning and appropriateness." They explain that increasing numbers of those claiming the collective identity tell such stories to coordinate membership growth, encourage new actors to affiliate, and solidify the collective identity itself.

In the third stage, formalization, dedicated social movement organizations are developed and participants continue to engage in collective action, in an increasingly organized and direct manner. During this stage, collective identities are important benchmarks for the types of actions that are appropriate for a given movement. For example, an anti-war movement is unlikely to engage in violent protest, as doing so is entirely incongruent with the movement's peace-focused collective identity. It is at this stage that legitimated practices come to be associated with a movement and emerging social structures become more codified. Finally, the fourth and last stage, institutionalization, is relatively self-explanatory, but it is worth noting that movements may "end" in various ways. Some movements may fizzle out after they achieve their goals, never developing the durable patterns of action necessary for institutionalization. Such movements may, however, influence existing institutions. The Occupy Wall Street movement, for example, raised awareness related to issues of economic inequality, yet never coalesced into an institution. Other movements may become formalized as organizations or even as institutions. The cannabis legalization movement, having successfully fought for cannabis legalization in 10 states, has created an institution that supports the identity of cannabis consumers and movement participants (Dioun, 2018). Another social movement organization, MADD (Mothers Against Drunk Driving), continues to mobilize support for stricter drunk driving laws, and has influenced public policy across the United States.

Identity and collective identity are perhaps most salient in the early phases of the social movement life cycle, during the social ferment and popular excitement stages, when individuals and small groups are beginning to come together, identify with each other, and articulate a common message. Identity is critical during these early stages, and its microfoundational power is evident. At a cognitive level, movement participants begin to articulate how the social movement relates to who they are as individuals, and they begin to craft a collective identity that adds clarity to the movement itself. In terms of communication, social movements utilize framing strategies to articulate their collective identity. Social movement organizers frame their causes by constructing narratives which detail why they are mobilizing for collective action (e.g., Wry et al., 2011), and by amplifying injustices or common needs within those narratives (Benford & Snow, 2000, p. 623). Fine (1995, p. 137) links cognition to communication, stating that "the content of the movement ideology affects [the movement's] narratives." Several scholars have taken initial steps at bridging the gap between the cognitive and communicative perspectives. Robnett (1996, p. 1661) explores "the ways in which individuals come to participate in movement organizations and identify with its issues and goals," while Snow, Rochford, Worden, and Benford (1986, p. 464) study "the various interactive and communicative processes that affect frame alignment." Finally, behavioral microfoundations can be seen in the actual activities of social movement participants. Identity is both a cognitive and behavioral microfoundation, something claimed as well as performed (Glynn, 2008). Collective identity is an inescapable construct within the social movement literature, and for good reason. Identification is a fundamental human tendency (Tajfel & Turner, 1985), and as such, it is unsurprising that our attempts to stimulate structural change rely so heavily on the formation of an effective and compelling collective identity.

While identity and lifestyle movements follow the same general stages (from Blumer, 1951) as more instrumental social movements, their goals and the processes through which they achieve their goals are markedly different (see Table 1, for a summary of these similarities and differences). Identity movements emerge when the cultural tools necessary to enact a given identity do not exist. Instrumental movements, on the other hand, emerge when actors notice and begin to oppose a social injustice. The formation of collective identities, an integral process in every movement's life cycle, is generally framed as oppositional to another (unjust) identity in instrumental movements, but framed as unique and/or forgotten by existing institutions in identity and lifestyle movements. The social movement organizations that are founded to support or represent instrumental movements are often politically minded, like think tanks or lobbyists, while those founded to represent identity movements are often more informal. Identity movements, thus, are concerned with initiating cultural change, by developing institutions and cultural tools that can be used to support and enact the focal identity. Instrumental movements are concerned with initiating public policy change, by gaining enough power to influence existing institutions. Identity and lifestyle movements often create "lifestyle institutions" – durable social structures which shape the cultural activities of those who claim the focal identity as their own – that are cognitive, communicative, and behavioral in their constitution.

Identity Movements

Rao et al. (2003) distinguish between identity movements and instrumental movements, characterizing the former as movements which strive for cultural change and the latter as movements which strive for legislative change. The authors argue that identity movements "disseminate identity-discrepant cues" that serve to either institutionalize a novel institutional logic or dismantle and modify an existing logic (Rao et al., 2003, p. 797). Although research on "identity movements" per se is scarce, other social movement scholars have noted the centrality of identity in many modern social movements. Johnston, Laraña, and Gusfield (1994, p. 7) posit that most, if not all "new social movements" rely heavily on identity: "[movements] often involve the emergence of new or formerly weak dimensions of identity." Common to both theorizations of identity movements is the notion that identity movements are cultural, both in origin and in their intended consequences. Bernstein (1997, p. 533) argues that identity movements are "defined as much by the goals they seek, and the strategies they use, as by the fact that they are based on a shared characteristic such as ethnicity or sex." Whether this "shared characteristic" is based on a nominal category like biological sex or on a more fluid and dynamic cognitive construct, like environmental sustainability, identity movements are – perhaps unsurprisingly – rooted in a strong sense of collective identity. Identity movements rely on cultural elements such as stories and symbols to build collective identity and affect cultural change (Rao et al., 2003; Wry et al., 2011); more generally, many identity movements are mainly concerned with creating spaces "where novel life-styles and social identities can be experienced and defined" (Johnston et al., 1994, p. 11). In other words, new social

Table 1. A Comparison of Movement Phases for Instrumental Social Movements and Identity/Lifestyle Movements.

Movement Phase	Instrumental Social Movements	Identity/Lifestyle Movements
Social ferment	• Awareness of social injustice	• Awareness of lack of cultural tools to enact identity
	• Collective identification begins	• Collective identification begins
Popular excitement	• Early stages of collective action	• Early stages of collective action
	• Framing of collective identity as oppositional	• Framing of collective identity as unique
Formalization	• Emergence of SMO's: political organizations	• Emergence of Social Movement Organizations (SMO's): cooperatives and informal networks
Institutionalization	• Regulatory institutions	• Lifestyle institutions
Institutional change	• Elimination of injustice	• Creation of cultural tools relevant to focal identity

movements and identity movements create sets of cultural elements from which actors construct patterns of action that reflect their ideal identity and lifestyle (Swidler, 1986).

Dugan (2008, p. 40) explores "how social movements actively create and deploy collective identity in an attempt to shape the public's perceptions." Again, the concepts of framing and identity appear to be tightly intertwined, reinforcing our proposition that identity is simultaneously a cognitive, behavioral, and communicative microfoundation of institutional formation and change. For instance, in a comparative study of the Christian Right movement and the gay rights movement, Dugan (2008) showed that both movements framed themselves as similar to the general public and different from each other. Similarly, Kaminski and Taylor (2008, p. 68) found that music and performance are important behavioral and practical "vehicles for expressing gay identity," arguing that practices such as performing and dancing to music can strengthen collective oppositional identities. Without collective identity, collective action is difficult, and without collective action, movements cannot hope to change anything. Collective identity is a potent cognitive, communicative, and behavioral mechanism that enables collective action to materialize. Collective identity "ensures the continuity and permanence of the movement over time" (Melucci, 1995, p. 49), and as such, represents a cornerstone upon which new institutions form.

From Identity Movements to Institutions

Identity has been implicated in theories of institutional change and formation by previous researchers. The identities claimed by institutional entrepreneurs, for instance, often imprint themselves on the institutions that they build. For example, Navis and Glynn (2010, p. 462) show that both Sirius and XM contributed to the development of a new market category – satellite radio – by embracing a "shared, collective identity." Maguire, Hardy, and Lawrence (2004) show that within the HIV treatment advocacy movement, HIV-positive constituents are particularly effective institutional entrepreneurs – they are perceived as legitimate by other movement adherents precisely because they identify so strongly with the movement's cause.

Lok (2010, p. 1331) recognized the power of identity to create and transform institutions, stating that "the particular ways in which actors understand themselves can influence the ways in which they reproduce and translate new institutional logics." Institutional logics are the specific "pattern of material practices, assumptions, values, beliefs, and rules" through which durable systems of meaning – institutions – are created and maintained (Thornton & Ocasio, 1999, p. 804). Logics are the musculoskeletal system to an institutional body: they dictate the types of activity that are legitimate and even possible within a given institution. Rao et al. (2003) found that identity movements have the power to replace dominant institutional logics – their study of French gastronomy shows that chefs engaged in the nouvelle cuisine movement both heeded and perpetuated identity-discrepant cues which significantly altered both their material and symbolic practices. Nouvelle cuisine chefs focused on fresh ingredients over traditional methods, emphasized individuality over conformity, and represented their food on menus in markedly more creative ways. Cerulo (1997, p. 393) describes identity movements similarly: "Spurred not by ideology or resource mobilization, identity-based movements act rather than react; they fight to expand freedom, not to achieve it; they mobilize for choice rather than emancipation." The notion that identity movements are fighting for "expansion" and "choice" holds intriguing connotations for how these movements can build novel institutions. Next, we apply these ideas to a specific identity movement: lifestyle movements.

LIFESTYLE MOVEMENTS

The concept of "lifestyle movements" is relatively new: Haenfler et al. (2012) define these as those movements which "consciously and actively promote a lifestyle, or way of life, as a primary means to foster social change," and consider them to be social movements which require individuals to modify the way they live their lives in order to support a broader societal-level goal. The emergence of lifestyle movements mirrors a broader cultural shift in the United States, from one sanctioning achievement to one of personality, based on their abilities as cultural entrepreneurs or "influencers." In other words, actors who are able to skillfully use culture to craft distinctive, original, yet still relatable identities exert considerable influence. Scholars in the humanities explain that consumers rely on organizations to organize cultural elements into neat packages which facilitate the adoption or elaboration of a given identity or lifestyle (see Bell & Hollows, 2005).

Organizations in several industries – politics, healthcare, cuisine, hospitality, entertainment, and others – systematically categorize consumers based on the lifestyles they adopt. For instance, in the 1990s, hotels, particularly those in the luxury segment, were refashioned to cater to a society that valued personalized and sometimes idiosyncratic lifestyles. Lockwood, Glynn, and Giorgi (2018, p. 30) note that these were focused on catering to guests' preferences that were tailored and unique; "luxury denoted staff 'invent[ing] a drink in your honor,'" for instance, or "re-creat[ing] the recipe from your favorite meal in Paris." These lifestyle preferences are driven, in many ways, by status differences and aspirations (Bell & Hollows, 2005, p. 6); individuals see certain lifestyles as offering various levels of cultural capital (Bourdieu, 1986), and thus lifestyle movements are concerned, first and foremost, with the acquisition of cultural capital. Individuals who participate in the "green living" movement, for instance, may be viewed as more conscientious and thus more valuable members of society than their non-green peers.

Lifestyle, "like other forms of high culture, combines concrete practices with a compelling story linking those practices to transcendent meanings and identities" (DiMaggio, 2006, p. 932). We conceptualize lifestyles as continuously enacted identities: actors transform identities into lifestyles by rationalizing and engaging in a set of practices that supports the rituals, narratives, and values upon which their identity is based. In this regard, lifestyles are both material and symbolic – both behavioral and cognitive – instantiations of individual identities. To illustrate the increasing prevalence of lifestyles in popular culture, we searched the *New York Times* for references to the term "lifestyle" and for references to a subset of the particular lifestyle movements identified by Haenfler et al. (2012).[1] Fig. 1 shows the frequency of references to the term "lifestyle" in the *New York Times* between 1970 and 2017. Around the turn of the millennium, we see the first significant spike in usage of the term, followed by a startling surge again in 2014. As lifestyles become increasingly salient in our society, we are likely to see existing institutions adapt in order to cater to practitioners of specific lifestyles, as did hotels, for example, as well as new institutions that form in response to especially novel lifestyles.

Fig. 2 shows the frequency of references in the *New York Times* to the subset of lifestyle movements we selected from Haenfler et al.'s (2012) analysis. Some movements, such as vegetarianism, have been a consistent presence over the last few decades; others, such as the slow food and locavore movements, are more recent phenomena, evidencing a rapid rise in the mid-2000s, before largely fading away a few years later.

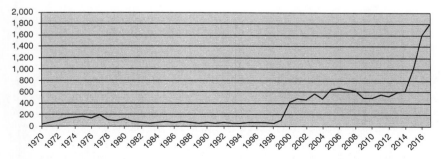

Fig. 1. References to the Term "Lifestyle" in the *New York Times*, 1970–2017.

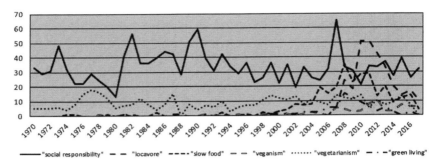

Fig. 2.   References to Specific Lifestyle Movements in the
New York Times, 1970–2017.

One early article (1972) focusing on vegetarianism – titled "Teenagers Choose the Meatless Diet" – focuses on the cognitive aspects of engaging with the lifestyle, indicating that some are motivated by moral reasons, others for environmental reasons, and others for spiritual reasons. A 2008 article on the slow food movement, "Slow Food Savors Its Big Moment," identifies the sort of practices that adherents adopt: "much of the organization's work involves identifying traditional foods, like Ethiopian white honey or Amalfi sfusato lemons, and designing ways to help the people who produce them." In response to the green living movement, a 2009 article titled "Felled Wood" discusses the "token rites of green living," including the need to purchase "curly light bulbs and brown napkins" – goods that have a significantly less deleterious effect on the environment than their high-intensity and bleached counterparts. Each of these lifestyle movements involves a set of practices that requires institutional support: without institutions to design and market efficient light bulbs, or import traditional foods from abroad, these lifestyles could not exist. The very existence of lifestyles such as locavorism, green living, vegetarianism, and slow food prompts a structural or institutional response. Perhaps, it is not that these lifestyles depend on institutions to support their continued existence, but rather that institutions develop organically in response to – or even in tandem with – the emergence of a novel lifestyle.

The Dynamics of Lifestyle Movements:
An Illustration from Martha Stewart Living

I think I started this whole category of lifestyle.– Martha Stewart (Malec, 2013)

Martha Stewart, founder of the eponymous media and merchandising company, Martha Stewart Living Omnimedia (MSLO), has been at the forefront of the lifestyle movement for more than three decades (Goldstein, 2005; Lockwood & Glynn, 2016; Mason & Meyers, 2001). She has been credited with being a *"Lifestyle maven"* (Forbes.com), *"Maker of middle-class manners"* (Credenda.org), *"Self-declared most tasteful person in the country"* (The Woman's Quarterly – iwf.org), *"Sociological Phenomenon"* (Pigtrail.Uark.edu), and *"Vampire-like cultural icon"* (ibar.com). In her magazines, television shows, radio programs, newspaper columns, numerous books, products for house and home (sold through K-Mart and Macy's), and furniture line, Martha Stewart advances a new, improved, hip and anti-Styrofoam image of home and domesticity – "...a life that isn't centered on fast food or. We take a different view of life, and you can, too." And, one that's for sale, "making the impossible purchasable." In Stewart's flagship product, her magazine, aptly entitled *Living*, she advances her concept of lifestyle, with a reach that is extensive: "Beautiful soups and how to make them, beautiful houses and how to build them, beautiful children and how to raise them." Because Martha Stewart has been engaged in the production of "lifestyle" that has been widely consumed by her magazine subscribers, television fans, and purchasers of her books and other products, we chose to draw on Martha Stewart and her company to offer an illustration of how the dynamics of lifestyle movements can function as microfoundations of institutions.

MSLO's mission is stated in terms of lifestyle:

> Martha Stewart Living is about the handmade, the homemade, the artful, the innovative, the practical and the beautiful. We are not just about lifestyle, but about tools for modern living – not just about the how-to but about the why-to.

It is a mission that fuels the movement. In their interview study with women who consume MSLO products, Mason and Meyers (2001, p. 814) found that the interviewees were attracted to, and excited by,

> the lifestyle she [Martha Stewart] both presents and represents. This lifestyle is one of wealth, luxury, and leisure – of immaculate homes, perfectly made beds, elegantly appointed furnishings, gorgeous landscaping, handmade gifts for the holidays, flawless dinner parties for 12, and the time to patiently pursue complex projects or recipes. ... Stewart's world is a fantasy of upper-class perfection.

Through her many offerings, for example, her magazines, television programs, and products for achieving the appealing lifestyle she sells, Stewart offers a variety of ways for realizing this aspirational lifestyle and the positive self-identity that can ensue. And yet, there is an inherent friction, as Stewart's fans "aspire to and emulate a fantasy lifestyle of wealth and luxury that ignores the systemic economic disparities that place real wealth beyond their reach" (Mason & Meyers, 2001, p. 820). Stewart puts in reach what seems elusive: access to an elite aesthetic that transcends some of the banality of their day-to-day routine. She does this through her framing of activities and offering her own life as a touchstone for theirs; her fans see this wealthy, corporate executive as approachable, because of her "natural appearance" (Mason & Meyers, 2001), making her seem more "real" and someone whom they might identify with, as a friend or neighbor. In a way that resembles the French chefs that Rao et al. (2003) studied, the identity movement that Stewart catalyzed seemingly held the power to replace the dominant institutional logic attending domestic work for its instrumentality and transforming the activities and roles of their mundane work into novel identities. Thus, the lifestyle movement led and mobilized by Martha Stewart and her followers was realized in a new institutional logic that recrafted the meaning of homekeeping and living, more generally. This was particularly apparent in the series of "101" articles that Stewart published in her flagship magazine, *Living*.

The 101 articles were introduced in the fifth year of *Living* (1995) and continued to appear over the next 17 years, until 2012; there were 98 in total (Lockwood & Glynn, 2016). The 101s takes a fairly routine pedestrian activity – such as cooking, cleaning, vacuuming, sewing or gardening – and juxtaposes an aspirational identity (the perfect chef, homemaker, or entertainer) to refashion its meaning cognitively (so as to transcend the ordinary) and prescribe a set of associated practices to be performed behaviorally. For instance, *Pizza 101* (October 1997) instructs that preparing this meal relates to the Italian lifestyle: "Making pizza is an ideal activity for those forced to live the Italian way vicariously. And for the lucky ones, it is a ritualistic way to return to their Italian roots." Or, for special occasions, *Magic 101* (October 1999) instructs more broadly on the lifestyle that it was once part of the practice:

> True parlor magic, intimate and civilized, was once commonplace in the elegant homes of nineteenth-century cognoscenti… Many of the techniques of modern magic are the offspring of the nineteenth-century Spiritualist movement. Spiritualism was a fad for séances and other communications with the spirit world. For decades nearly everyone in Europe and much of the eastern United States, from heads of state to the general populace, was caught up in the fervor ….

Thus, the creation of lifestyle involves both material (behavioral) and symbolic (cognitive) elements that enable the enactment of its institutional logic. As much as lifestyles shape people's everyday living and consumption, they also shape their "individuality, self-expression, and stylistic self-consciousness" (Featherstone, 1987, p. 55). Stewart serves as the lifestyle expert, the knowledgeable cultural authority, an "ordinary expert" (Lewis, 2010, p. 580) who is critical to the development of her followers' identity and lifestyle. For instance, in *Watering 101*(May 2000), Stewart is clear and firm in her direction:

> Give a plant too little water – or too much – and you will stunt or even kill it. Improper watering drastically diminishes a plant's bloom and ruins the flavor and texture of any fruits or vegetables it bears. Both overwatering and under-watering can depress a plant's defenses, making it more vulnerable to diseases and pests (indeed, insects are known to actively seek out water-stressed plants) …. Generally, you do best to let a plant tell you when it needs water.

And, it is this expertise that helps to catalyze Stewart's lifestyle movement and institutionalize its beliefs and practices in an enduring pattern of experiences and logic. As one fan commented on the occasion of the firm's 20th anniversary: "Martha has been the ultimate teacher in the fine art of living." (http://twenty.marthastewart.com/, retrieved July 29, 2011). To celebrate the anniversary, MSLO created a website where fans could respond to the prompt:

> Help toast the magazine's 20th year by sharing how Martha Stewart Living has influenced your life. Posts will appear on MarthaStewart.com and may be featured in our upcoming anniversary issue.[Complete the following sentence]…*Living* is ….

Some of the responses included:

- "I love this magazine because it contains just the way of living everybody should have."
- "The ideas are trendy enough, yet still traditional. Nothing is cute, but still fun. Appeals to more mature tastes with a touch of playfulness. Can tackle any project with confidence."

- "MS gives me sophisticated elegance to mirror in my life."
- "It has ingenious ways of using ordinary objects to spectacular tools!"

In addition to some of the specific ways in which Stewart's notion of lifestyle shaped the movement, fans acknowledge the "satisfying" sense of sharing in a collective identity – "I get to feel connected to other women who inspire me." – and the recognition of an "imagined community" (Anderson, 2006) coalescing and becoming institutionalized. Some fans' comments illustrate how Stewart's lifestyle had become institutionalized, as a durable pattern of living, over time: "Because the ideas from cooking to cleaning to decorating have become a part of my lifestyle for 20 years and counting." Stewart provided the cultural and identity elements that her followers could use to build and institutionalize the desired lifestyle. The collective identity shared by Stewart's fans and followers is powerful and likely durable; in this regard, Stewart's lifestyle movement has become institutionalized.

DISCUSSION

We explore the microfoundations of institutions by focusing on a critical institutional building block – the formation and deployment of identities, especially via social movements. We view identity as a key microfoundation of institutions, as it encompasses the cognitive, communicative, and behavioral aspects that are its essential components (Haack et al., this volume). Building on this insight, we examine identities in the context of social movements that are intended to activate and mobilize novel identities that, ultimately, can be institutionalized in later stages of a movement's advance.

We focus on a particular type of identity movement – the lifestyle movement – and observed its rise over the last several decades (see Figs. 1 and 2) and its emergence and institutionalization in the elite appeal of Martha Stewart's products, practices, and meaningful narratives that frame her offerings. Thus, we take a "full circle" look at the interplay of micro-and macro-foundations in processes of institutionalization; we see identities as playing a critical bridging role in linking the two. We propose that the study of social movements and, in particular, identity movements, could inform our understanding of the microfoundations of institutions.

Our work makes several contributions to both social movement theory and institutional theory. We integrate the identity literature in organization theory more generally with social movement theory, explaining the role of collective identity as a mechanism endemic to the microfoundations of institutions. In particular, we illuminate three key mechanisms through which identity functions as a microfoundation, building upon Haack et al.'s categorization of microfoundational research as communicative, cognitive, or behavioral (this volume). From the cognitive perspective, we argue that collective identities are perceptual constructions which help to solidify and potentially even institutionalize a particular pattern of meaning and action. From the communicative perspective, we show that the manner in which identities are framed influences how (or if) they become institutionalized. Finally, from a behavioral perspective, we argue that identities are materially enacted, contributing to the development and reinforcement of new institutional logics that undergird institutions. Additionally, we argue that social movement success or failure should not be treated as a dichotomy; even though some movements may fade away, the identities claimed and enacted by their participants can live on, becoming institutionalized in existing cultural or regulatory frameworks. While our theorization focuses on identity movements and lifestyle movements, future scholarship investigating social movements that are engendered by "contentious politics" can be equally informative. Future research could explore how identity becomes institutionalized in other social movements, especially those concerned with achieving political or regulatory change.

Methodologically, we focused on Martha Stewart's creation of a lifestyle-based institutional logic as an illustration of these dynamics. Future researchers might design studies to investigate the nuances suggested by the Stewart example. It could be especially illuminating to examine social movements over time in more fine-grained detail, to understand how the institutions created by social movements are created, how they change, and how they endure (or die out). Both qualitative and quantitative research designs would be informative. In-depth qualitative studies can help us to understand the nuances of the microfoundational mechanisms in specific social movements, but broader quantitative studies can help to make these dynamics more generalizable.

Our work highlights how collective identity is important to social movements and is a motor for the institutionalization effects of movements. Movements characterized by a strong sense of collective identity often create material and symbolic patterns of action that endure beyond the life cycle of the social movement itself, coalescing into an institution that permits the continued enactment of collective identity. Identification is an inescapable cognitive, communicative, and behavioral process, one that shapes and is shaped by the institutions of which we are part. As such, future scholarship at the intersection of identity, social movements, and institutional theory is ripe with opportunity.

NOTE

1. The lifestyle movements included in our search are: social responsibility, locavore, slow food, veganism, vegetarianism, and green living.

REFERENCES

Anderson, B. R. (2006). *Imagined communities* (rev. ed.). New York, NY: Verso.

Bell, D., & Hollows, J. (2005). Making sense of ordinary lifestyles. In D. Bell & J. Hollows (Eds.), *Ordinary lifestyles: Popular media, consumption and taste* (pp. 1–20). Maidenhead: Open University Press.

Benford, R. D., & Snow, D. A. (2000). Framing processes and social movements: An overview and assessment. *Annual Review of Sociology, 26*(1), 611–639.

Bernstein, M. (1997). Celebration and suppression: The strategic uses of identity by the lesbian and gay movement. *American Journal of Sociology, 103*(3), 531–565.

Blumer, H. (1951). Collective behavior. In A. M. Lee & H. Blumer (Eds.), *New outline of the principles of sociology* (pp. 166–222). New York, NY: Barnes & Noble.

Campbell, J. L. (2005). Where do we stand. *Social Movements and Organization Theory*, 41–68.

Carroll, G. R., & Swaminathan, A. (2000). Why the microbrewery movement? Organizational dynamics of resource partitioning in the US brewing industry. *American Journal of Sociology, 106*(3), 715–762.

Cerulo, K. A. (1997). Identity construction: New issues, new directions. *Annual Review of Sociology, 23*(1), 385–409.

Della Porta, D., & Diani, M. (2009). *Social movements: An introduction*. New York, NY: John Wiley & Sons.

DiMaggio, P. (2006). Book review of *"Accounting for Taste: The Triumph of French Cuisine." American Journal of Sociology, 112*(3), 932–934.

Dioun, C. (2018). Negotiating moral boundaries: Social movements and the strategic (re) definition of the medical in cannabis markets. In F. Briscoe, B. G. King, & J. Leitzinger (Eds.), *Social movements, stakeholders and non-market strategy* (pp. 53–82). Bingley: Emerald Publishing Limited.

Dugan, K. B. (2008). Just like you: The dimensions of identity presentations in an antigay contested context. *Identity Work in Social Movements, 30*, 21–46.

Featherstone, M. (1987). Lifestyle and consumer culture. *Theory, Culture & Society, 4*(1), 55–70.

Fine, G. A. (1995). Public narration and group culture: Discerning discourse in social movements. *Social Movements and Culture, 4*, 127–143.

Glynn, M. A. (2008). Beyond constraint: How institutions enable identities. In R. Greenwood, C. Oliver, T. B. Lawrence, & R. E. Meyer (Eds.), *The Sage handbook of organizational institutionalism* (pp. 413–430). New York, NY: Sage.

Glynn, M. A. (2011). The "Martha" moment: Wading into others" worlds. In A. Carlsen & J. Dutton (Eds.), *Research alive: Generative moments for doing qualitative research* (pp. 63–66). Copenhagen, Denmark: Copenhagen Business School Press.

Goldstein, D. E. (2005). Recipes for living: Martha Stewart and the new American subject. In D. Bell & J. Hollows (Eds.), In *Ordinary lifestyles: Popular media, consumption and taste* (pp. 47–64). Berkshire: Open University Press.

Haack, P., Sieweke, J., & Wessel, L. (2019). Microfoundations and Multi-level Research on Institutions. In P. Haack, J. Sieweke, & L. Wessel (Eds.), *Microfoundations of Institutions* (RSO V65A, pp. 11–42). Bingley: Emerald Publishing Limited.

Haenfler, R., Johnson, B., & Jones, E. (2012). Lifestyle movements: Exploring the intersection of lifestyle and social movements. *Social Movement Studies, 11*(1), 1–20.

Hedström, P., & Swedberg, R. (1998). Social mechanisms: An introductory essay. In P. Hedström, R. Swedberg, & G. Hernes (Eds.), *Social mechanisms: An analytical approach to social theory* (pp. 1–31). Cambridge: Cambridge University Press.

Johnston, H., Laraña, E., & Gusfield, J. R. (1994). Identities, grievances, and new social movements. *New Social Movements: From Ideology to Identity, 3*, 35.

Kaminski, E., & Taylor, V. (2008). 'We're not just lip-synching up here': Music and collective identity in drag performances. In J. Reger, D. J. Myers, & R. L. Einwohner (Eds.), *Identity work in social movements* (Vol. 30, pp. 47–76). Minneapolis, MN: University of Minnesota Press.

Laraña, E., Gusfield, J. R., & Johnston, H. (Eds.). (2009). *New social movements: From ideology to identity*. New York, NY: Temple University Press.

Lewis, T. (2010). Branding, celebritzation and the lifestyle expert. *Cultural Studies, 24*(4), 580–598.

Lockwood, C., & Glynn, M. A. (2016). The micro-foundations of mattering: Domestic traditions as institutionalized practices in everyday living. In J. Gehman, M. Lounsbury, & R. Greenwood (Eds.), *How institutions matter! Research in the sociology of organizations* (Vol. *48A*, pp. 201–232). Bingley: Emerald Publishing Limited.

Lockwood, C., Glynn, M. A., & Giorgi, S. (2018). *The cultural theorization of high market status: The discursive construction of luxury in U.S. hotels, 1790–2015*. Working Paper, University of Virginia.

Lok, J. (2010). Institutional logics as identity projects. *Academy of Management Journal, 53*(6), 1305–1335.

Lounsbury, M. (2007). A tale of two cities: Competing logics and practice variation in the professionalizing of mutual funds. *Academy of Management Journal, 50*(2), 289–307.

Maguire, S., Hardy, C., Lawrence, T. B. (2004). Institutional entrepreneurship in emerging fields: HIV/AIDS treatment advocacy in Canada. *Academy of Management Journal, 47*(5), 657–679.

Malec, B. (October 15, 2013). E! Martha Stewart's Gwyneth Paltrow Goop Diss? Retrieved from http://www.eonline.com/news/470428/martha-stewart-s-gwyneth-paltrow-goop-diss-i-think-i-started-this-whole-category-of-lifestyle. Accessed on October 18, 2013.

Mason, A., & Meyers, M. (2001). Living with Martha Stewart: Chosen domesticity in the experience of fans. *Journal of Communication*, *51*(4), 801–823.

Melucci, A. (1995). The process of collective identity. *Social Movements and Culture*, *4*, 41–63.

Navis, C., & Glynn, M. A. (2010). How new market categories emerge: Temporal dynamics of legitimacy, identity, and entrepreneurship in satellite radio, 1990–2005. *Administrative Science Quarterly*, *55*(3), 439–471.

Polletta, F., & Jasper, J. M. (2001). Collective identity and social movements. *Annual Review of Sociology*, *27*(1), 283–305.

Powell, W. W., & Colyvas, J. A. (2008). Microfoundations of institutional theory. In W. W. Powell, J. A. Colyvas, R. Greenwood, C. Oliver, K. Sahlin, & R. Suddaby (Eds.), *The Sage handbook of organizational institutionalism* (pp. 276–298). New York, NY: Sage.

Rao, H., Monin, P., & Durand, R. (2003). Institutional change in Toque Ville: Nouvelle cuisine as an identity movement in French gastronomy. *American Journal of Sociology*, *108*(4), 795–843.

Robnett, B. (1996). African-American women in the civil rights movement, 1954–1965: Gender, leadership, and micromobilization. *American Journal of Sociology*, *101*(6), 1661–1693.

Scott, W. R. (2008). *Institutions and organizations: Ideas and interests*. New York, NY: Sage.

Snow, D. A., Rochford, E. B., Jr, Worden, S. K., & Benford, R. D. (1986). Frame alignment processes, micromobilization, and movement participation. *American Sociological Review*, *51*(4), 464–481.

Swidler, A. (1986). Culture in action: Symbols and strategies. *American Sociological Review*, *51*(2), 273–286.

Tajfel, H., & Turner, J. C. (1985) The social identity theory of intergroup behavior. In S. Worchel & W. G. Austin (Eds.), *Psychology of intergroup relations* (2nd ed., pp. 7–24). Chicago, IL: Nelson-Hall.

Tarrow, S. G. (2011). *Power in movement: Social movements and contentious politics*. Cambridge: Cambridge University Press.

Thornton, P. H., & Ocasio, W. (1999). Institutional logics and the historical contingency of power in organizations: Executive succession in the higher education publishing industry, 1958–1990. *American Journal of Sociology*, *105*(3), 801–843.

Wry, T., Lounsbury, M., & Glynn, M. A. (2011). Legitimating nascent collective identities: Coordinating cultural entrepreneurship. *Organization Science*, *22*(2), 449–463.

CHAPTER 6

EMBODIED AND REFLEXIVE AGENCY IN INSTITUTIONAL FIELDS: AN INTEGRATIVE NEO-INSTITUTIONAL PERSPECTIVE OF INSTITUTIONAL CHANGE

Jan Goldenstein and Peter Walgenbach

ABSTRACT

Neo-institutional theory has been criticized for equating the macrolevel with the realm of unconsciously constraining institutions and the microlevel with the realm of actors' reflexive agency and the origin of change. Considering the co-constitution of the macro and micro, the authors propose that change can be explained through reflexivity at the microlevel and through unconscious processes that affect the macrolevel. This chapter contributes to neo-institutional theory's microfoundation by distinguishing four types of institutional changes. It will help institutionalists to become more explicit about what cognitive processes and what field conditions are related to what kinds of agency and change.

Keywords: Microfoundation; cognition; embodiment; reflexivity; institutional field; institutional change

Neo-institutional theory has been criticized for its lack of a microfoundation that considers the co-constitutive nature of institutional constraints and actors' agency (Powell & Colyvas, 2008; Powell & Rerup, 2017). A co-constitution of the

Microfoundations of Institutions
Research in the Sociology of Organizations, Volume 65A, 135–152
Copyright © 2020 by Emerald Publishing Limited
All rights of reproduction in any form reserved
ISSN: 0733-558X/doi:10.1108/S0733-558X2019000065A015

macro- and microlevels in sociological studies would account for the simultaneous instantiation of institutions and agency on both levels (Harmon, Haack, & Roulet, 2018; Jepperson & Meyer, 2011). However, the literature on the "paradox of embedded agency," which is currently the most promising avenue toward establishing a microfoundation for neo-institutional theory (Thornton, Ocasio, & Lounsbury, 2012), tends to neglect such a co-constitution. As Harmon and colleagues (2018) recently illustrated, this literature tends to equate the macrolevel with the realm of unconsciously constraining institutions and the microlevel with the realm of actors' reflexive agency (e.g., Abdelnour, Hasselbladh, & Kallinikos, 2017; Greenwood, Raynard, Kodeih, Micelotta, & Lounsbury, 2011; Seo & Creed, 2002; Smets & Jarzabkowski, 2013; Thornton et al., 2012). This implies that institutions and agency appear (at least) as semi-independent forces rather than co-constitutive (Lok & Willmott, 2018).

This seems problematic because by separating the macro- and microlevels, the theory needs to refer to mechanisms that explain when and how unconsciously enacted institutions enter the realm of conscious agency and, after re-institutionalization, become unconscious constraints again (Cardinale, 2018; Smets & Jarzabkowski, 2013; Suddaby, Viale, & Gendron, 2016; Voronov & Yorks, 2015). In neo-institutional theory, changes to institutions are usually explained by disruptions to the institutional order. External shocks (Zietsma, Groenewegen, Logue, & Hinings, 2017) or situations of institutional plurality and complexity (Greenwood et al., 2011) are considered to facilitate actors' reflexivity (Seo & Creed, 2002; Suddaby et al., 2016). Therefore, explaining an institutional change in situations that lack disruption of the institutional order or exhibit institutional plurality and complexity appears to be valuable. In this sense, it appears problematic to disregard the possibility that institutions may change without any recourse to reflexive agency and that agency may occur without reflexivity (cf., Harmon et al., 2018). In this chapter, we provide a theoretical apparatus with which to better understand why and when institutions evolve naturally and point out that this evolution might disrupt the institutional order.

We develop the following arguments. First, we argue that the taken-for-grantedness of institutions may involve their reflexive and unconscious maintenance (cf., Jepperson, 1991). Second, we argue that institutional change can be explained through both reflexive agency at the microlevel and through unconscious processes that become effective on the macrolevel (cf., Powell & Rerup, 2017). The background of our theoretical argument is the idea that institutions are cognitively represented in two distinct memories and that institutions are therefore accessible through two distinct modes of consciousness, namely discursive or practical consciousness (Giddens, 1984; Lizardo, 2017; Lizardo & Strand, 2010; Vaisey, 2009). Both types of memory represent institutions as different types of knowledge, and simultaneous representations of an institution in both types of memory are not required (Lizardo, 2017). Discursive consciousness is related to internalized knowledge about cultural symbols that signify institutions and that remains open for deliberate reflection – that is, discursive knowledge (Berger & Luckmann, 1967; Friedland & Alford, 1991). Practical consciousness, in turn, is related to internalized institution-related knowledge that has an impact on praxis but regularly is not reflected – that is, practical dispositions (Bourdieu, 1977). Based on this differentiation, we distinguish four basic types of institutional changes and outline the conditions under which each type is likely to occur.

We provide the following contributions. First, we contribute to neo-institutional theory's microfoundation (Powell & Colyvas, 2008; Powell & Rerup, 2017) by illustrating that institutional change does not require reflexive agency on the microlevel but may also occur as a macrolevel phenomenon, as a result of unconscious processes. Second, the theoretical framework we provide is aimed at helping institutional scholars to become more explicit in their research about what type of memory and consciousness are related to what kinds of agency and, consequently, to what kinds of institutional change.

In what follows, we will outline the basic arguments we use in this chapter and develop our framework of different types of institutional change. Finally, we discuss the consequences of our argument for institutional thinking and methodology.

UNPACKING THE RELATIONSHIP BETWEEN COGNITION AND INSTITUTIONAL CHANGE

The Dual Internalization of Institutions

Two Kinds of Taken-for-Grantedness

One of the main contributions of neo-institutional theory is the conceptualization of institutions as cultural-cognitive structures (Phillips & Malhotra, 2008), which achieve the status of *taken-for-grantedness* during their institutionalization (Jepperson, 1991). Institutions are *cultural* because they are socially constructed and considered an external cultural toolkit that forms a scaffold for actors' agency (Swidler, 1986; Thornton et al., 2012). They are *cognitive* because they order actors' perceptions of the social world (Berger & Luckmann, 1967; Friedland & Alford, 1991; Zucker, 1977).

Yet, the conceptualization of how taken-for-granted institutions inform actors' cognition and agency remains ambiguous. The existing literature tends to equate taken-for-grantedness with what we call practical consciousness, namely unconsciously enacted praxis that is regularly not reflected (Cardinale, 2018; Hirsch & Lounsbury, 1997; Micelotta, Lounsbury, & Greenwood, 2017; Smets & Jarzabkowski, 2013; Zucker, 1977). Indeed, Jepperson (1991, p. 147) argued that taken-for-grantedness may cause the unconscious enactment of institutions. However, he also pointed out that actors can consider an institution "with substantial scrutiny, but still take it for granted." Therefore, even if institutions have achieved the status of taken-for-grantedness, they may remain available to actors' discursive consciousness (Lizardo & Strand, 2010). To be maintained, institutions that are accessible via actors' reflexivity require support from convincing accounts (Phillips & Malhotra, 2008; Suddaby, 2010) and/or other forms of institutional work (Lawrence & Suddaby, 2006; Meyer, Jancsary, Höllerer, & Boxenbaum, 2018).

Building upon the differentiation above, we describe two ways in which institutions become internalized during actors' socialization and gain the status of taken-for-grantedness in either discursive or practical consciousness. We build on Lizardo's (2017) framework of cultural acquisition and propose that institutions, depending on how actors are exposed to them, are cognitively represented in two distinct types of memory. Consequently, and in contrast to recent suggestions (Cardinale, 2018; Smets & Jarzabkowski, 2013), we argue that the representations of institutions may only be loosely coupled and thus become accessible either through discursive or practical consciousness, but not necessarily through both (cf., Lizardo, 2017).

Discursive Consciousness and the Internalization of Institutions
The idea of a discursive consciousness is informed by the discovery of the so-called declarative memory in the human brain. This memory system stores networks of knowledge derived from a symbolically mediated macrolevel culture to which actors are exposed during their socialization. Knowledge of this kind is *generalized, reflexible*, and *verbalizable* (Evans, 2008; Squire, 2004). We argue that the idea of discursive knowledge fits an important conceptualization of cognition in neo-institutional theory well, namely that "culture is best understood as a network of learned knowledge structure, distributed amongst cultural members" (Thornton et al., 2012, p. 83).

Socialization in terms of declarative memory implies that institutions are internalized as generalized cognitive representations linked to an externalized and objectified system of cultural symbols (Berger & Luckmann, 1967; Friedland & Alford, 1991; Li, 2017). Li (2017) further condensed this idea by arguing that cultural symbols comprise a referent, a signified, and a signifier. The referent of a cultural symbol denotes the bundles of concrete events that are cognitively generalized and, in this way, become meaningful for an actor. The signified refers to the cognitive generalization of events, which form amodal cognitive representations (i.e., representations disconnected from concrete experiences). In neo-institutional research, these representations have been labeled as systems of typifications (Berger & Luckmann, 1967), categories (Loewenstein, Ocasio, & Jones, 2012), or content schemas (DiMaggio, 1997). The signifier, in turn, is the external form of a cultural symbol, which itself can take on an aural, visual, or kinesthetic gestalt (Höllerer, Daudigeos, & Jancsary, 2017). Yet, neo-institutional theory commonly focuses strongly on language as a primary medium for signifiers (Suddaby, 2010). Thus, as a result of socialization, institutions receive their meaning through the internalization of typifications that organize actors' experiences. These typifications, in turn, are learned through their connection to external signifiers, which support the typifications' legitimacy (Berger & Luckmann, 1967), such as vocabularies or frames (Cornelissen, Durand, Fiss, Lammers, & Vaara, 2015; Loewenstein et al., 2012; Purdy, Ansari, & Gray, 2017).

Thus, socialization in this context enables actors to access internalized institutions through reflection (Seo & Creed, 2002). This possibility becomes visible through the endemic phenomenon of decoupling in modern societies (Pope & Meyer, 2016). Decoupling implies that even if institutions are treated as being taken-for-granted, institutions' behavioral (i.e., praxis-based) and verbal reproduction (i.e., the signifiers) may be disconnected (Meyer & Rowan, 1977; Thornton et al., 2012). The simultaneous existence of taken-for-grantedness and reflexivity is also in line with the neo-institutional perspective that actors may need to actively work to maintain institutional arrangements (Lawrence & Suddaby, 2006; Loewenstein et al., 2012).

Practical Consciousness and the Internalization of Institutions
Not all institutions, however, are internalized in a way that keeps them accessible to reflection (Bourdieu, 2000). We follow Lizardo (2017) and argue for the parallel existence of practical consciousness. Practical consciousness refers to a certain brain area – the so-called non-declarative memory – that is destined for *non-contentual, schematic,* and *durable* dispositions, which actors internalize during their socialization (Evans, 2008; Squire, 2004). In what follows, we draw on Bourdieu's theory of practice and related insights from the philosophy of mind (Barsalou, 2008; Lakoff & Johnson, 1999) to highlight the unconscious instantiation of macrolevel structure at the actor level.

The effects of socialization in terms of non-declarative memory imply the internalization of institutions as unconscious dispositions for perception and praxis (Bourdieu, 1977; Giddens, 1984). Dispositions are durable and procedural competences internalized through bodily mediated exposure to a given experiential environment, namely the perceived and performed patterns of praxis (Bourdieu, 2000). Dispositions are grounded in the implicit meaning behind praxis. This implies that actors unconsciously understand what aims actors are pursuing and why they behave as they do (Tomasello, 2000).

Dispositions are embodied and situation-dependent (Barsalou, 2008). Bourdieu (1984) argued for the "embodiment" of praxis, which involves multimodal experiences of praxis via actors' visual, haptic, auditory, motor, and vestibular systems (cf., Barsalou, 2008). The experience of praxis therefore induces certain body states that are directly perceived as meaningful (Bourdieu, 1977) because the same brain area responsible for the comprehension and cognitive representation of praxis is also responsible for the (re)production of praxis (Gallese, 2006; Rizzolatti & Craighero, 2004). Dispositions are embodied because they are mapped within actors' sensomotoric system and represent the meaning of praxis, in terms of how the actor's body interacts with and perceives the world (Gallese & Lakoff, 2005; Lakoff & Johnson, 1999). Because dispositions are grounded in bodily mediated experiences of praxis, they greatly modify actors' abilities to act and consequently imprint a certain practical mode of perception and praxis (Bourdieu, 1990, 2000; Lakoff & Johnson, 1999). To illustrate the impact of dispositions, we briefly revisit Battilana and Dorado's (2010) study on two newly established microfinance organizations in Bolivia. Because these two organizations aimed to provide loans for the poor, they employed bankers and social workers who were expected to reconcile an economic banking logic with social development logic. However, Battilana and Dorado found that bankers in one organization suppressed this development logic. We argue that the bankers behaved in this way because they, in comparison to the bankers hired by the second organization, had long-term experiences as bank employees and thus strongly internalized dispositions related to the economic logic. Thus, these bankers, even if they should not have, drew upon their practical consciousness and enacted their economic mode of perception and praxis (Bourdieu, 1990, 2000) because it felt right (Bourdieu, 1984).

According to recent work in neo-institutional theory, institutions grounded in dispositions are transmitted through socialization via the mimesis of reoccurring praxis patterns and their implicit meanings (Sieweke, 2014). Consequently, institutions internalized this way achieve unconscious taken-for-grantedness (Jepperson, 1991) because actors mimic the meaning behind others' praxis and tend to accept praxis as externally given, without consciously reflecting it (Bourdieu, 1977, 1990).

It is important to note that actors do not just imitate scripts but instead unconsciously understand other actors' emotions, normative pressures, and intentions related to a praxis (Lizardo, 2007). In this sense, dispositions provide embodied descriptions of the social space in which they were internalized. In contrast to discursive consciousness, which draws upon contentual typifications that are generalized across certain events (DiMaggio, 1997), practical consciousness draws upon dispositions that represent situations as moments of purposefully intertwined and sequentially occurring praxis. In other words, praxis is linked to specific situations, which, in turn, evoke corresponding dispositions grounded by embodied representations that become (re)activated in similar situations. To put it in Bourdieu's words (1984, p. 474),

> Everything takes place as if the social conditionings linked to a social condition tended to inscribe the relation to the social world in a lasting, generalized relation to one's own body.

Institutional Fields and Modes of Consciousness

We consider an institutional field as a social space where an institutional infrastructure is emerging or has already reached a certain status of coherence. Institutional fields exhibit *high coherence in their institutional infrastructure* if the institutions within the field are strongly linked to each other. In this status of a field, institutions reinforce one another and thus provide a "coherent sense of what is legitimate or not" (Hinings, Logue, & Zietsma, 2017, p. 169), whereby actors can easily move from one institutionalized form of praxis to another (Martin, 2003). In this sense, depending on their exposure to the institutions within a field, actors either (a) use cultural symbols and discursive consciousness to navigate fields (Ocasio, Loewenstein, & Nigam, 2015; Purdy et al., 2017) or (b) draw upon practical consciousness and thus unconsciously enact praxis due to their embodied dispositions toward perception and praxis (Bourdieu, 1977, 1990; Sieweke, 2014). Institutional fields with a coherent infrastructure enable actors to traverse institutions predictably and with minimal dislocation of subjectivity (Zietsma et al., 2017).

Fields with *low coherence in their institutional infrastructure* exhibit an unsettled status (Davis & Marquis, 2005; Lizardo & Strand, 2010). Consequently, actors are uncertain regarding the appropriateness of their praxis because of

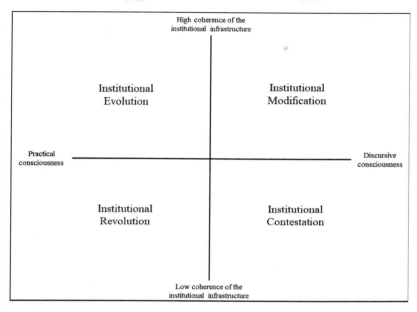

Fig. 1. An Integrative Framework of Institutional Change.

the existence of "competing conceptions of what is legitimate" (Hinings et al., 2017, p. 170). This implies that various actors, on the one hand, (a) may apply discursive consciousness and reflexively draw upon competing institutional logics (Thornton et al., 2012) or (b) draw upon practical consciousness and unconsciously enact contradicting praxis. In situations of incongruent embodied dispositions, actors mutually take their praxis for granted while opposing the praxis of others (Bourdieu, 1990). An institutional field of this kind is characterized by highly dislocated subjectivity (Martin, 2003).

Fig. 1 structures the following argument. We argue that four types of institutional change exist, with the occurrence of each type depending on the combination of modes of consciousness and the coherence of the institutional infrastructures within a field. Our discussion will reveal that neo-institutional theory has primarily focused on two types of institutional change, namely on what we call institutional modification and contestation (cf., Micelotta et al., 2017), while the two other types – institutional evolution and revolution – remained largely unnoticed.

Institutional Change and Discursive Consciousness

Institutional Modification

By institutional modification, we refer to a mode of change in which institutions evolve incrementally because actors intend to fill existing institutional voids or maintain their praxis but cause unintended institutional change by doing so.

A main argument in institutional literature holds that actors' reflexivity is central to institutional change (Battilana, Leca, & Boxenbaum, 2009). An important condition of institutional entrepreneurship is the existence of institutional voids – gaps in the institutional infrastructure that allow actors to exploit a certain lack of predictable and consistent institutional demands (Hinings et al., 2017) – even if a field exhibits a high degree of institutional coherence overall (Greenwood et al., 2011; Nicolini et al., 2016).

Regarding the two modes of consciousness, we argue that institutional entrepreneurship highlights the changes to taken-for-granted institutions that are represented in declarative memory and accessed by discursive consciousness. Actors use their capacity to "acquire moments of self-awareness in which they gain clear insight into the constraints imposed on them by the broader social structures (i.e., institutions) within which they are embedded" (Suddaby et al., 2016, p. 229). That is, even if reflexivity is constrained (Battilana, 2006; Greenwood & Suddaby, 2006; Lok, 2010), institutional entrepreneurs use cultural symbols as toolkits (Swidler, 1986; Thornton et al., 2012; Voronov, De Clercq, & Hinings, 2013) to incrementally fill institutional voids (Zietsma et al., 2017). For example, institutional entrepreneurs may change institutions by blending well-established frames that are taken for granted (Hargadon & Douglas, 2001; Khaire & Wadhwani, 2010). This is because a new frame is more likely to succeed if it is built upon frames that have already achieved a high degree of legitimacy (Werner & Cornelissen, 2014).

An additional argument in neo-institutional literature emphasizes the reflexive modification of institutions in terms of purposeful improvisation. Improvisation may lead to incremental institutional change, which, in contrast to institutional entrepreneurship, is primarily due to actors' intention to use reflexivity to maintain their praxis (Smets & Jarzabkowski, 2013; Wright & Zammuto, 2013). However, these efforts may result in an unintended and incremental reshaping of institutions.

P1. In a field with a coherent institutional infrastructure, institutions that are represented in declarative memory primarily change due to modifications that fill institutional voids or are caused by improvisation.

Institutional Contestation
In the context of institutional contestation, institutions tend to change quickly. This higher velocity is due to existing contradictions within an institutional field, which actors reflexively exploit to promote their institutionally defined interests. In contrast to modification, contestation requires an incoherent institutional infrastructure, in which the conflict between different institutional demands remains unresolved. Under such field conditions, actors use their reflective capabilities and choose, according to the situation, between possible ways to act in a web of contradictory demands (Greenwood et al., 2011). In contrast to modification, actors do not use their reflexivity to gain insights about the institutional arrangements but instead are already aware of existing contradictions (Seo & Creed, 2002; Suddaby et al., 2016).

Through effortful navigation, actors gain further insights into the strengths and weaknesses of different institutional arrangements and are also aware of the institutional infrastructure that best fits their interests (Fligstein & McAdam, 2012; Greenwood et al., 2011; Seo & Creed, 2002; Suddaby et al., 2016). Institutional fields with a contested institutional infrastructure also provide opportunities for outside actors to enter the field and import other ideas that are rooted in different logics (Garud, Hardy, & Maguire, 2007; Maguire, Hardy, & Lawrence, 2004). When various groups of actors operate within the same field, the likelihood of contestation between different logics further increases (Jones, Maoret, Massa, & Svejenova, 2012; Nicolini et al., 2016).

Many studies have examined how actors refer to and make use of cultural symbols as toolkits to support their interests (McPherson & Sauder, 2013; Thornton et al., 2012). Because these kinds of institutions are understood to be represented in declarative memory and accessed through discursive conscious- ness, neo-institutional research has emphasized the role of discursive strategies that actors apply to establish new meanings in an institutional field (Lawrence & Phillips, 2004; Loewenstein et al., 2012; Purdy et al., 2017; Reay & Hinings, 2005; Werner & Cornelissen, 2014). For example, Ocasio et al. (2015) argued that exist- ing cognitive representations of institutions are buttressed by bundles of practices and the vocabulary structures referring to these practices. To change institutions, actors may strategically apply means such as theorizing, narration, and sensegiv- ing to contest and replace the established meanings of vocabularies and practices (Ocasio et al., 2015; Suddaby & Greenwood, 2005; Tracey, 2016). The framing perspective in neo-institutional theory adds that discursive processes may change actors' cognitive representations (Purdy et al., 2017; Werner & Cornelissen, 2014). Institutional research has highlighted that when the taken-for-grantedness of institutions is questioned due to incoherence in institutional fields, various actors may mobilize different frames to contest and renegotiate the institutional order (Clemens, 1997; Hoffman, 1999; Seo & Creed, 2002).

P2. In an institutional field with an incoherent institutional infrastructure, institutions that are represented in declarative memory primarily change due to reflexive contestation.

Institutional Change and Practical Consciousness

Institutional Evolution

By institutional evolution, we refer to a mode of change in which institu- tions, without recourse to actors' reflexivity, naturally evolve due to the imper- fect transmission of dispositions from one institutional generation to the next. In this sense, institutional change may occur not through reflexive agency but through the accumulation of unconscious variations of praxis, that is, a mode, which we call institutional evolution at the macrolevel. In what follows, we will discuss two interrelated theoretical concepts that enable institutional evolution. We first introduce the concept of embodied metaphors as a mechanism that enables actors to unconsciously enact appropriate praxis for specific situational

conditions (Lakoff & Johnson, 1999). Second, we reintroduce the idea of institutional generations, namely the notion that groups of actors may differ depending on the length of time for which they were socialized in an institutional field
(Lizardo & Strand, 2010).

Bourdieu's (1977) basal notion of practical consciousness implies that actors
in an institutional field with a coherent institutional infrastructure internalize
situation-dependent and embodied dispositions in non-declarative memory. The
(re)activation of praxis always involves *embodied metaphors*, namely the match
between embodied representations and a situation's actual conditions (Gallese &
Lakoff, 2005; Lakoff & Johnson, 1999). In this sense, the embodied meaning
of praxis helps actors to understand whether a given situation and the praxis
observed in it correspond with their internalized dispositions (Bar, 2007;
Bourdieu, 1990). An embodied metaphor enables actors to apply the practical
capacity that they have internalized during their socialization. A coherent institutional infrastructure is maintained in a field because actors pass on their dispositions to subsequent generations. We argue that this effect is based on what we
call *institutional generations*. The "old" generation, which was socialized in an
institutional field, transmits institutions to the "younger" generation, which is not
yet entirely socialized in the field's praxis (Lizardo & Strand, 2010).

In this process, institutional change may unconsciously occur during the *process of transmission* from one institutional generation to the next. This is because
transmission may not be confused with copying. Transmission involves the possibility that the embodied metaphors will differ between institutional generations.
The transmission of an institution within an institutional field depends on the
embodied representations and, consequently, on actors' embodied metaphors.
Embodied metaphors, however, are fuzzy; therefore, the transmission of praxis
across institutional generations will remain incomplete. As a result, the praxis
enacted in certain situations may change. These changes may accumulate over
time.

Recent evidence from the philosophy of mind suggests that not all facets of
praxis are transmitted across institutional generations with the same probability.
Rather, praxis may be subject to unconscious selection and transformation
processes (Mesoudi, 2016). *Selection* refers to the fact that actors usually do
not reproduce the praxis of all actors they observe with the same probability.
Consequently, actors may not internalize all facets of the earlier generation's dispositions that form the basis of certain praxis within an institutional field. For
example, actors prefer to mimic others who stand out or whom they perceive
as superior (Henrich & McElreath, 2003). This selective mimicry influences the
internalization of actors' dispositions. Furthermore, the frequency with which
a distinct variant of a praxis is observed affects its selection by the subsequent
institutional generation (Boyd & Richerson, 1985).

The term *transformation* implies that the transmission of praxis is error-prone
(Giddens, 1984). This was visible in Zucker's (1977) seminal experiment, in which
she found that institutionalized praxis loses importance after a certain number
of transmissions to subsequent generations and may dissolve completely without
any variation in the transmission's context. Indeed, Zucker (1977) argued that

such change is because the institutionalized praxis is not optimally transferred from one generation to the next. We underline her argument and claim that transformations of praxis are not exceptions but rather the rule. In this way, even marginal transformations of a praxis by subsequent generations may accumulate and change the nature of a given institutional infrastructure (cf., Tomasello, 2000).

P3. In an institutional field with a coherent institutional infrastructure, institutions that are represented in non-declarative memory primarily change due to the imperfect transmission of dispositions from one institutional generation to the next.

Institutional Revolution

In the context of institutional revolution, institutions tend to change fast because actors from different institutional generations, who stick to diverging modes of praxis, stand in radical opposition to one another. According to Bourdieu (1984), this mode of change is prompted by a dramatic change in the factual contingencies of an institutional field. In this context, Bourdieu (1984, 2000) highlighted actors' propensity to maintain the praxis in which they were socialized. This has important implications. An institutional generation's embodied metaphors ensure that the actors enact a praxis that fits the situation's contingencies. However, the fit may become worse over time. Under contingencies in which an institutional generation's praxis becomes strongly ill-suited, a radical form of hysteresis may occur (Bourdieu, 1990). Hysteresis implies that actors sense that the praxis they are enacting no longer fits the situation's demands. However, because hysteresis is a phenomenon of practical consciousness, it does not lead to reflexivity. Consequently, actors (nearly defiantly) stick to their internalized dispositions, even if "previously developed modes of perception and appreciation are applied under circumstances which are no longer objectively appropriate" (Lizardo & Strand, 2010, p. 221). The next institutional generation, however, lacks the strong socialization that the preceding institutional generation experienced (for an example of the acquisition of diverging dispositions across institutional generations, see Tilcsik, 2010). Therefore, the following institutional generation unconsciously recognizes the ill fit of praxis with field conditions; their practical dispositions differ from those of the preceding generation. The ill fit of praxis does not necessarily cause problematic tensions in institutional fields because the next institutional generation mimics the praxis selectively and subsequently internalizes dispositions that better fit the field's contingencies.

However, dramatic changes to the contingencies of institutional fields over time may cause serious tensions within the field. The previous institutional generation will experience a shock, which will not lead to reflexivity and which will support changes to generalized cognitive representations. Rather, the hysteresis caused by dramatic changes to the contingencies of an institutional field will generate "an anti-institutional cast of mind" (Bourdieu, 1984, p. 144). Because old and young institutional generations significantly differ in their dispositions and hysteresis puts them in a state of mutual refusal of the other generation's praxis (Strand & Lizardo, 2017), they stand in radical opposition to each other – the institutional field becomes a place of revolutionary and (potentially) counter-revolutionary acting.

> *P4.* In an institutional field with dramatic incoherence in its institutional infrastructure, institutions that are represented in non-declarative memory are more likely to change because different institutional generations will radically oppose the praxis of the other generations.

DISCUSSION

In our chapter, we explored actors' cognition and its relationship with macrolevel institutional processes by unpacking two distinct memories and modes of consciousness (Giddens, 1984; Lizardo, 2017; Lizardo & Strand, 2010; Vaisey, 2009). We argued that, on the one hand, institutions signified by a scaffold of cultural symbols may be utilized in actors' reflexive agency on the microlevel. On the other hand, institutions as macrolevel phenomena also exist as actors' durable and embodied dispositions. Because institutions are instantiated on both the macro- and microlevels, agency should also be understood as a two-pronged phenomenon. Agency, on the one hand, may be reflexive in nature. On the other hand, agency may also involve unconscious components that account for institutional processes at the macrolevel (cf., Jepperson & Meyer, 2011).

We pointed to the fact that neo-institutional theory, in its attempt to clarify "the details of micro-level action [that] are needed to explain how macrolevel institutions change" (Hirsch & Lounsbury, 1997, p. 412), has tended to theorize about institutional change primarily at the level of discursive consciousness. However, we argue that the ways in which institutions change depend, first, on the mode of consciousness through which they are accessed and, second, on the coherence of the institutional infrastructure. In detail, we argued that institutional change may also occur at the level of practical consciousness. However, this stream of research in institutional theory, which focuses on practical consciousness, has remained underdeveloped in neo-institutional theory (e.g., Sieweke, 2014). To elaborate on it, we linked neo-institutional theory to insights from Bourdieu's theory of practice and related insights from the philosophy of mind. By doing so, we were able to provide a more fine-grained microfoundation to neo-institutional theory. Our theoretical approach will help institutional scholars to become more explicit in their research about how the nature of an institutional field and the mode of consciousness influence the kinds of agency and institutional change they are observing.

In detail, our conceptualization of institutional evolution and revolution differs significantly from earlier approaches that link institutional change with discursive consciousness. Furthermore, we illustrated the boundary conditions under which institutional evolution and revolution are likely to be the sources of institutional change. The unconscious initiation of institutional change may facilitate further research to better understand the conditions under which institutional evolution may cause institutional contradictions and plurality, which will open space for actors' reflexivity, or the conditions under which institutional evolution may lead to institutional revolution.

The outlined differentiation between discursive and practical consciousness as well as between different types of institutional change also has significant methodological implications. For example, interviews (McPherson & Sauder, 2013; Smets & Jarzabkowski, 2013), the analysis of visual imageries (Höllerer et al., 2017), and text analysis (Meyer & Höllerer, 2010) are suitable ways to study reflexive and verbalizable discursive knowledge.

We suggest utilizing three approaches to study practical consciousness: (1) ethnographic studies, (2) forced-choice surveys, and (3) experimental studies.

We consider *ethnography* to be a fruitful avenue with which to study the emergence of dispositions and their changes over time. One way to dig deeply into actors' dispositions is to undergo the same socialization process as the actors they are studying did (e.g., see Dalton, 1959; Wacquant, 2004). A meaningful complement to this kind of ethnographic research is a joint analysis of the researcher and the actors observed, to approach the unconscious (for methodological avenues of doing so, see McDonnell, 2014). Another method of analyzing practical consciousness is *forced-choice survey studies* (Bourdieu, 1984). Vaisey (2009) suggested that real-time decisions force actors to decide quickly and provide answers that feel right. To ensure that researchers implicit assumptions do not bias the construction of survey questions, survey questions should be constructed with reference to situations that can be observed as being part of actors' lifeworld and/or by asking experts to describe the specific lifeworld under consideration. For example, in his real-time decision study on the impacts of dispositions on prosocial behavior, Miles (2015) found that internalized dispositions and their unconscious enactment significantly influenced whether actors were willing to share their achievements. However, because even forced-choice surveys may be distorted by situations governed by social desirability (Srivastava & Banaji, 2011), it appears reasonable to buttress forced-choice surveys with techniques from experimental designs that will minimize the impact of discursive consciousness. Several scholars have already highlighted the relevance of *experiments* to neo-institutional theory (Bitektine & Haack, 2015; Glaser, Fast, Harmon, & Green, 2016; Green, 2004; Lauer, Rockenbach, & Walgenbach, 2008; Thornton et al., 2012; Zucker, 1977). Experiments are well suited to isolate cognitive processes from the interference of external variables and thus to provide the evidence of causality. As in forced-choice surveys, to investigate practical consciousness, the influence of discursive consciousness must be minimized. To this end, experimental designs may apply cognitive loading, which requires a design in which researchers first ask participants to accomplish tasks that deplete their discursive consciousness. For example, a task such as remembering numbers significantly impairs the participants' capacities to reflect. Subsequently, participants are asked to complete relevant tasks to investigate practical consciousness (Miles, 2015; Srivastava & Banaji, 2011). Moreover, experimental designs in general should focus on the construction of situations as cues in which actors are forced to (re)produce praxis patterns. Experimental designs should thus focus on directly measuring praxis because measurements that do not rely on introspective experience (such as self-reports by participants) is considered essential for clarifying the unconscious mechanisms underlying praxis (for an overview, see Nosek, Hawkins, & Frazier, 2011). Experimental designs of this kind minimize the reflective influence of discursive consciousness and thus investigate practical consciousness more directly (Lizardo et al., 2016).

ACKNOWLEDGMENTS

We would like to thank editor Jost Sieweke, an anonymous reviewer, and participants at the first meeting of the Microfoundations of Institutions network at VU Amsterdam who provided helpful comments.

Funding: This work was supported by the Deutsche Forschungsgemeinschaft under Grants WA 2139/16-1.

REFERENCES

Abdelnour, S., Hasselbladh, H., & Kallinikos, J. (2017). Agency and institutions in Organization Studies. *Organization Studies, 38*(12), 1775–1792.

Bar, M. (2007). The proactive brain: Using analogies and associations to generate predictions. *Trends in Cognitive Sciences, 11*(7), 280–289.

Barsalou, L. W. (2008). Grounded cognition. *Annual Review of Psychology, 59*(1), 617–645.

Battilana, J. (2006). Agency and institutions: The enabling role of individuals' social position. *Organization, 13*(5), 653–676.

Battilana, J., & Dorado, S. (2010). Building sustainable hybrid organizations: The case of commercial microfinance organizations. *Academy of Management Journal, 53*(6), 1419–1440.

Battilana, J., Leca, B., & Boxenbaum, E. (2009). How actors change institutions: Towards a theory of institutional entrepreneurship. *Academy of Management Annals, 3*(1), 65–107.

Berger, P. L., & Luckmann, T. (1967). *The social construction of reality: A treatise in the sociology of knowledge.* London: Penguin Press.

Bitektine, A., & Haack, P. (2015). The "macro" and the "micro" of legitimacy: Toward a multilevel theory of the legitimacy process. *Academy of Management Review, 40*(1), 49–75.

Bourdieu, P. (1977). *Outline of a theory of practice.* Cambridge: Cambridge University Press.

Bourdieu, P. (1984). *Distinction: A social critique of the judgement of taste.* Cambridge, MA: Harvard University Press.

Bourdieu, P. (1990). *The logic of practice.* Cambridge: Polity Press.

Bourdieu, P. (2000). *Pascalian mediations.* Stanford, CA: Stanford University Press.

Boyd, R., & Richerson, P. J. (1985). *Culture and the evolutionary process.* Chicago, IL: Chicago University Press.

Cardinale, I. (2018). Beyond constraining and enabling: Towards new microfoundations for institutional theory. *Academey of Management Review, 43*(1), 132–155.

Clemens, E. S. (1997). *The people's lobby: Organizational innovation and the rise of interest group politics in the United States, 1890–1925.* Chicago, IL: Chicago University Press.

Cornelissen, J. P., Durand, R., Fiss, P. C., Lammers, J. C., & Vaara, E. (2015). Putting communication front and center in institutional theory and analysis. *Academy of Management Review, 40*(1), 10–27.

Dalton, M. (1959). *Men who manage: Fusions of feeling and theory in administration.* New York, NY: Wiley.

Davis, G. F., & Marquis, C. (2005). Prospects for organization theory in the early twenty-first century: Institutional fields and mechanisms. *Organization Science, 16*(4), 332–343.

DiMaggio, P. J. (1997). Culture and cognition. *Annual Review of Sociology, 23*(1), 263–287.

Evans, J. S. B. T. (2008). Dual-processing accounts of reasoning, judgment, and social cognition. *Annual Review of Psychology, 59*(1), 255–278.

Fligstein, N., & McAdam, D. (2012). *A theory of fields*. Oxford: Oxford University Press.

Friedland, R., & Alford, R. R. (1991). Bringing society back in: Symbols, practices, and institutional contradictions. In W. W. Powell & P. J. DiMaggio (Eds.), *The new institutionalism in organizational analysis* (pp. 232–263). Chicago, IL: Chicago University Press.

Gallese, V. (2006). Intentional attunement: A neurophysiological perspective on social cognition and its disruption in autism. *Brain Research, 1079*(1), 15–24.

Gallese, V., & Lakoff, G. (2005). The brain's concepts: The role of the sensory-motor system in conceptual knowledge. *Cognitive Neuropsychology, 22*(3), 455–479.

Garud, R., Hardy, C., & Maguire, S. (2007). Institutional entrepreneurship as embedded agency. *Organization Studies, 28*(7), 957–969.

Giddens, A. (1984). *The constitution of society: Outline of a theory of structuration*. Cambridge: Polity Press.

Glaser, V. L., Fast, N. J., Harmon, D. J., & Green, S. E. (2016). Institutional frame switching: How institutional logics shape individual action. In J. Gehman, M. Lounsbury, & R. Greenwood (Eds.), *Research in the sociology of organizations: How institutions matter!* (pp. 35–69). Bingley: Emerald.

Green, S. E. (2004). A rhetorical theory of diffusion. *Academy of Management Review, 29*(4), 653–669.

Greenwood, R., Raynard, M., Kodeih, F., Micelotta, E. R., & Lounsbury, M. (2011). Institutional complexity and organizational responses. *Academy of Management Annals, 5*(1), 317–371.

Greenwood, R., & Suddaby, R. (2006). Institutional entrepreneurship in mature fields: The big five accounting firms. *Academy of Management Journal, 49*(1), 27–48.

Hargadon, A. B., & Douglas, Y. (2001). When innovations meet institutions: Edison and the design of the electric light. *Administrative Science Quarterly, 46*(3), 476.

Harmon, D. J., Haack, P., & Roulet, T. J. (2018). Microfoundations of institutions: A matter of structure vs. agency or level of analysis? *Academy of Management Review, 44*(2), 464–467.

Henrich, J., & McElreath, R. (2003). The evolution of cultural evolution. *Evolutionary Anthropology, 12*(3), 123–135.

Hinings, C. R., Logue, D. M., & Zietsma, C. (2017). Fields, governance and institutional infrastructure. In R. Greenwood, C. Oliver, T. B. Lawrence, & R. E. Meyer (Eds.), *The Sage handbook of organizational institutionalism* (2nd ed., pp. 163–189). Los Angeles, CA: Sage Publications.

Hirsch, P. M., & Lounsbury, M. (1997). Putting the organization back into organization theory: Action, change, and the "new" institutionalism. *Journal of Management Inquiry, 6*(1), 79–88.

Hoffman, A. J. (1999). Institutional evolution and change: Envrionmentalism and the U.S. chemical industry. *Academy of Management Journal, 42*(4), 351–371.

Höllerer, M. A., Daudigeos, T., & Jancsary, D. (2017). Multimodality, meaning, and institutions. In M. A. Höllerer, T. Daudigeos, & D. Jancsary (Eds.), *Research in the sociology of organizations: Multimodality, meaning, and institutions* (pp. 1–24). Bingley: Emerald.

Jepperson, R. L. (1991). Institutions, institutional effects, and institutionalism. In P. J. DiMaggio, & W. W. Powell (Eds.), *The new institutionalism in organizational analysis* (pp. 143–163). Chicago, IL: Chicago University Press.

Jepperson, R. L., & Meyer, J. W. (2011). Multiple levels of analysis and the limitations of methodological individualism. *Sociological Theory, 29*(1), 54–73.

Jones, C., Maoret, M., Massa, F. G., & Svejenova, S. (2012). Rebels with a cause: Formation, contestation, and expansion of the de novo category "Modern architecture," 1870–1975. *Organization Science, 23*(6), 1523–1545.

Khaire, M., & Wadhwani, R. D. (2010). Changing landscapes: The construction of meaning and value in a new market category – Modern Indian art. *Academy of Management Journal, 53*(6), 1281–1304.

Lakoff, G., & Johnson, M. (1999). *Philosophy in the flesh. The embodied mind and its challenges to western thought*. New York, NY: Basic Books.

Lauer, T., Rockenbach, B., & Walgenbach, P. (2008). Not just hot air: Normative codes of conduct induce cooperative behavior. *Review of Managerial Science, 2*(3), 183–197.

Lawrence, T. B., & Phillips, N. (2004). From Moby Dick to free willy: Macro-cultural discourse and institutional entrepreneurship in emerging institutional fields. *Organization, 11*(5), 689–711.

Lawrence, T. B., & Suddaby, R. (2006). Institutions and institutional work. In S. R. Clegg, C. Hardy, W. R. Nord, & T. Lawrence (Eds.), *The Sage handbook of organization studies* (pp. 215–254). London: Sage Publications.

Li, Y. (2017). A semiotic theory of institutionalization. *Academy of Management Review, 42*(3), 520–547.

Lizardo, O. (2007). "Mirror neurons," collective objects and the problem of transmission: Reconsidering Stephen Turner's critique of practice theory. *Journal for the Theory of Social Behaviour, 37*(3), 319–350.

Lizardo, O. (2017). Improving cultural analysis: Considering personal culture in its declarative and nondeclarative modes. *American Sociological Review, 82*(1), 88–115.

Lizardo, O., Mowry, R., Sepulvado, B., Stoltz, D. S., Taylor, M. A., Van Ness, J., & Wood, M. (2016). What are dual process models? Implications for cultural analysis in sociology. *Sociological Theory, 34*(4), 287–310.

Lizardo, O., & Strand, M. (2010). Skills, toolkits, contexts and institutions: Clarifying the relationship between different approaches to cognition in cultural sociology. *Poetics, 38*(2), 205–228.

Loewenstein, J., Ocasio, W., & Jones, C. (2012). Vocabularies and vocabulary structure: A new approach linking categories, practices, and institutions. *Academy of Management Annals, 6*(1), 41–86.

Lok, J. (2010). Institutional logics as identity projects. *Academy of Management Journal, 53*(6), 1305–1335.

Lok, J., & Willmott, H. (2018). Embedded agency in institutional theory: Problem or paradox? *Academy of Management Review, 44*(2), 470–473.

Maguire, S., Hardy, C., & Lawrence, T. B. (2004). Institutional entrepreneurship in emerging fields: HIV/AIDS treatment advocacy. *Academy of Management Executive, 47*(5), 657–679.

Martin, J. L. (2003). What is field theory? *American Journal of Sociology, 109*(1), 1–49.

McDonnell, T. E. (2014). Drawing out culture: Productive methods to measure cognition and resonance. *Theory and Society, 43*(3), 247–274.

McPherson, C. M., & Sauder, M. (2013). Logics in action: Managing institutional complexity in a drug court. *Administrative Science Quarterly, 58*(2), 165–196.

Mesoudi, A. (2016). Cultural evolution: A review of theory, findings and controversies. *Evolutionary Biology, 43*(4), 481–497.

Meyer, J. W., & Rowan, B. (1977). Institutionalized organizations: Formal structure as myth and ceremony. *American Journal of Sociology, 83*(2), 340–363.

Meyer, R. E., & Höllerer, M. A. (2010). Meaning structures in a contested issue field: A topographic map of shareholder value in Austria. *Academy of Management Journal, 53*(6), 1241–1262.

Meyer, R. E., Jancsary, D., Höllerer, M. A., & Boxenbaum, E. (2018). The role of verbal and visual text in the process of institutionalization. *Academy of Management Review, 43*(3), 392–418.

Micelotta, E., Lounsbury, M., & Greenwood, R. (2017). Pathways of institutional change: An integrative review and research agenda. *Journal of Management, 43*(6), 1885–1910.

Miles, A. (2015). The (re)genesis of values: Examining the importance of values for action. *American Sociological Review, 80*(4), 680–704.

Nicolini, D., Delmestri, G., Goodrick, E., Reay, T., Lindberg, K., & Adolfsson, P. (2016). Look what's back! Institutional complexity, reversibility and the knotting of logics. *British Journal of Management, 27*(2), 228–248.

Nosek, B. A., Hawkins, C. B., & Frazier, R. S. (2011). Implicit social cognition: From measures to mechanisms. *Trends in Cognitive Sciences, 15*(4), 152–159.

Ocasio, W., Loewenstein, J., & Nigam, A. (2015). How streams of communication reproduce and change institutional logics: The role of categories. *Academy of Management Review, 40*(1), 28–48.

Phillips, N., & Malhotra, N. (2008). Taking social construction seriously: Extending the discursive approach in institutional theory. In R. Greenwood, C. Oliver, K. Sahlin-Andersson, & R. Suddaby (Eds.), *The Sage handbook of organizational institutionalism* (pp. 702–720). Los Angeles, CA: Sage Publications.

Pope, S., & Meyer, J. W. (2016). Local variation in world society: Six characteristics of global diffusion. *European Journal of Cultural and Political Sociology, 3*(2–3), 280–305.

Powell, W. W., & Colyvas, J. (2008). Microfoundations of institutional theory. In R. Greenwood, C. Oliver, K. Sahlin-Andersson, & R. Suddaby (Eds.), *The Sage handbook of organizational institutionalism* (pp. 276–298). Los Angeles, CA: Sage Publications.

Powell, W. W., & Rerup, C. (2017). Opening the black box: The microfoundations of institutions. In R. Greenwood, C. Oliver, T. B. Lawrence, & R. E. Meyer (Eds.), *The Sage handbook of organizational institutionalism* (2nd ed., pp. 311–337). Los Angeles, CA: Sage Publications.

Purdy, J., Ansari, S., & Gray, B. (2017). Are logics enough? Framing as an alternative tool for understanding institutional meaning making. *Journal of Management Inquiry, 28*(4), 409–419.

Reay, T., & Hinings, C. R. (2005). The recomposition of an organizational field: Health care in Alberta. *Organization Studies, 26*(3), 351–384.

Rizzolatti, G., & Craighero, L. (2004). The mirror-neuron system. *Annual Review of Neuroscience, 27*(1), 169–192.

Seo, M.-G., & Creed, W. E. D. (2002). Institutional contradictions, praxis, and institutional change: A dialectical perspective. *Academy of Management Review, 27*(2), 222–247.

Sieweke, J. (2014). Imitation and processes of institutionalization: Insights from Bourdieu's theory of practice. *Schmalenbach Business Review, 66*(1), 24–42.

Smets, M., & Jarzabkowski, P. (2013). Reconstructing institutional complexity in practice: A relational model of institutional work and complexity. *Human Relations, 66*(10), 1279–1309.

Squire, L. R. (2004). Memory systems of the brain: A brief history and current perspective. *Neurobiology of Learning and Memory, 82*(3), 171–177.

Srivastava, S. B., & Banaji, M. R. (2011). Culture, cognition, and collaborative networks in organizations. *American Sociological Review, 76*(2), 207–233.

Strand, M., & Lizardo, O. (2017). The hysteresis effect: Theorizing mismatch in action. *Journal of the Theory of Social Behaviour, 47*(2), 164–194.

Suddaby, R. (2010). Challenges for institutional theory. *Journal of Management Inquiry, 19*(1), 14–20.

Suddaby, R., & Greenwood, R. (2005). Rhetorical strategis of legitimacy. *Administrative Science Quarterly, 50*(1), 35–67.

Suddaby, R., Viale, T., & Gendron, Y. (2016). Reflexivity: The role of embedded social position and entrepreneurial social skill in processes of field level change. *Research in Organizational Behavior, 36*(1), 225–245.

Swidler, A. (1986). Culture in action: Symbols and strategies. *American Sociological Review, 51*(2), 273–286.

Thornton, P. H., Ocasio, W., & Lounsbury, M. (2012). *The institutional logics perspective: A new approach to culture, structure and process*. Oxford: Oxford University Press.

Tilcsik, A. (2010). From ritual to reality: Demography, ideology, and decoupling in a post-communist government agency. *Academy of Management Journal, 53*(6), 1474–1498.

Tomasello, M. (2000). *The cultural origins of human cognition*. Cambridge: Harvard University Press.

Tracey, P. (2016). Spreading the word: The microfoundations of institutional persuasion and conversion. *Organization Science, 27*(4), 989–1009.

Vaisey, S. (2009). Motivation and justification: A dual-process model of culture in action. *American Journal of Sociology, 114*(6), 1675–1715.

Voronov, M., De Clercq, D., & Hinings, C. R. (2013). Institutional complexity and logic engagement: An investigation of Ontario fine wine. *Human Relations, 66*(12), 1563–1596.

Voronov, M., & Yorks, L. (2015). "Did you notice that?" Theorizing differences in the capacity to apprehend institutional contradictions. *Academy of Management Review, 40*(4), 563–586.

Wacquant, L. J. D. (2004). *Body & soul: Notebooks of an apprentice boxer*. Oxford: Oxford University Press.

Werner, M. D., & Cornelissen, J. P. (2014). Framing the change: Switching and blending frames and their role in instigating institutional change. *Organization Studies, 35*(10), 1449–1472.

Wright, A. L., & Zammuto, R. F. (2013). Wielding the willow: Processes of institutional change in english county cricket. *Academy of Management Journal, 56*(1), 308–330.

Zietsma, C., Groenewegen, P., Logue, D. M., & Hinings, C. R. (2017). Field or fields? Building the scaffolding for cumulation of research on institutional fields. *Academy of Management Annals, 11*(1), 391–450.

Zucker, L. G. (1977). The role of institutionalization in cultural persistence. *American Sociological Review, 42*(5), 726–743.

CHAPTER 7

HOW DO INSTITUTIONS TAKE ROOT AT THE INDIVIDUAL LEVEL?

Osnat Hazan and Tammar B. Zilber

ABSTRACT

The authors explore self-identity construction as a mechanism of institutionalization at the individual level. Building on in-depth analysis of life stories of yoga practitioners who are at different stages of practice, the authors found that as yoga practitioners are more exposed to the yogic institution, yogic meanings gradually infuse their general worldview and self-concept. The authors follow the line of research which focuses on professional identity construction as institutional work, yet, opening the "black box," the authors argue that institutional meanings take root at the individual level beyond the institutional context and beneath the explicit level of identity.

Keywords: Institutions; identity work; meanings; life story; qualitative research paper; self-concept; social construction

In this chapter, we unpack institutional microfoundations (Powell & Colyvas, 2008; Powell & Rerup, 2017) at the individual level, focusing on identity. While most prior studies explore collective identities – whether professional, organizational, or role related – we expand significantly the scope of inquiry, looking at self-identity – the answer to the question: "Who am I?" Building on narrative psychology, we hold that individuals construct their self-identity through the narration of a life story (Lieblich, Tuval-Mashiach, & Zilber, 1998; McAdams, 1996). Although each individual formulates a unique life story, he or she inevitably enlists "institutional meanings" (Zilber, 2017b) – widespread understandings

Microfoundations of Institutions

Research in the Sociology of Organizations, Volume 65A, 153–176

Copyright © 2020 by Emerald Publishing Limited

All rights of reproduction in any form reserved

ISSN: 0733-558X/doi:10.1108/S0733-558X2019000065A016

and common beliefs – to make sense of his/her life. Furthermore, individuals are constantly involved in identity work to readjust their identity to their changing self-concept and worldviews (Snow & Anderson, 1987). Since their identity work also involves creative application of institutional meanings, using meanings from one institutional context, to make sense of other contexts of life, individuals' self-identity work may turn out to also be a form of institutional work. We explored self-identity work by collecting and analyzing life stories of 25 yoga practitioners who share an institutional context yet differ by their exposure to it, being at different stages along the path (beginners, experienced practitioners, and teachers). We found that as yoga practitioners are more exposed to the yogic institution, yogic meanings become more prevalent in practitioners' life stories, and further deeply rooted within them.

INSTITUTIONS AT THE INDIVIDUAL LEVEL: THE ROLE OF SELF-IDENTITY

From the very inception of new institutional theory (NIT), scholars held that institutionalization involves the production of identities (Berger & Luckmann, 1967; see Glynn, 2008, for a review). Recently, within the institutional logics' perspective, it is held that logics "condition actors' […] sense of self and identity" (Thornton, Ocasio, & Loundsbury, 2012, p. 2). Some institutional scholars relate to identity not only as an outcome but also as a mechanism of institutionalization, which actually crafts institutions. Scott (2003, 2014) theorizes identities as "carriers" of institutional elements, which "affect the meaning of acceptance of what they carry" (2003, p. 891). Lawrence & Suddaby (2006) theorize identity construction as a form of institutional work – identity work – through which identities construct the "relationship between an actor and the field in which that actor operates" (p. 223; for empirical examples, see Chreim, Williams, & Hinings, 2007; Creed, DeJordy, & Lok, 2010; Lok, 2010; Reay, Golden-Biddle, & Germann, 2006).

Creed and his colleagues (2010) exemplify, in their study, the merits – as well as the demerits – of the current inquiry of individuals' identity and institutional dynamics. They focus on the identity work of GLBT pastors, motivated by the need to resolve the contradiction between their sexual preferences and the conservative institutionalized role of a minister. The pastors emphasized an inclusive institutional logic of Christianity that would include themselves (highlighting themes of forgiveness, God as the father who loves all his sons equally, or the "calling" to be a minister as a sign of predestination). Through this sensemaking, GLBT pastors were involved in identity work, refocusing the role identity of a minister on teaching people to accept themselves regardless of society approval and on being a living model thereby inspiring people to be authentic and courageous. This identity work, which was aimed at reaching inner peace, may also have effects on the institutional order (Creed et al., 2010). Although insightful, we claim that same as this study, almost all studies that explore institutionalized identities at the individual level are limited in the scope and depth of their definition of identity, and thus – in their conceptualization of the process of identity work. While these limitations are evident in methodological choices, these choices both attest to a partial concept of identity work and further narrow our theoretical understanding of identity work as institutional work.

Scope wise, current studies explore professional, organizational, or role-related identities, which are collective identities embodied by individuals. Yet, these collective identities are only partial segments of one's *self-identity* (Giddens, 1991; Sveningsson & Alvesson, 2003), which encompasses the whole identity of a person.[1] Self-identity is multifaceted – as people belong to many collective categories beyond merely their role and profession – thereby integrating gender, ethnicity, ideologies, religion, etc. (Callero, 2003). Moreover, self-identity incorporates also non-categorical aspects of selfhood such as kinship, family history, fears, and hopes (McAdams, 1996), which are "the more vital aspects [of] how people define and re-define themselves" (Sveningsson & Alvesson, 2003, p. 1190). Further, self-identity binds all these aspects "in terms of an overall picture of the psychological make-up of the individual" (Giddens, 1991, p. 35).

In addition to limiting the scope of inquiry to one facet of identity, most previous studies are limited in terms of the levels of depth they assume and explore. They are based on direct interviewing, during which people are asked explicitly about their understandings regarding their collective identities. For example, studying the institutionalized role of physicians, by explicitly asking physicians what is it to be a physician (Chreim et al., 2007). Doing so, they tap into what Bruner (1986) calls "logical" or "paradigmatic" mode of thought that relates to formal knowledge, based on definitions and categorizations, relatively ordered and analytic. This methodological choice reflects the assumption that identity, and the meanings attached to it, is readily available for persons to reflect upon. Yet, as Bruner claims, the logical mode is but one mode of thought, whereas the "narrative mode of thought" evokes implicit understandings that are based on presuppositions. Both modes of though reflect institutional meanings, or "cultural knowledge" in Bruner's terms, yet the narrative mode may reveal the more taken-for-granted, implicit level. Thus, the explicit reflections of people on their identities portray only the surface layer. We are lacking representations of the unconscious, deeply rooted institutional meanings which individuals hold, that correspond with the taken-for-grantedness of institutions.

Theorizing identity as existing at various levels of consciousness resembles theories of faith and knowledge. Theories of organizational knowledge distinguish between "tacit" vs. "explicit" knowledge (Nonaka & Takeuchi, 1995; for a review see, McLean, 2004). An explicit form of knowledge is "objective, rational and created in the 'then and there', whereas a tacit form is actionable, subjective experiential and created in the 'here and now'" (Nonaka & von Krogh, 2009, p. 641). This literature theorizes the conversion of tacit to explicit knowledge (and vice versa), emphasizing the movement from the unconscious and personal participation in a "known" action (tacit) to a conscious, formally articulated and impersonal knowledge (explicit). Thus, although the tacit form relates to action and not to cognition, the concept of conversion along that continuum, in which the "explicit knowledge loses some of its 'explicitness' trough internalization"

(p. 643), implies that before transforming to an unconscious tacit practical knowledge, explicit knowledge first transforms to an unconscious understanding. Likewise, within the tradition of Cognitive Anthropology, Spiro (1987) offers a five-level model of the process through which a cultural doctrine becomes a "genuine belief" of individuals. Moving from (a) exposure to the doctrine; to (b) familiarity with its common meaning; through (c) a belief that it is true; and further (d) internalization of the doctrine to be one's worldview; and to the most "cognitive salient" level, in which (e) the doctrine becomes an initiating force for action. Thus, common cultural knowledge – institutional meanings – may exist on various levels of depth within individuals' cognition. Whereas current studies of institutions and individuals' identity theorize and explore only the explicit reflections of people on their identities, we build on the above conceptualizations regarding the internalization of culture, arguing that in the case of identity as well, going beyond the surface layer is needed. We hold that these deeper layers are vital for fully exploring institutional meanings at the individual level.

Finally, current studies are retrospective, asking interviewees to reflect upon the changes in their identity (e.g., Chreim et al., 2007). Yet, identity is an ongoing process, changing as life unfolds (Josselson, 2011), and looking back, people tend to reconstruct the past according to present understandings (Freeman, 2011). Therefore, when we document an identity process retrospectively, we actually get a story of a process, which do not necessarily indicate the process itself. Taking seriously the concept of identity *work*, we should make more effort to get as close as possible to the process as it unfolds.

To conclude, we hold that current conceptualization restricts identity work to the negotiation of the boundaries and contents of a particular collective identity, limiting the influence of institutions on individuals and vice versa only to the specific institutional context and to the explicit level of consciousness. Such a conceptualization completely ignores that "actors can creatively use cultural resources as 'building blocks'" (Lok, 2020, p. 14), and therefore we get only a partial picture of the broad and deep interconnectedness of institutional meanings and individuals. Whereas deep and broad influences are recognized – for example, in Lok's suggestion to conceptualize the actor as "institutional bricoleur" – they have "not yet been formulated into a formal theory" (Lok, 2020, p. 13). In this chapter, we correspond with Lok's call and offer to conceptualize identity work as the gradual internalization of institutional meanings, and their integration within one's self-conception at its various facets and levels.

To theorize and explore such expanded concept of identity work, we draw on narrative perspective on self-identity, according to which humans are storytellers who construct their identity through the narration of their lives (Bruner, 1987; Lieblich et al., 1998; McAdams, 1996). People weave their life story from events and circumstances to make sense of their lives, understand who they are, and communicate this understanding to others. Life stories are narrated over and over again while reconstructing the past, integrating the unfolding present, and anticipating possible futures (Lieblich et al., 1998). Constructing a life story is a meaning-making process of reinterpreting the past according to present understandings, thereby involving many selections (Randall, 1999; Spector-Marsel, 2011), which are reflected in content, temporal order, and linguistic forms of the story (Bruner, 1987). These selections are not necessarily conscious; nevertheless, they indicate individuals' present beliefs (Josselson, 2011).

While narrating their identity stories, individuals are bound to create meanings from available cultural materials, stretching beyond their personal experience (Hammack, 2008); otherwise, their story will make no sense (Bruner, 1987; Gergen & Gergen, 1988). The application of a cultural material is also a selection that attests to one's present understanding. For example, Cain (1998) shows how people dealing with alcohol addiction in Alcoholic Anonymous programs, learned to produce an "AA story" using a field-level model to understand self and reinterpret the past.

Thus, identity work in this expanded conceptualization, leaning on insights from narrative psychology enables us to explore the microfoundations of institutions – as they are lived, crystallized and disseminated by individuals who inhabit institutions (Hallett & Ventresca, 2006) while (among other things) constructing their self-identity through storytelling.

METHOD

The Case: Yoga as an Institutional Context

Since the study of institutionalization at the individual level is quite a new area of exploration, choosing an outlier case may be rewarding (Yin, 1994). Hence, we locate our exploration in a rather exclusive field – yoga in Israel. Yoga is a school of philosophy originating in ancient India. It involves physical and mental disciplines mostly directed inward (Sen-Gupta, 2013). Over the centuries, yoga has been practiced through various traditions, all directing practice toward transforming the "ordinary" state of the mind and the common knowing-the-truth, ultimately aiming at gaining radical clarity and equanimity (Grinshpon, 2002). Yoga is deeply rooted in Indian institutions as asceticism, radical non-violence, and non-self (Eliade, 1969). All stand in a salient contradiction to well established Western institutions such as individualism, materialism and hedonism (Halbfass, 1988), which are common in Israel as well (Ram, 2013).

Yoga has been progressively spreading to the Western world (De Michelis, 2005) including Israel, where it is nowadays very common (Werczberger & Huss, 2014). There are numerous yoga centers across Israel, as well as yoga classes in recreation centers; there are many hundreds of yoga teachers all over Israel, and dozens of programs for training yoga teachers that are recognized by the Israeli Yoga Teachers Association – an active organization of yoga teachers (www. isyoga.co.il). Nevertheless, to date yoga has not been recognized as a mainstream activity at the societal level, but rather as a unique or exclusive discipline. Yoga is neither included in the formal education program, nor provided among the public healthcare services, nor is it surveyed in any formal statistics.

Thus, being a core issue among a growing community that negotiates its practices and meanings, we conclude that yoga is indeed an institutionalized field in Israel (Wooten & Hoffman, 2008), yet it is an exclusive institution. Israelis, who practice yoga, need to engage in identity work in order to translate and modify yoga institutional meanings to "Israelish" (DuPertuis, 1987), and to adjust their understanding of themselves to yoga (Pagis, 2009). The seemingly long process that Israeli practitioners are expected to undergo before yogic meanings becomes taken-for-granted to them, makes yoga a suitable case study for exploring nuances of identity work individuals undergo while becoming embedded in an institution.

Data Collection

We interviewed 25 (23 women) yoga practitioners that were at three different "moments" along their practice: beginners, who practice yoga regularly for 2 years; experienced practitioners, who practice yoga regularly for at least 7 years; and teachers, who practice yoga for at least 8 years and teach it regularly for at least 3 years. All interviewees practice at Vijnana Yoga centers. Their ages varied, and were not necessarily congruent with their seniority in yoga.[2]

The first author conducted a two parts interview with all the interviewees. First, she collected interviewees' life stories (identity stories) (Josselson, 2011). Next, conducting a structured interview, she focused on yoga asking all interviewees a similar set of questions regarding their understandings of yoga. Interviews lasted between 2 and 6 hours, held through 1–3 sessions. They were tape-recorded and transcribed. Altogether, we had 55 recorded hours and 720 transcript pages that were the raw materials for analysis.

Analytical Procedures

Our framework consists of three phases of analysis. In the first phase, we identified representations of yogic meanings in the interviews, at three different levels of depth. Looking first at interviewees' *definitions of yoga* using the answers to some of the direct questions we asked in the second part of the interview. Next, we moved to analyze *taken-for-granted beliefs regarding yoga*, using the meanings interviewees assigned to yoga along their life story. We content analyzed (Lieblich et al., 1998) both sets of data into three themes of meaning: (1) "Yoga as a path" – refers to yoga as a discipline for transforming the self; (2) "The fruits of yoga" – refers to the notable positive outcomes of yoga to the body, mind, and awareness; and (3) "Yoga as serving the self" – refers to yoga as a mean to glorify and upgrade the unique personalized "self". Finally, within this first phase, we moved to unpack *yogic interpretive schemes* (Scott, 2008), which are deeply internalized meanings evident from the schemes practitioners actually applied to make sense of their stories (Bruner, 1986; Gergen & Gergen, 1988). These schemes are often not explicit in the content of a story, yet they are implicit in the text and therefore can be deduced through interpretation (Zilber, Tuval-Mashiach, & Lieblich, 2008). We identified yogic interpretive schemes in episodes along the life stories which resonate with the above yogic meanings, without explicitly mentioning "yoga." We suggest that those implicit yogic meanings attest to an extremely deep level of internalization – deeper than the level of taken-for-grantedness that is reflected in the contents assigned to yoga along the life stories.

Altogether, we analyzed three types of representations of yogic meanings at the individual level – definitions (172 sections), taken-for-granted beliefs (198), and interpretive schemes (67) –which we regard as laying at three levels of depth of consciousness (for elaboration and examples, see the Appendix).

In the second phase, we explored the integration of yogic meanings within identity stories, relating to two dimensions: depth and importance.

Comparing Yogic Meanings across Different Levels of Depth to Explore How
Deeply Have Yoga Trickled Down into Individuals' Identity Stories
Following Spiro (1987), the more similar the meaning of yoga is across levels of depth, the deeper the institution of yoga has been internalized into one's identity. To compare the meaning of yoga across levels of depth, we mapped the meaning of yoga (for a similar procedure, see Zilber, 2006): at each level of depth, counting how many segments are classified to each one of the themes of meaning we identified above. Based on that counting, we composed prominence pies that map the meaning of yoga at each level of depth, for each group of interviewees. Then we compared the prominence pies across different levels of depth. We presume that if yogic meanings have trickled down from a surface to a deeper level, the prominence pies indicating the meaning of yoga should be identical across different levels of depth.

Widening the Scope to Explore How Important Is Yoga as a Facet
of Individuals' Self-identity
We explore the importance of yoga which is evident from the extent to which yoga is prevalent in practitioners' identity stories. While constructing their life story, individuals make many selections (Spector-Marzel, 2011). The (often unconscious) selections individuals make by elaborating early, more, less, or non on each facet of identity, or by applying one or another meaning system, may reflect which meanings are available to them and what they perceive – in the time of narrating the story – to be important and thus suitable for describing who they are (Josselson, 2011). The more yoga is prevalent in the story, the more important and significant the yogic institution is as a facet of identity.

We explored two indicators for the importance of yoga in individuals' identity stories. First, we explored the moment at which yoga enters the story (Rosenthal, 1993) – the first time the word "yoga" is mentioned, and the point of the story at which the interviewee relates the time she began to practice yoga. Second, we explored the volume of yoga within the life stories (Spector-Marzel, 2011). We measured an explicit volume (sections along the life stories in which interviewees related to yoga) and an implicit volume (episodes within which we could identify application of an interpretive yogic scheme).

In the third phase of analysis, we followed the traces of the process of identity work of individuals. The process of identity work is actually not accessible to us, since it takes place in the minds of individuals. However, we can explore its traces. To that end, we compared the life stories of yoga practitioners who differ by their level of exposure to the yogic institutional context, and whom we classified to three seniority groups–beginners, experienced practitioners, and teachers. The three groups of stories enabled us to "visit" three moments along the course of identity work yoga practitioners undergo. These moments are different both in terms of the time span practitioners are exposed to yoga as an institution, and in terms of the extent of involvement within the institutional context (Everitt, 2012). We compared the three groups of stories according to the indicators of depth and importance of yogic meanings within identity stories, described above. Doing that, we follow the traces of the process of identity work individuals undergo while adopting institutional meanings.

IDENTITY WORK: ASSIMILATING YOGIC MEANINGS INTO ONE'S SELF-CONCEPT

We unpack the identity work yoga practitioners undergo, showing how they assimilate institutional meanings within their self-conception. We begin by elaborating the outcomes of the process of identity work, and then we turn to explore the process itself.

Outcomes of Identity Work: Various Representations of Institutional Meanings at the Individual Level

What does it mean that yoga practitioners internalize yogic meanings, which are available at the institutional context? We show different types of representations of yogic meanings at the individual level, indicating different levels of internalizing yoga – from a surface level to a very deep level: (a) *definitions* of yoga, (b) *taken-for-granted beliefs* regarding yoga, and (c) *interpretive yogic schemes*.

Take, for example, the meaning of yoga as "developing awareness" (within the theme "the fruits of yoga"). This yogic meaning was represented along the interviews in all three types. First, as a definition – when directly asked about yoga in the structured interview – Na'ama expresses that idea straightforward:

It [yoga] really develops the awareness of the body and the awareness of the mind-body. [Na'ama, a beginner, structured interview]

Second, as a taken-for-granted belief – Lin assigns to yoga the same meaning, while relating along her life story to the first year of practicing yoga, yet she does so indirectly:

I can also say that after two month of yoga my husband and me, we began to lose weight, and we didn't do anything in particular for that end. Bit by bit we changed what we were eating. But not intentionally... we just realized what our body needs. [Lin, a beginner, life story]

Although both Na'ama and Lin relate to yoga explicitly, in Lin's phrase the meaning of yoga is not articulated directly, as a theoretical proposition, but is unfolding as a personal insight. While Na'ama seems to define yoga, Lin is not making any effort to explain yoga in an abstract manner. She speaks about her own experience, and by the way reveals her actual belief regarding yoga.

Also note that Na'ama is using the yogic concepts by the book (*Awareness, mind-body*), whereas Lin says the same, but in her own words: "we just *realized* what our body needs."

And third, the same idea is manifested in even a subtler manner as an interpretive scheme – in the following story, Ela conveys recalling her early childhood:

> I remember that I got this scar here when my brother was chasing me, and I bumped into the corner of a table in the living room. Then I remember that a neighbor physician, came over and that I was sitting on the kitchen counter, and in the hospital, I remember being tied to the bed with some kind of device to keep me from moving, and they gave me anesthetic-fluid, and I remember that it seeped into my ear, I mean...this is my memory...that it seeped into my ear. [Ela, a teacher, life story]

Ela conveys a rather hectic tale of a childhood injury. However, the point of the story relates to her somatic awareness: "I mean...*this* is my memory... that it seeped into my ear." She emphasizes the notion of awareness of subtle bodily sensations – like the dripping of the anesthetic-fluid into her ear – such that her story implicitly resonates with the yogic meaning of developing awareness to the body. Surely, Ela as a young child did not acknowledge that idea. However, when telling her life story retrospectively, Ela reinterprets that childhood memory according to the presuppositions she holds at the moment of telling. As a yoga teacher, who may have internalized that idea of developing awareness so deeply, she applies it as an interpretive yogic scheme to make sense of her childhood memory.

The three quotes above are examples of the outcomes of identity work at the individual level (for more examples, see the Appendix). All three of them indicate that individuals have been taking the institutional meanings (yoga) in, however, to a different level of depth of consciousness. In the literature, institutional meanings at the individual level are usually restricted to what we call here "definitions," indeed indicating bold and clear meanings individuals attach to the institution. However, it seems that when integrated into individuals' self-identity, institutional meanings may manifest in richer ways, sometimes being explicit, yet personalized and nested within concrete events, and in some occasions, they may be implicit, not apparent at all, just resonating from the stories. Thus, it is valuable to explore institutional meanings at the individual level in various levels of depth.

Tracing the Process of Identity Work as Institutional Work

After acknowledging the outcomes of identity work, we now move to unpack the process. We visit the process of identity work yoga practitioners undergo at three moments, by comparing stories of beginners, experience practitioners, and yoga teachers. We found that identity work of individuals involves a process through which yogic institutional meanings trickle down more deeply to practitioners' identity and become a more important facet of identity.

Depth

If the meaning of yoga has trickled down from a surface to a deeper level, it should be similar across different levels of depth. Thus, the pies representing the meaning of yoga by the prominence of each theme ("yoga as a path," "the fruits of yoga," and "yoga as serving the self") should be similar when comprised from definitions, taken-for-granted beliefs, and interpretive schemes.

Focusing first on the definitions of yoga, we see that the three seniority groups of interviewees share the definition of yoga, conceptualizing yoga mostly as a path, secondly as having fruits and modestly as serving the self (see Fig. 1, first row).

Spiro (1987) asserts that when people internalize a doctrine to a surface level, they are able to articulate its "traditional understanding" that is represented by the interpretation given by "recognized specialist" to that doctrine (p.164). Accordingly, the group of yoga teachers – as specialists – represents the traditional understanding of yoga, which we consider to be the institutionalized version of the meaning of yoga. Thus, we argue that the shared definition of yoga among the three groups indicates that practitioners along all three moments of identity work adopt the institutionalized meaning of yoga (at least) to a surface level of consciousness.

However, comparing the definition of yoga with the taken-for-granted beliefs regarding yoga, we find dramatic differences, such that the taken-for-granted belief regarding yoga resembles the definition of yoga only in the group of

Yogic meanings	Beginners	Experienced practitioners	Teachers
Definitions of yoga (Contents of the answers in the structured interview regarding yoga)			
Taken-for-granted beliefs regarding yoga (Contents assigned to yoga Along the life stories)			
Similarity between definitions and beliefs	**No similarity**	**No similarity**	**Very similar**
Implicit yogic schemes (Schemes that resonate with yogic definitions in episodes along the life stories)			
Similarity between definitions and schemes	**No similarity**	**No similarity**	**Fairly similar**

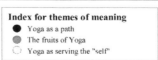

Index for themes of meaning
- Yoga as a path
- The fruits of Yoga
- Yoga as serving the "self"

Fig. 1.   Definitions of Yoga, Taken-For-Granted Beliefs Regarding Yoga, and Interpretive Yogic Schemes at the Individual Level.

teachers (see Fig. 1, second row). In the beginners' and experienced practitioners' groups, the theme yoga-as-serving-the-self seems to "take over" and comprise about half of the meanings attached to yoga along the life stories; whereas, meanings of yoga-as-a-path and of the-fruits-of-yoga are common in the discourse of yoga (Grinshpon, 2002; Sen-Gupta, 2013), meanings of yoga-as-serving-the-self do not appear in yogic texts. On the contrary, they contradict meanings expressed in the discourse of yoga, which construct yoga as fundamentally transforming the known "self" and demanding the yogini to "... 'die' to this life, and sacrifice the 'personality'" (Eliade, 1969, p. 363). Apparently, the meanings of yoga at the individual level reflect some new understandings that individuals assign to yoga, which are not institutionalized.[3]

Turning to the representations of yogic meanings as interpretive schemes,[4] again the meaning of yoga reflected in the definitions interviewees gave is replicated in the interpretive yogic schemes they applied, only in the group of teachers (see Fig. 1, third row). Since the combinations of the interpretive yogic schemes beginners and experienced practitioners apply do not resemble the common definition of yoga, we take it that the institutionalized meaning of yoga did not trickle down to inform their general worldview (Spiro, 1987).

In sum, yoga practitioners – beginners, experienced, and teachers – seem to share the common definition of yoga. They seem to be familiar with the institutionalized meaning of yoga, so they are able to provide quite the same definition. But, it may be the case that they actually recitea cliché, which they do not fully internalize. It seems that institutional meanings are more deeply internalized only after practitioners are long exposed to the institution and are actively engaged in it. We argue that this pattern is but a trace of the process of identity work through which yoga practitioners internalize yogic meanings to a deeper level of consciousness as the exposure to yoga grows.

Importance
The growing importance of yoga in practitioners' identity is reflected in two indicators: the point at which yoga enters the stories and the volume of yoga within the stories.

Point of Entrance. Our data suggest that as the exposure to yoga grows, yoga enters the stories earlier in two senses: the word "yoga" is firstly mentioned earlier in the stories; and the speaker conveys the story about beginning to practice yoga earlier (see Fig. 2).

Early mention of yoga in the life story, even before conveying the story about beginning to practice yoga, indicates that yoga is an available meaning to the speaker, which she finds relevant as a point of referral, even when she speaks about herself before encountering yoga. Similarly, the early or late point in the story at which the beginning of yoga practice is told about, indicates how important yoga practice is for explaining "who I am." Naturally, the story about how one began to practice yoga has to do with the length of time one actually practices yoga. Thus, it makes sense

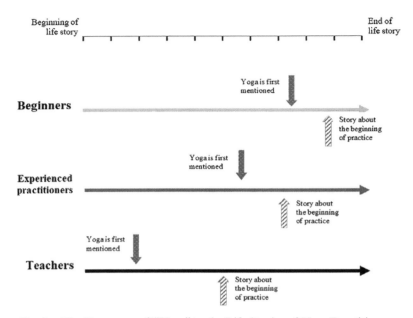

Fig. 2. The Entrances of "Yoga" to the Life Stories of Yoga Practitioners.

that beginners, who began practicing yoga about two years prior to the interview, would speak about it closer to the end of their life story. However, teachers did not necessarily begin practicing yoga earlier than experienced practitioners did, yet in average teachers relate the time they began practicing yoga earlier in the story. Thus, we conclude that these findings point to the growing importance of yoga in practitioners' identity, as their exposure to yoga grows.

Volume. We found that both explicit and implicit volumes of yoga in the stories are greater as the exposure to yoga grows. Counting the sections along the life stories, within which practitioners relate explicitly to yoga, we found that as the exposure to yoga grows, yoga practitioners tend to relate to yoga more often: yoga is explicitly mentioned in three episodes within life stories of beginners (on average per a life story), four – among experienced practitioners, and 17 – among teachers (see Fig. 3). Relating to yoga more frequently in the story indicates how central yoga is in characterizing "me" and in constructing the story about "who I am" at the time of the interview (Freeman, 2011; Randall, 1999).

Similarly, we found that the life stories of yoga practitioners resonated more often with yogic meanings, through interpretive yogic schemes, as the exposure to yoga grows: within life stories of beginners, less than one episode (on average

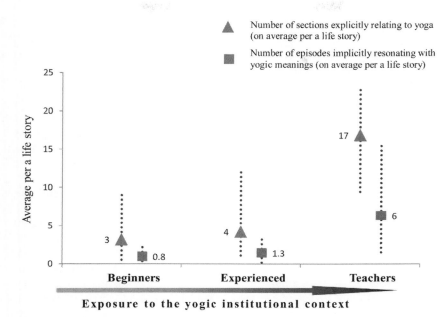

▲ Number of sections explicitly relating to yoga
(on average per a life story)

■ Number of episodes implicitly resonating with
yogic meanings (on average per a life story)

Fig. 3.   Explicit and Implicit Volume of Yoga within Life Stories of Yoga
Practitioners.

per a life story) implicitly resonates with yogic meanings, more than one – among experienced practitioners, and six – among teachers (see Fig. 3). The growing implicit volume of yoga in practitioners' identity stories, as the exposure to yoga grows, indicates that yoga is becoming a more available interpretive system to them, and therefore they use yogic schemes more often to make sense of their lives.

Altogether, the two indicators of importance consistently point out that the more practitioners are exposed to yoga, the greater yoga is prevalent in their stories; hence, we conclude – the more important facet of identity yoga becomes. Indeed, the context of being interviewed as a yoga practitioner might have primed yoga as a subject of speech (Mishler, 2004). Yet, although it was equal to all, practitioners differed extensively in how early and how much they spoke about yoga or resonated with its meanings (including two interviewees – beginners – who did not mention yoga explicitly at all along their life story).

Thus, we interpret the growing prevalence of yoga within identity stories as a trace of the process of identity work. As a process through which as yoga practitioners progress in their yogic journey, yoga is becoming a more important facet of their identity, and therefore yogic meanings become more fundamental and available to them for explaining who they are.

CONCLUSIONS AND DISCUSSION

While NIT refocuses its attention on microfoundations (Hallett & Ventresca, 2006; Powell & Colyvas, 2008), we still know very little about how institutions operate at the individual level (Suddaby, 2010). Following others (Creed et al., 2010; Lawrence & Suddaby, 2006), we view individuals' identity work as institutional work, through which individuals may adopt an institutionalized identity and negotiate its boundaries and contents. Aiming to expand this line of research, we analyzed individuals' life stories to explored how institutional meanings are entangled in individuals' understandings of themselves (their self-identity), going beyond the explicit contents related to the institutionalized (role/professional) identity only.

Our case study was the institutionalization of yoga at the individual level. We found that as yoga practitioners are more exposed to the yogic institution, yogic meanings take wider and deeper root in their self-concept. Yoga becomes more prevalent in practitioners' life stories, and more relevant to a broader array of issues: practitioners relate to yoga more often – and earlier – in the story, whether elaborating on their encounter with yoga, or referring to yoga while talking about themselves as teenagers, parents or "just" human beings coping with life; they also implicitly apply yogic schemes more often while making sense of episodes in their lives, which have nothing (explicit) to do with yoga. Second, with exposure, practitioners internalize the institutionalized meaning of yoga to a deeper level of consciousness: when they relate to yoga spontaneously along their life stories, the meanings they assign to yoga are more similar to their formal definition of yoga; and the yogic schemes they apply implicitly to convey various episodes along their stories also resemble more closely that definition. We conclude then, that institutionalization at the individual level involves making the institution a more important facet of identity and internalizing institutionalized beliefs to a deeper level of consciousness.

Our study involved several choices and compromises, which led to some limitations. First, we focus on Israeli yoga practitioners and their identity work. One may argue that the gradual process we found has to do with the foreignness of the yogic institution, since yogic meanings are not easy to comprehend thereby not easily internalized by newcomers or part-timers. And thus, our findings may not be generalized to other institutions. Yet, we chose yoga to serve as an extreme case, which allowed us a nuanced exploration (Yin, 1994), of a broader phenomenon. While the course of identity work in the case of more familiar institutions may be less dramatic, we still expect a fairly similar process.

Our study is also limited in our ability to follow the actual *process* of identity work as it unfolds. We did not follow the same individuals along the process they have undergone, starting when they are beginners as yoga practitioner, coming back to them after several years, as they are experienced practitioners and lastly after (and if) they become yoga teachers. As we did not collect the life stories of the same individuals at three different moments, we could not explore how the patterns of integrating yoga in one's life story actually changes, as she becomes a more senior yoga practitioner. Longitudinal research that follows the construction of individuals' life story along a life span of 15–20 years is rare and difficult to pursue (for a rare exception, see Josselson, 2000). Instead, we interviewed yoga practitioners that were differently exposed to yoga, and compared their stories. Although we were limited in exploring the actual process individuals undergo, it seems a reasonable compromise that allowed us to treat each group of interviewees as representing one "moment" along that process.

Last, our study explores the cognitive aspect of taking yoga in by individuals, being silent on the bodily aspect. Since yoga is a body-mind practice, the body must have been also an arena of institutionalization. Furthermore, since the body is a "memory pad" (Bourdieu, 2000, cited in Sieweke, 2014, p. 539), adopting yogic bodily practices – such as certain types of breathing (prolonged, deep), standing posture, sitting posture, etc. – may very well indicate and reinforce the engravement of yogic meanings in the mind. While beyond our scope in this chapter, future research is needed for exploring also the bodily aspect of the institutionalization of yoga, as a step toward realizing multimodality of institutions (Zilber, 2017a).

Nevertheless, our study has important contributions to the understanding of microfoundations of institutions. First, this study supports a broader concept of identity work as institutional work. Past research already established the understanding that identity work of individuals is a form of institutional work (e.g., Creed et al., 2010, Lok, 2010). Yet, current understanding of identity work restricts the role of individuals in the process of institutionalization to the institutional context only, as if their identity work may affect exclusively the meaning of the specific professional/role identity. However, since institutions are taken-for-granted beliefs (Scott, 2014), individuals use institutional meanings without being aware at all that they apply them. Furthermore, since individuals may pick up ideas from one setting and transpose them to another (Powell & Colyvas, 2008), being "artful in their mobilization of different institutional logics to serve their purpose" (Glynn 2008, p. 423), they are probe to apply institutional meanings "out of context". For example, Zilber (2009) shows how volunteers in a rape-crisis center used implicit feminist institutional logics of sexual harassment – common and institutionalized in the organization – to make sense of their relationships in general, not necessarily in contexts of sexual assault. Hence, one cannot adopt an institution restricting its influence to the institutional context only; yet, as Pratt and his colleagues stress "little is said about how members actively use identity-related information to construct their own identity" (Pratt et al., 2006, p. 237). Studying the "black box" of individuals (Pernkopf-Konhaeusner, 2014) in this chapter, we trace the infusion of institutional "information" in self-identity stories of individuals, showing that identity work is unbounded, affecting selfhood in general. Since identity work goes beyond the boundaries of the institutional context and beneath the explicit level of content, we suggest revisiting the concept of identity work as institutional work. Such that, in addition to reaffirming and changing the institutionalized identity, identity work of individuals involves also a mechanism of *expanding the relevance of the institution* – that is, spreading institutional meanings to further spheres of selfhood and deeper levels of consciousness.

Second, in this chapter, we develop a conceptual and methodological framework to study the role of individuals in the maintenance and change of the ideational aspect of institutions. While the two scholarly traditions we drew on – NIT and narrative psychology (life stories as self-identity stories) – provided a solid theoretical ground for our exploration of institutional meanings at the individual level, none of them established analytical tools for such exploration. Scholars within NIT emphasize the importance of exploring the individual level; yet, since the empirical research on that level is scarce, we are called to borrow tools from other traditions and develop them for use within the institutional perspective (Boxenbaum, 2014). Looking for such tools within the rich narrative literature, in which there is a strong agreement that life stories are authored using common cultural meanings, we find that there are no common tools for exploring these cultural meanings within life stories (McAdams, Josselson, & Lieblich, 2006). Therefore, in this chapter, based on past understandings in both literatures, we offer a new analytical framework to explore more comprehensively the role of individuals in the institutional drama.

In this chapter, we turned our gaze toward the intra-individual elements of the institutional course. Showing the traces of a cognitive process through which institutions are integrated within individuals' self-concept, our study joins the pioneer literature on emotions (Creed et al., 2010; Voronov & Vince, 2012), pointing at the significance participation of selfhood in its most broad sense, in processes of institutionalization.

NOTES

1. When scholars refer to the most broad and inclusive form of identity, they tend to use the generic term "identity" (McAdams, 1996; Pratt, Rockmann, & Kaufmann, 2006) without any specifying adjectives such as "social," "personal," "professional," etc. For example, McAdams explains: "Identity reflects the I's efforts to integrate the various tellings of self, both private and public, into a larger narrative framework that suggests life unity and purpose." (1996, p. 308). Yet, in order to be clear and avoid misunderstandings, we shell use the term "self-identity" to emphasize our focus on the holistic form of identity that encompasses selfhood.

2. The interviewees have been given pseudonyms to protect their identity.

3. We ought to take into consideration, however, that since a life story is a platform upon which individuals construct their identity (Lieblich et al., 1998; McAdams, 1996), it especially evokes meanings related to identity and self. Thus, assigning to yoga meanings related to the self may reflect – at least to some extent – the medium in which yoga is discussed, and not necessarily meanings of yoga that individuals take for granted. Yet since the prominence of this theme along the life stories varies extensively among the three groups of yoga practitioners, we assume that the domination of the serving-the-self theme is not exclusively due to the context of a life story interview.

4. We could not identify interpretive schemes for the serving-the-self theme and for few categories within the other two themes, since such meanings do not necessarily represent yogic meanings. Thus, to be able to compare the representations of yogic meaning as interpretive schemes with the definition of yoga, we ignored the serving-the-self theme and compared only the two other themes: "yoga as a path" and "the fruits of yoga" (including only the relevant categories – see the Appendix).

REFERENCES

Berger, P. L., & Luckmann, T. (1967). *The social construction of reality: A treatise in the sociology of knowledge.* London: Penguin.

Boxenbaum, E. (2014). Toward a situated stance in organizational institutionalism: Contributions from French pragmatist sociology theory. *Journal of Management Inquiry, 23*(3), 319–323.

Bruner, J. S. (1986). *Actual minds, possible worlds.* Cambridge, MA: Harvard University Press.

Bruner, J. S. (1987). Life as narrative. *Social Research, 54*(1), 11–32.

Cain, C. (1998). Personal stories in alcoholics anonymous. In D. Holland, W. Lachicotte, D. Skinner, & C. Cain (Eds.), *Identity and agency in cultural worlds* (pp. 66–97). Cambridge, MA: Harvard University Press.

Callero, P. L. (2003). The sociology of the self. *Annual Review of Sociology, 29*, 115–133.

Chreim, S., Williams, B. E., & Hinings, C. R. (2007). Interlevel influences on the reconstruction of professional role identity. *Academy of Management Journal, 50*(6), 1515–1539.

Creed, W. D., DeJordy, R., & Lok, J. (2010). Being the change: Resolving institutional contradiction through identity work. *Academy of Management Journal, 53*(6), 1336–1364.

De Michelis, E. (2005). *A history of modern yoga: Patanjali and western esotericism.* London: Continuum International Publishing Group.

DuPertuis, L. G. (1987). American adaptations of Hinduism. *Comparative Social Research, 10*, 101–111.

Eliade, M. (1969). *Yoga: Immortality and freedom* (2nd ed.). Princeton, NJ: Princeton University Press.

Everitt, J. G. (2012). Teacher careers and inhabited institutions: Sense-making and arsenals of teaching practice in educational institutions. *Symbolic Interaction, 35*(2), 203–220.

Freeman, M. (2011). Stories, big and small: Toward a synthesis. *Theory & Psychology, 21*(1), 114–121.

Gergen, K. J., & Gergen, M. M. (1988). Narrative and the self as relationship. *Advances in Experimental Social Psychology, 21*, 17–56.

Giddens, A. (1991). *Modernity and self-identity: Self and society in the late modern age.* Stanford, CA: Stanford University Press.

Glynn, M. A. (2008). Beyond constraint: How institutions enable identities. In R. Greenwood, C. Oliver, K. Sahlin, & R. Suddaby (Eds.), *The Sage handbook of organizational institutionalism* (pp. 413–430). London: Sage.

Grinshpon, Y. (2002). *Silence unheard: Deathly otherness in Pātañjala-yoga.* Albany, NY: State University of New York Press.

Halbfass, W. (1988). *India and Europe.* New York, NY: State University of New York Press.

Hallett, T., & Ventresca, M. J. (2006). Inhabited institutions: Social interactions and organizational forms in Gouldner's patterns of industrial bureaucracy. *Theory and Society, 35*(2), 213–236.

Hammack, P. L. (2008). Narrative and the cultural psychology of identity. *Personality and Social Psychology Review, 12*(3), 222–247.

Josselson, R. (2000). Stability and change in early memories over 22 years: Themes, variations, and cadenzas. *Bulletin of the Menninger Clinic, 64*(4), 462–481.

Josselson, R. (2011). Narrative research: Constructing, deconstructing, and reconstructing story. In K. Charmaz, & L. M. McMullen (Eds.), *Five ways of doing qualitative analysis: Phenomenological psychology, grounded theory, discourse analysis, narrative research, and intuitive inquiry* (pp. 224–242). New York, NY: Guilford.

Lawrence, T. B., & Suddaby, R. (2006). Institutions and institutional work. In S. R. Clegg, C. Hardy, T. B. Lawrence, & W. R. Nord (Eds.), *The Sage handbook of organization studies*, (Vol. 2, pp. 215–255). London: Sage.

Lieblich, A., Tuval-Mashiach, R., & Zilber, T. (1998). *Narrative research: Reading, analysis and interpretation.* Thousand Oaks, CA: Sage Publications.

Lok, J. (2010). Institutional logics as identity projects. *Academy of Management Journal, 53*(6), 1305–1335.

Lok, J. (2020). Theorizing the 'I' in institutional theory: Moving forward through theoretical fragmentation, not integration. In *The Oxford handbook of identities and organizations.* New York, NY: Oxford University Press.

McAdams, D. P. (1996). Personality, modernity, and the storied self: A contemporary framework for studying persons. *Psychological Inquiry, 7*(4), 295–321.

McAdams, D. P., Josselson, R., & Lieblich, A. (Eds.). (2006). *Identity and story: Creating self in narrative* (*Vol. 4*). Washington, DC: American Psychological Association.

McLean, L. D. (2004). A review and critique of Nonaka and Takeuchi's theory of organizational knowledge creation. In *5th UFHED/AHRD Conference*, Limerick, Ireland.

Mishler, E. G. (2004). Historians of the self: Restorying lives, revising identities. *Research in Human Development*, *1*(1), 101–121.

Nonaka, I. & Takeuchi, H. (1995). *The knowledge creation company: How Japanese companies create the dynamics of innovation*. New York, NY: Oxford University Press.

Nonaka, I., & von Krogh, G. (2009). Tacit knowledge and knowledge conversion: Controversy and advancement in organizational knowledge creation theory. *Organization Science*, *20*(3), 635–652.

Pagis, M. (2009). Embodied self-reflexivity. *Social Psychology Quarterly*, *72*(3), 265–283.

Pernkopf-Konhaeusner, K. (2014). The competent actor: Bridging institutional logics and French pragmatist sociology. *Journal of Management Inquiry*, *23*(3), 333–337.

Powell, W. W., & Colyvas, J. A. (2008). Microfoundations of institutional theory. In R. Greenwood, C. Oliver, K. Sahlin, & R. Suddaby (Eds.), *The Sage handbook of organizational institutionalism* (pp. 276–298). London: Sage.

Powell, W.W., & Rerup, C. (2017). Opening the black box: The microfoundations of institutions. In R. Greenwood, C. Oliver, T. B. Lawrence, & R. Meyer (Eds.), *The Sage handbook of organizational institutionalism* (2nd ed., pp. 311–335). London: Sage.

Pratt, M. G., Rockmann, K. W., & Kaufmann, J. B. (2006). Constructing professional identity: The role of work and identity learning cycles in the customization of identity among medical residents. *Academy of Management Journal*, *49*(2), 235–262.

Ram, U. (2013). *The globalization of Israel: McWorld in Tel Aviv, Jihad in Jerusalem*. New York, NY: Routledge.

Randall, W. L. (1999). Narrative intelligence and the novelty of our lives. *Journal of Aging Studies*, *13*(1), 11–28.

Reay, T., Golden-Biddle, K., & Germann, K. (2006). Legitimizing a new role: Small wins and microprocesses of change. *Academy of Management Journal*, *49*(5), 977–998.

Rosenthal, G. (1993). Reconstruction of life stories: Principles of selection in generating stories for narrative biographical interviews. *The Narrative Study of Lives*, *1*, 59–91.

Scott, W. R. (2003). Institutional carriers: Reviewing modes of transporting ideas over time and space and considering their consequences. *Industrial and Corporate Change*, *12*(4), 879–894.

Scott, W. R. (2008). Lords of the dance: Professionals as institutional agents. *Organization Studies*, *29*(2), 219–238.

Scott, W. R. (2014). *Institutions and organizations: Ideas, interests, and identities* (4th ed.). Los Angeles, CA: Sage.

Sen-Gupta, O. (2013). *Patanjali's Yoga sutras*. Jerusalem, Israel: Vijnana Books.

Sieweke, J. (2014). Pierre Bourdieu in management and organization studies – A citation context analysis and discussion of contributions. *Scandinavian Journal of Management*, *30*(4), 532–543.

Snow, D. A., & Anderson, L. (1987). Identity work among the homeless: The verbal construction and avowal of personal identities. *American Journal of Sociology*, *92*(6), 1336–1371.

Spector-Mersel, G. (2011). Mechanisms of selection in claiming narrative identities: A model for interpreting narratives. *Qualitative Inquiry*, *17*(2), 172–185.

Spiro, M. E. (1987). Collective representations and mental representations in religious symbol systems. In B. Killborne & L. L. Langness (Eds.), *Culture and human nature: Theoretical papers of Melford E. Spiro* (pp. 161–184). Chicago, IL: University of Chicago Press.

Suddaby, R. (2010). Challenges for institutional theory. *Journal of Management Inquiry*, *19*(1), 14–20.

Sveningsson, S., & Alvesson, M. (2003). Managing managerial identities: Organizational fragmentation, discourse and identity struggle. *Human Relations*, *56*(10), 1163–1193.

Thornton, P. H., Ocasio, W., & Loundsbury, M. (2012). *The institutional logics perspective: A new approach to culture, structure, and process*. Oxford: Oxford University Press.

Voronov, M., & Vince, R. (2012). Integrating emotions into the analysis of institutional work. *Academy of Management Review*, *37*(1), 58–81.

Werczberger, R., & Huss, B. (2014). New age culture in Israel. *Israel Studies Review*, *29*(2), 1–16.

Wooten, M., & Hoffman, A. (2008). Organizational fields: Past, present and future. In R. Greenwood, C. Oliver, K. Sahlin, & R. Suddaby (Eds.), *The Sage handbook of organizational institutionalism* (pp. 130–148). London: Sage.

Yin, R. K. (1994). Discovering the future of the case study method in evaluation research. *Evaluation Practice, 15*(3), 283–290.

Zilber, T. B. (2006). The work of the symbolic in institutional processes: Translations of rational myths in Israeli High Tech. *Academy of Management Journal, 49*(2), 281–303.

Zilber, T. B. (2009). Institutional maintenance as narrative acts. In T. B. Lawrence, R. Suddaby, & B. Leca (Eds.), *Institutional work: Actors and agency in institutional studies of organizations* (pp. 205–235). Cambridge: Cambridge University Press.

Zilber, T. B. (2017a). A call for "strong" multimodal research in institutional theory. *Research in the Sociology of Organizations* (special issue on *Multimodality, Meaning, and Institutions*), *54A*, 63–84.

Zilber, T. B. (2017b). The evolving role of meaning in theorizing institutions. In R. Greenwood, C. Oliver, T. B. Lawrence, & R. E. Meyer (Eds.), *The Sage handbook of organizational institutionalism* (2nd ed., pp. 418–444). London: Sage.

Zilber, T. B., Tuval-Mashiach, R., & Lieblich, A. (2008). The embedded narrative – Navigating through multiple contexts. *Qualitative Inquiry, 14*(6), 1047–1069.

APPENDIX

Table A1. Institutional Meanings at the Individual Level, at Three Levels of Depth.

Category of Meaning	Definitions of Yoga (From Structured Interview)	Taken-for-Granted Beliefs Regarding Yoga (From Life Story)	Interpretive Yogic Schemes (From Life Story)
1. Yoga as a path			
A practice	"Yoga is a physical and mental practice, systematic and repeating" [Genia, an experienced practitioner]	"I learned to play the violin for about two years. It was very difficult for me. One thing was that it is always on one side of the neck. And another thing I think… it's something that bothers me in many contexts and theoretically in yoga as well. That state of 'practicing'. Why do I say theoretically? Because now it seems to me less… but it was a thing that practicing is difficult, but if you wish to… I don't know, to play beautifully, so you must… I don't agree with that. Once someone in yoga told me: "Don't you want sometimes to have that feeling of the end of the yoga class, but to have it at the beginning of class?" and it wasn't clear to me what is it she wanted – of course I don't! Why should I want to miss the class? It's not that you do all the class only for the feeling at the end of it… I really believe that when you do things that you love doing, you enjoy them also when they are difficult" [Eilat, an experienced practitioner]	"At eleventh grade, I decided to go over that year again, because since the eighth grade I was doing fun, enjoying life, boys, action and everything. So I practically didn't study. And at some point I did want to pass the final exams. So I moved to an external high school and went over that year again. I calmed down a bit. And I took that study very seriously. It was suddenly a transformation to uniform, to discipline. I just realized that I want the high school diploma, and if I were to continue what I was doing, there is going to be nothing at all. And then, I remember, with my friend Alia we decided that we are doing this move together. She was my friend from scratch. So this change, suddenly studying together for the exams, making homework… I simply began to teach myself how to write…" [Ruthi, a teacher] *The story resonates with the yogic belief that transformation is reached through disciplined practice.*
Yogic way of life	"Yoga helps not to lose the trail in the forest. Doing it daily, it really puts life in order. There is a great need in organizing around a center" [Annabel, a teacher]	"I understood that I didn't want to go back to India, because… it is so valuable to practice in the world. In some ways, life in India enables a sterilized yoga practice. You know, living there is effortless, you don't have to work, you can just be there, live with so little money, practice, and that is it. But, it is very satisfying to… even making a living and teaching and raising children and practicing. I mean, putting sincere genuine practice into tax reporting and supermarket and garage – into life…. I mean, maintaining a car and raising children, and yet sustaining a genuine practice." [Rothem, a teacher]	"I had the deepest knowing that staying at the [Buddhist] monastery is not the way I think. It is not… I mean it's a possible way, but not my own way of learning and growing. I said, OK, you got the drill at the monastery, now let us see you smart, going back to filthy ugly Israel. And here, with Intifada and occupation, which is racism and alienation, militant and violent, with all that catastrophe going on in our society… Here, attain the same state that you realized at the monastery!" [Roei, a teacher] *The story resonates with the yogic notion that transformation requires practice in every aspect of living.*

Category of Meaning	Definitions of Yoga (From Structured Interview)	Taken-for-Granted Beliefs Regarding Yoga (From Life Story)	Interpretive Yogic Schemes (From Life Story)
Vijnana principles	"Yoga is a practice of… it is really a practice. It is to be in a state that I am sitting with you right now and I am relaxing my body and relaxing my mind. Directing consciousness, and being aware to my connectedness with the ground, and also feeling my extension and my connection with all the centers… this work with the principles it… it really directed me towards a way of life" [Aimee, a teacher]	"I think that this turning inward makes a change… it moves mountains in yoga. It takes time. The thing that happened with my teacher was really that along with this turning inward and being patient, much clarity has arisen. Also I think that with her I went through a process of calming down [...]. I let myself work with less effort. I let myself not wanting to succeed always. I let myself making mistakes, taking a step back and moving more slowly." [Annabel, a teacher]	"At the beginning it was very important for me that my kids get some kind of a religious experience so they would have something to throw away. To know who is this God that they are not going to believe in… I wanted to give them the options. To tell them… what these people think and what these think, and what I think. Without apologizing and without… you know my partner does not believe in God and I do, and that is fine, the world is complex. But, since it's only me, had I wanted them to have the experience of going to the synagogue, it meant that I had to take them. Had I wanted them to have 'Kidush' [A Jewish ceremony of blessing the wine], I had to do 'Kidush'. So, at the beginning I felt very guilty about that… about not performing enough of those religious practices. We tried all sorts of things, but at the end I understood that OK you cannot have it all. You cannot have it all. I can do only what I can do. So I have to let it go for the time being." [Annabel, a teacher] *The story resonates with the yogic principle of relaxation – here in the sense of letting go and accepting one's limits – as necessary for transformation.*
Yogic worldview	"Yoga is… The glasses that I wear are different… I look at the world totally different. In the past I would check whether my life are good… my inner indicator would be reaching goals–do I have a degree, a husband, children, status. Now, my inner thermometer is tuned to noisy against still; grounded versus distracted; How much loss of control and anger against precision and connectedness; how open or closed my heart is." [Yifat, an experienced practitioner]	"I began to do yoga, and it really caught me […] particularly it was a kind of a different language that I understood very well intuitively… a language that I actually spoke already yet without words" [Ayala, teacher]	"So I felt I needed to take a sabbatical. It started with the decision about a sabbatical, but nevertheless I left everything… I uprooted myself, uprooted from the very root. I have quit my job with retirement grant. I left my home. I scattered all my possessions. I departed with a bag pack, to a journey towards the unknown. And I left everything. And then, then I departed to a journey towards the unknown, which I meant to last for a year, but it rolled longer, much longer than a year." [Aimee, a teacher] *The story resonates with the ancient yogic ideal(!) of asceticism as a preferable condition for dedicated practice and as supporting radical transformation.*

(Continued)

Category of Meaning	Definitions of Yoga (From Structured Interview)	Taken-for-Granted Beliefs Regarding Yoga (From Life Story)	Interpretive Yogic Schemes (From Life Story)
Anchor	"There is no other meaning to life. It establishes for me a sense that being here has a meaning. Yoga is beyond just mental processes, it connects me with eternity. And without the resonance of eternity in my life, I cannot live." [Hilla, a teacher]	"I cannot tell you where I would be in this world without yoga. That is the anchor, that is the friend… this is the safest place in the world. Already in that story of mine of losing a baby in your belly… that your body with which you work so much betrays you… It's so… you know, why just a moment before you are supposed to hug him?… And returning back to life was largely thanks to the practice. Thanks to having something to go back to. You have the mattress – you have yourself" [Ruthi, a teacher]	Not relevant
A whole	"Yoga has few tracks that go alongside: philosophy, 'asanna' and 'pranna'" [Lea, an experienced practitioner]	"And you suddenly learn about a cultural whole, that yoga is one of its components. And then connecting yoga to the culture was very interesting for me. The practice of meditation, of breathing, of 'asanna'…" [Yaeli, an experienced practitioner]	Not relevant
2. Fruits of yoga			
Body: strength, flexibility and good health	"Yoga is good for protecting the body. I do additional things – I swim, I walk, but yoga is the best for me" [Shullamit, an experienced practitioner]	"Yoga helped me a lot. After the problems I had with my back and with my neck…. I felt I needed that for my strength and flexibility" [Sharon, an experienced practitioner]	Not relevant
Mind: joy and calmness	"Yoga is a practice that brings a kind of peace and happiness" [Ehud, a beginner]	"It was an international peace walk. They were walking across the [occupied] territories with signs 'we refuse to be enemies'. At the beginning I thought I would join them for a day or two. Eventually I walked for three and a half weeks, and cried. I cried about my ignorance, that I did not know anything, I cried because of guilt, shame, anger… I cried as a Jewish Israeli. When I walked across the territories and saw and heard and understood the Palestinian narrative… It was a hell of an experience… so deep…. because I cried a lot. I cried… everyone at this walk remember me as a washing machine since I was crying all the time. And then… I overcame a tremendous fear. At the first night I slept in the territories, not yoga, not meditation, nothing could stop my body from trembling" [Aimee, a teacher]	Not relevant

Category of Meaning	Definitions of Yoga (From Structured Interview)	Taken-for-Granted Beliefs Regarding Yoga (From Life Story)	Interpretive Yogic Schemes (From Life Story)
Awareness: developing awareness of the body, the mind and the connectedness of the mind-body	"It is a practice that helps reaching awareness and mindfulness to one self" [Efrat, an experienced practitioner]	"Yoga for pregnancy it's the breathings and all that stuff... it suddenly brought me back to that bodily awareness, to the consciousness of the body, to look what is happening within." [Annabel, a teacher]	"I have early memories that are related to specific sensations in specific situations... of... I think of elementary observations of the world – of sounds, of the tone of voice of my parents and friends, of the kind of light that gets into my room at morning through the blinds... Ah...the feeling of myself, of my body.... For example, one of the earliest memories I have, but it's an enduring memory of...the light which enters the blinds... a kind of light, and that thing of pausing... I am still in bed and a long long observation of the light... My breath, its sound in my ears." [Hilla, a teacher] *The memory resonates with the yogic attention to very subtle sensations.*
Clarity and stillness of consciousness	"The insight that there is a gap between the body and the consciousness is so powerful. You feel the body – there is itchiness, there is a pain... the pain does not have to be suffering. The insight that it is possible to separate them, and to create a consciousness state of quietness within the world of pain, is so powerful and curing. And then, even when it is very very difficult around – there is that understanding." [Rothem, a teacher]	"The chaos settled gradually over these years. At twenty-five years old Ben and I got married, and still the chaos was there.... [laughs] You know what? I really can say ... It is also a matter of age, but certainly also the practice [yoga]. The awfully extreme fluctuations are better endorsed, even if they happen, there is a center" [Hilla, a teacher]	"Half a year into dating my partner, we broke up for a week. And it was awfully difficult for me. But even in the midst of this difficulty I told myself 'OK'.... I mean... I did not know whether it was going to last, but I put myself into a state of hold. That is, not.... If in the past, I would really get into a great emotional turmoil such as having to speak about it – going to a friend and telling her, thinking and analyzing with myself, waiting and everything, so it wasn't like that. I mean, I had difficulties on that weak, and I cried and stuff like that. Yet, I functioned as usual, and moreover, in terms of my inner feeling – it was not as if I was sitting and waiting... holding my breath. Rather, it was coming from a quieter state, with expectation or questions and wondering.... But it was much quieter. And I think that this is the reason that it was easier for me afterwards when we decided to speak and check what was going on, it was simpler for me to say things from my own stance. Because.... I knew that OK that is the case right now, and if we are going to break up, I'll handle it – it enabled me to bring things as they are" [Efrat, an experienced practitioner]. *The story resonates with the yogic appreciation of gaining some equanimity facing troubling circumstances.*

(Continued)

Table A1. *(Continued)*

Category of Meaning	Definitions of Yoga (From Structured Interview)	Taken-for-Granted Beliefs Regarding Yoga (From Life Story)	Interpretive Yogic Schemes (From Life Story)
3. Yoga as serving the self			
Therapy	"Sometimes I need yoga in order to heal myself" [Roy, a teacher]	"Actually yoga is… and this is happening along the last two years… it is funny because actually the psychological therapy had ended, and yoga began. And I felt that in a way yoga was replacing the therapy for me…. Because I felt that things that I do in yoga – it is really an alternative to the psychological therapy. The things it brings up, the coping it requires…." [Ehud, a beginner]	Not relevant
A key element of who I am and what I cherish	"I cannot imagine myself anymore without yoga. When a day passes without yoga – something is missing" [Shullamit, an experienced practitioner]	"I consider myself a feminist, and it is important to me to teach feminist yoga, so that women will not feel as if having personal space for which they take time, is stealing from someone, as if this time is coming on the expense of someone else, which is something that shouldn't be done. It's very difficult to feel that way because we are strongly socialized to the contrary. It's exactly Virginia Woolf´s 'A room of one's own' in the metaphorical sense, a kind of turning inwardly. Generally, you have the right to turn inward" [Hilla, a teacher]	Not relevant
Personality balance	"I really like the issue of order in yoga. Something within you gets organized according to some rules and schedule, and I really am drawn to that. It is something that I personally lack – you see how many times I wrote 'confusion'" [Yaeli, an experienced practitioner]	"I think that many times you turn to something that gives you a response for something… I mean. I go to teach yoga, because I need to learn how to let go, learn to relax, to be calm. And through teaching and practicing, it gives me that thing." [Ela, a teacher]	Not relevant
Quality time, laser, interest	"Yoga is an hour for myself from toes to top – everything there gets attention" [Reut, an experienced practitioner]	"I was quit bored and lonely at that time. For example, at evenings, I was trying to attend all kinds of courses, but my husband could not guarantee that he would stay at home with the kids – sometimes he did and sometimes he did not…. Although for a short period I did go to yoga." [Rita, a beginner]	Not relevant
Useful tools	"It helps me to calm down in stressful situations. It helps me to fall asleep. So I use the breathing exercises." [Na'ama, a beginner]	"Yoga gave me many tools. Like… you know, once I was suffering from a terrible pain. I had a migraine. I am not used to it, but in my life I had difficulties… I remember that I sat in the room; I closed it, shut down the lights. I was laying down on the carpet and doing relaxation, and the migraine stopped" [Jacqueline, an experienced practitioner]	Not relevant

CHAPTER 8

SENSEGIVING AND SENSEMAKING OF HIGHLY DISRUPTIVE ISSUES: ANIMAL RIGHTS EXPERIENCED THROUGH PETA YOUTUBE VIDEOS

Yanfei Hu and Claus Rerup

ABSTRACT

This study examines how highly disruptive issues cause profound dissonance in societal members that are cognitively and emotionally invested in existing institutions. The authors use PETA's (People for the Ethical Treatment of Animals) entrepreneurial advocacy for animal rights to show how this highly disruptive issue interrupted and violated taken-for-granted interpretations of institutions and institutional life. The authors compare 30 YouTube videos of PETA's advocacy to explore pathways to effective sensegiving and sense-making of highly disruptive issues. The findings augment the analytical synergy that exists between sensemaking and institutional analysis by unpacking the micro-level dynamics that may facilitate transformational institutional change.

Keywords: Highly disruptive issues; sensemaking; sensegiving; sensebridging; emotions; microfoundations of institutions

Microfoundations of Institutions
Research in the Sociology of Organizations, Volume 65A, 177–195
Copyright © 2020 by Emerald Publishing Limited
All rights of reproduction in any form reserved
ISSN: 0733-558X/doi:10.1108/S0733-558X2019000065A018

INTRODUCTION

Highly disruptive issues, such as anti-slavery in the eighteenth century (King & Haveman, 2008), women's movements in the nineteenth and early twentieth centuries (Clemens, 1993, 1997), and animal rights (Jasper & Poulsen, 1993), call for fundamental change in how we organize society and impose moral challenges for societal members. Such issues are "highly disruptive" because they interrupt and violate taken-for-granted interpretations of a wide swathe of institutions and institutional life. For example, "almost all of us grew up eating meat, wearing leather, and going to circuses and zoos. We never considered the impact of these actions on the animals involved" (PETA website). This begs the question: how might highly disruptive issues transform deeply rooted institutions?

Institutional change analysis within neo-institutional theory (NIT) has captured incremental change but has only started to grapple with more disruptive problems that require radical change (de Rond & Lok, 2016; Lawrence, 2017; Whelan & Gond, 2016). Highly disruptive issues are distinct in their effects on societal members: they generate dissonance and resistance within an audience that is cognitively and emotionally invested in existing institutions (Voronov & Vince, 2012; Voronov & Weber, 2015; Zietsma & Toubiana, 2018). Therefore, such issues pose challenges to "the purposive action of individuals and organizations aimed at creating, maintaining and disrupting institutions" (Lawrence & Suddaby, 2006, p. 215). Institutional entrepreneurs – "agents who initiate, and actively participate in the implementation of, changes that diverge from existing institutions" (Battilana, Leca, & Boxenbaum, 2009, p. 72) – are one type of actors that sponsor highly disruptive issues. Understanding how highly disruptive issues might transform deeply rooted institutions is important, because such a change often drives the evolution of societies. However, changes in the context of highly disruptive issues have been underexplored. For instance, such change likely hinges on a distributed process through which a critical mass of society needs to experience cognitive and moral transformation; yet, it is unclear how institutional entrepreneurs facilitate this transformational change of societal members.

Institutional entrepreneurs often attempt to convey highly disruptive issues to a wide audience through numerous micro-episodes (e.g., through media and social media platforms). These episodes constitute sensegiving attempts to "influence the sensemaking and meaning construction of others toward a preferred redefinition of … reality" (Gioia & Chittipeddi, 1991, p. 442). These attempts trigger sensemaking – the social process "through which people work to understand issues or events that are novel, ambiguous, confusing, or in some other way violate expectation" (Maitlis & Christianson, 2014, p. 57). Everyday activities aimed at "sensemaking, alignment and muddling through" (Powell & Rerup, 2017, p. 12) are significant microfoundations of institutional change (Haack, Sieweke, & Wessel, 2019). In this study, we explore the process of micro-level sensemaking during institutional change.

Sensemaking scholars have focused on how people respond to violations of expectations (Patriotta & Gruber, 2015). But it is unclear how a wide and distributed audience makes sense of interruptions since existing research has privileged the study of sensemaking in co-located groups (Sandberg & Tsoukas, 2015). For highly disruptive issues to reach distributed societal members, institutional entrepreneurs need to craft discursive accounts – interpretations or explanations that may justify and enable actions (Cornelissen, 2012; Maitlis, Vogus, & Lawrence, 2013) – to attract broad-based attention and prompt positive involvement in the focal issue. Unfortunately, little is known about what accounts constitute sensegiving of highly disruptive issues as well as how these accounts stimulate the audience to make sense differently. This provokes our first research question: how do institutional entrepreneurs' sensegiving accounts stimulate distinctive sensemaking in the audience about highly disruptive issues?

While the first research question aims to explore the relational patterns between sensegiving accounts and the outcomes of subsequent sensemaking stimulated by these accounts, we are also interested in unpacking the processes through which these patterns emerge. During sensemaking, sensemakers are cognitively engaged (Maitlis & Christianson, 2014) but they are also emotionally involved. Emotional involvement is especially salient when the focal issue is highly disruptive (Bartunek, Balogun, & Do, 2011; Cornelissen, Mantere, & Vaara, 2014; Maitlis & Sonenshein, 2010). This leads to our second research question: how does the audience cognitively and emotionally make sense of accounts about highly disruptive issues?

To explore these questions, we examined 30 micro-episodes through which an institutional entrepreneur – People for the Ethical Treatment of Animals (PETA) – used YouTube videos to nudge viewers' sensemaking of animal rights. We developed an empirically grounded typology that explains how PETA's sensegiving accounts triggered distinctive modes of audience sensemaking. We paid particular attention to sensegiving accounts and mechanisms that generated *positive engaged sensemaking* – sensemaking that not only resulted in positive evaluations of the accounts but also deeply engaged the audience. This mode of sensemaking is central to our inquiry: an audience member will consider change only when he or she starts to view an issue in a positive light and with serious engagement. Therefore, *positive engaged sensemaking* signals potential transformation of audience members' views on animal rights.

We contribute to NIT by explicating micro-processes that suggest pathways to transformational change. We found that sensegiving accounts that conveyed disruptive raw truths of animal cruelty stimulated *positive engaged sensemaking* only when combined with *high forms of sensebridging*. In other words, these accounts incorporated materials that resonated with the audience's existing higher values and sentiments (rather than lower pursuits such as sex). These blended accounts broke existing sense, while providing generative materials that the audience could use to update their sensemaking (Christianson, 2019). We also found that such accounts elicited complex issue arousals comprising negative and positive emotions, as well as cognitive processes of judging and layering.

SENSEMAKING OF INSTITUTIONS AND THE ROLE OF EMOTIONS

The microfoundation movement highlights how explanations of higher level phenomena can benefit from involving micro-phenomena and actors (Bitektine & Haack, 2015; Felin, Foss, & Ployhart, 2015; Harmon, Haack, & Roulet, 2018). Specifically, to build microfoundation research within NIT we need systemic approaches to link micro with macro and vice versa (Haack et al., 2019).

Sensemaking research is highly compatible with institutional theory because both traditions share an orientation toward cognitive and social processes. In addition, scholars within both communities recently emphasized the role of emotions. Despite the fact that scholars largely studied local sensemaking (Strike & Rerup, 2016), the potential synergy between sensemaking and institutional analysis has regularly been noted. For example, Weber and Glynn (2006) proposed that institutions impact sensemaking through mechanisms of priming, editing, and triggering. Powell and Rerup (2017, p. 322) specified that

> [s]ocial movements take hold when individuals doubt a settled aspect of the world that is taken for granted .... Doubt might rupture the frames that currently provide the foundation for interpretation and reality construction.

Accordingly, in this study we employ the sensemaking perspective to address recent calls in institutional theory to "reinvigorate institutionalism's phenomenological roots by populating institutional processes with emotionally and socially embedded people" (Creed, Hudson, Okhuysen, & Smith-Crowe, 2014, p. 276).

Sensegiving of Highly Disruptive Issues

Sensegiving is an important construct within the sensemaking perspective. Current sensegiving research provides limited insights on sensegiving accounts and their outcomes (Maitlis & Christianson, 2014) although some studies acknowledge the importance of such accounts. For instance, in a study of postmerger acquisition, management sensegiving resulted in organizational members accepting, resisting, or distancing themselves from a new frame of justice; these reactions played a crucial role in determining the enactment of management-preferred norms of justice (Monin, Noorderhaven, Vaara, & Kroon, 2013). This finding suggests that we need to know how diverse accounts influence receivers' sensemaking.

In conveying highly disruptive issues, sensegiving accounts necessarily comprise novel and jarring interpretations of institutions. Sensebreaking, "the destruction or breaking down of meaning" (Pratt, 2000, p. 464), will be necessary to stimulate the audience to make sense of issues that drastically depart from existing meanings. Indeed, in studying the network marketing organization Amway, Pratt (2000) uncovered how senior Amway distributors first disrupted new members' sense of self to create a meaning void and "seekership," and then impregnated them with ideal new selves to drive identification with Amway. In contrast, research on frames has illuminated the importance of frame resonance; that is, an audience reacts positively to cognitive frames that align with their beliefs and values (Cornelissen & Werner, 2014). For instance, in a study of the effects of framing on audience evaluations, Giorgi and Weber (2015) found that analysts adopting frames that resonated with investors' needs were more likely to be positively evaluated (i.e., being shortlisted as best analysts of the year). Therefore, when giving sense to highly disruptive issues, the institutional entrepreneur will need to leverage both sensebreaking and frame resonance in order to positively engage a wide audience. Yet, little is known about how these different tactics might be deployed together to convey the same issue as well as their effects on the audience.

Sensemaking of Highly Disruptive Issues as Emotion-laden Events

Sensemaking occurs in the minds and through emotions (Sandberg & Tsoukas, 2015). Emotions are likely to be particularly salient when people make sense of highly disruptive issues. Within the sensemaking literature, scholars have only recently paid attention to emotion, defined as "a transient feeling state with an identified cause or target that can be expressed verbally or non-verbally" (Maitlis et al., 2013, p. 2). Intense negative emotions, such as panic, fear, and anxiety, forestall sensemaking by consuming cognitive capacity (Maitlis & Sonenshein, 2010; Weick, 1993), and may trigger escalation of commitment to faulty frames (Cornelissen et al., 2014). Maitlis et al. (2013) suggested that moderately intense negative emotions can energize sensemaking by signaling problems without exhausting cognitive resources. Indeed, Schabram and Maitlis (2017), in a process study of how animal shelter workers pursued challenging careers, found that when these workers encountered setbacks, manageable negative emotions (e.g., sorrow) fueled subsequent sensemaking.

Just like scholars working within the sensemaking literature, institutional scholars have also started to pay attention to emotions (Harmon, 2018; Zietsma & Toubiana, 2018). Voronov and Vince (2012) proposed that emotional scripts are integral parts of institutional structures, and people engage in institutional change only when they have lowered both emotional and cognitive investments in existing arrangements. Toubiana and Zietsma (2016) described how members of a nonprofit organization responded to a disappointing event by expressing negative emotions on Facebook, which amplified those emotions and energized members to promote change. In a study of Ontario's cool-climate wineries, Massa, Helms, Voronov, and Wang (2017) found that wineries drew from institutionalized vinicultural templates to craft rituals that led to inspiring emotional experiences for audiences, converting them into evangelists of this emerging wine practice. Overall, scholars have paid limited attention to how diverse *sensegiving accounts* generate emotions that fuel or stifle sensemaking and institutional processes, despite the significance of such accounts in communicating highly disruptive issues and driving transformational change.

METHODS

We used a case study to understand how institutional entrepreneurs' sensegiving accounts stimulate distinctive sensemaking in the audience about highly disruptive issues, and how the audience cognitively and emotionally makes sense of such accounts. Our goal was to compare patterns across diverse sensegiving and sense-making contexts. For this purpose, we analyzed 30 sensegiving and sensemaking micro-episodes of PETA's video communication to a general audience through its YouTube channels. We chose this type of data because YouTube is an important social media platform on the Internet. Further, the rise of Internet-mediated communication has generated questions about how such communication is playing an increasingly significant role in societal change (Dutton, 2013).

Research Context

In Western cultures, humans and animals have long been considered as distinct and human exceptionalism is taken-for-granted (Smith, 2012). This deeply insti-tutionalized view has served as the foundational justification for a broad range of human practices exploiting animals (Descola, 2013; Purser, Park, & Montuori, 1995). The rise of factory farming after World War II, combined with the preva-lent use of animals in scientific research, education, and entertainment, prompted small groups of societal members in America and European countries to voice concerns about the abuse of animals (Jasper & Nelkin, 2007). While some groups merely wanted to raise animal welfare without fundamentally challenging the institutionalized view on human exceptionalism, other groups contended the equal moral standing of humans and animals (Whelan & Gond, 2016).

The concept of animal rights was popularized by utilitarian philosopher Peter Singer. Singer's book, *Animal Liberation* (first published in 1975), argued that ani-mals' capacity for suffering gives them the right to equal consideration of interests: "we would be on shaky ground if we were to demand equality for blacks, women, and other groups of oppressed humans while denying equal consideration to nonhumans" (Singer, 1995, p. 3). Another philosopher, Tom Regan, extended the Kantian ideal of rights to animals. He suggested that just like humans, animals are "subjects of a life" that have "intrinsic value"; as such, they must be treated as ends in themselves, and "the fundamental wrong is the system that allows us to view animals as our resources, here for us to be eaten, or surgically manipulated, or exploited for sport or money" (Regan, 1986, p. 179).

These theorizations fueled the growth of animal rights organizations that acted to oppose the use of animals for human ends in any form. One such organization is PETA. Founded in 1980, PETA has been known for its perseverance in com-municating highly disruptive issues of animal rights to the public (Smith, 2012). As a consequence of PETA and other similar institutional entrepreneurs, animal rights as "a belief system, an ideology" have "seeped into the bone marrow of Western culture" (Smith, 2012, p. 3). It has led to fundamental legislative change in some contexts. For example, Switzerland amended its constitution in 1992 so that animals were acknowledged as "beings" rather than things; similarly, in 2002, Germany changed its constitution to add animals, alongside human beings, as beings who have a life that are subject to state protection (Connolly, 2002). These changes partially acknowledges rights to animals, indicating the gradual erosion of the dominant institution that views and treats animals as being distinct from, and inferior to, human beings.

Data Collection

We collected the top 30 videos with the highest viewer counts from PETA's YouTube channel and transcribed them noting visual and audio elements. For each video, we collected the numbers of "likes" and "dislikes" and the top 15 comments. These data were pulled on June 6, 2015. In addition, we examined PETA websites and publications, read media coverage and books on PETA, and viewed a large number of PETA videos. These broader data were not directly used in this study, but provided important anchors for reliably interpreting PETA's sensegiving and viewers' sensemaking related to its top 30 videos. The production and dissemination of texts is central to the process of institutionalization (Phillips, Lawrence, & Hardy, 2004), but institutional analysis has predominantly focused on verbal texts when studying the role of communications in institutional processes. Recently, scholars have emphasized that multimodal texts (e.g., video content that include not only verbal, but also visual and audio, texts) may stimulate emotional and bodily involvement in addition to cognitive processing (Meyer, Jancsary, Höllerer, & Boxenbaum, 2017). The presence of multimodal data in our dataset allowed us to explore multimodal communications during a microfoundational process of institutional change.

Data Analysis

Our analysis comprised three steps. In the first step, we explored viewers' sensemaking modes by looking at how they evaluated and engaged with the video. The ratio of likes and dislikes established a measure of viewers' collective evaluation, with ratios higher than "1" signaling positive evaluation and ratios lower than "1" signaling the opposite. The total number of likes and dislikes, divided by viewcounts, established an indicator of viewers' engagement level; a high ratio suggested that a higher percentage of viewers were propelled to "like" or "dislike" the video rather than just browsing it, which indicated higher engagement. When looking across *viewer evaluation* and *viewer engagement*, we found viewer sensemaking followed four modes: *positive engaged sensemaking* (positive evaluation and high engagement), *positive superficial sensemaking* (positive evaluation but low engagement), *contested sensemaking* (negative evaluation and high engagement), and *ineffective sensemaking* (negative evaluation and low engagement).

In the second step, we identified four distinct types of sensegiving accounts by iteratively comparing video transcripts (Strauss & Corbin, 1998).We first noted *fact-based sensebreaking*, in which undercover footage of animal cruelty was used to break viewers' existing perceptions (e.g., footage showing workers pulling fur from screaming Angora rabbits). Relatedly, *meaning-based sensebreaking* broke viewers' perception of an issue by linking two domains that were generally thought to be unrelated in meaning (e.g., showing women on a dance floor exposing milk-dripping breasts which look like cow udders).

We also identified a variety of bridging elements in videos that resonated with existing viewer desires, values or sentiments. We called this "sensebridging" and found that bridging elements had patterns. One group of videos sought to appeal

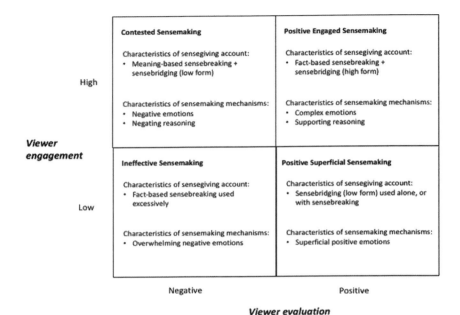

Fig. 1. Four Modes of Sensegiving and Sensemaking for Highly Disruptive Issues.

to viewers' interests in sex. Another appealed to shared higher values such as loyalty, justice, and tenderness toward children. We labeled the former *low forms of sensebridging*, and the latter *high forms of sensebridging*. Teasing out these differences allowed us to see that distinct accounts, or certain combinations of accounts, were linked to different modes of viewer sensemaking. By linking steps 1 and 2, we inductively established four modes of sensegiving and sensemaking of highly disruptive issues (see Fig. 1). The first two steps of our analysis addressed our first research question.

In the third step, we coded viewer comments to identify sensemaking mechanisms in each mode of sensegiving and sensemaking (see Fig. 1). In order to distill the predominant mechanism of sensemaking, we focused on what the commentator was saying in entirety and tried to capture the overall tone of his or her comment (Toubiana & Zietsma, 2016).

Most codes were highly emotive, and we developed three categories – "negative emotions," "positive emotions," and a much smaller, third, category for comments expressing both negative and positive emotions. Examples of negative emotions included "feeling sad," "feeling shocked or disgusted," "feeling angry," "feeling shameful," "feeling helpless," etc. Examples of positive emotions comprised "feeling motivated," "feeling hopeful," "feeling compassionate," etc. A comment containing both negative and positive emotions can be illustrated with the following:

Can someone stop this madness? I'm crying. Poor animals? What have they done to deserve this? NOTHING!!!!!!! They have feelings, they have a soul. They deserve better!!! so much better. this is so horrible. I just want to go and help all those poor horses and take them with me back to Norway. (Comment for video "Horse Racing Exposed: Drugs and Death")

While the first half of the comment expressed negative emotions including feeling sad and feeling angry, the latter half contained the positive emotion of feeling motivated to take actions (to help the horses).

In addition to emotions, we also identified cognitive mechanisms. We identified two predominant mechanisms: "judging" and "layering." "Judging" concerned making an explicit judgment, for instance, "That's abuse." "Layering" was more subtle and concerned offering additional layers of meaning that would expand and enrich the video message. The following is an example of "layering":

> I've known how animals were slaughtered since grade school ... I went with my parent's to Mcdonalds (for the WiFi basically and didn't eat) and while my parents scarfed down cheeseburgers I had the image of them grabbing flesh out of a hole in a cows chest like zombies devouring a human. (Comment for video "Peter Dinklage: Face Your Food")

Importantly, both "judging" and "layering" can either negate or support the message conveyed in the video. By looking across our codes for emotions and cognitions, we identified patterns in each of the four modes of sensegiving and sensemaking. Consequently, the third analytical step addressed our second research question.

FINDINGS: SENSEMAKING OF HIGHLY DISRUPTIVE ISSUES

We identified four types of sensegiving accounts that PETA used to convey highly disruptive issues of animal rights, including *fact-based sensebreaking*, *meaning-based sensebreaking*, *low forms of sensebridging*, and *high forms of sensebridging*. In some videos, PETA used these accounts alone, but it was also common to blend two types of accounts in one video. We related these accounts, in pure or blended forms, with viewer sensemaking, in terms of whether viewers positively or negatively evaluated the sense being given and how engaged they were. The outcome of this process was a typology that captured four modes of sensegiving and sensemaking of highly disruptive issues. Below, we explain each mode and the emotional and cognitive arousals (sensemaking mechanisms) related with each mode.

Positive Engaged Sensemaking

In this mode, viewers' collective evaluation was positive and engagement level high. Sensegiving tended to be a combination of *fact-based sensebreaking* and *high forms of sensebridging*. Viewer comments demonstrated both positive and negative emotions as well as cognitive responses. We illustrate this combination with a video in which actor Alec Baldwin called for boycotting circuses that use animals.

Sensegiving Account
This video used undercover footage to break viewers' existing perception of circuses (i.e., fact-based sensebreaking). Baldwin's explanations of animal abuse

are accompanied by footage showing, for example, terrified baby elephants being slammed to the ground and shocked with electric prods, circus elephants lining up with a trainer repeatedly hitting them, and elephants being hit repeatedly in the face. Dramatic sound effects include trainers shouting: "Tear that off! Make them scream!," "When he starts squirming too f—ing much..," and "... Hurt them!"

The video richly uses high forms of sensebridging. For example, viewers are shown an elephant family roaming in the wild with Baldwin explaining "the bond between these animals is strong and females spend their entire lives with their mothers." These images resonate because they resemble the free life we all cherish. The frequent use of the images of baby elephants also resonates as general viewers are expected to care about children. Alternatively, baby elephants may evoke the image of an endearing pet. Also in this video, "Dr. Mel Richardson, Veterinarian with 40 years of experience with elephants," claims that allowing careless treatment of elephants in circuses is "absolutely inappropriate for the American people." The opinion of an expert and the reference to the American people (and their values) constitutes high forms of sensebridging as well.

Sensemaking Mechanisms

Baldwin's sensegiving account elicited both emotional and cognitive responses. Negative emotions included three types: 1) *feeling sad*: "I couldn't bear to watch it," or "This is very sad"; 2) *feeling disgusted or shocked*: "Good god this is sickening," "Horrendous!!!!," or "I had no idea this type of abuse goes on"; 3) *feeling angry*: "I'd love to see the same done to those heartless 'trainers'!"

Viewers also demonstrated two positive emotions: (1) *feeling motivated:* "We need to ban circuses," or "Because Animals can't defend themselves – That's why we're here" and (2) *feeling enthusiastic*: "Well said Alec!," or "Good for him! That's what we need to help stop animal torture.... CELEBRITIES!." Sometimes, the same comment contained both negative and positive emotions. For instance, "This is sick and I never dreamed all this went on. I want the elephants to go back to Africa where they can roam free."

We also identified significant cognitive mechanisms of judging and layering. (1) *judging*: "This should be outlawed," or, "People need to stop abusing animals for entertainment" and (2) *"layering"*: examples included personal reflections such as the following:

> I own horses and have raised many from birth. I have never needed to inflict pain during my training .... Instead I develop a loving bond where my animals know I will never hurt them. Once they understand this they will do anything for me. What I don't understand is this: these huge animals when in the wild would kill a human so why don't these animals fight back and hurt of kill the people...?

Layering also included attempts to follow up on the video message for issue solutions:

> [...] getting celebrities involved. Just think of how much good they could do if they would get behind stopping the torture and killing of animals in China and other countries ....

In sum, the sensemaking mechanisms associated with *positive engaged sensemaking* were characterized by a complex range of negative and positive emotions as well as active cognitive processing that concurred on the video message.

Positive Superficial Sensemaking

In this mode, viewers made positive evaluations of issues but displayed low levels of engagement. Low forms of sensebridging constituted the predominant sensegiving account. It was sometimes mixed with a small amount of undercover footage (fact-based sensebreaking). We use the PETA video "Model Vida Guerra's naked photo shoot" to unpack this mode of sensemaking.

Sensegiving Account
The video shows behind-the-scene footage of Vida's photo shoot "Spice up your life," including footage of her talking to the camera about vegetarianism. The video shows Vida lying naked on top of a bed of hot chilies, with close-ups of her breasts and legs, and showing her face with a pepper seductively placed in her mouth. When Vida mentions PETA's anti-fur campaign, viewers were shown undercover footage including a fox in a cage and a fox being struck repeatedly on the head. Overall, the video is dominated by sexy images of a naked Vida on hot chilies from various angles.

Sensemaking Mechanisms
Viewer sensemaking was characterized by positive emotions. Unlike *positive engaged sensemaking* in which viewers felt motivated, enthusiastic, or compassionate, two emotions displayed here were superficial in terms of engagement with the core message from the video: (1) *feeling (superficially) excited*: "She so right," "Great video! We just started showing the hot legs and feet...," or "If I wasn't vegan, I would now...Dammmm she's sexy" and (2) *feeling humorous*: "Veggies alone did not grow that sweet ass Vida, cmon now," or "You crushing the chilies!! Those poor, poor chilies..."

There were occasions when cognitive mechanisms of judging and layering seemed to take place, but they were often irrelevant to the message the video intended to convey. Examples included sexist judgments (e.g., "she looks old now").

Overall, the dominant characteristic of sensemaking in this mode seemed to include positive, but superficial, emotions with limited cognitive processing of the focal message.

Contested Sensemaking

In this mode, viewers were highly engaged but negatively evaluated the video. Typical sensegiving accounts were meaning-based sensebreaking combined with low forms of sensebridging. We use the video "Milk gone wild" to unpack this mode of sensemaking.

Sensegiving Account
The video breaks viewers' perception of milk by showing milk being produced in an apparently unrelated scene, that is, women on the dance floor. The video appeals to general viewers' interests in sex, though its intention is to disrupt the meaning of "milk." It shows a group of young women wearing small tops, dancing in a club. One woman lifts up her shirt to reveal what looks like cow's udders, and then quickly covers back up. Another woman does the same. Five women are on stage with their tops up and one is taking hers off while guys are heard hooting and hollering at them. Then, a man is sprayed with milk as he is yelling. Another man is on the floor with milk all in his mouth and over his body.

Sensemaking Mechanisms
Viewer comments were dominated by one negative emotion: *feeling disgusted*. For examples: "That's awful and milk isn't from women," "that's just gross," "awful and very disgusting," and "No ... Bad PETA. No Oh GOD."

Cognitive reactions were largely about *negatively judging* the video message: "There is nothing you can eat that doesn't involve eating animals. Nothing. Nothing," or "I'm glad this video has the dislikes it deserves. My faith in humanity is restored."

There were some simple positive emotions (e.g., "Love this!!!") and one occasion of *layering* ("To show how gross it is to drink cow's milk. Their milk isn't for us, it's for their babies"). But overall, contested sensemaking featured negative emotions and negating reasoning.

Ineffective Sensemaking

This type of sensemaking was ineffective because viewers displayed a low degree of engagement and also evaluated the message negatively. Typical accounts exclusively and excessively used undercover footage (fact-based sensebreaking). We use the video entitled "Dogs killed for leather" to unpack this mode of sensemaking.

Sensegiving Account
This video intends to break viewers' perception of "leather gloves, belts ... and other accessories" by linking these everyday items with inhumane practices. It shows workers in a Chinese slaughterhouse grab one terrified, yelping dog after another with metal pinchers before bashing them over the head with a wooden pole, rendering some unconscious but leaving others to writhe in agony. Workers cut dogs' throats and drain their blood before throwing their bodies onto a pile. Some of the dogs are still alive and struggling. Screams from the dogs can be heard in the background.

Sensemaking Mechanisms
Viewers displayed three intense negative emotions: (1) *feeling upset*: "I can't really finish watching this video. It hurts me," or "I feel really sad after watching this";

(2) *feeling shocked*: "I ... I don't know what to say...," or "This is the most shocking dog abuse video I've ever seen"; and (3) *feeling angry*: "Fuck people that support this shit," "These people are some of the most disgusting, vile creatures on Earth ... Let them rot in jail ...," or "wtf? They do that and they go home and play with kids?" On one occasion a viewer blamed China: "I really hate China!!! The Chinese people are so cruel!" But for most viewers, the anger was so overwhelming it intermingled with a shameful feeling toward the entire human race. (4) *Feeling shameful*: "The human being is the most insidious and evil creature of God :(, " "I just threw up. Fuck the human race," or "Who the hell would buy this kind of 'leather'? Oh wait, idiots and about 90% of the human population...yeah that pretty much sums up humanity."

To summarize, ineffective sensemaking was characterized by overwhelming negative emotions with limited cognitive processing.

DISCUSSION

We studied micro-episodes of PETA's interactions with a wide audience on highly disruptive issues. Such issues call for fundamental re-interpretation of aspects of society and impose profound moral challenges to people. Limited work has explored micro-processes of how such issues were conveyed to, and processed by, societal members. By investigating these micro-level processes, our study makes contributions to NIT and sensemaking.

Contribution to the Microfoundations of Institutions

We contribute to NIT by explicating micro-processes that are linked to macro-institutional phenomena (Cardinale, 2018; Raaijmakers, Vermeulen, Meeus, & Zietsma, 2015). Positive and engaged sensemaking points to potential transformational change, and we identified pathways to this mode of sensemaking. Our results indicated that sensegiving accounts solely containing disturbing raw truths (in our case, footage of animal cruelty) led to *ineffective sensemaking*. The audience was overwhelmed with negative emotions that drove out cognitive reasoning and lowered engagement. These accounts also elicited negative evaluations, despite the unequivocal material evidence presented to the audience.

Research has pointed out that frames need to resonate with the audience to get their attention, engagement and positive evaluation (Giorgi, 2017; Giorgi & Weber, 2015; Snow, Rochford, Worden, & Benford, 1986). In contrast, we found that not all resonance leads to *positive engaged sensemaking*. In our case, when the institutional entrepreneur leverages people's interests in sexual images to establish resonance, the audience evaluated the sensegiving accounts positively but their engagement was low. *Positive but superficial sensemaking* does not promise a path to transformational change.

Our findings further illustrated that when the accounts appealed to the audience on commonly shared higher values such as loyalty, justice, and tenderness toward children, the audience was willing to engage with disrupting raw facts and they were likely to positively evaluate the message. These blended accounts presented hard facts to the audience, on one hand, and deployed high-forms of resonating elements, on the other hand. While the former elicited negative emotions such as anger, disgust, or sadness, the latter evoked positive emotions (e.g., feeling motivated) and stimulated cognitive efforts – the audience actively *judged* the message and *layered* it with additional meanings. This leads to the mode of *positive engaged sensemaking* which is a most desirable pathway for the audience members to make transformational change. One illustration is PETA's use of undercover footage from fur farms in China. An earlier video ("China fur trade exposed in 60 seconds") exclusively used such footage, showing dogs beaten in the head and skinned alive. This video generated *ineffective sensemaking*. A later video blended similar footage with high-forms of sensebridging: actress Olivia Munn started the video by saying:

> [a]s a proud person of Chinese decent it broke my heart to learn just how terribly animals suffer and die on Chinese fur farms and there are no penalties for this abuse. Please join me in taking a look at where most of the world's fur originates....

By contexualizing disturbing footage with meanings of justice and compassion, this video scored very high in viewer engagement and evaluation. Videos in the mode of *positive engaged sensemaking* consistently showed the characteristics of blending fact-based sensebreaking with high-forms of sensebridging.

Correspondingly, a key insight from our study is to elaborate the role of sensebridging in conveying disrupting truth. We empirically distinguished low forms and high forms of sensebridging, showing that in order to orient an audience to the path of transformational change the institutional entrepreneur needs to establish resonance in the audience with high forms of values and sentiments, as opposed to using sex appeal or other low-form equivalents.

We focused on micro-mechanisms, but our findings have implications for macro-level change. It is well understood that micro-moments have a cumulative effects on macro-structures (Haack et al., 2019). In our case, sensemaking via public spaces such as YouTube is likely to shape collective appraisals of events. We found that emotions were prominent mechanisms for making sense of highly disruptive issues. Research suggests that emotional contagion takes place in groups small (e.g., project teams) or large (e.g., demographic groups); with every sharing of an emotion, the appraisal of the event that elicited the emotion is also transmitted (Menges & Kilduff, 2015). Although we did not directly study emotional contagion, our results provide insights into how micro-level sensemaking processes may shape, or fail to shape, collective appraisals of institutions.

We make an additional contribution to NIT by using multimodal texts to explore institutional processes. Recent conceptual work suggests that visual texts tend to stimulate engagement and generate emotional responses which override cognitive processing (Meyer et al., 2017). We empirically extended this insight. Using multimodal texts (i.e., video content that included verbal, visual, and audio texts), we inductively identified distinct sensegiving accounts and explicated their varied effects on viewers of those texts. For example, we found visual (and audio) texts of animal abuse indeed incited powerful emotional responses. We further found that when used alone and excessively, disturbing visual texts led to over-whelmingly negative emotions that blocked viewers from processing the core message; but similar texts, when combined with verbal and visual texts of high-forms of sensebriding, generated complex emotional and cognitive processes that encouraged the audience to process the message delivered by the institutional entrepreneur. Future research needs to further explore blended use of multimodal texts during institutional interactions.

Contribution to Sensemaking

We introduced a grounded typology of four modes of sensegiving and sensemak-ing of highly disruptive issues. In studying the sensemaking process of social issues that are steeped in institutional practices and meanings, we contribute to the sensemaking literature by adding an "explicit account of...the embeddedness of sensemaking in social space and time" (Weber & Glynn 2006, p. 1639). In our study, hard truths alone failed to prompt effective sensemaking. Such truths drastically broke down existing meanings of modern institutional life (such as the meaning of meat, milk, wool, and leather belts), eliciting overwhelming negative emotions, such as felt shame toward the human race (Creed et al., 2014). These intense emotions seemed to "paralyze" the audience when they were given noth-ing to reconstruct meanings. We further showed that when the sensegiver con-textualized hard facts with inspiring institutional meanings (i.e., high forms of sensebridging), the audience responded with complex emotions and active cogni-tive processing. Vogus, Rothman, Sutcliff, and Weick (2014) proposed that a joint feeling of negative and positive emotions signals that an environment is both safe and problematic, making individuals more receptive to alternative perspectives. Our study resonates with their proposition. We add to it by suggesting which sensegiving accounts may instigate complex emotional states, and we provide evi-dence that such a state of feeling indeed leads to *positive engaged sensemaking*. Accordingly, sensemaking does not happen in a meaning void; sensegivers must package "naked truth" with inspiring institutional elements with which the audi-ence can reconstruct meanings. This explains why it is important to distinguish low- and high-forms of sensebridging. Despite the fact that both forms of sense-bridging resonate with the audience and lead to positive evaluations, only high-forms of sensebridging provide generative materials that inspire the audience to develop new meanings.

Limitations and Boundary Conditions

We drew on a small sample of videos and our findings are explorative. While sample sizes in *positive engaged sensemaking* and *positive superficial sensemaking* were fairly robust, they were small in *contested sensemaking* and *ineffective sense-making*. We addressed this issue by examining PETA videos beyond the top 30 list. After developing the constructs and their relations from our sample, we com-pared how our initial findings aligned with other similar PETA videos. This step validated our initial findings, but studies with larger samples are clearly needed to further augment this line of research.

Another limitation concerns data from online forums. License holders of YouTube channels can delete offensive comments. In our case, PETA likely did so to some videos; for example, comments for one video with footage of extreme animal cruelty were disabled. In the other 29 videos, we found a variety of negative and positive comments. Despite a lack of total control over social media data, we believe they still provide valuable insights that otherwise would be inaccessible to researchers (Kozinets, 2010).

Our study can be generalized to audiences similar to YouTube users: individuals representative of the general demographics of Internet users that are largely untrained on animal issues. Extant research suggests that issue specialists focus on empirical evidence rather than sweeping claims, applying clear criteria and knowledge to rationally assess a specific claim (Crilly, Hansen, & Zollo, 2015). It has also been demonstrated that organizational leaders or officials are less prone to emotional expressions than average members (Toubiana & Zietsma, 2016). We therefore anticipate different sensemaking patterns for audiences distinct from average YouTube users. Examples of such audiences may include regulators, veterinarians, and academics, who are well trained on issues and who by profession would favor cognitive, over emotional, processing of sensegiving accounts.

ACKNOWLEDGMENTS

We gratefully acknowledge the insightful guidance of Editor Jost Sieweke and one reviewer. We also thank PETA employees in Los Angeles and Norfolk for their generative comments and insights. This chapter is part of a larger project on PETA. We gratefully acknowledge helpful comments from Marlys Christianson, Sally Maitlis, Mike Pratt, and Tim Vogus on an earlier version of a manuscript from the project. We acknowledge with gratitude the financial support provided by the Ivey Business School, Canada. The authors declare no potential conflicts of interest with respect to the research, authorship, and/or publication of this chapter.

REFERENCES

Bartunek, J. M., Balogun, J., & Do, B. (2011). Considering planned change anew: Stretching large group interventions strategically, emotionally, and meaningfully. *The Academy of Management Annals*, 5(1), 1–52. doi:10.1080/19416520.2011.567109

Battilana, J., Leca, B., & Boxenbaum, E. (2009). How actors change institutions: Towards a theory of institutional entrepreneurship. *The Academy of Management Annals*, 3(1), 65–107. doi:10.1080/19416520903053598

Bitektine, A., & Haack, P. (2015). The "macro" and the "micro" of legitimacy: Toward a multilevel theory of the legitimacy process. *Academy of Management Review*, 40(1), 49–75. doi:10.5465/amr.2013.0318

Cardinale, I. (2018). Beyond constraining and enabling: Toward new microfoundations for institutional theory. *Academy of Management Review*, 43(1), 132–155. doi:10.5465/amr.2015.0020

Christianson, M. K. (2019). More and less effective updating: The role of trajectory management in making sense again. *Administrative Science Quarterly, 64*(1), 45–86. doi:10.1177/0001839217750856

Clemens, E. S. (1993). Organizational repertoires and institutional change: Women's groups and the transformation of U.S. politics, 1890–1920. *American Journal of Sociology, 98*(4), 755–798.

Clemens, E. S. (1997). *The people's lobby: Organizational innovation and the rise of interest group politics in the United States, 1890–1925*. Chicago, IL: University of Chicago Press.

Connolly, K. (2002). German animals given legal rights *The Guardian*, June 22. Retrieved from https://www.theguardian.com/world/2002/jun/22/germany.animalwelfare

Cornelissen, J. P. (2012). Sensemaking under pressure: The influence of professional roles and social accountability on the creation of sense. *Organization Science, 23*(1), 118–137. doi:10.1287/orsc.1100.0640

Cornelissen, J. P., Mantere, S., & Vaara, E. (2014). The contraction of meaning: The combined effect of communication, emotions, and materiality on sensemaking in the stockwell shooting. *Journal of Management Studies, 51*(5), 699–736. doi:10.1111/joms.12073

Cornelissen, J. P., & Werner, M. D. (2014). Putting framing in perspective: A review of framing and frame analysis across the management and organizational literature. *The Academy of Management Annals, 8*(1), 181–235. doi:10.1080/19416520.2014.875669

Creed, D. W. E., Hudson, B. A., Okhuysen, G. A., & Smith-Crowe, K. (2014). Swimming in a sea of shame: Incorporating emotion into explanation of institutional reproduction and change. *Academy of Management Review, 39*(3), 275–301. doi:10.5465/amr.2012.0074

Crilly, D., Hansen, M., & Zollo, M. (2015). The grammar of decoupling: A cognitive-linguistic perspective on firms' sustainability claims and stakeholders' interpretation. *Academy of Management Journal, 59*(2), 705–729. doi:10.5465/amj.2015.0171

de Rond, M., & Lok, J. (2016). Some things can never be unseen: The role of context in psychological injury at war. *Academy of Management Journal, 59*(6), 1965–1993. doi:10.5465/amj.2015.0681

Descola, P. (2013). *The ecology of others*. Chicago, IL: University of Chicago Press.

Dutton, W. (2013). *Internet studies: The foundations of a transformative field*. Oxford: Oxford University Press.

Felin, T., Foss, N. J., & Ployhart, R. E. (2015). The microfoundations movement in strategy and organization theory. *The Academy of Management Annals, 9*(1), 575–632. doi:10.1080/19416520.2015.1007651

Gioia, D. A., & Chittipeddi, K. (1991). Sensemaking and sensegiving in strategic change initiation. *Strategic Management Journal, 12*(6), 433–448.

Giorgi, S. (2017). The mind and heart of resonance: The role of cognition and emotions in frame effectiveness. *Journal of Management Studies, 54*(5), 711–738. doi:doi:10.1111/joms.12278

Giorgi, S., & Weber, K. (2015). Marks of distinction: Framing and audience appreciation in the context of investment advice. *Administrative Science Quarterly, 60*(2), 333–367. doi:10.1177/0001839215571125

Haack, P., Sieweke, J., & Wessel, L. (2019). Microfoundations and Multi-level Research on Institutions. In P. Haack, J. Sieweke, & L. Wessel (Eds.), *Microfoundations of Institutions (Research in the Sociology of Organizations*, Vol. 65A, pp. 11–40). Bingley: Emerald Publishing.

Harmon, D. (2018). When the Fed speaks: Arguments, emotions, and the microfoundations of institutions. *Administrative Science Quarterly, 64*(3), 542–575. doi:10.1177/0001839218777475

Harmon, D., Haack, P., & Roulet, T. J. (2018). Microfoundations of institutions: A matter of structure vs. agency or level of analysis? *Academy of Management Review, 44*(2), 464–467. doi:10.5465/amr.2018.0080

Jasper, J. M., & Nelkin, D. (2007). The animal rights crusade. In J. M. Henslin (Ed.), *Life in society* (pp. 225–232). Boston, MA: Pearson.

Jasper, J. M., & Poulsen, J. (1993). Fighting back: Vulnerabilities, blunders, and countermobilization by the targets in three animal rights campaigns. *Sociological Forum, 8*(4), 639–657. doi:10.1007/bf01115215

King, M. D., & Haveman, H. A. (2008). Antislavery in America: The press, the pulpit, and the rise of antislavery societies. *Administrative Science Quarterly, 53*(3), 492–528.

Kozinets, R. V. (2010). *Netnography: Doing ethnographic research online*. Los Angeles, CA: Sage Publications.

Lawrence, T. B. (2017). High-stakes institutional translation: Establishing North America's first government-sanctioned supervised injection site. *Academy of Management Journal, 60*(5), 1771–1800. doi:10.5465/amj.2015.0714

Lawrence, T. B., & Suddaby, R. (2006). Institutions and institutional work. In S. R. Clegg, C. Hardy, T. B. Lawrence, & W. Nord (Eds.), *The Sage handbook of organization studies* (pp. 215–254). London: Sage Publications.

Maitlis, S., & Christianson, M. (2014). Sensemaking in organizations: Taking stock and moving forward. *Academy of Management Annals*, 8(1), 57–125.

Maitlis, S., & Sonenshein, S. (2010). Sensemaking in crisis and hange: Inspiration and insights from Weick (1988). *Journal of Management Studies*, 47(3), 551–580.

Maitlis, S., Vogus, T. J., & Lawrence, T. B. (2013). Sensemaking and emotion in organizations. *Organizational Psychology Review*, 3(3), 222–247. doi:10.1177/2041386613489062

Massa, F. G., Helms, W. S., Voronov, M., & Liang, W. (2017). Emotions uncorked: Inspiring evangelism for the emerging practice of cool-climate winemaking in Ontario. *Academy of Management Journal*, 60(2), 461–499. doi:10.5465/amj.2014.0092

Menges, J. I., & Kilduff, M. (2015). Group emotions: Cutting the Gordian knots concerning terms, levels of analysis, and processes. *The Academy of Management Annals*, 9(1), 845–928. doi:10.1080/19416520.2015.1033148

Meyer, R. E., Jancsary, D., Höllerer, M. A., & Boxenbaum, E. (2017). The role of verbal and visual text in the process of institutionalization. *Academy of Management Review*, 43(3), 392–418. doi:10.5465/amr.2014.0301

Monin, P., Noorderhaven, N., Vaara, E., & Kroon, D. (2013). Giving sense to and making sense of justice in postmerger integration. *Academy of Management Journal*, 56(1), 256–284. doi:10.5465/amj.2010.0727

Patriotta, G., & Gruber, D. A. (2015). Newsmaking and sensemaking: Navigating temporal transitions between planned and unexpected events. *Organization Science*, 26(6), 1574–1592. doi:10.1287/orsc.2015.1005

Phillips, N., Lawrence, T. B., & Hardy, C. (2004). Discourse and institutions. *The Academy of Management Review*, 29(4), 635–652. doi:10.2307/20159075

Powell, W., & Rerup, C. (2017). Opening the black box: Micro-foundations of institutional theory. In R. Greenwood, C. Oliver, K. Sahlin-Andersson, & R. Suddaby (Eds.), *The SAGE handbook of organizational institutionalism* (2nd ed., pp. 311–337). Thousand Oaks, CA: Sage Publications.

Pratt, M. G. (2000). The good, the bad, and the ambivalent: Managing identification among amway distributors. *Administrative Science Quarterly*, 45(3), 456–493.

Purser, R. E., Park, C., & Montuori, A. (1995). Limits to anthropocentrism: Toward an ecocentric organization paradigm? *Academy of Management Review*, 20(4), 1053–1089. doi:10.5465/amr.1995.9512280035

Raaijmakers, A. G. M., Vermeulen, P. A. M., Meeus, M. T. H., & Zietsma, C. (2015). I need time! Exploring pathways to compliance under institutional complexity. *Academy of Management Journal*, 58(1), 85–110. doi:10.5465/amj.2011.0276

Regan, T. (1986). A case for animal rights. In M. W. Fox & L. D. Mickley (Eds.), *Advances in animal welfare science* (pp. 179–189). Washington, DC: The Humane Society of the United States.

Sandberg, J., & Tsoukas, H. (2015). Making sense of the sensemaking perspective: Its constituents, limitations, and opportunities for further development. *Journal of Organizational Behavior*, 36(S6-S32). doi:10.1002/job.1937

Schabram, K., & Maitlis, S. (2017). Negotiating the challenges of a calling: Emotion and enacted sensemaking in animal shelter work. *Academy of Management Journal*, 60(2), 584–609. doi:10.5465/amj.2013.0665

Singer, P. (1995). *Animal liberation*. London: Random House.

Smith, W. J. (2012). *A rat is a pig is a dog is a boy: The human cost of the animal rights movement*. New York, NY: Encounter Books.

Snow, D. A., Rochford, E. B., Jr, Worden, S. K., & Benford, R. D. (1986). Frame alignment processes, micromobilization, and movement participation. *American Sociological Review*, 51(4), 464–481.

Strauss, A., & Corbin, J. (1998). *Basics of qualitative research: Techniques and procedures for developing grounded theory*. Thousand Oaks, CA: Sage Publications.

Strike, V. M., & Rerup, C. (2016). Mediated sensemaking. *Academy of Management Journal*, 59(3), 880–905.

Toubiana, M., & Zietsma, C. (2016). The message is on the wall? Emotions, social media and the dynamics of institutional complexity. *Academy of Management Journal, 60*(3), 922–953. doi:10.5465/amj.2014.0208

Vogus, T., J., Rothman, N., B., Sutcliffe, K., M., & Weick, K., E. (2014). The affective foundations of high-reliability organizing. *Journal of Organizational Behavior, 35*(4), 592–596. doi:10.1002/job.1922

Voronov, M., & Vince, R. (2012). Integrating emotions into the analysis of institutional work. *Academy of Management Review, 37*(1), 58–81. doi:10.5465/armr.2010.0247

Voronov, M., & Weber, K. (2015). The heart of institutions: Emotional competence and institutional actorhood. *Academy of Management Review, 41*(3), 456–478. doi:10.5465/amr.2013.0458

Weber, K., & Glynn, M. A. (2006). Making sense with institutions: Context, thought and action in Karl Weick's theory. *Organization Studies, 27*(11), 1639–1660.

Weick, K. E. (1993). The collapse of sensemaking in organizations: The Mann Gulch disaster. *Administrative Science Quarterly, 38*(4), 628–652.

Whelan, G., & Gond, J.-P. (2016). Meat your enemy: Animal rights, alignment, and radical change. *Journal of Management Inquiry, 26*(2), 123–138. doi:10.1177/1056492616671828

Zietsma, C., & Toubiana, M. (2018). The valuable, the constitutive, and the energetic: Exploring the impact and importance of studying emotions and institutions. *Organization Studies, 39*(4), 427–443. doi:10.1177/0170840617751008

CHAPTER 9

CONNECTING THE TREE TO THE RAINFOREST: EXAMINING THE MICROFOUNDATIONS OF INSTITUTIONS WITH CULTURAL CONSENSUS THEORY

Joshua Keller

ABSTRACT

The author introduces cultural consensus theory as a theoretical and methodological tool for examining the microfoundations of institutions by linking variance in individuals' micro-level conditions with cross-level variance in individuals' adoption of macro-level socially constructed knowledge. The author describes the theory and methods, which include the use of cultural and subcultural congruence as cross-level variables. The author then provides an illustrative example of the theory and methods' application for studying institutions, incorporating primary survey data of US-based ethics and compliance officers (ECOs). Results of the survey revealed variance in ECOs' level of congruence associated with their direct communication with executives, their experience implementing ethics practices, and their educational background. Finally, the author discusses additional ways to use this approach for researching the microfoundations of institutions.

Keywords: Microfoundations; institutions; cultural consensus theory; agency methodology; corporate ethics practices; multi-level

Microfoundations of Institutions
Research in the Sociology of Organizations, Volume 65A, 197–215
Copyright © 2020 by Emerald Publishing Limited
All rights of reproduction in any form reserved
ISSN: 0733-558X/doi:10.1108/S0733-558X2019000065A019

INTRODUCTION

There is wide acceptance among scholars that institutions operate at multiple levels of analyses, from the individual to the organization to the field to the society (Bitektine & Haack, 2015; Gehman, Lounsbury, & Greenwood, 2016; Harmon, Haack, & Roulet, 2018; Jepperson & Meyer, 2011; Powell & Rerup, 2017). How to decipher the relationships between the various levels of analyses, however, remains a question that is fraught with debate (Cardinale, 2018b; Harmon et al., 2018). Much of the debate centers on how much agency individuals have in adopting and transforming institutions (Abdelnour, Hasselbladh, & Kallinikos, 2017). Some scholars have looked at individuals' experience on the ground to demonstrate they have agency to transform macro-institutions through purposive actions (Battilana, Leca, & Boxenbaum, 2009; Garud, Hardy, & Maguire, 2007; McPherson & Sauder, 2013) or day-to-day routines (Jarzabkowski, 2008; Powell & Rerup, 2017; Smets & Jarzabkowski, 2013; Spee, Jarzabkowski, & Smets, 2016). However, other institutional scholars argue that even individuals engaged in purposive actions on the ground have a predisposed approach to agency (Jepperson & Meyer, 2011) and day-to-day practice (Cardinale, 2018a) that is shaped by macro-institutions. Consequently, while most institutional scholars agree that individuals are neither "cultural dopes" nor "heroic change agents" (e.g., Powell & Colyvas, 2008; Powell & Rerup, 2017), the question of how much agency remains a "chicken vs. egg" debate.

One underlying cause of this "chicken vs. egg" debate, which I address here, is the limited empirical scope of microfoundation studies, which primarily focus on individuals' cognitions, emotions, and actions within specific spatiotemporal contexts. While focusing on the ground provides insight on individuals' relationship with institutions and the micro-level processes that facilitate institutional adoption and transformation, two critical issues limit the approach's capacity to delineate the various micro and macro-factors that enable or constrain agency. One issue arises because micro-level instantiations of macro-structures include both cultural and socio-structural elements (Abdelnour et al., 2017), and focused attention on the specific spatiotemporal context limits our capacity to disentangle the two elements. For example, when an MBA student has a socially constructed worldview and social ties to a community that shares a similar worldview, it is difficult to assess which element is enabling or constraining the student's agency without comparing both the thoughts and social experiences of other MBA students. A second issue arises because macro-level aggregations of socially constructed knowledge are pluralistic and fragmented (Kraatz & Block, 2008; Thornton, Ocasio, & Lounsbury, 2012). Micro-level processes that form socially constructed knowledge within a particular spatiotemporal context may not necessarily translate across other contexts (Ocasio, Loewenstein, & Nigam, 2015). For example, an MBA student may alter the worldviews of her classmates through participating in a sustainability program, but the same processes may not translate across other schools and hence may limit the aggregation of the student's agency in the institution transformation process. This empirical approach, therefore, limits our capacity to disentangle either the micro-level instantiations of structure or the macro-level aggregations of agency.

To transcend the empirical limitations of focusing on the ground when addressing the micro-level instantiations of macro-level structures and the macro-level aggregations of micro-level agency, I propose that more research incorporates a variance-based cross-level empirical approach (Klein, Tosi, & Cannella, 1999; Kozlowski & Klein, 2000; Rousseau, 1985). This approach focuses on variance in individuals' relationship to macro-level patterns. Rather than conceptualizing an individual as a tree within a single-specie forest, thus assuming that the individual represents the collective, I propose conceptualizing the individual as a tree within a grove within a larger rainforest – a forest that comprises an interconnected ecosystem of multiple species with varying levels of access to water, sun, soil, and animals. Analogously, I conceptualize macro-institutions as heterogeneously distributed forms of knowledge that are socially constructed within interconnected yet varying micro-contexts with varying micro-instantiations of socio-structural conditions. The interplay between the micro- and the macro-contexts enable or constrain agency in multiple ways. This approach shifts our attention from questions about *how* micro-contexts are associated with institutions to questions about *which* micro-contexts are associated with *which* components of institutions and to *what degree*.

My proposed approach, however, requires a conceptual vocabulary and set of methodological tools that, on the one hand, recognize the socially constructed foundation of institutions (Berger & Luckmann, 1967), while, on the other hand, enable us to capture variance associated with the social construction and its relationship to socio-structural conditions. The concept of "taken-for-grantedness," which is often used to refer to cultural-cognitive based institutionalization (e.g., Tolbert & Zucker, 1983), is a particularly insufficient indicator of variance because "taken-for-grantedness" only arises after individuals across the environment no longer recognize any alternative to their constructed reality (Canales, 2016; Dacin, Goodstein, & Scott, 2002). This makes it difficult to assess individual-level variance in "taken-for-grantedness" as it assumes that others share the same perception. "Institutional logics" has been more explicitly defined as a multi-level concept with a capacity to include pluralism in its application (Thornton et al., 2012), but does not have an easily discernible associated variance-based concept. In other words, individuals can have access to one or more logics, but it is difficult to assess what it means if someone has access "to a degree."

CULTURAL CONSENSUS THEORY

To provide a vocabulary and associated set of methods that enable variance-based cross-level examinations into the microfoundations of institutions, I turn to CCT, which is a theoretical and empirical framework that was originally developed by cognitive anthropologists to address a similar set of issues (e.g., Romney, Batchelder, & Weller, 1987; Romney & Moore, 1998; Romney, Weller, & Batchelder, 1986). Cognitive anthropologists recognized that knowledge was culturally conditioned, which was a view of knowledge that was ontologically analogous to a socially constructed view of knowledge found in sociological work (e.g., Berger & Luckmann, 1967). At the same time, they also wrestled with the question of how to determine ontologically "what is culturally true," as they wanted to assess the viability of individual informant's cultural knowledge as a "true" representation of the collective's socially constructed views. In response, they concluded that knowledge should be considered to be "culturally true" when there was consensus across informants, and thus they developed a set of associated methods to determine whether, in fact, there was consensus. CCT research has since expanded across other domains, including the study of organizations (e.g., Keller & Loewenstein, 2011; Liu, Keller, & Hong, 2014; Loewenstein & Mueller, 2016) and organizational levels (e.g., Borgatti & Carboni, 2007; Lahneman, 2015).

A major component of CCT research recognizes that cultural knowledge is distributed heterogeneously, even when an overall consensus has been reached. They recognize that some informants are more likely to be considered "cultural experts" because their views and beliefs are more representative of the overall culture (Medin, Ross, Atran, Burnett, & Blok, 2002). Others, due to a lack of competency, opportunity, or interest, are less likely to have beliefs and ideas that reflected the overall culture. In addition, an assortment of micro-level factors could influence how and why individuals varied in their "cultural expertise." For example, some individuals are more likely than others to be recognized as an official expert (Medin, Lynch, Coley, & Atran, 1997) or have a more central position within the community's social network (Hopkins, 2011). CCT researchers have responded to the question of heterogeneity by developing the concept of "cultural competence," which indicates a varying level of alignment between each individual's ideas and beliefs with the collective's consensus ideas and beliefs. To avoid the conceptual confusion attributed to research on intercultural competence that refers to an ability to work with people in other national cultures (Lustig & Koester, 2003), some CCT scholars have begun to use the term "cultural congruence" instead (e.g., Keller, Wong, & Liou, 2019), which I hereafter do as well. Recent CCT scholarship also recognizes that there can also be areas of consensus within a subculture that is distinct from the wider culture (e.g., Anders & Batchelder, 2012; Batchelder & Anders, 2012). Individuals therefore do not only vary in their level of cultural congruence but also in their level of subcultural congruence.

Finally, CCT also includes an assortment of methodological tools that operationalize the cultural and subcultural congruence concepts (Anders, 2013). Researchers first collect qualitative data to determine the range of "culturally true" beliefs and follow-up with a questionnaire with content derived from the qualitative data to determine the distribution of beliefs (Weller, 2007). Researchers than use a set of statistical techniques to analyze data from the questionnaire, which determines: a) the absence or presence of two or more subcultures, b) the general beliefs that represent the cultural consensus and the subcultural consensus, and c) the cultural congruence and subcultural congruence scores for each individual. Areas of consensus are determined by a Bayesian algorithm that assesses a best-fit model based on the probability that respondents in the survey agree with each other across items, adjusting for individuals' response bias across items. Congruence scores are then calculated as a probability of agreement with the culture or specific subcultures. For each congruence score, a "1" indicates complete congruence with the culture or subculture, a "–1" indicates complete incongruence, and a "0" indicates orthogonality. Because these scores indicate an individual's cross-level relationship with macro-patterns, the congruence scores can then be inserted into other statistical models that can then analyze the relationship between congruence and other variables (e.g., the individual's demographic background). This demonstrates the range of variables associated with macro- level patterns, as individuals who are more congruent with the culture or subculture are more likely to influence and be influenced by the consensus.

CCT APPROACH TO MICROFOUNDATIONS

The macro-level concepts of cultural and subcultural consensus, the associated cross-level concepts of cultural and subcultural congruence, and their respective statistical measures provide new ways of examining the multi-level foundations of institutions. A CCT approach separates heterogeneous macro-level patterns of socially constructed knowledge (i.e., cultural and subcultural consensus) from individuals' material conditions, which disentangles the cultural-cognitive and socio-structural elements of macro-institutions. A CCT approach also provides cross-level measures of individuals' congruence with the cultural and subcultural consensus, which connects micro-level instantiations of macro-socio-structural conditions with macro-level aggregations of socially constructed knowledge. This approach therefore enables scholars to examine the micro-level instantiations of macro-level structures and the macro-level aggregations of micro-level agency without compromising the ontological and epistemological principles of institutional theory. It also avoids the "chicken vs. egg" debate about micro- versus macro-factors because it enables researchers to ask questions instead about degrees of micro- and macro-influences. An abstract depiction of this cross-level approach is presented in Fig. 1.

However, the effective use of CCT as a multi-level approach to examining institutions requires two important steps in designing the study.

First, while cultural consensus can be used to demonstrate the "cultural truth" in any domain, institutional theorists are most concerned with questions about how much agency individuals have in the adoption and transformation of practices (Leca, Battilana, & Boxenbaum, 2008). As a growing number of institutional theorists contend, the biggest constraint on individuals' agency is not their own beliefs but their perceived beliefs of other stakeholders (e.g., Canales, 2016). Psychologists refer to this collective set of beliefs as intersubjective consensus (Wan, Torelli, & Chiu, 2010), where actors, irrespective of their own beliefs, respond to consensus that others would object to violations of the norm. If there was consensus that stakeholders reject a practice, then the majority of individuals would have limited agency in adopting the practice; but, if there was consensus

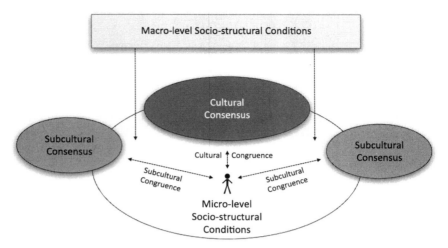

Fig. 1. Abstract Model of a CCT Approach to Microfoundations of Institutions.

that stakeholders accept the practice, individuals would have greater agency in adopting the practice. Consequently, culturally congruent individuals would more likely than others adopt the practice if the consensus view about stakeholder beliefs was positive and less likely if the consensus view was negative. At the same time, if there is a lack of consensus but there are instead subcultures with contrasting perceptions of stakeholder beliefs, individuals' agency would depend on both *whether* individuals' perceptions are congruent with a subculture and *which* subculture. For instance, some individuals may perceive stakeholders' beliefs as enabling (if one subculture's consensus belief is positive), others as constraining (if the other subculture's consensus belief is negative), and yet others as neither enabling nor constraining.

Second, while the relationship between cultural congruence and any individual-level variable can be analyzed statistically, analyzing relationships with variables that capture micro-level instantiations of macro-level socio-structural conditions are most effective at enabling researchers to disentangle the cultural and socio-cultural elements of macro-forces operating at the micro-level. These include, for example, individuals' status within the organization, their experience within the field, or their ties to other organizations. Statistical associations between individuals' micro-conditions and individuals' congruence to the wider culture or subcultures across the field demonstrate that systematic patterns on the ground are more likely to contribute to particular forms of field-level institutions. This enables researchers to demonstrate how macro-level socio-structural factors are related to macro-level cultural-cognitive factors, with micro-level cross-level relationships playing a mediating role. CCT, therefore, does not only have the potential to help examine micro-level antecedents of macro-level institutionalization outcomes but also the potential to help examine micro-level mediations of macro-level antecedents.

MICROFOUNDATIONS OF ECO AGENCY

To illustrate how CCT can be used as an approach to examining the microfoundation of institutions, I participated in the design and implementation of a study of the perceptions of corporate ethics practices among Ethics and Compliance officers (ECOs) in the United States, using primary data collected from members of the Ethics and Compliance Officers Association (ECOA) in 2013, the largest association of ECOs in the United States. I report an unpublished subset of these findings to demonstrate how CCT can be used to provide new insights into the microfoundations of institutions.

The ECOA was founded in 1992, in response to the introduction of new US laws that required corporations to ensure that they comply with ethics-related laws and rewarded corporations that engaged in discretionary ethics-related practices (Weaver, Trevino, & Cochran, 1999). As Chandler (2014) found in a mixed-method longitudinal study of the development of the ECO position over the course of 20 years, the adoption of the position quickly became widely distributed across the United States; yet, ambiguity on how corporations should use the position to respond to external pressures for ethicality created variance in financial and administrative support for the ECO during implementation. To examine how the environment influenced the day-to-day activities of ECOs on the ground, Trevino and colleagues (2014) interviewed 40 ECOs. The results of their investigation revealed that ECOs faced a number of internal legitimacy challenges that centered on their relationship with top executives, including clashing interests with market-related interests and overcoming a "legal' mindset. ECOs responded to these challenges by engaging in a number of tactics to enhance the legitimacy of the practices and the position.

The studies from Chandler (2014) and Trevino and colleagues (2014) demonstrated that ECOs had some yet limited agency in institutionalizing corporate ethics practices and the limited agency was experienced by ECOs on the ground. To understand how the ECOs' micro-level experience informed their macro-level role in the shaping of corporate ethics practices as a field-wide institution, however, we needed to further investigate the entire field, including ECOs across the field's intersubjective beliefs about the field and the micro-level conditions that shaped these beliefs.

By examining beliefs across the field and about the field, we can understand the status of the role of the ECO as a field-wide institution and its impact on the ground. For example, if there was consensus among ECOs that top executives across the field valued the ECO role, then ECOs would more likely take-for-granted their own authority in implementing practices within their own firm. If, on the other hand, there was consensus among ECOs that top executives across the field did not value the ECO role, then ECOs would more likely doubt their own authority in implementing practices within their own firm. By examining the overall consensus patterns, we could gain better insight on ECOs' overall agency as institutional actors (Lawrence, Suddaby, & Leca, 2009). Furthermore, by examining whether variance in ECOs' micro-level conditions were associated with variance in ECOs' congruence with the consensus, we can gain better insight on the micro-level conditions that shape ECOs' institutional role (Powell & Rerup, 2017). To answer these questions, I turned to CCT as a theoretical and empirical guide.

Theory and Hypotheses

The initial inception of the ECO position was based on top executives' fear of legal non-compliance in their corporate practices (Chandler, 2014). The development of discretionary ethics practices, on the other hand, was in response to a general incentive by the government to encourage executives to implement discretionary practices by rewarding such behavior in case there was a transgression. Discretionary ethics could do more in enhancing the overall ethicality of the firm, but it required additional resources that were not necessary in order to comply by laws. Top executives were, therefore, likely to have consensus on the value of compliance practices, yet were unlikely to have consensus on discretionary ethics practices or on whether the ECO should play an important role in the organization.

I contend that the extent to which consensus beliefs among top executives shaped the intersubjective beliefs of ECOs depended on whether ECOs were in micro-conditions that facilitated a knowledge transfer between the top executives and the ECOs. If ECOs were in constant communication with their CEO, for example, they were more likely to learn about top executives' views, as well as top executives' perceptions of other firms' executives' views. They would learn that top executives generally value compliance practices and coalesce around a field-wide consensus among ECOs about top executives' valuing compliance. Therefore:

> *H1.* ECOs with more direct communication with top executives were more likely to be culturally congruent to a field-wide consensus that top executives value compliance.

Since collective ambiguity reduces the likelihood that consensus is reached (Liu et al., 2015), ECOs' uncertainty about top executives' views on discretionary ethics' practices was likely to result in a lack of consensus on how they viewed the field. Other factors, however, could facilitate the formation of subcultures with consensus within each subculture. Some ECOs may coalesce around the idea that top executives are co-champions of enhancing discretionary ethics practices, whereas others coalesce around the idea that top executives only care about the bottom line and will do anything they can to minimize investing in ethics-related efforts.

One factor that may lead ECOs to coalesce around a particular view of top executives is their education background, as having a legal versus managerial educational background can influence the type of institutional logics that ECOs carry with them to their profession (Meyer & Hammerschmid, 2006). While managerial logics may emphasize the normative discretionary aspects of executive decision-making, legal logics will more likely emphasize the importance of rules and regulations over voluntary action as a mechanism for controlling firm behavior (Quack, 2007; Suddaby, Cooper, & Greenwood, 2007). ECOs with a legal background may personally advocate discretionary ethics practices because they also personally value enhancing the ethicality of the firm; yet, they are more likely to be preconditioned to believe that the only way firms adhere to norms is to implement laws and regulations (Quack, 2007; Suddaby et al., 2007).

H2. ECOs with a legal educational background were less likely to be congruent with a subculture consensus that top executives value discretionary ethics.

While ECOs may bring with them a predisposition toward viewing top executives in a positive or negative light, experience on the ground will also influence their adherence to a particular view. Specifically, ECOs are going to make inferences about the field based on their own experience with top executives (King & Whetten, 2008). If they have experience successfully implementing discretionary ethics practices, they are not only more likely to attribute some of the success to cooperative top executives within the firm, but will also more likely see other top executives as similarly cooperative. If, on the other hand, they fail to implement discretionary ethics practices, they will attribute some of the failure to their own top executives and make general inferences about the uncooperativeness of top executives across the field.

H3. ECOs with experience implementing discretionary ethics practices were more likely to be congruent with a subculture consensus that top executives value discretionary ethics.

Survey Design and Sample

A web-based questionnaire was sent to all 414 members of the ECOA, which was the primary US-based association for ECOs (Weber & Fortun, 2005). Included in the questionnaire were 12 items encompassing perceptions of the field (Table 1), based on interviews of 20 ECOs used in a previous study (Chandler, 2014). The use of interview data within the same sample to design CCT survey items is common (Weller, 2007), as it provides the range of "answers" that are potentially "culturally true" within the specific context. All 12 items were about their perceptions of top executives' views. Two items related to what ECOs perceived as top executives' views on mandatory compliance practices; six items related to what ECOs perceived as executives' views of specific discretionary practices (including training, compensation, and resources devoted to ethics); and, finally, four items related to what ECOs perceived as executives' views of the legitimacy of the ECO role itself as an implementer of ethics practices.

Of the ECOA's 414 organizational members, we received responses from 174 ECOs, each representing a unique organization, which resulted in an overall response rate of 42%.

Methods

To measure aggregate patterns of cultural and subcultural consensus and individual cross-level measures for cultural and subcultural congruence, I followed recently adapted analytical procedures used in CCT research

Table 1. Factor Loadings and Subculture Mean Scores for Eco Intersubjective Beliefs.

Perceived beliefs about top executives	Factor 1	Factor 2	Mean Subgroup 1	Mean Subgroup 2
Compliance practices				
1. A primary reason for ECOs is to signal to stakeholders that the organization is ethical	0.077	0.792	4.36	4.31
2. A primary reason for ECOs is to comply with laws	0.211	0.469	5.03	4.95
Discretionary practices				
3. Ethics and compliance codes should apply to suppliers and distributors	0.613	−0.010	4.94*	3.92
4. Organizations should have managerial-level and board-level ethics committees	0.672	−0.308	5.09*	3.83
5. Ethics should be a metric for managerial and board compensation	0.715	−0.238	4.42*	3.20
6. Important to invest significant financial and employee resources into ethics	0.722	−0.219	4.40*	2.95
7. ECOs should be given a prominent status in the organizations	0.794	−0.072	4.86*	3.53
8. ECOs should meet regularly with executives and board members	0.772	−0.143	5.25*	3.97
ECO strategic role				
9. ECOs provide competitive advantage	0.715	0.201	5.06*	3.83
10. ECOs improve ethical standards	0.755	0.163	5.22*	4.50
11. ECOs are a strategic asset	0.769	0.274	4.81*	3.77
12. ECOs no longer provide differentiation	−0.517	−0.140	2.63	3.33*

* Significantly higher than the other subculture based on one-tailed t-test results at $p < 0.05$.

(Anders & Batchelder, 2012; Batchelder & Anders, 2012), and most recently applied to organizational research (Keller et al., 2019; Loewenstein & Mueller, 2016). I used CCTpack, a hierarchical Bayesian model that tests probabilities of agreement between dyads across the sample and controls for item-level and respondent-level idiosyncratic noise across 10,000 iterations (Anders, 2013). I found that a two-subculture model (DIC = 3,841.3) was a better fit than either a single-culture model (DIC = 3,950.7) or three-subculture model (DIC = 5,946.4). The number of respondents in each subculture was evenly distributed at 50% and 50%, respectively, of the entire sample.

Congruence to Field-wide Consensus
I used the CCTpack measure of "cultural competence" to measure "cultural congruence." CCTpack assesses the mean probability that the individual's patterns of responses matches the consensus pattern.

Congruence to Subgroup Consensus
To measure congruence with a subculture consensus, I used CCTpack to measure the mean probability of each individual agreeing with members of one subculture more than the other (i.e., Omega Score).

Direct Interaction with CEO
I asked the number of times a year the ECO meets formally (i.e., a meeting scheduled in advance, rather than, for example, in response to a crisis) with the CEO to indicate the level of interaction that the two parties have with each other (and thus opportunities to communicate).

Organization's Implementation of Discretionary Ethics Practices
To measure the implementation of practices, I aggregated 10 measures of discretionary ethics' practices based on qualitative assessments of various practices in the field (Chandler, 2014). They included dichotomous measures based on whether the organization currently has CEO ethics training, board ethics training, a management-level ethics committee, a board-level ethics committee, ethics metrics as a component of CEO compensation, ethics metrics as a component of board compensation, an external audit of ethics practices, ethics requirements for suppliers, ethics requirements for distributors, and an ethics anonymous reporting system.

Legal Educational and Professional Background
I had two measures that indicated that an ECO possessed a legal educational and professional background that may influence how they frame their perceptions. The first was the reported possession of a Juris Doctor (J.D.) degree. The second

was a self-report selection of "legal/government relations" professional background. Because the two measures were highly correlated ($r = 0.71$) and they both had similar predictive power, I used the possession of a J.D. as the final measure.

Control Variables
Finally, I included other variables that may contribute to the microfoundation, but I list them as controls to ensure parsimony in my analyses. These included whether the organization was for-profit (coded 1) or non-profit (coded 0), as that could impact the ECO's access to information about the field at large and organization size (measured by the number of employees) because larger organizations may engage in different ethics practices and thus lead to different perceptions of how practices are across the field. I included ECO tenure (i.e., tenure as an ECO) because individuals may have different bases of experience within the profession and thus may have different sources of knowledge about the norms. I also included ECO organizational tenure (i.e., tenure within the organization) because some ECOs are promoted internally, which suggests a different set of professional experience than those ECOs who had previously been an ECO elsewhere. I also included ECO age (five-year increments) and ECO gender (female coded as 1) as demographic-related controls that influence access to knowledge of the field.

Results

Results for Consensus Content
Once I concluded that there were two aggregate consensus patterns (field-wide and two subcultures), I examined the specific perceptions associated with each aggregate pattern. First, I ran an exploratory factor analysis of the 12 items and found two factors explaining 61% of all variance, as shown in Table 1. There were 10 items loading on one factor (with one in reverse) that combined all six of the items associated with discretionary ethics practices and all four of the items associated with the value of the ECO role. ECOs who believed top executives valued discretionary ethics practices also believed that top executives treated the ECO role as strategically important. The other two items associated with compliance practices loaded on a second factor, and thus indicated that ECOs perceptions on compliance and discretionary ethics practices were orthogonal. An ECO could believe top executives value one, both or neither. My next step was to examine how each set of items was related to the aggregate consensus patterns to determine the content of each aggregate pattern. I aggregated the means for items within each factor and examined their association with field-wide and subculture consensus. I found that there was a positive relationship between cultural congruence and the aggregate score of the two items on compliance ($r = 0.36$, $p < 0.05$). I also found that there was a positive correlation between subcultural congruence for one of the two subgroups and the aggregate mean of the 10 items associated with discretionary ethics practices and the strategic role of the ECO ($r = 0.72$, $p < 0.05$). Therefore, there was field-wide consensus that top executives valued compliance practices, while one subculture (and not the other) had consensus that top executives valued discretionary ethics practices and the strategic role of the ECO.

Results for Micro-level Factors Influencing Field-wide Cultural Congruence
I conducted an ordinary least squares (OLS) linear regression analysis with the cultural congruence as the dependent variable. As presented in Table 2, the results found that frequency of interaction between the ECO and the CEO was associated with field-wide cultural congruence ($B = 0.02$, $p < 0.05$), thus supporting *H1*. No other independent variables were associated with cultural congruence.

Results for Micro-level Factors Influencing Subcultural Congruence
I used a linear regression analysis with the Omega score as the dependent variable. The results of these analyses are presented in Table 3. Specifically, the results indicate that ECOs who had a legal education background were less likely to be congruent with the subculture that perceives top executives as valuing discretionary ethics practices ($B = -0.13$, $p < 0.05$), thus supporting *H2*. The results also found that ECOs who implemented more discretionary practices within the

Table 2. Results of Linear Regression for Congruence with Field-wide Consensus.

	B	SE
Control variables		
For profit firm	−0.13	0.14
Organization size	−0.01	0.01
ECO organizational tenure	0.01	0.01
ECO professional tenure	−0.01	0.01
ECO age	0.05*	0.02
ECO gender	0.01	0.06
Independent variables		
Interaction with CEO	0.02*	0.01
R Square	0.12	

* = $p < 0.05$.

Table 3. Results of Linear Regression for Congruence with Subculture Consensus.

	B	SE
Control variables		
For profit firm	−0.1	0.12
Organization size	−0.01	0.01
ECO organizational tenure	−0.01	0.01
ECO professional tenure	−0.01	0.01
ECO age	0.02	0.03
ECO gender	0.02	0.08
Independent variables		
Implementation of discretionary practices	0.60*	0.17
Legal background	−0.13*	0.07
R Square	0.16	

* = $p < 0.05$.

participant's organization was associated with congruence with the subculture that perceives top executives as valuing discretionary ethics practices ($B = 0.60$, $p < 0.05$), thus supporting *H3*. I found no significant results for other variables and no support for any interaction between variables.

DISCUSSION OF RESULTS

The results from the study pointed to two different types of cross-level relationships between ECOs' experience on the ground and the institutionalization of corporate ethics' practices across the field. I found that there was consensus across the field that compliance practices are valued, and the link between ECOs communication with the CEO and ECO's cultural congruence suggests that communication with top executives facilitates the formation of a taken-for-granted view that ECOs' have agency to implement practices that help comply with laws. At the same time, I found that views on discretionary ethics practices were far from taken-for-granted, but characterized instead by variance in how ECOs viewed their agency. Those who had a legal background or were less successful in implementation were more likely than others to view top executives as a barrier to agency. These heterogeneous views do not necessarily reflect the structures that materially enabled or constrained the ECOs, but they do reflect the ECOs' socially constructed realities that informed their institutional roles and goals. Given the critical role of the ECO in the institutionalization of corporate ethics practices (Chandler, 2014), this socially constructed reality is central to the overall institutionalization of the practices.

The study of ECOs' intersubjective beliefs provided an exemplar illustration of how CCT can be used to connect micro-level factors to macro-level institutionalization patterns. Prior research had already examined the emerging institutionalization of the ECO role within a single organization qualitative study (Treviño et al., 2014). However, field-level perceptions of ECO's agency cannot be automatically inferred from insights on the ground, as some of the micro-level experiences were likely to vary. By examining the extent to which the variance in experiences was associated with variance in individuals' congruence with macro-level patterns (i.e., cultural and subcultural congruence), my study provided a link between the micro-conditions and the macro-institutions that inform the ECO's experience.

One limitation of this particular study is the cross-sectional design. While I was able to find an association between individuals' micro-conditions and their congruence to macro-level patterns, I was unable to decipher any causal relationship between the two levels of analyses. For example, ECOs' growing understanding of the field may also precipitate them to communicate more with top executives to further refine their understandings of the field. By examining the cross-level relationships over time, future research could examine the dynamic relationship between ECOs' experience on the ground and their predisposed beliefs. This can be captured empirically by testing the interactive effects of the variables on changes in ECOs' cultural or subcultural congruence. Other micro-instantiations of macro-structures, such as ECOs' embeddedness within networks of ECOs, or reactions to industry-level events, would also provide further insight on the interplay between micro-conditions and macro-institutions.

In sum, by using CCT, I was able to demonstrate how the institutionalization of corporate ethics' practices was distributed heterogeneously and demonstrate the micro-level factors that contributed to this pattern. In other words, I was able to conceptualize the corporate ethics field as a rainforest with different species of trees with different micro-conditions tied to the forest in different ways.

EXPANDING MICROFOUNDATIONAL RESEARCH WITH CCT

The study of ECOs, as described above, provides only one illustration of how CCT can be used to examine the microfoundation of the institutionalization of practices. The potential areas of inquiry are vast. However, there are some issues that researchers must pay attention to when deciding how to use CCT.

Sample Frame and Macro-level of Analysis

In the illustration, I used the population of ECOs within the US as the macro-level of analysis, which was plausible because the data sample were drawn from members of the largest professional association of ECOs. Primary data are critical for determining both the distribution of beliefs and the individual-level factors that provide the basis of a microfoundation. Therefore, ensuring that the sample reflects a population that is meaningful for elucidating macro-level patterns is critical. However, the type of population can vary, as the distribution of perceptions can apply to institutionalization processes at multiple levels of analyses, from the division to the organization to the industry to the field to the society.

Questionnaire Content

In the illustration, I included 12 items in a survey that was derived from earlier interviews of 20 ECOs used in a prior study (Chandler, 2014). A more robust study integrates the qualitative elements in the questionnaire design in a more systematic way, as described by Weller (2007). The purpose of the questionnaire design is not to produce generalizable constructs, but to produce a range of "answers" that can be tested by an "exam without an answer key" (Borgatti & Carboni, 2007). When addressing the agency of the participant in the institutionalization process, capturing intersubjective data is critical. In the case of ECOs, the critical concern of agency pertained intersubjective views of top executives. However, other stakeholders (e.g., shareholders) may be more pertinent, or in some cases, the population's views themselves are most pertinent. Because CCT involves a "test without an answer key," it is critical to provide questions that are highly contextualized and concrete in meaning. Otherwise, researchers run the risk of conflating verbalized meanings from meanings incorporated into practice (Lizardo et al., 2016). For example, asking questions about specific corporate ethics practices (e.g., "do executives support having CEO remuneration tied to ethics") are more pertinent than asking general questions about discretionary practices (e.g., "do executives support ethics"), as it ensures that all respondents are interpreting the questions in the same way.

Microfoundational Variables

Of course, the most critical component of examining microfoundations of institutionalization using CCT is the micro-level factors that explain macro-level patterns. This requires the use of questionnaires or other sources to capture individual-level data. Theoretically, any psychographic or demographic variable qualifies as a potential microfoundational factor. However, in addition to general issues surrounding parsimony in quantitative methods, attention must be made to ensure that the variance-based link between the micro-level factor and the cultural competence measure reflects a microfoundational process. An underlying assumption must be met that an individual who thinks like everyone else is contributing to the macro-level thinking in a heightened way. This relationship is mutually constitutive, as it suggests that the individual is more likely to be influenced by and influence others within the population. The micro-level variables that are linked to this measure must be theoretically consistent. For example, a link between interaction with the CEO and cultural competence suggests that the individual is learning more and/or contributing to knowledge diffusion among ECOs more because of the interaction. Of course, while difficult, multi-stage data collection that can demonstrate changes in cultural competence over time is likely to provide a more robust causal explanation of microfoundational patterns.

Stage of Institutionalization

Finally, as demonstrated in the illustration, a CCT study is best utilized when the level of consensus is weak enough to still allow some variability in perceptions. It is, therefore, critical to use in stages when practices have already begun to diffuse across a population yet before it has become taken-for-granted across the entire population. Otherwise, there is insufficient variance to determine whether micro-level factors contribute to variance explained.

CONCLUSION

The microfoundational wave in institutional research and the growing attention to examining the multiple levels of analyses has been a boon in enhancing our understanding of how factors on the ground contribute to broader macro-level processes (e.g., Bitektine & Haack, 2015). Bridging the micro to the macro, however, remains a lingering issue that is best addressed through further empirical inquiry. Shifting our questions from "how does the micro-shape the macro" to "which micro-shapes which macro" enables us to gain more nuanced theoretical insights that consider the heterogeneous nature of institutions. Furthermore, by borrowing from the theoretical and empirical approach developed by anthropologists to examine what is "culturally true" across a population provides the right set of tools to enable a variance-based cross-level approach. I hope that more future answers to the question of "what shapes institutions" include the "who" and the "where."

ACKNOWLEDGMENTS

I would like to thank David Chandler and John Mezias for their participation in data collection and enabling me access to the data to be used for the illustrative example used in the chapter. I would also like to thank Judith Walls and Melodie Cartel for their feedback.

REFERENCES

Abdelnour, S., Hasselbladh, H., & Kallinikos, J. (2017). Agency and institutions in organization studies. *Organization Studies*, *38*(12), 1775–1792.

Anders, R. (2013). CCTpack: Cultural consensus theory applications to data. *R package version*.

Anders, R., & Batchelder, W. (2012). Cultural consensus theory for multiple consensus truths. *Journal of Mathematical Psychology*, *56*(6), 452–469.

Batchelder, W., & Anders, R. (2012). Cultural Consensus Theory: Comparing different concepts of cultural truth. *Journal of Mathematical Psychology*, *56*(5), 316–332.

Battilana, J., Leca, B., & Boxenbaum, E. (2009). 2 how actors change institutions: Towards a theory of institutional entrepreneurship. *Academy of Management annals*, *3*(1), 65–107.

Berger, P. L., & Luckmann, T. (1967). *The social construction of reality: A treatise in the sociology of knowledge*: London: Anchor.

Bitektine, A., & Haack, P. (2015). The "macro" and the "micro" of legitimacy: Toward a multilevel theory of the legitimacy process. *Academy of Management Review*, *40*(1), 49–75.

Borgatti, S. P., & Carboni, I. (2007). On measuring individual knowledge in organizations. *Organizational Research Methods*, *10*(3), 449–462. doi:10.1177/1094428107300228

Canales, R. (2016). From ideals to institutions: Institutional entrepreneurship and the growth of Mexican small business finance. *Organization Science*, *27*(6), 1548–1573.

Cardinale, I. (2018a). Beyond constraining and enabling: Toward new microfoundations for institutional theory. *Academy of Management Review*, *43*(1), 132–155.

Cardinale, I. (2018b). Microfoundations of institutions and the theory of action. *Academy of Management Review*, *44*(2), 467–470.

Chandler, D. (2014). Organizational susceptibility to institutional complexity: Critical events driving the adoption and implementation of the ethics and compliance officer position. *Organization Science*, *25*(6), 1722–1743.

Dacin, M. T., Goodstein, J., & Scott, W. R. (2002). Institutional theory and institutional change: Introduction to the special research forum. *Academy of Management Journal*, *45*(1), 45–56.

Garud, R., Hardy, C., & Maguire, S. (2007). *Institutional entrepreneurship as embedded agency: An introduction to the special issue*. London: Sage Publications.

Gehman, J., Lounsbury, M., & Greenwood, R. (2016). How institutions matter: From the micro foundations of institutional impacts to the macro consequences of institutional arrangements. In *How institutions matter!* (pp. 1–34). Bingley: Emerald Publishing Limited.

Harmon, D., Haack, P., & Roulet, T. J. (2018). Microfoundations of institutions: A matter of structure vs. agency or level of analysis? *Academy of Management Review*, *44*(2), 464–467.

Hopkins, A. (2011). Use of network centrality measures to explain individual levels of herbal remedy cultural competence among the Yucatec Maya in Tabi, Mexico. *Field Methods*, *23*(3), 307–328. doi:10.1177/1525822x11399400

Jarzabkowski, P. (2008). Shaping strategy as a structuration process. *Academy of Management Journal, 51*(4), 621–650.

Jepperson, R., & Meyer, J. W. (2011). Multiple levels of analysis and the limitations of methodological individualisms. *Sociological Theory, 29*(1), 54–73.

Keller, J., & Loewenstein, J. (2011). The cultural category of cooperation: A cultural consensus model analysis for China and the United States. *Organization Science, 22*(2), 299–319.

Keller, J., Wong, S.-s., & Liou, S. (2019). How social networks facilitate collective responses to organizational paradoxes. *Human Relations*. doi: 0018726719827846.

King, B. G., & Whetten, D. A. (2008). Rethinking the relationship between reputation and legitimacy: A social actor conceptualization. *Corporate Reputation Review, 11*(3), 192–207.

Klein, K. J., Tosi, H., & Cannella, A. A. (1999). Multilevel theory building: Benefits, barriers, and new developments. *Academy of Management Review, 24*(2), 248–253.

Kozlowski, S. W., & Klein, K. J. (2000). A multilevel approach to theory and research in organizations: Contextual, temporal, and emergent processes. In K. J. Klein & S. W. J. Kozlowski (Eds.), *Multilevel theory, research, and methods in organizations: Foundations, extensions, and new directions* (pp. 3–90). San Francisco, CA: Jossey-Bass.

Kraatz, M. S., & Block, E. S. (2008). Organizational implications of institutional pluralism. *The SAGE handbook of organizational institutionalism*, (p. 840). London: Sage Publications.

Lahneman, B. (2015). In vino veritas understanding sustainability with environmental certified management standards. *Organization & Environment*, 1086026615578008.

Lawrence, T. B., Suddaby, R., & Leca, B. (2009). *Institutional work: Actors and agency in institutional studies of organizations*. Cambridge: Cambridge University Press.

Leca, B., Battilana, J., & Boxenbaum, E. (2008). *Agency and institutions: A review of institutional entrepreneurship*: Cambridge, MA: Harvard Business School.

Liu, X.-x., Keller, J., & Hong, Y.-y. (2015). Hiring of personal ties: A cultural consensus analysis of China and the United States. *Management and Organization Review, 11*(1), 145–169. doi:10.1111/more.12055

Lizardo, O., Mowry, R., Sepulvado, B., Stoltz, D. S., Taylor, M. A., Van Ness, J., & Wood, M. (2016). What are dual process models? Implications for cultural analysis in sociology. *Sociological Theory, 34*(4), 287–310.

Loewenstein, J., & Mueller, J. (2016). Implicit theories of creative ideas: How culture guides creativity assessments. *Academy of Management Discoveries, 2*(4), 320–348.

Lustig, M. W., & Koester, J. (2003). Intercultural competence. *Interpersona Communication across Cultures*. New York, NY: Harper Collins College Publishers.

McPherson, C. M., & Sauder, M. (2013). Logics in action managing institutional complexity in a drug court. *Administrative Science Quarterly, 58*(2), 165–196.

Medin, D. L., Lynch, E. B., Coley, J. D., & Atran, S. (1997). Categorization and reasoning among tree experts: Do all roads lead to Rome? *Cognitive Psychology, 32*(1), 49–96.

Medin, D. L., Ross, N. O., Atran, S., Burnett, R. C., & Blok, S. (2002). Categorization and reasoning in relation to culture and expertise. In B. Ross (Ed.), *The psychology of learning and motivation* (pp. 1–38). London: Academic Press.

Meyer, R. E., & Hammerschmid, G. (2006). Changing institutional logics and executive identities a managerial challenge to public administration in Austria. *American Behavioral Scientist, 49*(7), 1000–1014.

Ocasio, W., Loewenstein, J., & Nigam, A. (2015). How streams of communication reproduce and change institutional logics: The role of categories. *Academy of Management Review, 40*(1), 28–48. doi:10.5465/amr.2013.0274

Powell, W. W., & Colyvas, J. A. (2008). Microfoundations of institutional theory. *The SAGE handbook of organizational institutionalism* (p. 840). London: Sage Publications.

Powell, W. W., & Rerup, C. (2017). Opening the black box: The microfoundations of institutions. *The SAGE handbook of organizational institutionalism* (p. 2). London: Sage Publications.

Quack, S. (2007). Legal professionals and transnational law-making: A case of distributed agency. *Organization, 14*(5), 643–666. doi:10.1177/1350508407080313

Romney, A. K., Batchelder, W. H., & Weller, S. C. (1987). Recent applications of cultural consensus theory. *American Behavioral Scientist, 31*(2), 163–177. doi:10.1177/000276487031002003

Romney, A. K., & Moore, C. C. (1998). Toward a theory of culture as shared cognitive structures, *Ethos*, *26*(3), 314–337.

Romney, A. K., Weller, S. C., & Batchelder, W. H. (1986). Culture as consensus: A theory of culture and informant accuracy. *American Anthropologist, 88*, 313–338.

Rousseau, D. M. (1985). Issues of level in organizational research: Multi-level and cross-level perspectives. *Research in Organizational Behavior, 7*(1), 1–37.

Smets, M., & Jarzabkowski, P. (2013). Reconstructing institutional complexity in practice: A relational model of institutional work and complexity. *Human Relations, 66*(10), 1279–1309.

Spee, P., Jarzabkowski, P., & Smets, M. (2016). The influence of routine interdependence and skillful accomplishment on the coordination of standardizing and customizing. *Organization Science, 27*(3), 759–781.

Suddaby, R., Cooper, D. J., & Greenwood, R. (2007). Transnational regulation of professional services: Governance dynamics of field level organizational change. *Accounting, Organizations and Society, 32*(4–5), 333–362. doi:http://dx.doi.org/10.1016/j.aos.2006.08.002

Thornton, P. H., Ocasio, W., & Lounsbury, M. (2012). *The institutional logics perspective: foundations, research, and theoretical elaboration.* Oxford: Oxford University Press.

Tolbert, P. S., & Zucker, L. G. (1983). Institutional sources of change in the formal structure of organizations: The diffusion of civil service reform, 1880–1935. *Administrative Science Quarterly*, 22–39.

Treviño, L. K., den Nieuwenboer, N. A., Kreiner, G. E., & Bishop, D. G. (2014). Legitimating the legitimate: A grounded theory study of legitimacy work among Ethics and Compliance Officers. *Organizational Behavior and Human Decision Processes, 123*(2), 186–205. doi:http://dx.doi.org/10.1016/j.obhdp.2013.10.009

Wan, C., Torelli, C. J., & Chiu, C.-y. (2010). Intersubjective consensus and the maintenance of normative shared reality. *Social Cognition, 28*(3), 422–446. doi:10.1521/soco.2010.28.3.422

Weaver, G. R., Trevino, L. K., & Cochran, P. L. (1999). Corporate ethics programs as control systems: Influences of executive commitment and environmental factors. *Academy of Management Journal, 42*(1), 41–57.

Weber, J., & Fortun, D. (2005). Ethics and compliance officer profile: Survey, comparison, and recommendations. *Business and Society Review, 110*(2), 97–115.

Weller, S. C. (2007). Cultural Consensus Theory: Applications and frequently asked questions. *Field Methods, 19*(4), 339–368. doi:10.1177/1525822x07303502

CHAPTER 10

SPECIFYING THE "WHAT" AND SEPARATING THE "HOW": DOINGS, SAYINGS, CODES, AND ARTIFACTS AS THE BUILDING BLOCKS OF INSTITUTIONS

Omar Lizardo

ABSTRACT

The author distinguishes between state, process, and object perspectives on institutions and institutionalization. While all-purpose process approaches dominate the literature, the author argues that these are analytically insufficient without theorizing the nature of "institutional objects." Building on recently developed analytic disaggregations of the culture concept in cultural sociology, the author argues that doings, sayings, codes, and artifacts exhaust the broad classes of potential objects subject to institutionalization processes. The proposed approach provides a coherent ontology for future empirical work, features robust microfoundations, places institutional routines and practices in a material context, and acknowledges the importance of semiotic codes and vocabularies in organizational fields.

Keywords: Institutions; culture; practices; codes; vocabularies; artifacts

Microfoundations of Institutions
Research in the Sociology of Organizations, Volume 65A, 217–234
Copyright © 2020 by Emerald Publishing Limited
All rights of reproduction in any form reserved
ISSN: 0733-558X/doi:10.1108/S0733-558X2019000065A021

BEYOND THE "HOW" AND THE "THAT"

Institutional theory is distinctive among approaches to the study of formal (and informal) organizing in that "culture" or the "cultural-cognitive" dimension plays a key role (Phillips, Lawrence, & Hardy, 2004; Scott, 2013, p. 67; Zilber, 2012). As Barley and Tolbert (1997, pp. 93–95) once noted, institutional theory in sociology and organization studies stands out because it highlights "cultural influences on decision making and formal structure" while seeing both individuals and organizations as "suspended in a web of values, norms, rules, beliefs, and taken for granted assumptions ... [t]hese cultural elements define the way the world is and should be." Institutional theory is also unique in conceptualizing the core phenomenon of *institutionalization*, in both state (e.g., static property) and process (e.g., a sequence of events) terms (Jepperson, 1991, p. 145). The state version of institutionalization tells us *that* something has been institutionalized (or not), while the process version outlines the *mechanisms* enabling or preventing its occurrence (Weber, 2006).

Cultural processes are central to both state and process accounts of institutionalization. Mechanisms of collective belief attribution, taken-for-grantedness, typification, and collective constraints on cognition and decision-making are central to theorizing institutionalization as a steady-state (Berger & Luckmann, 1966; Scott, 2013), with one of the most influential takes on institutionalization conceiving of it as a one of the main drivers of "cultural persistence" (Zucker, 1977). Cultural processes of theorization, legitimation, endorsement, and social construction are also central to understanding how things go from not-being institutionalized to being institutionalized (Powell & Colyvas, 2008; Strang & Meyer, 1993), while processes of delegitimation, devaluation, erosion, and entropy are crucial for shedding light on deinstitutionalization processes (Oliver, 1992).

However, institutionalization pertains not only to processes and outcomes but also to the *what* of institutionalization. When people speak of institutionalization processes and outcomes, what is the object they are speaking of? As Li (2017) has recently noted, it turns out that the primary objects of institutionalization are cultural elements. This means that most of institutional theory deals with cultural processes operating on cultural "objects." According to this account, when we consider the things that organization theorists say are institutionalized we come up with three broad categories: *practices* (what people do), *vocabularies* (what people say), and the public meanings attached to doing and sayings via well-established semiotic codes (Sewell, 2005; Swidler, 2001b), and discourses (Phillips et al., 2004; Zilber, 2012), especially when these pertain to ways and modes of organizing or justifying the existence of specific organizational arrangements and structures (Meyer & Rowan, 1977).[1]

It turns out that the three elements of doings – sayings, public meanings, and discourses – in addition to artifacts[2] (and their relationships) have been the subject of much theorizing in recent sociological work on culture (Bourdieu, 1990; Khan & Jerolmack, 2013; Patterson, 2014; Spillman, 1995; Swidler, 2001b). Lizardo (2017) has recently proposed that the "omnibus" conception of culture sociologists usually deploy decomposes into one of these classes of cultural elements. On the personal side, we have sayings and doings, and on the public side, we have such things as public codes, vocabularies, and other collective ways of fixing the "meanings" of both sayings and practices (Weber, Heinze, & DeSoucey, 2008), in addition to tools, material technologies, and artifacts. This convergence provides an exciting opportunity to develop accounts of institutions that are unabashedly cultural in terms of the *what* of institutions in addition to the "how" and the "that."

Building on these distinctions, I provide an analytically useful and parsimonious account of the object-side of institutions based on a developing theory bringing together insights from the sociology of culture, cultural models theory in psychological anthropology, and cognitive science (Bourdieu, 1990; Strauss & Quinn, 1997; Swidler, 2001b). I show how specifying the "what" of institutions can help us resolve perennial issues related to the link (or lack thereof) between institutional processes and institutional objects.

DEFINING INSTITUTIONS AND INSTITUTIONALIZATION

Despite being "core concepts" in social science, the notion of an institution and the allied concept of institutionalization have been notoriously hard to define; this is a "conceptual variety" and vagueness Jepperson (1991, p. 143) once found "striking" in a seminal theoretical contribution to the subject. The main problem is that different analysts emphasize disjoint aspects of both concepts, leading to a cacophony of definitions. For instance, Lawrence, Suddaby, and Leca (2011, p. 53) define institutions as

> enduring elements of social life ... [affecting] the behavior and beliefs of ... actors by providing templates for action, cognition, and emotion...nonconformity with which is associated with some kind of costs.

Greenwood, Oliver, Lawrence, and Meyer (2017, p. 4), on their part, propose that institutions are "[...] *taken-for-granted repetitive social behaviour [sic.] that is underpinned by normative systems and cognitive understandings that give meaning to social exchange and thus enable self-reproducing social order*" (italics in original).

Settling the question of whether there is a "best" definition of institution (or whether on crafting one is worthwhile) is beyond the scope of this chapter. One thing to note is that many of these definitions combine state (e.g., "enduring" and "repetitive"), process ("self-reproducing," and "nonconformity"), object ("behavior," "belief," and "action"), and effects ("affect behavior" and "give meaning to") descriptions in mutually incompatible ways. The only thing on which there is some agreement is that institutions have to do with processes bringing some kind of patterning, repetition, and order to social and organizational life and that institutionalization as a state or property is not a binary on/off situation but admits to "more or less" gradation so that something can be more or less or even "semi" institutionalized.

State Approaches

Some analysts take the individual/society opposition as the critical dimension in defining institutions. From this perspective, institutionalization is a *steady state* enjoyed by some practice or organizational arrangement. In this respect, a key aspect of institutions and institutionalization is the quality of some set of social arrangements or practices as appearing to individuals as exogenous, obdurate realities. This is "Durkheimian" approach is common among those who depart from the social phenomenological tradition of institutional theory inaugurated by Berger and Luckmann (1966), such as Meyer and Rowan (1977). Here, something is an institution if it is treated as exogenous to action and even as "constructing" the actors who perform the actions (Meyer & Jepperson, 2000). This *externalization* theory is probably the most influential version of the state approach to institutions.

Externalization theorists have been (rightly) criticized because they propose too sharp a split between institutions as they exist "in the world" and as enacted and practiced by people. In this last respect, while institutions do have an external aspect, they also have an interactional or even "personal" aspect, and these two must be linked in any satisfactory account; microfoundations are required not optional (Powell & Colyvas, 2008). Recent lines of institutional theory focus on bringing individuals actors back into the picture (in many ways, coming closer to Berger and Luckmann's original account). This may happen by emphasizing micro-level processes of interaction, negotiation, and meaning-making in institutions (as with "inhabited" accounts; Hallett & Ventresca, 2006); pointing to the dialectic between institutions as grammar or templates and institutions as situated performances both producing and reproducing those patterns (as in "structuration" accounts; Barley & Tolbert, 1997); or via the myriad of activities, whether habitual, reactive, or projective, enacted by agents in their everyday attempts at creating, challenging, reproducing, tinkering, or otherwise affecting institutionalized structures and practices (as in "work" accounts; Lawrence et al., 2011).

Process Approaches

Other analysts hone-in on some generically defined set of *processes*, and define institutions as the things that owe the core quality they have, usually some relatively unproblematic "persistence" (Zucker, 1977), to those processes being regularly activated to keep the arrangement or practice going. Jepperson belongs to this camp, defining institutions as "a social pattern that reveals a particular reproduction process" (Jepperson, 1991, p. 145). The processes he refers to are "repeated activated, social constructed, controls – that is ... some set of rewards and sanctions." Therefore, institutions are "social pattern that ... owe their survival to relatively self-activating social processes."

Process theorists reject conceptions of institutions specifying that only a particular type of "object" gets to be institutionalized. They usually proceed, like Jepperson (1991, p. 144), by listing a laundry list of practices, collective actors, routines, and categories that don't seem to be at all related and asking what they may have in common. Finding that they crosscut the usual divisions of social science (e.g., some are "cultural" and others are "structural") process theorists point out that there is nothing about the object properties that lends itself to institutionalization. Instead, what institutionalized objects have in common is the way they are maintained in a relatively unproblematic way, locking in the process definition (Jepperson, 1991, p. 145). Process theorists also reject the conflation between the concept of an institution and *institutional effects*, which, as we saw earlier, are sometimes run together by analysts. For instance, the fact institutions produce "constraints on the options that individuals and collectives are likely to exercise" (Barley & Tolbert, 1997, p. 94) is a kind of institutional *effect*, but it is not a core element of what an institution is as a process.

Tolbert and Zucker (1996) have extended the process perspective by reconstructing the process theory implicit in Berger and Luckmann (1966). They begin with Berger and Luckman's (1966, p. 54) famous definition of steady-state institutionalization as a "reciprocal typification of habitualized action types by actors." According to Tolbert and Zucker (1996), this definition of institutionalization as a state implies the operation at least three processes (pp. 174–175).

First, there are mechanisms leading to the *habitualization* of specific actions so they are automatically and effortless elicited in particular contexts as the primary way to go about doing things. Second, there are typification mechanisms leading actors to develop shared public meanings about those behaviors, and the actors who perform them, as "types" or categories and not as indexical performances tied to context:

> [s]ince typifications entail classifications or categorizations of actors with whom the actions are associated, this concept implies that the meanings attributed to habitualized action have come to be generalized, that is, to be independent of the specific individuals who carry out the action.

The process of generalized assignment is what Tolbert and Zucker, following Zucker (1977), refer to as *objectification*. In this respect, institutionalization entails both habitualization and objectification processes. Finally, when objectified patterns acquire a taken-for-granted reality as "just the way things are" and cease to be questioned, they are said to be *sedimented*. Tolbert and Zucker thus provide a continuum of institutionalization processes progressing from the stages of habitualization, to objectification, and finally to sedimentation which allows for some things to be partially institutionalized (e.g., habitualized and objectified but not sedimented).

Object Approaches

If state definitions focus on the qualities characteristic of things that are institutionalized (e.g., being exogenous), and process definitions focus on the mechanisms that keep it that way, object definitions point to the actual *things* to which properties and processes apply. In this respect, object theorists implicitly contend, contra process theorists such as Jepperson, that only particular class of things can enjoy the quality of being institutionalized. In this respect, they make an argument concerning the "ontology" of institutions (Searle, 2006).

Object theorists are also process and state theorists since they must supply an account of how is it particular objects become institutionalized and what keeps them that way. However, as we saw earlier the reverse is not the case, since both state and process theorists can be agnostic as to what are the objects that are the subject of institutionalization processes, with the limit case being those who say *anything* can be institutionalized (Jepperson, 1991, p. 145). Subtypes of object theorists and even historical lineages separating different object institutionalisms in sociology can be distinguished by looking at the things they say are the objects of institutionalization as a process or a state. For instance, according to the "old" institutionalism of Talcott Parsons the primary object of institutionalization where norms and values at the level of the social system. The "new" institutionalism broke with this, replacing the main object of functionalism with a new one: "cognitive templates" or "schemas" at the level of organizational fields (DiMaggio & Powell, 1991; Scott, 2013).

The main problem faced by object theorists is whether to go restrictive (e.g., saying that only a small set of objects is subject to institutionalization) or go omnibus (proposing a large number of objects). However, object theorists cannot provide a completely unprincipled laundry list of objects, because if that were the case, object theory would reduce to a Jeppersonian process theory (as an open-ended list of objects is tantamount to saying "anything"). So, the primary task of the object theorist is to pick some delimited set of objects and mount a theoretical argument as to why these are the ones that can enjoy the property of being institutionalized and not some other ones.

Scott (2013, p. 48) provides what is arguably the most influential object-based account of institutions: "*Institutions are composed of regulative, normative and cultural-cognitive elements that, together with associated activities and resources, provide stability and meaning to social life*" (italics in the original). According to Scott, regulative, normative, and cultural-cognitive elements are the "building blocks" of institutions (this is the object-based ontological point), and it is these that are the object of self-reproducing processes. Some of these elements, such as "rules, norms, and cultural-cognitive beliefs" are closer to those emphasized by Durkheimian/phenomenological externalization theorists. Others, however, such as "social activities" and "associated behaviors" (Scott, 2013, p. 49) bring "people back in" so his definition is not subject to the standard critique of the externalization approach posed by process-based structuration, "work," or "inhabited" institutionalisms (e.g. Barley & Tolbert, 1997; Hallett & Ventresca, 2006; Lawrence & Suddaby, 2006).

That said, Scott's object perspective remains vague as to the nature of the three broad classes of objects that constitute the "pillars," and how they interface with activities and resources. Scott's brand of object theory also has a hard time accommodating the role of other types of objects central to vibrant lines of institutional and organization theory, such as techno-material artifacts, semiotic codes, vocabularies or organizing, organizational routines, and practices. This will be the main task of the "refurbished" object-based account to be developed in what follows

Can We Have an Object-Neutral Account of Institutions?

As we have seen, process theorists attempt to reduce the concept of institutions and institutionalization to a (relatively small) generic set of processes and activities. They also, sometimes implicitly or explicitly, say that we do not need to worry about theorizing the "what" (objects of) institutional analysis, because what matters is the *way* certain patterns are maintained not the nature of the things subject to these self-correcting processes. If this were true, then it would make object-based attempts to specify the "building blocks" of institutions (e.g., what institutions are "made of") either superfluous or misguided. Here, I show that a pure process perspective that is neutral on theorizing the objects of institutionalization is a non-starter.

Pure process accounts face some problems. The most important of which is that they err on the side of over-specificity and thus produce overly restrictive definitions of the core phenomenon of institutions. In this respect, it is unlikely that there is a single process, however generic, that keeps institutions going (or that makes institutionalization happen), much less one that would be sufficient to count as *definitional* of the broad concept of an institution (Lawrence & Suddaby, 2006). Take Jepperson's (1991, p. 145) proposed meta-process: "repeatedly activated, socially constructed controls...some set of rewards and sanctions." It is odd that Jepperson proposes this particular process as the main candidate mechanism for institutional persistence. First, "rewards and sanctions" are just one of many mechanisms that can sustain a given institutional pattern. They fall under a somewhat restrictive category, especially for sociological institutionalism, in that they belong mainly to the "regulative" pillar in Scott's (2013) terms. Jepperson (1991) himself goes on to emphasize the standard phenomenological mechanisms of "taken-for-grantedness" and "social construction" later on (pp. 153–157), breaking his definitional bounds. Second, rewards and sanctions have been pinpointed by those who prefer processes with a more "cultural-cognitive" flavor, such as Zucker (1977) as precisely the sort of indicators that something is *not* institutionalized. If you have to engage in so much overt incentivizing, rewarding, and sanctioning to get people to do the required thing, then maybe that is not taken-for-granted or objective (Sieweke, 2014, p. 26). In Jepperson's terms, rewards and sanctions sound much more like effortful "action" rather than self-activating "enactment."

What's a process theorist to do? One approach is to propose a more well-rounded set of processes. For instance, we can combine Jepperson's emphasis on self-reproducing sanctions and equilibrium restoration mechanisms with Tolbert and Zucker's processes of habitualization, objectification, and sedimentation, thus producing a more general and robust account. This has been a more or less coherent line of development in institutional theory since the 1990s, in which processes operating across every level of aggregation have proliferated (Greenwood et al., 2017).

However, this line of process theory ultimately cannot avoid turning into a type of object theory because the principal substantive claim is that there is an elective affinity between a given process and a given object. This is more or less the key to the synthetic approach taken by Scott (2013). In that rendering, for instance, specific legal codes are sustained via reward-and-sanction processes, but highly generalized schemata, such as the notion of "organization" (Meyer & Bromley, 2013) are institutionalized via cultural-cognitive mechanisms. In this respect, no matter how hard they try, process theorists cannot avoid the task of theorizing the object of institutionalization processes.

A REFURBISHED OBJECT ACCOUNT OF INSTITUTIONS

What Gets Institutionalized?

The proposed account of the "what" of institutionalization is summarized in Fig. 1. The approach suggested here requires us, with Scott (2013), to not be shy about theorizing the nature and properties of the broad types of things that are the subject of institutionalization processes, thus providing an ontology of institutions. In this respect, the object approach emphasizes a sharp distinction between object and processes, avoiding the object/process "conflationism" that sometimes besets structuration and inhabited accounts (Archer, 1996) so that we can develop coherent theories of the way particular processes operate on specific objects, to produce institutionalization outcomes and associated institutional effects. This is reflected in the figure in the separation of object ("what") questions (shown at the top) from process questions regarding the origins of, or the reproductive processes that keep institutions going (Jepperson, 1991) (shown at the bottom).

As shown in the figure, the primary substantive claim that I make is that at the most general level, what gets institutionalized is *culture*.[3] So, institutional theories are theories about the way culture gains pattern and organization in social life (as stated at the outset). If culture were an "amorphous mist," (Ghaziani, 2009), a homogeneous blob with no clear ontological status or internally differentiated elements this claim would be both vacuous and counter-productive. Unfortunately, some have dismissed object approaches emphasizing the cultural status of the building blocks of institutions as providing such a non-substantial account in which "social structure" is lost (Hirsch, 1997).

Thankfully, recent advances in cultural theory have been devoted precisely to dealing with the issue of "cultural ontology." That is specifying the culture concept by isolating the various ways culture shows up for empirical inspection, and by grounding the notion of culture in non-problematic entities and objects existing in the world (Lizardo, 2017; Patterson, 2014; Strauss & Quinn, 1997). At the same time, the distinction between "culture" and "structure" has come into question as a conceptual dead end (Hays, 1994), since all types of culture have their specifiable form of structure; the *opposition* of culture and structure is a thing of the past (Sewell, 2005). In this way, institutional theorists can safely declare institutional theory to be a branch of cultural theory without hanging their head in shame (Weber & Dacin, 2011).

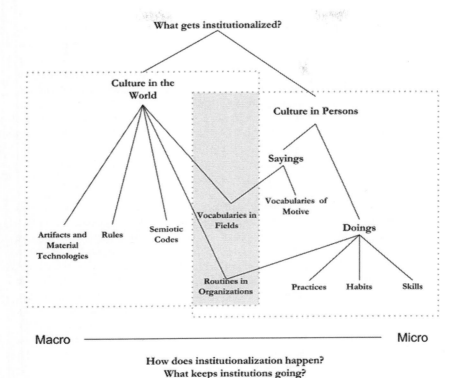

Fig. 1. Diagram Showing How the Different Objects of Institutionalization Process and their Relations.

The key substantive point of the proposed object approach is that culture disaggregates into two broad categories based on "location" (the two main branches in the figure). Culture can be *in* people or culture can be *in* the world (Lizardo, 2017; Strauss & Quinn, 1997). Culture gets into people via internalization and learning processes (Lizardo, 2017; Quinn, Sirota, & Stromberg, 2018), and culture gets in the world (from people) via people's meaning-construction and objectification processes (Shore, 1996). This approach to culture thus provides robust microfoundations for key cultural processes (Sieweke, 2014).

Artifacts and Material Technologies
As shown on the left-hand side of the figure, culture in the world can be found in three primary forms. First, culture exists as embodied in the myriad of material artifacts that populate organized settings (Orlikowski, 2000; Pentland & Feldman, 2005, p. 797). As used here, the notion of artifact covers *all forms of material culture* depending on human intervention, labor, and ingenuity constructed as signatures along a physical medium (archaeologists, for instance, only have access

to artifacts; Malafouris, 2013). This conception of artifact is maximal; for example, both the "material" side of spoken and written language (see e.g., Clark, 2006), buildings, tools, maps, books count as an artifact in this sense.[4] The human body especially its effectors like hands, lips, and tongue (most notably, in the production of "signals" with representational import) is the artifact par excellence. In this respect, the use, disposition, and arrangement of bodies, material objects, and technologies is another important site where institutionalization operates. This has been a leitmotif of recent lines of theorizing attempting to link insights from science and technology studies to institutional analysis (Pinch, 2008).

Rules and Semiotic Codes
Second, there are externally defined semiotic codes fixing the meaning of both sayings and doings in organized settings by shared convention (Swidler, 2001b; Weber et al., 2008). This is the account of institutionalization (as a linkage between public semiotic codes and patterned sayings and doings) that has been central to the more "macro" oriented phenomenological tradition of institutional theory since the consolidation of the new institutionalism (Li, 2017; Tolbert & Zucker, 1996). However, semiotic codes are not the only way in which culture acquires external form in organizations. As noted by object theorists (Scott 2013), rules and procedures are one of the primary "things" that get institutionalized in organizations, sometimes to great effect.

Sayings and Vocabularies in Fields
For purposes of institutional analysis, culture that has been internalized by people – what cognitive anthropologists Strauss and Quinn (1997) – refer to as "personal culture," is found in both their routine or habitualized activities (or "practices"), and via linguistic externalization (in the talk and text and text they produce): essentially, in people's *doings* or in their *sayings* (Li, 2017); note that while all sayings are a type of doing, not all doings are sayings since some practices are non-linguistic. This is the second branching on the people side.

Sayings are personal in that they are ultimately produced by people drawing on their internalized knowledge of conventional forms of linguistic expression. However, due to their linguistic nature sayings are in the world because they require embedding in a semiotic system (usually, a natural language) to be perceived as patterned and meaningful. In sociology, researchers primarily study sayings in the form of "vocabularies of motive" or "accounts" used by individuals to justify and provide meaning to their patterns of activity and ways of life (Mills, 1940; Scott & Lyman, 1968). Accounts are forms of personal culture that can enjoy greater or lesser degrees of institutionalization (Swidler, 2001a). In the figure, these "vocabularies in people" stand toward the personal side of the divide.

Institutional theorists draw on this tradition of studying sayings but focus on particular forms of collective account-making used to communicate the propriety or correctness of a set of organizational structures and practices to external audiences so that they appear as "prudent, rational, and legitimate" (Meyer & Rowan, 1977, p. 349). Recently, researchers have become interested in the specifically linguistic structure of these types of collective sayings in organized settings, both in terms of the diffusion of particular words (and associated concepts) used by organized actors, and the dynamic evolution of patterns of word co-occurrence and linkages as proxy for changing meanings of key terms (Loewenstein, Ocasio, & Jones, 2012). These "vocabularies of organizing" therefore represent an important class of objects that may be subject to institutionalization processes (Ocasio & Joseph, 2005). All of these types of vocabularies (of motive, structure, organizing, and so on) stand squarely in the personal/public culture boundary (shaded gray area); I refer to them as "vocabularies in fields," and they are one of the primary objects of institutionalization processes.

Practices and Organizational Routines

Following practice theory, science and technology studies, and recent developments in the study of organizational routines, doings are seen as embodied in people's "procedural" skills, habits, and capacities (Bourdieu, 1990; Cohen & Bacdayan, 1994; Pinch, 2008; Sieweke, 2014). They are thus located toward the "strong" side of the personal continuum as these would not exist as such without being deeply internalized by individuals via processes of learning and training. However, when habits and skills are assembled as publicly recognized *organizational routines*, especially those that rely on the distributed, interlinked, and interdependent pattern of activities enacted by multiple people (Hutchins, 1995), then they also straddle the boundary of persons and the world (Pentland & Feldman, 2005, p. 795); hence, the location of this variant of culture in the shaded gray area between people and the world.

ADVANTAGES OF THE PROPOSED SCHEME

Personal Culture (and thus People) Is Central to Institutions

The proposed classification of potential objects of institutionalization processes has several advantages. The main one is that people, and thus microfoundations, come for free. This deals with one of the major lines of criticism of state approaches emphasizing the purely external aspects of institutions, which somehow lost track of the fact that people are required to keep institutions going (Hallett & Ventresca, 2006; Lawrence et al., 2011). However, inhabited, structuration, and work approaches have mainly focused on adding to the process toolbox of institutional theory (e.g., by pointing out that core institutionalization processes require people and their situated interactions to make them happen and keep them going). My point is more fundamental, and that is that a lot of what is *subject* to institutionalization process is embodied and produced in and by people in either habitualized actions and practices and patterned ways of constructing meaning in language and interaction for purposes of legitimation, sense-making, accounting, justifying, and so on.

Artifacts (and thus Technologies and Material Culture)
Is Central to Institutions

Materiality also comes for free. In this respect, the approach proposed here is fully compatible with the "material and visual turn" in organizations studies (Boxenbaum, Jones, Meyer, & Svejenova, 2018). A sticking point in institutional analysis, even for approaches emphasizing the fact that institutions are composed of "material practices" (e.g., Thornton, Ocasio, & Lounsbury, 2012), is that materiality is hard to find. Instead, analysts focus on *talk* about objects and practices and not on the material bases of institutions as embodied in material objects (Jones, Boxenbaum, & Anthony, 2013). This is not to say that studying the institutionalization of field-level vocabularies taking material practices are their referent is not worthwhile; however, substituting them for actual artifacts and practices is a category mistake at the level of institutional ontology.

In the refurbished approach, we do not have to choose. Practices engaged in by people, the material location and the artifacts involved in those practices (a relatively neglected aspect of the microfoundations of institutions), and sayings and vocabularies taking the practices, and the material objects as their referents are all elements potentially subject to institutionalization processes (Orlikowski, 2000). These all three are distinct elements, some closer to personal culture, others closer to public culture; whether linkages between them exist is an empirical question, not an analytical issue.

Specifying the Objects Helps Clarify State Accounts

State accounts point to the static or contemporaneous aspect of something as a definitional aspect of institutions. As we saw above, phenomenological theorists look to people considering a given way of doing things as "taken-for-granted" or external as just such a signature. This type of state account is limited because it does not apply to all possible objects. For instance, a variety of practices, habits, and routines, may enjoy the quality of being a pervasive and reliable reproduced part of social life without anybody necessarily having a particular phenomenological attitude toward them. This was a "mark" of institutionalization in evolutionary theories of institutions developed in the nineteenth century. While this does not work as a general theory, it does apply to the "non-declarative" set of habits and practices and routines that make up the "doings" part of personal culture.

Overall, theorizing the objects of institutionalization leads us to realize that there are as many "signatures" of this state as there are types of cultural objects and analytically distinct process-object linkages. Some states are stronger diagnostic markers of institutionalization for some objects. For instance, the traditional phenomenological markers used by externalization theorists are probably a more powerful signature for semiotic codes than they are for routines, or artifacts. In the same way, when it comes to vocabularies, a more significant mark of institutionalization is having acquired a stereotypical structure reducing variance in both lexical choice and the sequential links between different concepts. This applies to both vocabularies in persons and vocabularies in fields (Loewenstein et al., 2012; Swidler, 2001a). In the case of material culture and technologies, diffusion, adoption, and in particular *embeddedness* into the routine practices of a field is a stronger a mark of institutionalization than the collective belief they are the only way of doing things (Colyvas & Jonsson, 2011); a set of material artifacts can be firmly embedded in a given field (and thus count as strongly institutionalized) even if people believe that there are better options out there.

The refurbished approach can also help us clarify what is meant by "more or less" or "stronger versus weaker" forms of institutionalization (Tolbert & Zucker, 1996). For instance, theories limiting themselves to specifying the conditions for any subtype of culture to count as institutionalized make weaker claims than those that require *couplings* or linkages across different types of culture (e.g., personal and public culture). One may propose that a mark for the "full" institutionalization of a pattern requires the creation of a *link* between at least two types of institutional objects in a field. This could be a link between a set of practices or routines and semiotic codes "fixing" the meaning of the practice for external audiences (Li, 2017), or a link between certain skills and habits and set of material artifacts and technologies in an organized setting (Pinch, 2008). Even stronger forms of institutionalization may involve entire "circuits" linking multiple types of institutional objects such as external codes, artifacts, their practices in mutually sustaining (actor)networks resilient to disruption (Lawrence & Suddaby, 2006). However, note that the more links proposed, and thus the stronger the criteria for institutionalization used, the less likely it is that we will see them realized empirically since the number of mechanisms and processes required to generate and sustain those linkages increases exponentially in the number of elements that are supposed to be connected, and is the likelihood of entropy, decay, and erosion.

Specifying the Objects Helps Clarify Process Accounts

The refurbished approach to the objects of institutionalization also helps to clarify existing process accounts. Different processes operate preferentially on different institutional objects, and this is something that process theorists seldom articulate clearly. By the same token, the same process (e.g., diffusion) can operate on distinct objects in analytically separable ways. Finally, some processes are (by definition) incapable of operating on some objects.

Take, for instance, Tolbert and Zucker's (1996) phenomenological process account as summarized earlier. It is clear that habitualization processes fall closer to the realm of personal culture as they are grounded in people's habits and practices. Within formal organizations, this pertains to the formation of routines encoded in procedural memory (Cohen & Bacdayan, 1994) and performed "by specific people, at specific times, in specific places" (Feldman & Pentland, 2003, p. 93). As Tolbert and Zucker note, the development of new habits and routines is usually a response to local exigencies and problems by either individual institutional entrepreneurs or organizational actors. This means that the first stage of institutionalization in their account starts with the internalization of novel forms of personal culture externalized as practices, which may be then strongly linked to local vocabularies and codes fixing their meaning (Li, 2017).

This is different from objectification processes because these are closer to the realm of public culture. Objectification, in its essence, requires the development of a consensual semiotic code disambiguating the meanings of habitualized actions for external audiences outside of the context of use (Li, 2017). Thus, what was previously a "performative" and localized activity pattern can now be referred to in an "ostensive" manner as if it was an externally existing "thing"; hiring, firing, designing, consulting, investing, and so on (Feldman & Pentland, 2003). Objectification also requires the development of more or less stereotyped sayings in the form of vocabularies of motive and justification produced by actors when queried as to the meanings of their practices (Mills, 1940). These may in their turn blossom into full-blown field-level vocabularies endowed with specifiable structure, consensual meaning, and a restricted lexical choice set (Ocasio & Joseph, 2005).

Reconstructing the phenomenological process account in this way helps us realize that the full complement of institutionalization processes leading to the strongest forms of institutionalization as a steady-state requires patterning, repetition, relative homogeneity, linkage, and self-reproduction across a broad set of *distinct* institutional objects (e.g., habits, vocabularies, semiotic codes). As noted earlier, this would entail the operation of different mechanisms activities and structures working at multiple levels and not necessarily operating in tandem (Weber & Glynn, 2006). But, this should also be expected to be a rare phenomenon. In this respect, the institutionalization and linkage of a set of objects in a field (e.g., material technologies and associated routines) does not have to be accompanied by the institutionalization of a related but distinct set of objects (e.g., vocabularies of organizing taking these as their referent), and will usually involve a panoply of distinct processes enacted by different actors (Lawrence & Suddaby, 2006).

One implication of this, not necessarily explicit in extant process accounts is that, empirically, we will be unlikely to observe many "institutions" in the sense of the simultaneous locking-in of the full complement of institutional objects depicted in Fig. 1 into a mutually supportive dialectic of self-reproduction. Instead, the institutionalization of some objects may grind against the lack of institutionalization of others; in the same way, different processes operating selectively on particular objects means that institutionalization will proceed at "different speed, stability, and variation" (Li, 2017, p. 521). Exploiting gaps, contradictions, disjunctions, and "loose couplings" between different institutionalization processes operating on distinct institutional objects at different time-scales thus becomes a natural avenue from which people can enact institutional change in a given field (Lawrence & Suddaby, 2006).

Specifying the Objects Helps to Discover New Object/Process Links

Finally, the proposed object approach allows us to enact a sharper and more empirically accurate separation between mechanisms (how) and objects (what) of institutionalization. This can lead to the consideration of process/object linkages that have been excluded in previous process theories by fiat. For instance, Tolbert and Zucker (1996, pp. 176–177) implied that the diffusion process did not apply to habits, skills, and routines. In their analysis, only explicit public typifications (semiotic codes) of these patterns of action diffused.

Keeping in mind that diffusion as a process does not in itself imply institutionalization as an outcome (Colyvas & Jonsson, 2011), recent theoretical and empirical work mitigate against this restriction. As Sieweke (2014) has argued, procedural routines and skills may diffuse via mechanisms of mimicry, embodied simulation, and "mirroring" (Lizardo, 2007). The *diffusion* mechanism (related to process) is distinctive in having no particular affinity to any of the broad classes of institutional objects, as doings, sayings, material artifacts, and their use, or particular ways of assigning public meanings to either sayings or doings can diffuse. This may even be the reason for its centrality in empirical work on institutionalization. However, this does not imply that the specific diffusion mechanism will be the same for types of institutional objects. We should expect that spread of doings, sayings, and public semiotic codes to be governed by distinct variants of the diffusion process at both the micro and macro levels.

CONCLUSION

In this chapter, I have proposed a "refurbished" object account of the building blocks of institutions, synthesizing across a number of lines of organization theory and institutional analysis (Jones et al., 2013; Loewenstein et al., 2012; Pinch, 2008), and recent developments in cultural theory in cultural sociology, cognitive anthropology (Lizardo, 2017; Patterson, 2014; Quinn et al., 2018). The proposed approach relies on an analytic disaggregation of the culture concept to specify the possible set of "objects" that can be said to be institutionalized and thus be said to be the "building blocks" of institutions.

Broadly, I argue for an analytic distinction between "doings" (practices, habits, and routines), "sayings" (vocabularies), semiotic codes, rules of the game, and material technologies and artifacts as the broad types of objects that could be subject to institutionalization as a state and on which institutionalization processes operate. I argued that state and process accounts need to be decoupled from object accounts, because the same process (e.g., diffusion, theorization, and endorsement) may work on different objects via distinct pathways. In the same way, different "marks" of institutionalization as a steady state (e.g., taken for grantedness) are stronger diagnostics for particular object types (codes). Some processes, on the other hand, such as habitualization, can only work on a restricted set of objects (practices, routines). Other processes work by forging linkages between different types of institutional objects (e.g., practices linked to semiotic codes fixing their meaning, vocabularies linked to material artifacts serving as their referent).

This leads to a distinction between "weak" and "strong" criteria for institutionalization, with the former merely stating that a single class of objects enjoys some level of organization or pattern and latter proposing in addition to this that there are specifiable linkages across different types of objects hooking them together into a mutually supportive loop. This last situation should be uncommon, as most organizational fields will feature temporally discontinuous and only partially overlapping levels of institutionalization across their constitutive objects, with different institutionalization processes operating preferentially on some subset of those objects. These gaps, discontinuities, and "loose couplings" in levels and mechanisms of institutionalization across objects then become the natural raw material for people's attempts at institutional innovation, maintenance, disruption, and change.

NOTES

1. While using the term "people," I do not mean to restrict the following account to institutionalization to pure "individual-level" action and cognition. After all, the distributed, independent performance of practices by multiple generate "organizational routines," (Feldman & Pentland, 2003, p. 96) while highly patterned vocabularies shared across agents generate field-level codes and discourses (Loewenstein, Ocasio, & Jones, 2012) (see Fig. 1).

2. The inclusion of "artifact" as an object of institutionalization processes is meant to make room for institutionalization processes operating on material culture and technologies (Pinch, 2008). I provide a broad definition of the term later in the chapter.

3. I understand that the term "culture" is subject to a similar definitional morass as "institution." However, recent work in cultural analysis has begun to cut through that morass, mostly by abandoning the idea that there is a single "thing" called culture and following a *disaggregation strategy instead*. Readers interested in the theoretical foundations of the approach offered here should consult Lizardo (2017), Patterson (2014), Strauss and Quinn (1997), and Shore (1996).

4. This notion of artifact thus comes very close to the way that term "equipment" is used in strands of the Philosophy of Mind inspired by (Heideggerian) existentialism (Dreyfus, 1991) and embodied phenomenology (Merleau-Ponty, 1962).

REFERENCES

Archer, M. S. (1996). *Culture and agency: The place of culture in social theory*. Cambridge: Cambridge University Press.

Barley, S. R., & Tolbert, P. S. (1997). Institutionalization and structuration: Studying the links between action and institution. *Organization Studies*, *18*(1), 93–117.

Berger, P. L., & Luckmann, T. (1966). *The social construction of reality: A treatise in the sociology of knowledge*. New York, NY: Doubleday.

Bourdieu, P. (1990). *The logic of practice*. Stanford, CA: Stanford University Press.

Boxenbaum, E., Jones, C., Meyer, R. E., & Svejenova, S. (2018). Towards an articulation of the material and visual turn in organization studies. *Organization Studies*, *39*(5–6), 597–616.

Clark, A. (2006). Language, embodiment, and the cognitive niche. *Trends in Cognitive Sciences*, *10*(8), 370–374.

Cohen, M. D., & Bacdayan, P. (1994). Organizational routines are stored as procedural memory: Evidence from a laboratory study. *Organization Science*, *5*(4), 554–568.

Colyvas, J. A., & Jonsson, S. (2011). Ubiquity and legitimacy: Disentangling diffusion and institutionalization. *Sociological Theory*, *29*(1), 27–53.

DiMaggio, P. J., & Powell, W. W. (1991). Introduction. In W. W. Powell & P. J. DiMaggio (Eds.), *The new institutionalism in organizational analysis* (pp. 1–38). Chicago, IL: University of Chicago Press.

Dreyfus, H. L. (1991). *Being-in-the-world: A commentary on Heidegger's being and time, división I*. Cambridge, MA: MIT Press.

Feldman, M. S., & Pentland, B. T. (2003). Reconceptualizing organizational routines as a source of flexibility and change. *Administrative Science Quarterly, 48*(1), 94–118.

Ghaziani, A. (2009). An "amorphous mist"? The problem of measurement in the study of culture. *Theory and Society, 38*(6), 581–612.

Greenwood, R., Oliver, C., Lawrence, T. B., & Meyer, R. E. (2017). *The SAGE handbook of organizational institutionalism*. London: SAGE.

Hallett, T., & Ventresca, M. J. (2006). Inhabited institutions: Social interactions and organizational forms in Gouldner's patterns of industrial bureaucracy. *Theory and Society, 35*(2), 213–236.

Hays, S. (1994). Structure and agency and the sticky problem of culture. *Sociological Theory, 12*(1), 57–72.

Hirsch, P. M. (1997). Review essay: Sociology without social structure: Neoinstitutional theory meets brave new world. *The American Journal of Sociology, 102*(6), 1702–1723.

Hutchins, E. (1995). *Cognition in the wild*. Cambridge, MA: MIT Press.

Jepperson, R. L. (1991). Institutions, institutional effects, and institutionalism. In W. W. Powell & P. J. DiMaggio (Eds.), *The new institutionalism in organizational analysis* (pp. 143–163). Chicago, IL: University of Chicago Press.

Jones, C., Boxenbaum, E., & Anthony, C. (2013). The immateriality of material practices in institutional logics. *Research in the Sociology of Organizations, 39*, 51–75.

Khan, S. R., & Jerolmack, C. (2013). Saying meritocracy and doing privilege. *The Sociological Quarterly, 54*(1), 9–19.

Lawrence, T. B., & Suddaby, R. (2006). Institutions and institutional work. In S. R. Clegg, C. Hardy, T. Lawrence, & W. R. Nord (Eds.), *The Sage handbook of organization studies* (pp. 215–254). Thousand Oaks, CA: Sage.

Lawrence, T., Suddaby, R., & Leca, B. (2011). Institutional work: Refocusing institutional studies of organization. *Journal of Management Inquiry, 20*(1), 52–58.

Li, Y. (2017). A semiotic theory of institutionalization. *Academy of Management Review, 42*(3), 520–547.

Lizardo, O. (2007). "Mirror neurons," collective objects and the problem of transmission: Reconsidering Stephen Turner's critique of practice theory. *Journal for the Theory of Social Behaviour, 37*(3), 319–350.

Lizardo, O. (2017). Improving cultural analysis: Considering personal culture in its declarative and nondeclarative modes. *American Sociological Review, 82*(1), 88–115.

Loewenstein, J., Ocasio, W., & Jones, C. (2012). Vocabularies and vocabulary structure: A new approach linking categories, practices, and institutions. *The Academy of Management Annals, 6*(1), 41–86.

Malafouris, L. (2013). *How things shape the mind: A theory of material engagement*. Cambridge, MA: MIT Press.

Merleau-Ponty, M. (1962). In C. Smith (Trans.), *Phenomenology of perception*. New York: Routledge.

Meyer, J. W., & Bromley, P. (2013). The worldwide expansion of "organization." *Sociological Theory, 31*(4), 366–389.

Meyer, J. W., & Jepperson, R. L. (2000). The "actors" of modern society: The cultural construction of social agency. *Sociological Theory, 18*(1), 100–120.

Meyer, J. W., & Rowan, B. (1977). Institutionalized organizations: Formal structure as myth and ceremony. *The American Journal of Sociology, 83*(2), 340–363.

Mills, C. W. (1940). Situated actions and vocabularies of motive. *American Sociological Review, 5*(6), 904–913.

Ocasio, W., & Joseph, J. (2005). Cultural adaptation and institutional change: The evolution of vocabularies of corporate governance, 1972–2003. *Poetics, 33*(3), 163–178.

Oliver, C. (1992). The antecedents of deinstitutionalization. *Organization Studies, 13*(4), 563–588.

Orlikowski, W. J. (2000). Using technology and constituting structures: A practice lens for studying technology in organizations. *Organization Science, 11*(4), 404–428.

Patterson, O. (2014). Making sense of culture. *Annual Review of Sociology, 40*(1), 1–30.

Pentland, B. T., & Feldman, M. S. (2005). Organizational routines as a unit of analysis. *Industrial and Corporate Change, 14*(5), 793–815.

Phillips, N., Lawrence, T. B., & Hardy, C. (2004). Discourse and institutions. *Academy of Management Review, 29*(4), 635–652.

Pinch, T. (2008). Technology and institutions: Living in a material world. *Theory and Society, 37*(5), 461–483.

Powell, W. W., & Colyvas, J. A. (2008). Microfoundations of institutional theory. In R. Greenwood, C. Oliver, R. Suddaby, & K. Sahlin-Andersson (Eds.), *The Sage handbook of organizational institutionalism* (pp. 276–298). Thousand Oaks, CA: Sage.

Quinn, N., Sirota, K. G., & Stromberg, P. G. (2018). Conclusion: Some advances in culture theory. In N. Quinn (Ed.), *Advances in culture theory from psychological anthropology* (pp. 285–327). London: Palgrave Macmillan.

Scott, R. W. (2013). *Institutions and organizations: Ideas, interests, and identities*. London: Sage.

Scott, M. B., & Lyman, S. M. (1968). Accounts. *American Sociological Review, 33*(1), 46–62.

Searle, J. R. (2006). Social ontology: Some basic principles. *Anthropological Theory, 6*(1), 12–29.

Sewell, W. H., Jr. (2005). The concept (s) of culture. In *Practicing history: New directions in historical writing after the linguistic turn* (pp. 76–95). New York: Routledge

Shore, B. (1996). *Culture in mind: Cognition, culture, and the problem of meaning*. Oxford: Oxford University Press.

Sieweke, J. (2014). Imitation and processes of institutionalization. *Schmalenbach Business Review, 66*(1), 24–42.

Spillman, L. (1995). Culture, social structures, and discursive fields. *Current Perspectives in Social Theory, 15*(1), 129–154.

Strang, D., & Meyer, J. W. (1993). Institutional conditions for diffusion. *Theory and Society, 22*(4), 487–511.

Strauss, C., & Quinn, N. (1997). *A cognitive theory of cultural meaning (Vol. 9)*. Cambridge: Cambridge University Press.

Swidler, A. (2001a). *Talk of love: How culture matters*. Chicago, IL: University of Chicago Press.

Swidler, A. (2001b). What anchors cultural practices. In K. K. Cetina, T. R. Schatzki, & E. von Savigny (Eds.), *The practice turn in contemporary theory* (pp. 74–92). London: Routledge.

Thornton, P. H., Ocasio, W., & Lounsbury, M. (2012). *The institutional logics perspective: A new approach to culture, structure, and process*. Oxford: Oxford University Press.

Tolbert, P., & Zucker, L. G. (1996). The institutionalization of institutional theory. In S. Clegg, C. Hardy, & W. R. Nord (Eds.), *The handbook of organization studies* (pp. 175–190). London: Sage.

Weber, K. (2006). From nuts and bolts to toolkits: Theorizing with mechanisms. *Journal of Management Inquiry, 15*(2), 119–123.

Weber, K., & Dacin, M. T. (2011). The cultural construction of organizational life: Introduction to the special issue. *Organization Science, 22*(2), 287–298.

Weber, K., & Glynn, M. A. (2006). Making sense with institutions: Context, thought and action in Karl Weick's theory. *Organization Studies, 27*(11), 1639–1660.

Weber, K., Heinze, K. L., & DeSoucey, M. (2008). Forage for thought: Mobilizing codes in the movement for grass-fed meat and dairy products. *Administrative Science Quarterly, 53*(3), 529–567.

Zilber, T. B. (2012). The relevance of institutional theory for the study of organizational culture. *Journal of Management Inquiry, 21*(1), 88–93.

Zucker, L. G. (1977). The role of institutionalization in cultural persistence. *American Sociological Review, 42*(5), 726–743.

CHAPTER 11

IDENTITY WITHIN THE MICROFOUNDATIONS OF INSTITUTIONS: A HISTORICAL REVIEW

Anna E. Roberts

ABSTRACT

Identities provide a human link between macro-level mechanisms and micro-foundations of institutions. Yet, as the literature on identity within the micro-foundations of institutions has developed, scholars have begun to shift their understanding of "who" populates the microfoundations of institutions. This chapter offers a historical review of this niche, but growing, area of research. More specifically, the author identifies and discusses three phases of research on identity within the microfoundations of institutions, their ontological and epistemological assumptions, and their implications for the area. To conclude, the author reflects on the possible theoretical avenues for future research on identities within the microfoundations of institutions.

Keywords: Historical review; identity; institutional theory; microfoundations; microfoundations of institutional theory; social identity theory (SIT); social constructivist theory of identity

Identity, at its core, answers the question "Who am I?" Identities serve as an important part of way that people produce and are produced by their social and institutional contexts, and how they seek to exercise their agency over it. Understanding

Microfoundations of Institutions
Research in the Sociology of Organizations, Volume 65A, 235–249
Copyright © 2020 by Emerald Publishing Limited
All rights of reproduction in any form reserved
ISSN: 0733-558X/doi:10.1108/S0733-558X2019000065A023

identities and how they shape institutional processes, therefore, are crucial for any meaningful understanding of the microfoundations of institutions. Empirical research at the intersection of people's identities, identity work, and institutions has been an influential area of scholarship for over a decade (Creed, DeJordy, & Lok, 2010; Creed, Scully, & Austin, 2002; Giorgi & Palmisano, 2017; Kyratsis, Atun, Phillips, Tracey, & George, 2017; Leung, Zietsma, & Peredo, 2013; Lok, 2010; Meyer & Hammerschmid, 2006; Rao, Monin, & Durand, 2003; Reay & Hinings, 2009;). Yet, as the literature on identity within the microfoundations of institutions has developed, scholars have shifted their understanding of "who" populates the microfoundations of institutions.

The aim of this chapter is twofold. The first goal is to identify and review, despite its scarcity,[1] exemplars of past empirical scholarship related to identity *within the microfoundations of institutions*. By this, I mean studies engaging with concepts and theories of identity at the level of individuals or persons, such as their self- or personal identities. With acknowledgement that no level of analysis should be more "real" than the others (Friedland & Alford, 1991), I focus on people's identities, and, therefore, do not focus on research at the intersection of organizational identity and institutional theory.[2] Part of this goal is also to provide other scholars with a theoretical overview of the empirical work on identities within the microfoundations of institutions that has been done to date. This historical approach permits a critical discussion of the past, present, and possible future state of identity research within the microfoundations of institution. It also allows me to draw implications more broadly for research on the microfoundations of institutions.

The second aim for this chapter is to shed light on the paradigmatic shifts behind the changing "who" of institutions through historical review and analysis of each period's scholarly frames of identity within the microfoundations of institutions. By engaging in a historical review of the concept of identity within the microfoundations of institutions, I find that the concept of identity underwent a progressive evolution. Nearly absent in foundational and early literature, identity within the microfoundations of institutions began with the domination of social identity theory (SIT) (Phase 1), which implied a top-down, cognitive, and psychology-based approach. Then, a turn toward a social constructivist concept of identity within the microfoundations of institutions (Phase 2) was marked by the publication of Lok (2010) and Creed et al. (2010). In the most contemporary period, the microfoundations of identity within institutionalism has taken a more intellectually pluralistic approach to the concept of identity, including both top-down and bottom-up conceptualizations (Phase 3). The ensuing plethora of definitions and concepts of identity within the microfoundations of institutions draws from microsociology, discourse, symbolic interactionism, and critical theory.

This chapter is organized as follows: for each phase that I identified, I denote the dominant theoretical approach to identity and the empirical chapters from the period that exemplify this approach ("exemplars"). Then, I detail and discuss the theoretical approach to identity, its ontological and epistemological assumptions related to identity, and its implications for the microfoundations of identity within institutionalism. For context, I start with the foundational and early literature in institutional theory and its connections to identity within the microfoundations of institutions. I then detail each phase in chronological order. I conclude with a reflection on the possible theoretical avenues for future research on identities at the microfoundations of institutions.

FOUNDATIONAL AND EARLY LITERATURE IN INSTITUTIONS (PRIOR TO 2003)

To theorize the role of the individual in institutions as different from other rational actor models, early institutional scholars engaged lightly with social psychology and micro-sociology research related to identity and related topics, particularly Zucker (1977) in her work on role identities. Influential foundational scholars for institutional theory, such as Mead (1934), Cooley (1902/1956), Berger and Luckmann (1967), Parsons (e.g., 1951), and Goffman (e.g., 1983) engaged with identity in their own work. Yet, as exemplified by Creed et al., (2002) and their studies of legitimating accounts for and against workplace anti-discrimination policies for LGBT people, the scholars' focus on elucidating institutional dynamics meant that identity was conceptualized as a self-evident concept, rather than explicitly defined.

Assumptions. The assumption existed among early scholars that "the psychology of mental structures" provided an implicit microfoundation to the sociology of institutions (DiMaggio, 1997, p. 271). Early scholars envisioned identity at the microfoundations as cognitive; however, that may be an artifact of the cognitive emphasis in psychology at the time. Zucker (1991, p. 105) wrote, "without a solid, cognitive, microlevel foundation, we risk treating institutions as a black box at the organization level, focusing on content at the exclusion of developing a systematic explanatory theory of process." Identities, though not articulated in depth, also were envisioned as doubly embedded in institutions. Jepperson (1991), for example, suggested that institutions conferred identities and the actors themselves are constructed institutions.

Exemplar. Creed et al. (2002) drew upon Goffman, social movement theory, and other micro-sociological theories to connect the production of identities with institutions. The authors adopted a "framing approach to identities," but did not explicitly define the concept of identity. Their study found that identity within the microfoundation of institutions relies on "'tailor-made' legitimating accounts, defined as cultural narrations and myths, dominant assumptions, inherent ideologies, and 'master frames'." Thus, identities were depicted as mutually constitutive with institutionalizing processes (Creed et al., 2002, p. 480). Identities were also conceived as situated in time and space and involving attributes, relationships, and actions (Creed et al. 2002, p. 480). Their findings led to theorization of identities as dynamic processes, not static.

Implications. Identity within the microfoundations of institutions lacked a cohesive theoretical understanding of identity itself. Yet, interest in identities within the microfoundations of institutions was building. Scholars at the time called for an examination of "the interdependence between institutions and individual identity and roles" (Dacin, Goodstein, & Scott, 2002, p. 52).

PHASE 1 (2003–2009): SOCIAL IDENTITY THEORY (SIT) DOMINATES

With the greater concern for agency and actors (e.g., Battilana, 2006; DiMaggio, 1988), institutional theorists began to turn toward a concern for individuals and how they understand themselves within institutions (e.g., Seo & Creed, 2002; Zilber, 2002). To theorize how people understand themselves, scholars within this period primarily relied on SIT and its variants (SIT) (Ashforth & Mael, 1989; Tajfel, 1982; Tajfel & Turner, 1986; Turner, 1984). Three empirical works that employ the SIT during this period act as exemplars. First, Rao et al. (2003) studied the influence of identity movements and institutional change by studying elite chefs' identity changes from classical to nouvelle cuisine. Second, Meyer and Hammerschmid (2006) examined how shifts in institutional logics can be examined by changes in public-sector workers' identities. Third, Reay and Hinings (2009) found how physicians and regional health authority managers maintain separate identities to maintain the rivalry between two competing institutional logics in a field.

Assumptions. SIT and its variants stress "how people form identities in relation to others through cognitive attachments to social categories – that is, in groups and outgroups" (Ashcraft, 2013, p. 11), despite some recent refinements (Ashforth, 1998; Bartel & Dutton, 2001; Haslam & Reicher, 2007).[3] Once a group identity is made salient in a given situation, all other identities recede and that single group identity, or social identity, guides the behavior (Tajfel & Turner, 1985). The concept of the self is treated as containing two separable elements of "personal identity" and "social identity" (Ashford & Mael, 1989). All three exemplars explicitly cite SIT and its variants as the definition of identity and engage, in varying degrees, with its theory of identity.

Three embedded assumptions in SIT influence its onto-epistemic approach related to the role of cognition, the nature of identity targets, and the understanding of identity as a resource. First, SIT treats identification as a nearly entirely cognitive process. Because identities encompass one's affiliation to specific social groups, identities are the result of deliberate and conscious affinities (e.g., Chattopadhyay, Tluchowska, & George, 2004; George & Chattopadhyay, 2005). As a result, individuals are assumed to possess the agency and the ability to resist identification and reshape identities, including sexual orientation, and racial and gender identities (Ashcraft, 2013; Nkomo, 1992). Thus, this cognitive emphasis assumes that during identification, a person is deciding among well-defined groups.

Second, because social groups provide identities, a person is assumed to choose an identity among well-established unified identities. Thus, SIT implicitly conceptualizes identities as objective, stable, and unchanging targets, including race and gender (Chattopadhyay et al., 2004; George & Chattopadhyay, 2005).

This relatively stable and static view of identities treats the associated levels of identification between a person and her targeted group(s) to be fairly uniform across people (Alvesson, Ashcraft, & Thomas, 2008) and regardless of institutional context and material bodies.

Third, the two previous assumptions – identities as discrete, largely static mental resources that encompass one's affiliation to groups – reveal a conceptualization of identities where identities act as freely available and controllable resources. By framing identities as *mental* resources tied to affinities, rather than embodied phenomena, SIT scholars implicitly claim what is important is how I *think* of my race or gender (Ashcraft, 2013; Nkomo, 1992). Identities are conceptualized as fully available to those who mentally and consciously "target" the social group, regardless of their own body or physical attributes. In addition, identities rarely are conceptualized as able to commingle with, to be interdependent of, or to be mutually dependent on other identities. Because an identity arises only when a social group is salient in a person's mind, identities are only constrained by institutions or organizations when such entities influence cognitive functioning.

Exemplars. In the Phase 1 exemplars, SIT's reliance on cognition allowed for the strong connection between logics and identities. These exemplars viewed identity as top-down and deterministic process, where identities are drawn directly from associated institutional logics. Rao et al. (2003) defined identity using a variant of SIT (p. 797) and explicitly tied identification to logics and cognition. Identification occurred when "situational logics create distinctive categories, beliefs, expectations, and motives and thereby constitute the social identity of actors" (Rao et al., 2003, p. 797). Explicitly defining identities using SIT, Meyer and Hammerschmid (2006, p. 1001) depicted identities as cognitively tied to logics because identities "change with the logics that shape them." Although they minimally engaged with SIT in its text, Reay and Hinings (2009) also depicted a physician's identity as connected to logics in a deterministic fashion. Because a physician cognitively identified as a physician, a physician was assumed to support the logic of medical professionalism, despite the new dominant field logic of business-like health care. These logic-specific elements of cognition (i.e., expectations, categories, and vocabularies) deliberately influence which social identities people claim. Thus, in this study, logic-specific elements of cognition are the primary essence of identities.

Furthermore, the connections between logics, identities, and social groups in the exemplars support SIT's assumption related to stable and enduring nature of identities. In the Phase 1 exemplars, identities within the microfoundations of institutions are concomitant with logics and with social groups. Therefore, a stability and commonality between logics, identities, and groups to connect must exist at some point. To sustain the connection, identities must map onto the social groups created by associated institutional logics. For instance, if a person encounters multiple institutional logics, multiple matching social identities then become available to her (Meyer & Hammerschmid, 2006; Rao et al., 2003; Reay & Hinings, 2009). These multiple logics give cognitive access to identity by providing vocabularies and the legitimating accounts that people can draw up on to indicate to others their identity (Meyer & Hammerschmid, 2006, p. 1005).

Identities are provided by institutions in this view; identities are not seen as intertwined or co-constitutive of logics.

However, the Phase 1 exemplars did challenge the conceptualization of identities, logics and groups as perpetually static, particularly as depicted in SIT. Rao et al. (2003) borrowed from social movement theory to challenge the idea of group identity to be unitary in nature. As an increasing number of classical cuisine chefs responded to identity-discrepant cues, more chefs defected to the nouvelle cuisine identity. The "groupness" of nouvelle cuisine, thus, was variable rather than fixed (Rao et al., 2003, p. 838). Meyer and Hammerschmid (2006) adhered to SIT's conceptualizations of identities as multiple additive mental resources, but emphasized the instability and impermanence of the institutional realm. Reay and Hinings (2009) noted that the dominant field-level logic had changed to business-like health care and political pressures existed for doctors to switch logics. However, the individual doctor's identity remained a physician and, thus, she instead was guided by the medical professionalism logic instead. Thus, identity within the microfoundations of institutions was more fragile than SIT, depending on the state of the logic within the field and the state of the group itself.

However, this flexibility did not extend to the nature of the identity itself. Identities in the Phase 1 exemplars were depicted as discrete entities and multiple identities cannot exist simultaneously, as in SIT. For instance, a person with an identity as a doctor cannot also identify as a businessperson. Identities are conceptualized as "contingent, flexible resources in interaction" (Meyer & Hammerschmid, 2006, p. 1001), and thus, to a degree, can be chosen. Multiple identities are not simultaneously understood considering each other. Rather, identities must compete or be reconciled into a singular identity produced by "hybridization" of the two competing identities (Meyer & Hammerschmid, 2006, p. 1006; Rao et al., 2003, p. 836).

In sum, employing SIT to theorize identity within the microfoundations of institutions did not challenge SIT's view of identification. People primarily were seen as freely choosing their identification, albeit to the extent allowed by institutional context. Identities were also experienced as cognition and as objective, stable, and unchanging targets. In doing so, employing SIT continued to depict people within institutions as primarily cognitive and rational actors, despite ongoing shifts away from such view in the literature.

Implications. If the use of SIT undercut the shift away from the primarily cognitive and rational approach that the microfoundations movements held promise for, what advantages did SIT confer upon the exemplars of identity within microfoundations research in this phase? SIT provided early institutionalists exploring the microfoundations of identity with an explicit definition of identity and theoretical approach to identities at the microfoundational level. Theories from psychology and organizational behavior (OB) are often borrowed to form microfoundations of organizational theory; institutional theorists have advocated such borrowing (Powell & Colyvas, 2008; Powell & Rerup, 2017). At this time, SIT reigned as the dominant theory of identity (Nkomo, 1992). By extending the presumed macro-level theory of institutional theory to the individual level, these scholars risked being perceived as illegitimate. Thus, SIT and its exceedingly well-established literature was a prime candidate for understanding identity in the microfoundations of institutional theory.

However, this cognitive emphasis limited the role of emotion and "felt" social experience. Cognition and emotion require each other. Feeling is not free of thought and thought is not free of feelings (Zajonc, 1980). Identification solely through cognition ignores the material conditions of the body and its relationship to identities. It ignores how particular identities, such as race and gender, require a certain type of body to enact it. These bodies come with constraints and implications which alters how a person maneuvers the implications of her body in social interaction and in institutions, no matter what she thinks (Ashcraft, 2013; Nkomo, 1992). By perpetuating a view of identities as purely cognitive tools, Phase 1 reinforced cognitive bias in institutionalism.

By viewing access to identities as merely access to logics, the exemplars gave remarkable agency toward people and their creativity, abilities, and energies as they navigate multiple logics. This certainly departed from the notion of "cultural dopes" (Powell & Colyvas, 2008, p. 277) found in "old" institutionalism. However, this concept of identities as freely and equally available to all was also problematic. In sum, the Phase 1 approach supported the rational actor model, deemphasized the role of emotions and feelings in identification, and privileged macro-processes over microfoundations.

PHASE 2 (2010): SOCIAL CONSTRUCTIVIST IDENTITY TURN BEGINS

Social constructivists believe that the question "Who am I?" implicates another question: "how should I act?" (Cerulo, 1997). A person's ongoing attempts to address both questions are important to microfoundational institutionalist approach. In contrast to SIT's static and fixed conceptualization, this view emphasizes identities as "becoming, rather than being" (Alvesson et al., 2008, p. 15). In this approach, individuals are bound to create meanings, from available cultural material beyond their personal experience (Cerulo, 1997), such as "cultural frames" (Callero, 2003) or "social-identities" (Watson, 2008). Thus, this approach views the self as a social construction that is mutually constituted by internal, personal elements and external, cultural elements.

Two empirical works ushered in the social constructivist approach to identity within the microfoundations of institutions, and thus, are the exemplars of this brief and important phase (Creed et al., 2010; Lok, 2010). Lok (2010) found that as investors engaged in micro-level identity work, their practices transformed new institutional logics. Creed et al. (2010) found how gay and lesbian ministers, as embedded marginalized actors, use cultural resources to engage in embodied identity work that creates experiences of contradictory institutional prescriptions.

Assumptions. Incorporating the external aspects of identity brought institutionalism to bear on social constructivist aspects of identities at the microfoundations. Watson's (2008) theory of social identity linked aspects of "internal" personal identity work and the "social-identities" that individuals draw on in identity construction. Originating in context and external to selves, social-identities are cultural, discursive, or institutional notions of who any person might be. Social-identities pertain to all people in the various environments in which they live their lives. Implicit in his theory was a critique of the tendency of identity research to deemphasize the contextual, external, and/or social influences on the processes of identity work. Watson (2008) strengthened the analytical power of the concept of identity by incorporating an explicit recognition that identity work shapes both the external and internal elements of identity.

In social constructivism, identification arises from the processes of identity work. Identity work is defined as

> the mutually constitutive processes whereby people strive to shape a relatively coherent and distinctive notion of personal self-identity and struggle to come to terms with and, within limits, to influence the various social-identities which pertain to them in the various milieu in which they live their lives. (Watson, 2008, p. 129)

People themselves make these institutional meanings underlining their identities through these identity resources: people have the scope to interpret or even modify the role given to them in the "script" of any given identity.

Watson (2008) also takes a more critical bent to identities: identities exist and are acquired, claimed and allocated within power relations because identity work occurs as others attempt to tell us who or what we are. A person may utilize identities as institutional resources to advance their own objectives. However, people do not utilize identities completely out of free will or as a matter of personal whim (Watson, 2008). Because of the many diverse, competing and contradictory discursive pressures upon and resources available to every individual in the contemporary world (Giddens, 1991), engagement in identity work is unavoidable and plurality of often competing social-identities exists (Alvesson et al., 2008, p. 6). The use of these identity-making cultural resources also varies.

Exemplars. For exemplars in this phase, identities and identity work exist when both internal self-reflection and external engagement come together – through talk and action – with various institutional "building blocks." Creed et al. (2010) explicitly operationalized the term "identity" using the definition by Watson (2008) to emphasize the "internal" and external aspects of identity work. The authors' engagement with Watson (2008) allowed them to incorporate the idea in their analysis that through personal identity work actors can influence, within limits, the various institutionally prescribed social-identities that pertain to them. In other words, individuals' notions of who and what they are, accomplished through identity work, can act back on the institutional notions of who or what any individual might or should be, and affect institutional structure.

Identities entwined feelings, values and behaviors, and point them in particular, and sometimes conflicting, directions (Alvesson et al., 2008). Creed et al. (2010) pushed against the notion of identities as purely cognitive structures and employed Watson (2008) to theorize about how identities are not purely mental resources. In this study, identities were highly emotionally charged, where contradictions are embodied and "lived, rather than merely cognitive experiences" (Creed et al., 2010, p. 1356). LGBT ministers were not purely heroic change agents or cultural dopes; instead, they were both enabled and constrained by their embeddedness and commitment to their denominations. This study contradicted the notion that identities are purely cognitive and normative structures experienced in the form of behavioral assumptions, expectations, or norms. Instead, the subjectively lived experience and emotions were crucial to an understanding of identities and identity work in institutional theory.

Lok's (2010) study showed how SIT no longer fit the needs of institutional research. The study's strong conception of identities as derived from logics could have allowed the study to employ SIT and its associated assumptions, as the Phase 1 exemplars did. Instead, Lok (2010) drew directly from the social constructivist approach to identity. In turn, his findings significantly departed from prior understandings of the microfoundations. Lok's (2010) illustrated that identities are no longer defined purely by their relation to social units or related logics. People within the microfoundations of institutions encountered a multiplicity of logics which influence and shape their identities. Because logics are another source of cultural scripts, as in Creed et al. (2002), identities did not emerge from the logic as a fully formed mirror of the logic. Instead, logics acted as "inputs" to the self-identity. In this study, changing logics still influenced how actors reproduce and translate new institutional logics into their identities, but did not result in a wholesale transformation into identical identities.

Implications. Unlike Phase 1, the Phase 2 approach to identities portrayed identities as not only an outcome but also as a mechanism of institutionalization. Identities, in turn, craft institutions. Cognition did play a role in the Phase 2 approach to identity within the microfoundations of institutions, but not in the same way as in Phase 1. In Phase 1, identities are mental resources that are internal to selves, but mirroring external social conditions. However, in Phase 2, external engagement brings people into contact with institutional, discursive, and cultural resources that become part of their identity work, and eventually become incorporated into internal notions of the self.

PHASE 3 (2011-PRESENT): MULTIPLE THEORIES AT PLAY

In the most contemporary period, the microfoundations of identity within institutionalism has taken a more intellectually pluralistic approach to the concept of identity (Phase 3). Some scholars continued to engage with the SIT (Phase 1) and social constructivist (Phase 2) approaches to identity, while others brought new theories to play. Rather than solidifying into one approach, identity within the microfoundations of institutions continued to be defined in a variety of ways.

Three empirical works exemplify this phase. Leung et al. (2013) researched people content with one institutionally prescribed identity and no other identity targets in sight: Japanese housewives. Giorgi and Palmisano (2017) studied people who participated in mystic Catholic communities in Italy. Kyratsis et al. (2017) analyzed how individual physicians from five European countries navigated shifts in institutional logics during the transition from Soviet to Western health care system model.

Assumptions. This multiple paradigmatic approach did not create a cohesive set of assumptions operating in Phase 3. For instance, Kyratsis et al. (2017) defined identity akin to Phase 1 scholars and relied on SIT research (p. 611). Leung et al. (2013) defined identity similar to Phase 2 scholars, defining identity as consisting of external and internal components (p. 3). In contrast, Giorgi and Palmisano (2017) provided no explicit definition and treated the concept of identity as self-evident, but the scholars did engage with discourse and critical research on identities. The assumptions of Phase 3, thus, were characterized by the theory at play in the exemplar, rather than being able to be characterized cohesively.

Exemplars. Leung et al. (2013) found that by engaging in actions to obtain healthier food and products for their families as part of enacting their house-wife identity, the women also interacted with the multiple institutional pressures. These interactions eventually sparked an emotionally driven conflict with the housewife identity, reshaping their personal identity along with their institutional identity. Giorgi and Palmisano (2017) found that rather than the experience of institutional contradictions acting as motivation for mystic Catholics to engage in endogenous change, identity work to achieve a coherent sense of self also acted as institutional maintenance work. Even if such identity work was "costly," mystic Catholics also experienced an intensity of emotions such as joy, love, and awe and were not willing to forgo them (Giorgi & Palmisano, 2017, p. 813). In an empirical context with a highly contested shift in professional logic with powerful actors championing the change, Kyratsis et al. (2017) found that some profession-als worked to change their identities, while others actively worked to maintain all or part of their original identities. The degree to which doctors adopted the new professional identities associated with the new logics affected the degree to which they enacted logics at a local, including new work practices, vocabularies, and new professional titles.

Implications. Leung et al. (2013) relied upon social constructivist, structural interactionist, and structuration theories to theorize the recursive loop between social structures – such as institutional process, pressures, and opportunities – and identities in people. By emphasizing the recursive aspects of identities and institutions, Leung et al. (2013) explained how and why identities do not per-fectly mirror an institutionally prescribed logic and often depart from them in significant ways. Kyratsis et al. (2017) employed SIT initially, but its findings challenged SIT by positing interrelationships between multiple group identities. For doctors with a more pro-Western identity, the logic shift allowed them to be both a doctor and an entrepreneurial businessperson (p. 632). The authors are not alone in their continued use of psychology theories at the microfounda-tions of identity. Brandl and Bullinger (2017) wrote a theory article advocating for identity control theory, another psychology theory, as the microfoundations of identity within institutions. Alternatively, Giorgi and Palmisano (2017) used the term identity without a corresponding micro-theory of identity. Instead, the scholars theorized within institutional theory. Thus, Phase 3 raised the ques-tion: do we need a *single* theory of identity to undergird the microfoundations of institutionalism, at all?

DISCUSSION

Identity acts as a human link between macro-level mechanisms and microfoundations of institutions. To investigate this link, this historical overview illuminates the theories and assumptions underpinning this intersection. The Phase 1 exemplars adopted the cognitively heavy view of SIT; yet, SIT's dominance in OB conferred legitimacy on identity within the microfoundations of identity. Phase 2 exemplars had a more socially constructed approach to identity; this allowed identities to be envisioned as a recursive mechanism of institutionalization. The exemplars in Phase 3 employed prior approaches and experimented with new ways of conceptualizing identity, even complicating the identity concepts that it employed. Thus, this research on identity within the microfoundations of institutions allowed both theories to evolve in complexity and nuance. Institutional theory research has become less deterministic, top-down, and static, and identity research more frequently recognizes that institutions and the social world have impact on identity work and identity.

However, no paradigmatic consensus has emerged. Some may have hoped to find a declaration, particularly institutional scholars who consider the theory's "uninhibited" theorization dangerous (Alvesson, Hallett, & Spicer, 2019) and OB scholars who fear a similar encroachment of identity research (Alvesson et al., 2008; Brown, 2019). This historical review, however, suggests such a declaration would be premature. As institutional theory evolved and grew in directions difficult to foresee, different enabling theories of identity provided different implications for research and for our scholarly community. Institutional theory, thus, will continue to be a pluralistic field with multiple paradigms operating within its microfoundations.

Future scholars may want to consider which conceptualizations of identity are appropriate for the intellectual conversation and the research community within institutionalism. Institutional theory and organizational theory are growing in its appreciation of emotions (Voronov & Vince, 2012; Creed, Hudson, Okuysen, & Smith-Crowne, 2014; Voronov & Yorks, 2015; Zietsma, Toubiana, Voronov, & Roberts, 2019); many of the exemplars have been a crucial part of that appreciation. Identity within the microfoundations research may find insights from "institutional biography," studying accounts of identities in relation to the institutions that structured their lives and that they worked to create, maintain, or disrupt (Lawrence, Suddaby, & Leca, 2011). New approaches to identity within the microfoundations, such as Hazan and Zilber's narrative identity (this issue) and inhabited institutions (e.g., Delbridge & Edwards, 2013), may begin new phases.

As the "human link" between the microfoundations and macro-process of institutions, identities within the microfoundations of institutions will be important to scholarly understanding of ongoing social and organizational challenges. For example, as organizations and institutions become more fragmented due to the growing gig economy and industry disruptions, identities may be the most evident way to understand both connections to institutions (Roberts & Zietsma, 2018) and how workers can best cope with its toll (Petriglieri, Ashford, & Wrzesniewski, 2019). Perhaps by continuing to find ourselves and others' identities, we can continue to flesh out the people within the microfoundations of institutions.

ACKNOWLEDGMENTS

I am extremely grateful to Jost Sieweke, Patrick Haack, and Lauri Wessel for giving me the opportunity to pursue this project. I thank Jost and an anonymous reviewer for pushing me to sharpen my argument. I also grateful to the organizers and the participants of the 2015 EGOS Sub-Theme on Institutions and Identities and the 2016 EGOS Sub-theme on Bringing Emotions out of the Shadows of Institutions for their insights into earlier drafts of this manuscript and their help honing my ideas. I also appreciate the participants of the Brown Bag Seminar at the Schulich School of Business, York University, for their encouragement and thoughtful feedback at a very early stage of this chapter and my academic career.

NOTES

1. Theorization at the intersection of organizational identity and institutional theory examines the identification of organizational members, but only as a part of organizational identity and not as a process onto itself (see Glynn, 2008; Glynn, 2017, for review; Schilke, 2018, for recent empirical example). Although outside the microfoundational focus of this volume and chapter, institutional scholarship employing organizational identity theory (Albert & Whetten, 1985) also has relied on social identity theory-based concepts and theories of identity alongside institutional theory in their research explicitly and implicitly (e.g., Foreman & Whetten, 2002; Glynn, 2000, 2008). Therefore, I consider organizational identity related-research beyond the scope of this review.

2. The initial identification of empirical exemplars in 2015 used the Web of Science citation mapping to trace the influence of key social identity theory (SIT) and key micro-sociological articles in institutionalist empirical research. This allowed me to identify influential empirical articles that engaged with identity within the microfoundations of identity without being restricted to keyword searches. In 2018, the earlier identification of empirical articles was supplemented with a more systematic search using the keywords identity; identification; identities; self; ident* and institutionalism, institutional theory, institutions, institution, and institut* (with wildcards to catch variants) in the following journals with a significant institutionalist presence: *Academy of Management Journal, Administrative Science Quarterly, Journal of Management, Management Science, Organization Science, Organization Studies,* and *Research in the Sociology of Organizations.* I then read the abstracts and, if necessary, the text to identify relevant works. I excluded works that were either a theoretical article or did not explicitly engage with the institutions and identity at the individual-(or person-) level. For instance, much work was excluded because the article focused on the organizational-level, collective- or professional level, or field-level identity (see Footnote 1).

3. Recent research on SIT in OB has evolved to incorporate situational and processual interpretations (Ashforth, Kreiner, & Fugate, 2000; Ashforth, Rogers, & Corley, 2011; Kreiner et al., 2015). However, these approaches were not emphasized in the exemplars' use of SIT.

REFERENCES

Alvesson, M., Ashcraft, K. L., & Thomas, R. (2008). Identity matters: Reflections on the construction of identity scholarship in organization studies. *Organization, 15*(1), 5–28.

Alvesson, M., Hallett, T., & Spicer, A. (2019). Uninhibited institutionalisms. *Journal of Management Inquiry, 28*(2), 119–127.

Ashcraft, K. L. (2013). The glass slipper: "Incorporating" occupational identity in management studies. *Academy of Management Review, 38*(1), 6–31.

Ashforth, B. E. (1998). Becoming: How does the process of identification unfold. In D.A Whetten & P.C. Godfrey (Eds.), *Identity in organizations: Building theory through conversations* (pp. 213–222). Thousand Oaks, CA: Sage.

Ashforth, B. E., Kreiner, G. E., & Fugate, M. (2000). All in a day's work: Boundaries and micro role transitions. *Academy of Management Review, 25*(3), 472–491.

Ashforth, B. E., & Mael, F. (1989). Social identity theory and the organization. *Academy of Management Review, 14*(1), 20–39.

Ashforth, B. E., Rogers, K. M., & Corley, K. G. (2011). Identity in organizations: Exploring cross-level dynamics identity in organizations. *Organization Science, 22*(5), 1144–1156.

Barney, J., & Felin, T. (2013). What are microfoundations? *Academy of Management Perspectives, 27*(2), 138–155.

Bartel, C., & Dutton, J. (2001). Ambiguous organizational memberships: Constructing organizational identities in interactions with others. In M.A. Hogg & D.J. Terry (Eds.), *Social identity processes in organizational contexts* (pp. 115–130). Philadelphia, PA: Psychology Press.

Battilana, J. (2006). Agency and institutions: The enabling role of individuals' social position. *Organization, 13*(5), 653–676.

Berger, P., & Luckmann, T. (1967). *The social construction of reality.* London: Allen Lane.

Brandl, J., & Bullinger, B. (2017). Individuals' considerations when responding to competing logics: Insights from identity control theory. *Journal of Management Inquiry, 26*(2), 181–192.

Brown, A. D. (2019). Identities in organization studies. *Organization Studies, 40*(1), 7–22.

Callero, P. L. (2003). The sociology of the self. *Annual Review of Sociology,* (29), 115–133.

Cerulo, K. A. (1997). Identity construction: New issues, new directions. *Annual Review of Sociology, 23,* 385–409.

Chattopadhyay, P., Tluchowska, M., & George, E. (2004). Identifying the ingroup: A closer look at the influence of demographic dissimilarity on employee social identity. *The Academy of Management Review, 29*(2), 180–202.

Cooley, C. H. (1902/1956). *Human nature and the social order.* New York, NY: Scribner.

Creed, W. E. D., DeJordy, R., & Lok, J. (2010). Being the change: Resolving institutional contradiction through identity work. *Academy of Management Journal, 53*(6), 1336–1364.

Creed, W. E. D., Hudson, B., Okhuysen, G. A., & Smith-Crowe, K. (2014). Swimming in a sea of shame: Incorporating emotion into explanations of institutional reproduction and change. *Academy of Management Review, 39*(3), 275–301.

Creed, W. E. D., Scully, M. A., & Austin, J. R. (2002). Clothes make the person?: The tailoring and the social accounts legitimating of identity construction. *Organization Science, 13*(5), 475–496.

Dacin, M. T., Goodstein, J., & Scott, W. R. (2002). Institutional theory and institutional change: Introduction to the special research forum. *Academy of Management Journal, 45*(1), 45–56.

Delbridge, R., & Edwards, T. (2013). Inhabiting institutions: Critical realist refinements to understanding institutional complexity and change. *Organization Studies, 34*(7), 927–947.

DiMaggio, P. (1988). Interest and agency in institutional theory. In L. G. Zucker (Ed.), *Institutional patterns and organizations: Culture and environment* (pp. 3–21). Cambridge, MA: Ballinger.

DiMaggio, P. J. (1997). Culture and cognition. *Annual Review of Sociology, 23,* 263–287.

DiMaggio, P. (1988). Interest and agency in institutional theory. In L. G. Zucker (Ed.), *Institutional patterns and organizations: Culture and environment* (pp. 3–21). Cambridge, MA: Ballinger.

Foreman, P., & Whetten, D. A. (2002). Members' identification with multiple-identity organizations. *Organization Science, 13*(6), 618–635.

Friedland, R., & Alford, R. R. (1991). Bringing society back in: Symbols, practices and institutional contradictions. In W.W. Powell & P.J. DiMaggio (Eds.), *The new institutionalism in organizational analysis* (pp. 232–263). Chicago, IL: University of Chicago Press.

George, E., & Chattopadhyay, P. (2005). One foot in each camp: The dual identification of contract workers. *Administrative Science Quarterly, 50*(1), 68–99.

Giddens, A. (1991). *Modernity and self-identity. Self and society in the late modern age.* New York, NY: Polity Press.

Giorgi, S., & Palmisano, S. (2017). Sober intoxication: Institutional contradictions and identity work in the everyday life of four religious communities in Italy. *Organization Studies, 38*(6), 795–819.

Glynn, M. A. (2000). When cymbals become symbols: Conflict over organizational identity within a symphony orchestra. *Organization Science*, *11*(3), 285–298.

Goffman, E. (1983). The interaction order: American Sociological Association, 1982 presidential address. *American Sociological Review*, *48*(1), 1–17.

Greenwood, E. R., Oliver, C., Suddaby, R., & Sahlin, K. (2008). Introduction. In E. R. Greenwood, C. Oliver, R. Suddaby, & K. Sahlin (Eds.), *Sage handbook of organizational institutionalism* (pp. 1–46). Thousand Oaks, CA: Sage Publications, Inc.

Haslam, S. A., & Reicher, S. (2007). Beyond the banality of evil: Three dynamics of an interactionist social psychology of tyranny. *Personality and Social Psychology Bulletin*, *33*(5), 615–622.

Jepperson, R. L. (1991). Institutions, institutional effects and institutionalism. In P. J. DiMaggio & W. W. Powell (Eds.), *The new institutionalism in organizational analysis* (pp. 143–163). Chicago, IL: University of Chicago Press.

Kreiner, G. E., Hollensbe, E., Sheep, M. L., Smith, B. R., & Kataria, N. (2015). Elasticity and the dialectic tensions of organizational identity: How can we hold together while we are pulling apart? *Academy of Management Journal*, *58*(4), 981–1011.

Kyratsis, Y., Atun, R., Phillips, N., Tracey, P., & George, G. (2017). Health systems in transition: Professional identity work in the context of shifting institutional logics. *Academy of Management Journal*, *60*(2), 610–641.

Lawrence, T., Suddaby, R., & Leca, B. (2011). Institutional work: Refocusing institutional studies of organization. *Journal of Management Inquiry*, *20*(1), 52–58.

Leung, A., Zietsma, C., & Peredo, A. M. (2013). Emergent identity work and institutional change: The "quiet" revolution of Japanese middle-class housewives. *Organization Studies*, *35*(3), 423–450.

Lok, J. (2010). Institutional logics as identity projects. *Academy of Management Journal*, *53*(6), 1305–1335.

Mead, G.H. (1934). *Mind, Self, and Society from the Standpoint of a Social Behaviorist*. Chicago, IL: University of Chicago Press.

Meyer, R. E., & Hammerschmid, G. (2006). Changing institutional logics and executive identities: A managerial challenge to public administration in Austria. *American Behavioral Scientist*, *49*(7), 1000–1014.

Nkomo, S. M. (1992). The emperor has no clothes: Rewriting "race in organizations." *Academy of Management Review*, *17*(3), 487–513.

Parsons, T. (1951). *The social system*. Glencoe, IL: The Free Press.

Petriglieri, G., Ashford, S. J., & Wrzesniewski, A. (2019). Agony and ecstasy in the gig economy: Cultivating holding environments for precarious and personalized work identities. *Administrative Science Quarterly*, *64*(1), 124–170.

Powell, W. W., & Colyvas, J. A. (2008). Microfoundations of institutional theory. In E. R. Greenwood, C. Oliver, R. Suddaby, & K. Sahlin (Eds.), *Sage handbook of organizational institutionalism* (pp. 276–298). Thousand Oaks, CA: Sage Publications, Inc.

Powell, W. W., & Rerup, C. (2017). Opening the black box: The microfoundations of institutions. In R. Greenwood (Ed.), *Sage handbook of organizational institutionalism* (2nd ed., pp. 541–576). Thousand Oaks, CA: Sage Publishers, Inc.

Rao, H., Monin, P., & Durand, R. (2003). Gastronomy institutional change in Toque Ville: Nouvelle Cuisine as an identity movement in French. *American Journal of Sociology*, *108*(4), 795–843.

Reay, T., & Hinings, C. R. (2009). Managing the rivalry of competing institutional logics. *Organization Studies*, *30*(6), 629–652.

Roberts, A., & Zietsma, C. (2018). Working for an app: Organizational boundaries, roles, and meaning of work in the "on-demand" economy. In L. Ringel, P. Hiller, & C. Zietsma (Eds.), *Toward permeable boundaries of organizations?* (pp. 195–225). Bingley: Emerald Publishing Limited.

Schilke, O. (2018). A micro-institutional inquiry into resistance to environmental pressures. *Academy of Management Journal*, *61*(4), 1431–1466.

Seo, M., & Creed, W. E. D. (2002). Institutional contradictions, praxis, and institutional change: A dialectical perspective. *Academic of Management Review*, *27*(2), 222–248.

Tajfel, H. (1982). Instrumentality, identity and social comparisons. In H. Tajfel (Ed.), *Social identity and intergroup relations* (pp. 483–507). Cambridge: Cambridge University Press

Tajfel, H., & Turner, J. C. (1985). The social identity theory of intergroup behavior. In S. Worchel & W. G. Austin (Eds.), *Psychology of intergroup relations* (2nd ed., pp. 7–24). Chicago, IL: Nelson-Hall.

Turner, J. C. (1984). Social identification and psychological group formation. In H. Tajfel (Ed.), *The social dimension: European developments in social psychology* (Vol. 2, pp. 518–538). Cambridge: Cambridge University Press.

Voronov, M., & Vince, R. (2012). Integrating emotions into the analysis of institutional work. *Academy of Management Review, 37*(1), 58–81.

Voronov, M., & Yorks, L. (2015). "Did you notice that?" Theorizing differences in the capacity to apprehend institutional contradictions. *Academy of Management Review, 40*(4), 563–586.

Watson, T. J. (2008). Managing identity: Identity work, personal predicaments and structural circumstances. *Organization, 15*(1), 121–143.

Zajonc, R. B. (1980). Feeling and thinking: Preferences need no inferences. *American Psychologist, 35*(2), 151.

Zietsma, C., Toubiana, M., Voronov, M., & Roberts, A. (2019). *Elements in organization theory: Emotions in organization theory.* Cambridge: Cambridge University Press.

Zilber, T. B. (2002). Institutionalization as an interplay between actions, meanings, and actors: The case of a rape crisis center in Israel. *Academy of Management Journal, 45*(1), 234–254.

Zucker, L. G. (1977). The role of institutionalization in cultural persistence. *American Sociological Review, 42*(5), 726–743.

Zucker, L. G. (1991). Postscript: Microfoundations of institutional thought. In W.W. Powell & P.J. DiMaggio (Eds.), *The new institutionalism in organizational analysis* (pp. 103–107). Chicago, IL: University of Chicago Press.

CHAPTER 12

MICROFOUNDATIONS OF INSTITUTIONAL CHANGE IN THE CAREER STRUCTURE OF UK ELITE LAW FIRMS

Thomas J. Roulet, Lionel Paolella, Claudia Gabbioneta and Daniel Muzio

ABSTRACT

The authors investigate an institutional change as the co-occurrence of deinstitutionalization and institutionalization, while accounting for its determinants at multiple levels of analysis to further our understanding of how individual characteristics aggregated at the organizational level and organizational characteristics together account for the erosion and emergence of practices within the field. The authors empirically explore this question in a multilevel dataset of UK law firms and their employees, looking in particular at how the practice of equity partnership faded away and how non-equity partnership emerged as a new practice. The results contribute to the literature on institutional change and the microfoundation of institutions.

Keywords: Microfoundations of institutions; institutional change; deinstitutionalization; institutionalization; law firms; equity partnership

Recent scholarship in institutional theory in the past decade has examined the links between micro-processes, how they aggregate at the organizational level, and

Microfoundations of Institutions
Research in the Sociology of Organizations, Volume 65A, 251–268
Copyright © 2020 by Emerald Publishing Limited
All rights of reproduction in any form reserved
ISSN: 0733-558X/doi:10.1108/S0733-558X2019000065A025

institutional dynamics (Powell & Colyvas, 2008). The microfoundations agenda in institutional theory, in particular, has tried to inform the role played by everyday actions and processes carried out at a more micro-level in the institutionalization process (Powell & Rerup, 2017). However, how this micro-level exactly works, what matters there, and how it does remain to be fully understood. For some scholars, this perspective put more focus and importance to broadly defined agents (Battilana, 2006; Powell & Rerup, 2017), while others see it as an opportunity to focus on interactions at various levels of analysis (Gibson & vom Lehn, 2017). A recent work has framed this debate around the dichotomy of agency versus structure (Cardinale, 2018), while others have challenged this dichotomy to stress the importance of considering multiple levels (or a continuum of levels) of analysis in examining the microfoundations of institutions (Harmon, Haack, & Roulet, 2018). These authors call for multilevel analyses to advance our understanding of the microfoundations of institutions, taking into account that the characteristics of organizations are driven in part by the characteristics of their members and that the population of an organization, its composition, and attributes influence its decision-making and this, in turn, influences more macro-dynamics.

At the same time, research has examined institutional change (Micelotta et al., 2017), in particular through the prism of divergence and convergence of institutionalization and deinstitutionalization processes (Oliver, 1992). Institutions may erode under a variety of conditions, as they lose enactors and participants (Davis, Diekmann, & Tinsley, 1994), creating space for new institutions to emerge (Ahmadjian & Robinson, 2001). Existing work on deinstitutionalization focuses on a single level of analysis and looks at the characteristics of organizations that explain nonconformity (Maguire & Hardy, 2009). However, conceptual research suggests the existence of trickling up mechanisms as individual behaviors lead to collective decisions to disengage from a practice (Clemente & Roulet, 2015), that is, the aggregate behaviors of individuals within organizations may tilt their decisions with regards to institutions (Oliver, 1992). Similarly, we can expect that institutionalization involves trickling down mechanisms, from the structure to the group to the individuals engaging in a practice (Harmon et al., 2018). Deinstitutionalization and institutionalization can be seen as two faces of the same coin (Maguire & Hardy, 2009) as there is a recursive process alternating deinstitutionalization of old practices and institutionalization of new practices (Clemente, Durand, & Roulet, 2017; Zietsma & Lawrence, 2010). Because of these mechanisms of trickling up and trickling down, a focus on the microfoundations of institutional change as the co-occurrence of deinstitutionalization and institutionalization would inform more broadly the role of micro-level dynamics and their aggregation at the organizational level in institutional theory.

In this chapter, we aim at explaining the link between organizational and aggregated individual characteristics, on the one hand, and institutional change, as captured in the co-occurrence of deinstitutionalization and institutionalization of a new practice, on the other hand, as a way to advance the microfoundations agenda. In particular, we flesh out trickling up mechanisms that can ultimately explain why organizations deviate from existing practices because of their internal members and their idiosyncratic characteristics.

We empirically explore the question of how individuals, at the aggregate level, and organizational characteristics influence organizational decisions with regards to an institutionalized practice using an original and comprehensive multilevel dataset capturing the characteristics of organizations and their senior employees. Our quantitative study examines equity partnership in the UK legal industry and the growing number of firms engaging in a new practice: non-equity partnership (i.e., salaried partnership). Our dependent variable reflects the change of career structures and practices and the degree of engagement with the new practice, and thus the concurrent deinstitutionalization of the old practice (equity partnerships) and the institutionalization of the new one (non-equity partnership). The mutually exclusive transition from the collegial model of partnership (comprising only equity partnership) to the multi-tier partnership (including also non-equity partnership) is a strategically motivated change for law firms. We explore how demographic aspects of the organizational population such as profitability per equity partner, compensation disparity, percentage of partners on associates (normally referred to as leverage ratio), gender diversity, and partners' reputation are associated with the adoption, or the nonadoption, of the new practice of non-equity partnership.

Our work contributes to fleshing out organizational and aggregated individual determinants of institutional change, as they motivate and trigger organizations' deviance from institutionalized practices and the adoption and institutionalization of new practices. By looking at how individual populations influence organizational decisions with regards to institutionalized practices, we stress the importance of including a multiplicity of levels of analysis in the study of institutional change, and more broadly in the study of the microfoundations of institutional theory.

MICROFOUNDATIONS AND INSTITUTIONAL CHANGE

In the last decade, institutional theory has increasingly paid attention to its "microfoundations" (Powell & Rerup, 2017) although this call dates back to Zucker (1991) and DiMaggio and Powell (1991). However, limited progress has been made since then (Powell & Colyvas, 2008). The objective of the microfoundation movement is to

> understand how individual-level factors impact organizations, how the interaction of individuals leads to emergent, collective, and organization-level outcomes and performance, and how relations between macro-variables are mediated by micro actions and interactions (Felin, Foss, & Ployhart, 2015, p. 576).

In institutional theory, the starting point of the microfoundations agenda is the idea that institutions are modified and reproduced through the everyday actions of individuals (Powell & Colyvas, 2008). Individuals are not only cognitive carriers (DiMaggio & Powell, 1991) but also the actors that can bend or reproduce institutions (Lawrence et al., 2009). One reason why progress has been limited in the microfoundations of institutions is the lack of clarity with regards to what exactly microfoundations are. In particular, there has been an oscillation between focusing on interactionism (Gibson & vom Lehn, 2017) and a perspective considering agents as a broadly defined set of actors that can affect and reciprocally be affected by structure (Battilana, 2006) – "recurrent patterns of interaction or the mechanisms that cause them" (Cardinale, 2018, p. 137).

Microfoundations of Institutions: Agency and Levels of Analysis

A debate over the definition of microfoundations exists, reflecting the tensions between individualism, holism, and systemism (Reihlen, Klaas-Wissing, & Ringberg,2007). The microfoundations of institutions can be defined as the ways individual behavior can support or challenge institutions (Powell & Colyvas, 2008). For some authors, microfoundations are a way to solve the agency versus structure debate (Cardinale, 2018). Early work in this area indeed brought the role of agents to the front to explain endogenous institutional change (Battilana, 2006). Structure is the product of human agency but at the same time constrain human agency (DiMaggio & Powell, 1991). To solve this problem of embedded agency, Cardinale (2018) suggested that structure is not only a constrain to action but also a compass that orients agents, and provides them with pre-reflexivity. Empirical work has thus shown that institutional change can originate from the everyday action of individuals (Smets, Morris, & Greenwood, 2012). Structure and agency are, however, often equated to a macro–micro divide (Emirbayer & Mische, 1998) which limits our view of what agents can be and the way they can bend or reproduce structure. "Bottom-up change" (Smets et al., 2012, p. 879) is not only the consequences of individuals slowly changing field-level practices but also individuals changing the decisions made by organizations, as their effect on structure is mediated by the organizational level of analysis.

Beyond further theorization of the agency versus structure dichotomy, a focus on the role of agents needs to go beyond the sole role of individuals to take into account the way they affect organizational decision-making as a population (Harmon et al., 2018). This is consistent with a view of social theory as accounting for individual-, organizational- and field-levels of analysis (Friedland & Alford, 1991). In the case explored by Smets et al. (2012), the change at the organizational level, triggered by individual-level changes in practices, ultimately led to the field-level institutionalization of a new practice. It shows that macro-level phenomena are not only the consequences of individual behaviors (Coleman, 1986) but are also the result of individuals and organizations interrelatedly affecting institutions (Udehn, 2002).

Looking at the behavior of organizations through their micro-level composition is a way to move forward the research agenda on the microfoundations of institutions, considering the importance of intermediate levels of analysis between individuals and fields. We focus here on how the demography and population characteristics of organizations can help us understand organizational decision-making. Such a perspective also enables to account for the nestedness of levels of analysis as "everything is micro to something and macro to something else" (Harmon et al., 2018). Including multiple levels of analysis, when identifying the determinants of institutional processes, also ensure that key mechanisms at the organizational- or field-levels are not ignored beyond individual behaviors.

Institutional Change as the Co-occurrence of Deinstitutionalization and Institutionalization: A New Perspective on Microfoundations

In parallel to the debate on the microfoundations of institutional theory, a recent body of work has brought together institutionalization and deinstitutionalization as two sides of the same coin (Zietsma & Lawrence, 2010) to explain and understand institutional change (Micelotta et al., 2017). Cycles of stability – in which actors engage in practices that amount into the reproduction of institutions – succeed to cycles of change – during which new practices emerge. As noted by Zietsma and Lawrence (2010), existing work in institutional theory tends to focus solely on either stability or change and ignore the way in which one process leaves room for the other.

One of the processes at the core of institutional lifecycle is deinstitutionalization (Oliver, 1992; Maguire & Hardy, 2009). Deinstitutionalization is the process leading to the erosion or abandonment of a practice and can be triggered by either external pressures or internal agents (Maguire & Hardy, 2009). For Oliver (1992), deinstitutionalization refers to the erosion or discontinuity of an institutionalized organizational activity or practice. In fact, deinstitutionalization suggests a shift in existing practices and activities (Davis et al., 1994). Deinstitutionalization and institutionalization are two interrelated process, as a practice is institutionalized when it has gained enough legitimacy to become a norm, and is completely deinstitutionalized when its legitimacy has finished eroding (Oliver, 1992). Practices are rarely fully institutionalized or deinstitutionalized but are often in between, as the questioning of entrenched practices can give room for new practices to emerge (Ahmadjian & Robinson, 2001). In this sense, deinstitutionalization and institutionalization form the two versants of lifecycles in which practices emerge and erode, and form a broader conceptual picture to understand institutional change. Deinstitutionalization and institutionalization have, however, often been analyzed separately, without empirically accounting for the interrelation between the two processes as we attempt to understand the processes and the pathways of institutional change (Clemente et al., 2017). Yet, if a practice is falling into abeyance, it might leave space for new ones to emerge unless the purpose and objective of the deinstitutionalized practice has lost meaning and value for the agents. In sum, in a number of contexts, institutionalization and deinstitutionalization happen jointly.

Deinstitutionalization, as the erosion or discontinuity of an institutionalized activity or practice, has a multitude of determinants at both the macro- and the micro-levels (Oliver, 1992). Research on deinstitutionalization recognizes the key role of agents as they progressively disengage from the practice, until only a minority enacts it (Davis et al., 1994). Conceptual models of deinstitutionalization flesh out the mechanisms through which individual disengagement from a practice triggers a spiral of deinstitutionalization (Clemente & Roulet, 2015). This argument relies on the proposition that institutionalized practices rely on a majority enacting them, while deinstitutionalization is usually the sign of only a minority maintaining engagement in the practice. This mechanism relies on social control, as agents are punished for engaging in a practice that is marginalized and rewarded for engaging in a practice that has become a norm (Glynn & Huge, 2007). This approach also stresses the importance of the population of organizational members and its characteristics in the deinstitutionalization of practices.

We argue that a focus on the lifecycle of institutional change, with phases of deinstitutionalization and institutionalization, is a specifically informative context to understand the importance of multiple levels of analysis in advancing the microfoundations agenda in institutional theory. In this study, we acknowledge for agency at the employee level and its consequences for organizational decision-making, while exploring the co-occurrence of deinstitutionalization and institutionalization.

EMPIRICAL SETTING AND HYPOTHESES IN CONTEXT

Our empirical setting is the UK legal industry. Law firms are a prominent professional service firm industry, characterized by knowledge intensity and a professionalized workforce (Von Nordenflycht, 2010). The importance of human capital in this industry makes it a perfect case to study microfoundations, considering the key role played by individuals and groups of individuals. The global legal industry tends to follow an American model (Dezalay & Garth, 2004) dictating organizational practices, in particular with regard to their career system (Malhotra, Morris, & Smets, 2010; Malhotra, Smets, & Morris, 2016).

In this study, we focus on the progressive emergence of non-equity or salaried partnership as an alternative to equity partnerships. Equity partners own part of the partnership and are entitled to part of the earnings, which makes this stage in a career very attractive, and plays an important role in motivating senior employees of law firms. Associates naturally aspire to partnership as their careers progress (Malhotra et al., 2010; Malhotra et al. 2016). A decision to promote an associate to partner is risky and not taken lightly by the organization, and has a range of reputational and economic consequences (Hitt, Bierman, Shimizu, & Kochlar, 2001). Law firms can, however, only sustain a limited number of equity partners as equity partnership dilutes equity (Malhotra et al., 2010; Malhotra et al., 2016). Thus, the decision to abandon or reproduce the practice of equity partnership is crucial for a large majority of law firms, to attract and retain talent and with regards to how profits are shared.

Because of the difficulties to sustain a high number of equity partners, the institutionalized practice of equity partnership is progressively eroding. This lead to the progressive emergence of non-equity (or salaried) partnership (Malhotra et al., 2010; Malhotra et al., 2016), that is, a practice that is mostly aimed at retaining top talents by offering them an alternative career path to equity partnership. Such a practice offers a number of strategic and instrumental advantages to the firms adopting it by allowing them to increase leverage and often profits. Law firms can also frame the practice as fitting with different life choices. In this sense, the new practice is accepted and spreading (Colyvas & Jonnsson, 2011) thus signaling not only institutionalization but also diffusion, through its adoption. The rise of the non-equity partnership is concurrent with a reduced proportion of equity partners because the two are mutually exclusive. Our Fig. 1 shows how the percentage of non-equity partners on the total number of partners in the top 100 law firms in the UK rose from 35% to 50%.

We now turn toward looking at the different explanations for why specific organizations might start deviating from the norm of equity partnership and adopt non-equity partnership, seeing how different levels of analysis might be connected in triggering institutional change.

Individual and Organizational Characteristics and Institutional Change

As stressed in our theory section, individual and organizational levels of analysis are deeply interrelated. The population of an organization will necessarily affect its behavior (Felin et al., 2015), and, as individual-level behaviors aggregate, a critical mass of similarly minded individuals can orient organizational decisions. In our case, the partners are the ones that have been consecrated by the institution, and they also happen to have significant decisional power.

Some determinants of institutional change are expected to be distinct from and, at least to some extent, unrelated to the population within the organization. One important predictor of the career structure and opportunities in law firm is profitability, considering that equity partnership is aimed at sharing this profitability with an increasing number of individuals (Malhotra et al., 2010). We could expect that equity partners in profitable firms may want to avoid sharing the profit and that profitable firms may thus be more likely to abandon a practice that dilutes profits. Thus, we could expect that higher *profitability per partner* will make firms more likely to deviate from the existing practice of equity partnership, in order to avoid sharing profits. Profitable firms may also have more room and leeway to be at the forefront of the deinstitutionalization process and thus innovate

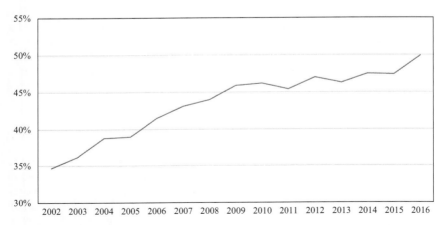

Fig 1. Percentage of Salaried Partners on Total Number of Partners.

by adopting a new practice and abandoning the old one (Spreitzer & Sonenshein, 2004). Alternatively, one could argue that profitability may enable firms to stick to existing practices, and not experience the need to change practices for survival, thus conforming to dominant existing practices. When looking at nonprofitable firms, these too may have incentives to adopt or nonadopt new practices. For example, nonprofitable firms may adopt non-equity partnership in order to avoid sharing more what is already a low pool of profit.[1] Campbell (2007), however, argues that from an institutional perspective, firms with poor profitability are unlikely to engage in new practices, because they lack slack resources. Thus, we see that there are theoretical arguments to link profitability and adoption of the new practice both positively and negatively and we thus intend to test those two sets of competing mechanisms.

H1a. Profitability per partner is positively associated with the adoption of non-equity partnership.

H1b. Profitability per partner is negatively associated with the adoption of non-equity partnership.

In addition, we can expect *compensation disparity* to affect disengagement from equity partnerships. Wide inequalities in wages are often associated with inequalities in the status of employees (Belliveau, O'Reilly III, & Wade, 1996) and with the fragmentation of the organizational population in subgroups of different salaries. In addition, as explained by Amis, Munir, Lawrence, Hirsch, and McGahan (2018), inequalities tend to reinforce themselves through the materialization and ultimately institutionalization of practices perpetuating inequalities. There are also significant evidences in economics that institutional change endogenously reinforces inequalities: Fortin and Lemieux (1997) found that a positive association between the rise in wage inequality and deunionization or economic deregulation. Finally, non-equity partnership enables the firms to give the partner title without the access to the profit pool, as a status benefit, to compensate for a noncompetitive remuneration at the industry level (Greenberg & Ornstein, 1983). Consequently, we can expect compensation disparity to be associated with the rise of non-equity partnership: this new practice increases inequality by fragmenting the population of partners as a function of their access to profit. In other terms, firms offer the title of partners but differentiate two pathways conditioning the incomes of the two groups.

H2. Compensation disparity is positively associated with the adoption of non-equity partnership.

In addition, the business model of the law firm could play a crucial role in triggering deviance from an institutionalized practice. Law firms as professional service firms are highly reliant on their human capital (Von Nordenflycht, 2010) but there is some variance in the extent to which human capital is used as a strategic lever (Bowman & Swart, 2001). Strategic human resources practices often become institutionalized because of the prevalent value proposition in an industry (Gill, Roulet, & Kerridge, 2018; Wright & McMahan, 1992). Some firms might decide to rely on cheaper, lower quality and thus less qualified associates to increase profitability. In this case, elite lawyers become expendable and the firm has an incentive in abandoning equity partnership as associates are a less crucial asset in such business model. *High leverage ratio* signals the large number of associates by contrast with the number of partners. It means that the business model is not based on the high quality of top partners. In this case, the firm will be more likely to disengage from equity partnership and engage in non-equity partnership as it would not fear a leakage of human capital. At the same time, if the business model is not based on the quality of partners, the willingness and incentives to retain and promote talent might be limited. Such a situation creates low strategic incentives for changing practices, so we could alternatively expect firms with high leverage ratio to stick to equity partnership.

H3a. A high leverage ratio is positively associated with the adoption of non-equity partnership.

H3b. A high leverage ratio is negatively associated with the adoption of non-equity partnership.

In addition, we could expect diversity within the organization, in particular **gender diversity**, to prompt disengagement with equity partnerships. Existing research has shown that a more diverse base in the relationships with outside stakeholders could prompt new practice adoption (Raffaelli & Glynn, 2014). A more diverse employee base may also be more open to institutional change, especially as individual members of an organization, in their diversity, can provide the basis for support to a new practice (Vican & Pernell-Gallagher, 2013). Law firms may also use non-equity partnership strategically to maintain the status quo with regards to diversity. Non-equity partnership can help prevent emerging minorities to reach the equity partnership level by giving them access to a second best option to retain them.

H4a. Gender diversity is positively associated with the adoption of non-equity partnership.

Positive evaluations might also play a role in deviation from the norm (Daudigeos, Roulet, & Valiorgue, 2018; Paolella & Durand, 2016). One of the key social evaluations playing a role in the engagement with institutions is reputation (Rao, 1998). Reputation is defined as the "stakeholders' perceptions about an organization's ability to create value relative to competitors" (Rindova, Williamson, Petkova, & Sever, 2005, p. 1033). The uncertainty about the quality of a service provider is compensated by the exchange of information that forms the basis for a reputation judgment (Rao, 1998). Reputation at the organizational level can be conceptualized as the aggregation of micro-level behaviors (Etter, Ravasi, & Colleoni, forthcoming), and in sectors in which human capital is so crucial such as in professional service firms (Von Nordenflycht, 2010) individuals can be the main drivers of reputation. In fact, in this case, high reputation of individuals can translate into high reputation for the organization.

In the case of law firms, partners are ranked and compared on a regular basis as experts in their areas. Partners are compared to their peers across firms, at the field level. They make or break the reputation of their organization as the individual interactions with institutionalized practices can yield organizational consequences that deter or encourage organizations to enact or refuse institutional change (Roulet, 2019). Although they form a collective for the organization, star lawyers can drive up the deference of stakeholders toward the organization. Higher reputation partners will tend to be conservative with regards to opportunities of institutional change. They will reproduce existing practices that have benefitted them and their reputation (as it enabled them to become partner) and will also align against new practices. Conformity to institutional practices is usually seen at odds with reputation as a signal of differentiation, but individual differentiation may compensate for a non-discriminating posture at the organizational level (Bergh, Ketchen Jr, Boyd, & Bergh, 2010). Thus, we expect that the higher the *average reputation of the partners* in an organization, the more reluctant their organization will be to disengage from the practice.

H5. The average reputation of the partners will be negatively associated with the adoption of non-equity partnership.

METHODS

Data Collection

We built a comprehensive dataset capturing the characteristics of organizations (UK law firms) and their senior employees (partners). We collected data on the reputation of UK lawyers in the legal directory *Chambers and Partners* for the period 2000–2016 (as in Paolella & Durand, 2016). This guide is an invaluable and indispensable source of guidance for in-house counsel in large corporations worldwide. It is designed primarily for firms that require access to pre-eminent practitioners in specific areas of law for instructing cases. Based on extensive independent research, *Chambers and Partners* provides rankings of the best lawyers operating in a specific practice area. We selected eight different practice areas (competition-antitrust, tax, litigation, employment, corporate, intellectual property, real estate, and bankruptcy) because they are independent and unrelated according to the experts and lawyers that we interviewed in preparation of this study. These practice areas not only cover conveniently all the scope of law firms but are also at the top of the list of work usually sent externally by clients and in-house counsels. In addition, we collected data on the law firms in which the ranked lawyers were affiliated with using the professional publication *Legal Business Week*.

Dependent Variable

Our dependent variable is the number of non-equity partners within a firm. The higher this number is the higher is the degree to which the firm has engaged with the new practice and disengaged from the institutionalized practice.

Independent Variables

As our independent variable, we first included *profit per equity partner* as a measure of firm performance. To capture *compensation disparity*, we included the spread between the top of equity partners and the bottom of equity partners in terms of compensation. *Leverage* is computed as the ratio associates to partners (Kor & Leblici, 2005). We use the percentage of female partners on total as a measure of *gender diversity*. Finally, to capture *reputation*, we used an average of the reputation of all partners across different practices. *Chambers and Partners* adopts an ordered scale for each practice area for each year ranging from 1 to 7, with 1 representing the highest rank. We inverted the scale to obtain an increasing value order from 1 (the lowest-ranked lawyer) to 7 for lawyers at the top of the guide's ranking. For example, in our dataset a lawyer ranked in "tax" with a value of 5 has a higher reputation than a lawyer with a value of 3 in the same practice area. We also included dummy variables to control for specific effect of each practice area. We finally captured *time fixed-effects* by including a set of dummy variables in our models.

RESULTS

To test our hypotheses, we ran random-effects negative binomial models. Descriptive statistics for the variables used are presented in Table 1, and correlations are presented in Table 2. Results testing hypotheses are reported in Table 3. Model 1 contains firm-level variables only and already yields interesting results to understand the deinstitutionalization process.

Importantly, profit per equity partner is negatively associated with non-equity partnership (significant at the $p < 0.01$ level) thus supporting *H1b*. Profitable

Table 1. Descriptive Statistics.

Variables	Obs	Mean	Std. Dev.	Min	Max
Non-equity partner	683	66.72	94.94	0	840
Profit per equity partner	683	447.96	241.30	65	1,832.5
Spread top/bottom eq. partners	683	410,495.60	308,309.30	9,000	3,550,000
Leverage	683	2.66	0.97	0.73	7.38
Lawyers gender	683	0.21	0.22	0	1
Lawyers reputation	683	2.79	0.91	1	6
Partnership size	683	159.01	178.16	18	1,302

Table 2. Pairwise Correlations.

Variables	1	2	3	4	5	6
1. Non-equity partner						
2. Profit per equity partner	0.28					
3. Spread top/bottom eq. partners	0.08	0.11				
4. Leverage	0.03	0.40	0.03			
5. Lawyers gender	0.00	−0.05	0.03	0.06		
6. Lawyers reputation	0.10	0.31	0.10	0.32	−0.02	
7. Partnership size	0.86	0.49	0.08	0.28	−0.01	0.27

firms conform to the dominant existing practice, as they do not need to adapt for survival. Nonprofitable firms may adopt non-equity partnership in order to avoid further sharing of the profits between partners.

While we would expect compensation disparity to be associated with the furthering of practice reproducing inequality within the firm – such as mixing non-equity partnership and equity partnership – we note that compensation disparity does not affect the propensity of firms to disengage from the institutionalized practice. We do not find support for *H2*.

Contrary to our first expectation, leverage ratio is negatively associated with deinstitutionalization (significant at the $p < 0.001$ level), meaning that when the ratio of associates to partner is high, the firm will stick to equity partnership. This result supports *H3b*. We might explain this result by the fact that firms with high leverage are focusing on commoditized services and thus have little need for

Table 3. Random-Effects Negative Binomial Models.

Variables	Model 1	Model 2	Model 3
Profit per equity partner	−0.002	−0.002	−0.002
	(0.010)	(0.009)	(0.009)
Spread top/bottom eq. partners	0.001	0.001	0.001
	(0.644)	(0.778)	(0.647)
Leverage	−0.25	−0.26	−0.26
	(0.000)	(0.000)	(0.000)
Lawyer gender		0.15	0.15
		(0.045)	(0.046)
Lawyer reputation			−0.08
			(0.000)
Partnership size	0.01	0.01	0.01
	(0.000)	(0.000)	(0.000)
Constant	3.38	3.43	3.78
	(0.000)	(0.000)	(0.000)
Log likelihood	−2,793.69	−2,785.2	−2,778.35
Wald chi-square	1,085.94	1,073.78	1,071.93
	(0.000)	(0.000)	(0.000)
Year fixed-effects	Yes	Yes	Yes
Observations	683	683	683
Number of firms	98	98	98

p-value in parentheses.

non-equity partnership to retain top talent. Thus, those firms stick to the institutionalized practice of equity partnership.

Model 2 adds another variable: the ratio of women among ranked partners in the *Chambers*. This variable has a positive and significant effect ($p < 0.05$) on the adoption of non-equity partnership, suggesting support for *H4*. This is aligned with our argument that diversity within organizations makes them more likely to adopt new practices because of the variety of contexts and backgrounds of their employees. The counter-argument concerning the use of non-equity partnership as a tool to discriminate against minority is invalidated.

Finally, Model 3 supports our theoretical argument regarding reputation (*H5*): we find that the average reputation of lawyers within an organization negatively affects the ratio of non-equity partners on total number of partners (significant at the $p < 0.001$ level). This result means that organization with members of higher reputation can afford to maintain a costly institution. In this case, law firms with partners of higher reputation are reluctant to engage in deinstitutionalization. This can be due to the fact that the existing practice of equity partner is seen as a positive asset that contributed to the higher reputation of its partners, thus making it likely to be maintained.

DISCUSSION

In this study, we focused on institutional change as a lifecycle of deinstitutionalization-institutionalization of equity and non-equity partnership in the UK legal industry. We explore the determinants of this process at the individual- and at the organizational-level by looking specifically at how the population of organizational members and its characteristics affect the strategic decision of the firm to disengage with an institutionalized practice to enact a new one.

We identified and discarded a number of factors that could explain institutional change toward non-equity partnership, mostly focusing on the pragmatic and economic reasons for adopting a new practice. We noted that wage inequality in the firm had no effect on the erosion of equity partnership. At the same time, profit per equity partner shows a negative relationship with the rise of non-equity partnership, meaning that profitable firms see limited incentives in switching to a new practice. Leverage shows an orientation of law firms toward selling commoditized services. Because of this orientation toward lower value-added services, these firms have a limited need to avoid high turnover and retain top talents who are trying to reach partner level. As a consequence, firms with high ratio of associates on partners will have limited incentives to abandon the practice of equity partnership. More gender balanced firms at the partner level are more likely to switch to non-equity partnership, suggesting that gender diverse firms are more prone to adopt the new practice. Finally, the aggregated reputation of a firm's lawyers is negatively associated with the deinstitutionalization of equity partnership. This result suggests that higher reputation lawyers will push their organization to stick to the practice of equity partnership, associating it with their success.

Contribution to Institutional Theory

While microfoundations have often been understood as, broadly speaking, a focus on agents, we further develop the idea that microfoundations do not necessarily only reside at the individual-level and that this individual level has consequences on organizational decision-making when averaged and aggregated at the organizational level. We started the chapter by stressing the existence of a continuum of levels affecting institutional processes – from individuals to organizations, finally trickling up to the field-level and triggering institutional change through the concurrent deinstitutionalization and institutionalization of practices. Our chapter expands on the role of multiple levels of analysis in the microfoundations of institutional theory (Harmon et al., 2018) by considering the characteristics of populations within organizations and how these populations influence organizational decision-making. We indeed tested how individuals, because of their biases, and as a collective, can influence an organization's decision to deviate from or conform to an institutionalized practice. Agents of deinstitutionalization can thus be organizations pushed by their composition and demography. For example, in our case, we looked at the sharing of profit, and the leverage of the firm, which are organizational-level aspects determined by the demography of the organization. A closer look to diversity within organizations may yield interesting results with regards to the behavior of these organizations with regards to institutions. For example, one could look at other forms of diversity beyond gender.

Suggesting a full continuum of levels of analysis to understand microfoundations of institutional theory opens a number of new questions and areas of research. Accounting for multiple levels of analysis recognizes that some levels might be more important than others depending on the setting and context. With a sole focus on individual as microfoundational determinants of (de)institutionalization we run the risk of missing a key explanatory mechanism. It is indeed crucial to look into the characteristics of populations within organizations to understand organizational behavior and ultimately field-level change.

Limitations and Future Research

We offer a broad empirical exploration of the factors that might explain the deinstitutionalization of equity partnership and the institutionalization of non-equity partnership. Further research could cover a wider time frame, and the legal industry in multiple countries, to capture more adequately the institutional dynamics. We chose an empirical context in which institutional change can be captured through a cycle of deinstitutionalization and institutionalization succeeding to each other, thus picking a specific "pathway" of institutional change (Micelotta et al., 2017). Previous studies of deinstitutionalization have recognized that the deinstitutionalization of institutionalized practices might not necessarily make room for new practices to emerge (Maguire & Hardy, 2009). In our case, non-equity (or salaried) partnership progressively replaced equity partnership

(Malhotra et al., 2010; Malhotra et al., 2016) and this might have favored the deinstitutionalization process. We could expect that without a new emerging practice to replace the old one, high reputation individuals will resist deinstitutionalization even harder as they know that the alternative is yet to be shaped. Future research could differentiate situation in which deinstitutionalization is followed by another period of institutionalization. In our empirical context, it is however difficult to disentangle whether the process of deinstitutionalization and institutionalization is due to a higher appeal of the multi-tier partnership (including both equity and non-equity partnership) or a lower appeal of the collegial partnership (including only equity partnership), or both.

As we stress the importance of studying a continuum of levels of analysis to understand the microfoundations of institutional theory, building upon Harmon et al. (2018), we call for future research to further this stream of work. How does individual resistance to an institutionalized practice shift toward group resistance? When does this resistance reach a critical mass or a threshold beyond which we can consider a practice (de)institutionalized (Clemente & Roulet, 2015)?

In addition, we could wonder whether our results are generalizable to other professional service firms (Von Nordenflycht, 2010). How do other professional service firms such as investment banks, audit firms or consulting firms differ in their determinants of engaging in institutional change? The perception of typical practices in the investment banking industry for example depends on the subgroups within this field (Roulet, 2015, 2019). In fact, within investment banks, we could expect senior executives in equity research to perceive more negatively typical practices such as bonuses and lobbying compared to executives in the mergers and acquisition teams. The stigmatization of minorities in audit firms also epitomizes the negative consequences of institutions and the resistance of employee groups (Stenger & Roulet, 2018).

CONCLUSION

In this study, we empirically examined how organizational deviance from equity partnership resulted in the erosion of this practice in the UK legal industry and the emergence of non-equity partnership as an alternative practice. By studying a specific institutional lifecycle and the co-occurrence of deinstitutionalization and institutionalization processes, while examining both demographic and organizational determinants, we acknowledge the diversity of microfoundational mechanisms in institutional theory. While microfoundations have often been understood, broadly speaking, as a focus on agents, we further develop the idea that microfoundations do not necessarily only reside at the individual level. In fact, we stress the importance of taking into account a continuum of levels affecting institutional processes, in particular as population within organizations influence their decision-making with regards to institutionalized practices, ultimately affecting institutional processes at the broader level.

ACKNOWLEDGMENTS

The authors are grateful for the feedback of the editor, Jost Sieweke, an anonymous reviewer, Michael Gill, and participants of the 2018 Oxford PSF conference and of the 2018 New Institutionalism Conference.

NOTE

1. We are grateful for the reviewer's suggestions to flesh out those mechanisms associating profitability and the adoption of the new practice.

REFERENCES

Ahmadjian, C. L., & Robinson, P. (2001). Safety in numbers: Downsizing and the deinstitutionalization of permanent employment in Japan. *Administrative Science Quarterly*, *46*(4), 622–654.

Amis, J. M., Munir, K. A., Lawrence, T. B., Hirsch, P., & McGahan, A. (2018). Inequality, institutions and organizations. *Organization Studies*, *39*(9), 1131–1152.

Battilana, J. (2006). Agency and institutions: The enabling role of individuals' social position. *Organization*, *13*(5), 653–676.

Belliveau, M. A., O'Reilly III, C. A., & Wade, J. B. (1996). Social capital at the top: Effects of social similarity and status on CEO compensation. *Academy of Management Journal*, *39*(6), 1568–1593.

Bergh, D. D., Ketchen Jr, D. J., Boyd, B. K., & Bergh, J. (2010). New frontiers of the reputation – Performance relationship: Insights from multiple theories. *Journal of Management*, *36*(3), 620–632.

Bowman, C., & Swart, J. (2007). Whose human capital? The challenge of value capture when capital is embedded. *Journal of Management Studies*, *44*(4), 488–505.

Burbano, V. C., Mamer, J., & Snyder, J. (2018). Pro bono as a human capital learning and screening mechanism: Evidence from law firms. *Strategic Management Journal*, *39*(11), 2899–2920.

Cameron, A. C., Gelbach, J. B., & Miller, D. L. (2011). Robust inference with multiway clustering. *Journal of Business & Economic Statistics*, *29*(2), 238–249.

Campbell, J. L. 2007. Why would corporations behave in socially responsible ways? An institutional theory of corporate social responsibility. *Academy of Management Review*, *32*(3), 946–967.

Cardinale, I. (2018). Beyond constraining and enabling: Toward new microfoundations for institutional theory. *Academy of Management Review*, *43*(1), 132–155.

Clemente, M., & Roulet, T. J. (2015). Public opinion as a source of deinstitutionalization: A "spiral of silence" approach. *Academy of Management Review*, *40*(1), 96–114.

Clemente, M., Durand, R., & Roulet, T. (2017). The recursive nature of institutional change: An annals school perspective. *Journal of Management Inquiry*, *26*(1), 17–31.

Coleman, J. S. (1986). Social theory, social research, and a theory of action. *American Journal of Sociology*, 1309–1335.

Colyvas, J. A., & Jonnsson, S. (2011). Ubiquity and legitimacy: Disentangling diffusion and institutionalization. *Sociological Theory*, *29*(1), 27–53.

Daudigeos, T., Roulet, T., & Valiorgue, B. (2018). How scandals act as catalysts of fringe stakeholders' contentious actions against multinational corporations. *Business & Society*.

Davis, G. F., Diekmann, K. A., & Tinsley, C. H. (1994). The decline and fall of the conglomerate firm in the 1980s: The deinstitutionalization of an organizational form. *American Sociological Review*, *59*(4), 547–570.

Dezalay, Y., & Garth, B. G. (2004). The confrontation between the Big Five and Big Law: Turf battles and ethical debates as contests for professional credibility. *Law & Social Inquiry*, *29*(3), 615–638.

DiMaggio, P. J., & Powell, W. W. (Eds.). (1991). *The new institutionalism in organizational analysis* (Vol. 17). Chicago, IL: University of Chicago Press.

Drukker, D. M. 2003. Testing for serial correlation in linear panel-data models. *Stata Journal*, *3*(2), 168–177.

Emirbayer, M., & Mische, A. (1998). What is agency? *American Journal of Sociology, 103*(4), 962–1023.

Etter, M., Ravasi, D., & Colleoni, E. (2019). Social media and the formation of organizational reputation. *Academy of Management Review, 44*(1), 28–52.

Faulconbridge, J. R., & Muzio, D. (2009). The financialization of large law firms: Situated discourses and practices of reorganization. *Journal of Economic Geography, 9*(5), 641–661.

Felin, T., Foss, N. J., & Ployhart, R. E. (2015). The microfoundations movement in strategy and organization theory. *The Academy of Management Annals, 9*(1), 575–632.

Fortin, N. M., & Lemieux, T. (1997). Institutional changes and rising wage inequality: Is there a linkage? *Journal of Economic Perspectives, 11*(2), 75–96.

Friedland, R., & Alford, R. R. (1991, October 25). Bringing society back in: Symbols, practices and institutional contradictions. In W. W. Powell & P. J. DiMaggio (Eds.), *The new institutionalism in organizational analysis* (pp. 232–263). Chicago, IL: University of Chicago Press.

Gibson, W., & vom Lehn, D. (2017). *Institutions, interaction and social theory*. London: Palgrave.

Gill, M. J., Roulet, T. J., & Kerridge, S. P. (2018). Mentoring for mental health: A mixed-method study of the benefits of formal mentoring programmes in the English police force. *Journal of Vocational Behavior, 108*, 201–213.

Glynn, C. J., & Huge, M. E. (2007). Opinions as norms applying a return potential model to the study of communication behaviors. *Communication Research, 34*, 548–568.

Greenberg, J., & Ornstein, S. (1983). High status job title compensation for underpayment: A test of equity theory. *Journal of Applied Psychology, 68*(2), 285.

Harmon, D. J., Haack, P., & Roulet, T. J. (2019). Microfoundations of institutions: A matter of structure versus agency or level of analysis? *Academy of Management Review, 44*(2), 464–467.

Hitt, M., Bierman, L., Shimizu, K., & Kochlar, R. (2001). Direct and moderating effects of human capital on strategy and performance in professional service firms: A resource-based perspective. *Academy of Management Journal, 44*, 13–28.

Kor, Y. Y., & Leblebici, H. (2005). How do interdependencies among human-capital deployment, development, and diversification strategies affect firms' financial performance?. *Strategic Management Journal, 26*(10), 967–985.

Lawrence, T. B., Suddaby, R., & Leca, B. (2009). *Institutional work: Actors and agency in institutional studies of organizations*. Cambridge: Cambridge University Press.

Maguire, S., & Hardy, C. (2009). Discourse and deinstitutionalization: The decline of DDT. *Academy of Management Journal, 52*(1), 148–178.

Malhotra, M., Morris, M., & Smets, M. (2010). New career models in UK professional service firms: From up-or-out to up-and-going-nowhere? *The International Journal of Human Resource Management, 21*(9), 1396–1413.

Malhotra, N., Smets, M., & Morris, T. (2016). Career pathing and innovation capacity in professional service firms. *Academy of Management Perspectives, 30*(4), 369–383.

Micelotta, E., Lounsbury, M., & Greenwood, R. (2017). Pathways of institutional change: An integrative review and research agenda. *Journal of Management, 43*(6), 1885–1910.

Mishina, Y., Block, E. S., & Mannor, M. J. (2012). The path dependence of organizational reputation: How social judgment influences assessments of capability and character. *Strategic Management Journal, 33*(5), 459–477.

Oliver, C. (1992). The antecedents of deinstitutionalization. *Organization Studies, 13*(4), 563–588.

Paolella, L., & Durand, R. (2016). Category spanning, evaluation, and performance: Revised theory and test on the corporate law market. *Academy of Management Journal, 59*(1), 330–351.

Polzer, T., Meyer, R. E., Hollerer, M. A., & Seiwald, J. (2016). How institutions matter in public sector reform: The sedimentation of administrative paradigms. In J. Gehman, M. Lounsbury, & R. Greenwood (Eds.), *How institutions matter* (Vol. 48B, pp. 69–99). *Research in the Sociology of Organizations*. Bingley: Emerald Publishing Limited.

Powell, W. W., & Colyvas, J. A. (2008). Microfoundations of institutional theory. In R. Greenwood, C. Oliver, R. Suddaby, & K. Sahlin-Andersson (Eds.), *The Sage handbook of organizational institutionalism* (pp. 276–298). London: Sage.

Powell, W. W., & Rerup, C. (2017). Opening the black box: The microfoundations of institutions. In R. Greenwood, C. Oliver, T. B. Lawrence, & R. E. Meyer (Eds.), *The Sage handbook of organizational institutionalism* (pp. 311–337). London: Sage.

Raffaelli, R., & Glynn, M. A. (2014). Turnkey or tailored? Relational pluralism, institutional complexity, and the organizational adoption of more or less customized practices. *Academy of Management Journal, 57*(2), 541–562.

Rao, H. (1998). Caveat emptor: The construction of nonprofit consumer watchdog organizations. *American Journal of Sociology, 103*(4), 912–961.

Reihlen, M., Klaas-Wissing, T., & Ringberg, T. (2007). Metatheories in management studies: Reflections upon individualism, holism, and systemism. *M@n@gement, 10*(3), 49–69.

Rindova, V. P., Williamson, I. O., Petkova, A. P., & Sever, J. M. (2005). Being good or being known: An empirical examination of the dimensions, antecedents, and consequences of organizational reputation. *Academy of Management Journal, 48*(6), 1033–1049.

Roulet, T. J. (2015). What good is Wall Street? Institutional contradiction and the diffusion of stigma over the finance industry. *Journal of Business Ethics, 130*(2), 389–402.

Roulet, T. J. (2019). Sins for some, virtues for others: Media coverage of investment banks' misconduct and adherence to professional norms during the financial crisis. *Human Relations, 72*(9), 1436–1463. https://doi.org/10.1177/0018726718799404

Smets, M., Morris, T., & Greenwood, R. (2012). From practice to field: A multilevel model of practice-driven institutional change. *Academy of Management Journal, 55*(4).

Spreitzer, G. M., & Sonenshein, S. (2004). Toward the construct definition of positive deviance. *American Behavioral Scientist, 47*(6), 828–847.

Stenger, S., & Roulet, T. J. (2018). Pride against prejudice? The stakes of concealment and disclosure of a stigmatized identity for gay and lesbian auditors. *Work, Employment and Society, 32*(2), 257–273. https://doi.org/10.1177/0018726718799404

Udehn, L. (2002). The changing face of methodological individualism. *Annual Review of Sociology, 28*(1), 479–507.

Vican, S., & Pernell-Gallagher, K. (2013). Instantiation of institutional logics: The "business case" for diversity and the prevalence of diversity mentoring practices. In *Research in the sociology of organizations*, Institutional Logics in Action, Part B (pp. 233–273). Bingley: Emerald Group Publishing Limited.

Von Nordenflycht, A. (2010). What is a professional service firm? Toward a theory and taxonomy of knowledge-intensive firms. *Academy of Management Review, 35*(1), 155–174.

Wooldridge, J. (2011). *Introductory econometrics*. Nashville, TN: South-Western.

Wooldridge, J. M. (2002). *Econometric analysis of cross section and panel data*. Cambridge, MA: MIT Press.

Wright, P. M., & McMahan, G. C. (1992). Theoretical perspectives for strategic human resource management. *Journal of Management, 18*(2), 295–320.

Zietsma, C., & Lawrence, T. (2010). Institutional work in the transformation of an organizational field: The interplay of boundary work and practice work. *Administrative Science Quarterly, 55*(2), 189–221.

Zucker, L. G. (1991, October 25). Postscript: Microfoundations of institutional thought. In W. W. Powell, & P. J. DiMaggio (Eds.), *The new institutionalism in organizational analysis* (pp. 103–106). Chicago, IL: University of Chicago Press.

CHAPTER 13

BASES OF CONFORMITY AND INSTITUTIONAL THEORY: UNDERSTANDING ORGANIZATIONAL DECISION-MAKING

Pamela S. Tolbert and Tiffany Darabi

ABSTRACT

This analysis investigates the micro-dynamics of organizational decision-making by exploring connections between institutional theory, on the one hand, and both social psychological research on conformity and recent work in economics on herd behavior and information cascades, on the other hand. The authors draw attention to the differences between normative and informational conformity as distinct motivational drivers of adoption behaviors by exploring their differential effects on the post-adoption outcomes of decoupling (e.g., Westphal & Zajac, 1994), customization (e.g., Fiss, Kennedy, & Davis, 2012), and abandonment (e.g., Ahmadjian & Robinson, 2001). The authors conclude that normative conformity leads to certain post-adoption outcomes while informational conformity is associated with others.

Keywords: Institutional theory; normative conformity; informational conformity; organizational decision-making; decoupling; customization; abandonment

Microfoundations of Institutions
Research in the Sociology of Organizations, Volume 65A, 269–290
Copyright © 2020 by Emerald Publishing Limited
All rights of reproduction in any form reserved
ISSN: 0733-558X/doi:10.1108/S0733-558X2019000065A027

INTRODUCTION

Institutional theory's foundational works (Meyer & Rowan, 1977; Zucker, 1977) drew on interactionist traditions such as phenomenology and ethnomethodology to argue that social norms and shared beliefs are an important source of formal organizational structure. Subsequent empirical research generated by these foundational articles, though, focused largely on the macro-level implications for explaining broad patterns of change in formal structure within and across populations of organizations. While more than 25 years have transpired since scholars began to call for more attention to the microfoundations of these patterns, or "the cognitive processes involved in the creation and transmission of institutions ... (and) their maintenance and resistance to change" (Zucker, 1991, p. 104; see also Zucker, 1977, 1987), to date, these processes remain relatively unexplored. Thus, in contrast to a common criticism made of early studies of organizations as "closed systems" – that is, predicated on a view of organizations operating in the absence of environmental influences – institutional theory has too often evoked the opposite imagery, environmental influences operating in the absence of (peopled) organizations.

We address this issue by exploring different kinds of organizational decision-making processes implied by theoretical arguments of the original formulations, examining the connection of these arguments to an older tradition of social psychological research on conformity, as well as to more recent work by economists on herd behavior and information cascades. This juxtaposition helps highlight an important distinction between normative and informational conformity (reflecting, respectively, a desire for social acceptance and a desire to make correct decisions), a distinction typically elided by institutional theorists. We argue that explicit recognition of this distinction adds to our ability to understand and integrate work that has documented varying outcomes of organizational decision-making in the context of institutional pressures. This includes studies of *decoupling* (e.g., Westphal & Zajac, 1994), *customization* (e.g., Fiss et al., 2012), and *abandonment* (e.g., Ahmadjian & Robinson, 2001). We argue that when the adoption of structures is driven primarily by normative conformity, certain post-adoption outcomes are more likely to occur, while informational conformity will be associated with other outcomes. Clarifying these micro-level processes of decision-making not only can enrich our understanding of why organizations adopt new policies and practices, a common focus of empirical work using institutional theory, but can also allow us to better predict post-adoption outcomes. Thus, based on our review of both older theoretical work and more recent empirical studies, we offer a number of propositions to be examined in further research, and discuss potential methodologies for exploring these.

To begin, in the next section, we sketch the view of organizational decision-making processes suggested in early work on institutional theory, contrasting this with one implied by then-dominant contingency-based approaches.

FROM CONTINGENCY TO INSTITUTIONAL THEORY: MODELS OF DECISION-MAKING

Institutional theory emerged in the late 1970s as a novel vantage point for explaining variations in the formal structure of organizations, a central preoccupation among macro-organizational theorists at the time. Embedded in the first major expression of this approach (Meyer & Rowan, 1977) was a very provocative – if not fully developed – view of organizational decision-making processes, one that was notably at variance with the view that underpinned the myriad analyses of formal structure conducted under the banner of contingency theory.

Contingency Theory's Implicit Model

Typically, research in the latter tradition focused on the relation between aspects of formal structure (e.g., the ratio of administrators to line personnel, the number of separate offices, the degree of specificity in job descriptions) and an array of predictor variables. Common predictors included measures of size, the nature of the core production technology used, and various environmental conditions (see summaries of this work in Aldrich & Ruef, 2006; Scott & Davis, 2007; Tolbert & Hall, 2009). Although these analyses rarely spelled out the model of decision-making implicitly underpinning them, it can be deduced from both the framing of hypotheses and interpretation of results (see Child, 1972; Donaldson, 1996; Schoonhoven, 1981; Scott, 1995).

This model is embodied by the phrase from Thompson's (1967) classic effort to distill general conclusions from this literature, one repeated with mantra-like frequency: "under norms of rationality." Formal structure was viewed as the result of decisions that presumably reflected individuals' independent and rational choices (at least boundedly rational ones). Such choices were intended to maximize efficient production through organizational design, taking into account particular conditions facing the organizations – for example, having a large number of employees or using technology that entailed high worker interdependence (Child, 1972; Donaldson, 1996; Scott, 1975). For example, the often-observed positive relation between organizational size and complexity was explained in terms of problems of duplication and coordination that accompanied increasing size, which led decision-makers to create separate subunits with explicitly differentiated responsibilities as a means of solving these problems (e.g., Blau, 1970).

These decisions were treated as being independent of those made in other organizations. In other words, organizational actors were viewed much as individual actors in classical economics, whose decisions and actions are assumed to be based on the isolated assessments of costs and benefits. When decisions were right, resulting in a structure that was efficient and effective for the conditions facing the organization, it survived; when they were wrong, the organization failed. The observed cross-sectional correlations between structural characteristics and various conditions were the consequence of such decisions.

Institutional Theory's Alternative Model

In contrast, institutional theory offered an explanation of formal structure that rested on a very different view of organizational decision-making, one strongly challenging this dominant one. It suggested that the adoption of components of formal structure is often driven by decision-makers' observations of other organizations, and pressures to meet the expectations of external constituents, rather than by independent calculations of how to accomplish work tasks efficiently. In Meyer and Rowan's words (1977, p. 343),

> Many of the positions, policies, programs and procedures of modern organizations are enforced by public opinion, by the views of important constituents, by knowledge legitimated through the education systems, by social prestige, by the laws and by definitions of negligence and prudence used by the courts.

Aspects of formal structure (job titles, written policies, etc.) associated with general social beliefs and understandings about what components well-run organizations *ought* to have are described as "institutionalized," and the adoption of such components is treated as the outcome of inter-organizational social influence processes that organizational decision-makers face (see David, Tolbert, & Boghossian, forthcoming).

This view of organizational decision-making is very much in line with a stream of research on conformity generated by social psychologists studying small groups, one that was prominent at Stanford University in the 1970s where early work on institutional theory was developed. Social psychological research provided ample documentation of the importance of perceived group consensus on a given issue as an influence on individuals' decisions. Meyer and Rowan's arguments reflected a key insight, that the operation of conformity pressures could (and should) be considered at the organizational level of analysis, with other groups and organizations outside the boundary of a focal organization – "important constituents," "educational systems," "courts," etc. – serving as sources of conformity pressures on organizational decision-makers.

NORMATIVE VERSUS INFORMATIONAL CONFORMITY: FROM SMALL GROUPS TO HERDS

However, perhaps because early institutional theorists did not elaborate on the way in which these external pressures played out in decision-making processes within organizations (let alone how they might relate to internally generated conformity pressures), the connections to the small groups research were unacknowledged. And as a result, one long-standing distinction in social psychology, between normative and informational conformity, was ignored. Failure to make this distinction led to a theoretical confound that continues to characterize work by institutional theorists to the present. To explain this further, some background on social psychological studies of conformity is needed.

Conformity Research in Social Psychology

Empirical research on individual conformity can be traced back to the beginning of the twentieth century (see Allen, 1965), but crucial work in this tradition is usually attributed to Asch who, in a series of studies in the 1950s (Asch, 1951, 1955, 1956), provided compelling demonstrations that individuals often adapt their behaviors to align with those of other group members, even when it is relatively easy to discern that those behaviors represent poor choices. In a classic design, Asch showed subjects a line, and asked them to identify which of three lines on a chart was of the same length – a task that 99% correctly accomplished on their own. However, when asked to give their responses after others (confederates) in the group all gave a different response, subjects often changed their answer, with over a third following the group and giving the same, incorrect response. This finding may be the most widely known of any social science research conducted to date and served as the source of inspiration for a voluminous literature on group influence processes, one whose outpouring continues well over half a century later (see Hodges & Geyer, 2006; Levine, 1999).

Although the majority of scholars interpreted the conformity of Asch's subjects as resulting from social pressures to go along with a view espoused by the group, despite its inconsistency with their own beliefs, Asch suggested that some subjects yielded to group pressure because they assumed the majority was right (Levine, 1999, p. 359). (Classic images and videos show subjects rubbing their eyes and staring intently at the lines as they listen to other respondents give incorrect answers.) These different interpretations were the geneses of the distinction drawn between normative and informational conformity, often credited to Deutsch and Gerard. As they expressed it (Deutsch & Gerard, 1955, p. 629), *normative conformity* is motivated by the wish to acquire "positive expectations of another" (i.e., a desire for social acceptance), while *informational conformity* reflects the use of information from others "as evidence about reality" (i.e., a desire to make the right decision, using all available data). The distinction implies important variations in motives for observed instances of conformity; this, in turn, has important implications for the stability of behavior.

The distinction between normative and informational conformity is related to another long-standing distinction in social psychology, between public and private behavior (Festinger, 1953). Research replicating Asch's work found that when subjects were removed from the group setting, and asked to perform the task again in private, they often abandoned the response they had given with the group (Allen, 1965; Luchins & Luchins, 1955, 1961). Such differences in public and private responses are consistent with the operation of normative conformity. When *only* normative conformity is operative, individuals are most likely to display a difference in public and private behaviors, and to readily abandon adopted behaviors once the normative pressure is removed (Nail & Van Leeuwen, 1993). On the other hand, work examining situations where the right answer is ambiguous – in which one might expect that informational conformity likely to be at work – have found a greater congruence between public and private responses, and continuing alignment of individual and group responses (Hardy, 1957; Raven, 1959; Zucker, 1977).

Social psychologists have continued to pursue research on each type of conformity, though relatively little work has focused on the problem of how to distinguish these different bases of conformity empirically. In fact, differing interpretations of research examining group size as a predictor variable suggest that the distinction is sometimes ignored. For example, some work treats increases in the number of confederates supporting a given choice as increasing the likelihood of social sanctions for contrarians – that is, as increasing normative conformity pressure (Campbell & Fairey, 1989; Latané, 1981; Rosenberg, 1961). In other studies, an increasing number of advocates are seen as providing greater evidence for the validity of the advocated position, and thus as representing informational influence (Asch, 1951; Mannes, 2009; Tanford & Penrod, 1984).

Informational Conformity: Herds and Cascades among Economists

More recent work by economists, who have also discovered the importance of social influences on decision-making, has concentrated largely on informational conformity. Like institutional theorists, however, they generally have downplayed or ignored connections to the older tradition of work from social psychology, and thus use different terminology, referring alternatively to "informational cascades" or "herd behavior" (Banerjee, 1992; Bikhchandani, Hirshleifer, & Welch, 1992). Both concepts refer to individuals' rejection of their private assessments of the right choice in response to observations of others' contrary choices.[1] One example of research in this tradition is provided in an experiment on sequential individual decision-making (Anderson & Holt, 1997). Undergraduate subjects in this study were given the task of making a correct choice between two possible options. After receiving private information about the probabilities of each option being correct, each was then asked to announce a choice. The decisions were made in sequence, and the choices of subjects whose turns came earlier were made known to subjects who chose later, providing them with another basis for assessing the probabilities of which option was correct. Thus, for example, a given subject might have private information indicating that "A" was the right answer but would also know how many subjects before her had chosen "B" rather than "A" before committing to a choice.

The researchers coded an information cascade as occurring when subjects (correctly) followed the choices made by earlier subjects, regardless of their own private information.[2] Cascades were found in nearly 75% of the rounds, a result interpreted in a way that meshes closely with work on informational conformity.

Although not acknowledged by the authors, such results could also be interpreted at least partly as the result of normative influences. Despite efforts to conceal which subjects were making which choices, experiments by social psychologists indicate that subjects often suspect that others can deduce who's making a given choice (Allen, 1965). Thus, subjects may have been concerned about how others would view them if their choices ran counter to a growing cascade. Because of the general neglect of differences between normative and informational conformity, economists have given little attention to the implications of this for cascades and herd behavior.

NORMATIVE AND INFORMATIONAL CONFORMITY IN INSTITUTIONAL THEORY AND RESEARCH
Theoretical Arguments

In contrast to economists' emphasis on informational conformity, early institutional theorists' arguments implicitly invoked the role of *both* informational and normative influences on organizational decision-making although, like economists, they did not acknowledge the distinction. While Meyer and Rowan (1977) generally emphasized normative pressure, they occasionally highlighted the role of informational conformity, for example, noting that (p. 347), "a particularly effective practice, occupational specialty or principle of coordination can be codified into mythlike form." Zucker's (1977, 1986) work, following a more phenomenological tradition, tended to emphasize informational conformity, at least insofar as "taken-for-grantedness" can be understood to imply the use of efficiency-based heuristics in decision-making, as highlighted by psychologists (Gigerenzer & Gaissmaier, 2011). Tolbert and Zucker (1983, p. 26), though, appear to have given more weight to normative influences in asserting,

> When some organizational elements become institutionalized, that is, when they are widely understood to be appropriate and necessary components of efficient, rational organizations, organizations are under considerable pressure to incorporate these elements into their formal structure in order to maintain their legitimacy.[3]

DiMaggio and Powell's (1983) well-known distinction between coercive, mimetic, and normative isomorphism also suggests the operation of the different conformity processes recognized in social psychology, although they do not make such differences explicit nor explore their implications. Isomorphism refers to the propensity of organizations to become structurally similar to one another over time. Coercive isomorphism, in their use (DiMaggio & Powell, 1983, p. 150), appears closely aligned with normative conformity:

> Coercive isomorphism results from both formal and informal pressures exerted on organizations by other organizations upon which they are dependent and by cultural expectations in the society within which organizations function.

Mimetic isomorphism, on the other hand, maps closely on to the notion of informational conformity – the use of others as data points, or a heuristic, in decisions under conditions of uncertainty.

> Uncertainty is also a powerful force that encourages imitation...The advantages of mimetic behavior are considerable; when an organization faces a problem with ambiguous causes or unclear solutions, problemistic search may yield a viable solution with little expense (DiMaggio & Powell, 1983, p. 151).

Their discussion of normative isomorphism, which they identify with decision-making shaped by professions and reflecting shared occupational standards and information, implies a little of both normative and informational conformity, although our interpretation of their arguments leads us to categorize this type of isomorphism as primarily reflecting normative conformity pressure. That is, professions, like social movement activists or other social groups advocating particular practices, often place pressure on organizational decision-makers to follow their prescriptions.[4] Professions differ from other groups in that they often have greater social credibility and are better organized to influence legislators to pass laws that reinforce practices and policies that they advocate (Abbott, 1988; Freidson, 2001). With few exceptions (e.g., Dobbin & Kelly, 2007; Kelly, 2003), much less attention has been given to occupationally driven (normative) isomorphism than to coercive or mimetic (Mizruchi & Fein, 1999).

Empirical Analyses

One consequence of this theoretical ambiguity is that there is a good deal of variability in empirical research drawing on institutional theory to explain organizations' adoption of various practices. Some work clearly implies normative conformity pressures as the primary source of adoption decisions. For example, in a study of organizations' responses to anti-discrimination laws, Edelman (1992, p. 1542) argues,

> As a strategy for achieving legitimacy, organizations adapt their formal structures to conform to institutionalized norms; the structures are symbolic gestures to public opinion, the views of constituents, social norms, or law,

and suggests (p. 1544) that the "quest for legitimacy is a primary motivation for structural elaboration" (although she notes this certainly is not the sole motivation). Her findings indicated that organizations that were more directly dependent on federal authorities for funding, as well as larger organizations (i.e., those apt to be more visible to authorities) were more likely to create resource-intensive formal offices, compared to other organizations which were more likely to simply adopt formal policies and statements of commitment to non-discrimination. Thus, her framing appears to emphasize normative conformity, and suggests a common disjuncture between public and private behavior, that is, the decoupling of formal structure and day-to-day practice (Festinger, 1953; Zucker, 1977).

Similarly, using a sample of 154 colleges and universities, Lounsbury (2001) examined the spread of recycling programs, which were strongly promoted by student environmental advocacy groups. He found that the majority of schools simply added recycling to the duties of an existing unit rather than creating a dedicated recycling unit, a seemingly ceremonial response.

More recently, along the same lines, Raaijmakers, Vermeulen, Meeus, and Zietsma (2015) drew on early theoretical arguments by Oliver (1991) in examining organizations' responses to legal mandates when other resource-controlling constituents and/or internal members opposed the mandates. Using an innovative combination of experimental and qualitative methods, they showed that such conflicts notably slowed the pace of compliance, and even increased the respondents' intentions to resist compliance. Overall, studies that equate institutional pressure with normative conformity often treat the adoption of new practices, policies, and structures as a strategic choice, a way of fending off sanctions by providing ceremonial or symbolic responses – very much akin to work on differences in public and private behaviors by social psychologists.

In contrast, other empirical research using institutional theory focuses on informational conformity, and often treats implementation of socially endorsed formal structures as unproblematic. For example, Greve's (1996) study of the adoption of a new programing format, Soft Adult Contemporary, by US commercial radio stations strongly emphasized rational calculations by managers based, in part, on observations of other stations' behavior. Referring to economists' work on herd behavior, he notes (p. 29), "The decision maker ... is influenced by others because they are also rational, so their actions reveal how they view the available opportunities." In line with his predictions of mimetic influence, his research showed evidence of significant contagion effects in the spread of the format, particularly among stations that had recently been sold or experienced a previous format change, suggesting that ones in an active "problemistic search" state were most likely to imitate others.

Likewise, a study by Compagni, Mele, and Ravasi (2015) of the decision-making processes underpinning the adoption of new robotic surgery technology by Italian hospitals underscores the use of others as sources of information in such decisions. Although their interviewees occasionally mentioned pressure from patients who demanded access to state-of-the-art treatment, more frequently they stressed competitive pressure as sources of their adoption decisions, a motive that is consistent with informational conformity insofar as respondents are seeking to accurately assess how to meet future service delivery requirements. Responses (p. 255) included comments such as: "Our hospital competes with [X]. Clearly, having the possibility to catch up from a technological point of view...and to be on equal footing was crucial;" and, "I do not want to miss the train." Moreover, the authors suggest that hospitals that adopted in later phases continued to critically evaluate the costs and benefits, based on observations of others' experiences before making such decisions (p. 262).

Interestingly, several studies have suggested that when adoption decisions are viewed as reflecting normative conformity, they are discounted as sources of evidence of the innovation's operational value by organizations that may still engage in informational conformity. In other words, adoptions seen as being driven by coercive isomorphic pressures will be less likely to engender mimetic isomorphism. Thus, for example, Briscoe and Safford (2008, p. 465), in a study of the spread of same-sex partner benefits among Fortune 500 companies around the turn of the twenty-first century, argued that,

> Information is more influential when it is seen as independent and not a result of normative pressure ... Activism-resistant adopters are likely to provide a stronger signal that a convincing logic of economic rationality has attached to the practice.

In support of this claim, their findings indicated that adoption of benefit policies by firms that had previously resisted overt influence efforts by external actors (and thus presumably had a reputation for recalcitrance to such efforts) significantly increased the likelihood of adoption by other firms, while adoption by firms with a record of capitulation to pressure had no effect.

In a similar vein, a later study (Briscoe, Gupta, & Anner, 2015, p. 302) examining colleges' and universities' decisions to participate in a boycott of an apparel manufacturer accused of workers' rights violations, argued that, "inferences about the merits of a controversial practice will be influenced by how prior practice adoptions are visibly associated with different activist tactics." Their results indicated that increases in the adoption of the boycott by schools that had experienced disruptive tactics by activists (sit-ins, picket lines at campus stores, demonstrations that shut down buildings) had no impact on the subsequent adoption of the boycott by other schools, but increases in adoptions by schools that had not experienced any activism, or had had information-only campaigns conducted by activists had significant effects. Their interpretation of these results is consistent with the notion of informational conformity (although it is not completely clear what specific benefits adopters expected to receive from imitation).

DIFFERENT TYPES OF CONFORMITY AND POST-ADOPTION BEHAVIORS

Thus, while couched in a shared set of theoretical concepts, arguments, and cited works, and focused on a similar problematic – decisions by organizations to adopt new policies and practices – different studies often highlight very different motives underlying adoption decisions and imply differences in decision-makers' private evaluations of the operational advantages of adoption. Such differences are critical to understanding post-adoption behavior: different types of conformity pressures are likely to affect subsequent decisions about how to implement new structures in an organization, as well as decisions about whether to retain or abandon them. Drawing upon existing empirical studies, we propose three hypotheses about how normative and informational conformity, as drivers of adoption decisions, are related to three outcomes, ones that have most often been examined in empirical studies: decoupling/implementation; customization/fidelity, and retention/abandonment. Although we discuss these as polarities, we want to emphasize that we conceive of each set as representing ends of a continuum. Thus, organizations decision-makers may choose to engage in decoupling to a greater or lesser degree; this is also true for customization and retention.

Decoupling/Implementation

Meyer and Rowan proposed decoupling as a common consequence of the adoption of formal structure that is driven by institutional pressure. They do not explicitly define decoupling, though their claim (1977, p. 357) that, "decoupling enables organizations to maintain standardized, legitimating formal structures while their activities vary in response to practical considerations" implies that decoupling involves limiting the impact of a structural change on the day-to-day behaviors and products of organizational activities, making its primary function a ceremonial one. We view decoupling and implementation as ends of a continuum, one that might be operationally defined by the amount of resources invested in some newly adopted program or policy, by the number of organizational members affected by it, or other such indicators (see Park, Sine, & Tolbert, 2010).[5]

In general, Meyer and Rowan's arguments about decoupling imply adoption decisions involving normative conformity, and their arguments parallel both the older social psychological literature on differences in public and private behavior (Festinger, 1953), and more recent, related work on impression management and facades of conformity. The latter studies explore contexts in which individuals overtly express values and attitudes to which they do not subscribe (and thus, presumably would not express in private) in order to ingratiate themselves with a larger group (Ferris, King, Judge, & Kacmar, 1991; Hewlin, 2009; Hewlin, Dumas, & Burnett, 2017). Such transient alterations in behavior in response to normative pressure are commonly referred to as "compliance" by social psychologists, which are contrasted with "internalization," denoting longer-term changes in beliefs about the factual correctness of the choice (Kelman, 1961; Nail & Van Leeuwen, 1993).

Empirical studies of decoupling provide support for treating it as compliance behavior, associated with normative conformity. In addition to work by Edelman (1992) and Lounsbury (2001) described above, studies by Westphal and Zajac (1994, 2001) of the adoption of CEO long-term incentive plans (LTIPs) and stock repurchase plans in the late twentieth century suggest these were driven largely by pressure from investors, who were increasingly swayed by the theoretical arguments of academics and other financial experts advocating them as a way to fix misalignments between managers' and shareholders' interests. LTIPs are arrangements that link CEO compensation to firms' share price, while stock repurchase plans (or buybacks) involve board approval for the firm to buy existing company shares from the market. Both have potentially negative consequences for CEOs, either putting a portion of their compensation at the mercy of market fluctuations or preventing their unrestricted control of corporate cash flows. As the authors point out, in practice, such policies were typically vague about the amount of CEO compensation that had to be part of the LTIP, and the date by which a specified amount of stock would be repurchased, thus potentially permitting decoupling.

Their research showed that while a large proportion of firms in their sample announced LTIPs and repurchase agreements, most engaged in very limited implementation of the plans. Many of the firms that announced adopting LTIPS did not actually compensate CEOs with shares of stock in a given year, and the proportion failing to do this rose considerably over time (Westphal & Zajac, 1994). Similarly, among firms announcing stock market repurchase plans, most purchased a very small proportion of available stock (Westphal & Zajac, 2001, p. 217). In both cases, indicators of CEO power were significantly, negatively related to measures of plan implementation. Thus, while ostensibly complying with pressures from external constituents to adopt practices that were accepted as signs of appropriately market-disciplined management, less publicly visible limits on implementation provided evidence of privately held managerial sentiments.

Chandler's (2014) study of firms' responses to field-level pressures to demonstrate commitments to ethical behavior yielded similar results. Four events that drew public attention to problems of unethical behavior by firms (including the passage of regulatory legislation and major court cases involving firm scandals) stimulated the diffusion of a new position among corporations, Ethics and Compliance Officer (ECO). Chandler's analyses indicated significant spikes in the creation of ECOs in the wake of each event. However, he also found that firms did not adequately resource the ECO position following adoption unless the firm received media coverage for its own specific ethical transgressions, thus upholding the relationship between normatively motivated practice adoptions and a propensity to engage in decoupling.

Studies that have focused on informational conformity (e.g., Briscoe et al, 2015; Greve, 1996) have not considered decoupling. Logically, and in line with social psychological research showing that informational conformity is usually identified with the alignment of public and private behavior, we would expect:

> *P1*. Decoupling is more likely to occur when the adoption of formal structures is driven by normative conformity pressures rather than informational.

Customization/Fidelity

Organizational innovations often (perhaps typically) consist not of one, single change option, but a bundle of interlinked changes. For example, the long-term incentive plans studied by Westphal and Zajac (1994) include options for CEOs to purchase shares in the company at a given price, appreciation rights allowing them to exchange options for a cash price, and outright grants of shares of common stocks, contingent on firm performance measures. Similarly, "golden parachutes," contractual agreements to provide CEOs with compensation if they leave their position because the firm is acquired by another, vary in the kinds of compensation they include – cash payouts, accelerated stock options, ongoing benefits, and coverage of legal fees, among others (Fiss et al., 2012). Likewise, tenure systems consist of rules about required probationary periods prior to promotion with tenure, how evaluations are to be conducted and the criteria to be considered, and which faculty members are eligible (Park et al., 2010).

Thus, when organizations follow the lead of other organizations in adopting a given innovation, decision-makers must also choose whether to tailor the practice to the specific needs, culture, and other aspects of their organization or not. While common bundles with standard options often emerge over time, decision-makers still make choices between what Westphal, Gulati, and Shortell (1997) refer to as customization and conformity (see also Ansari, Fiss, & Zajac, 2010). In the present context, since we have used "conformity" in other ways, we think it is clearer to refer to this as customization versus fidelity. Fidelity, in our use, denotes decisions to include only the bundle of elements and options that are most commonplace among other adopters.

We argue that these decisions are also likely to be affected by whether the initial adoption decision primarily reflects normative or informational conformity pressures. When organizations adopt innovations as a result of normative conformity, they are unlikely to devote time and effort to adapting them to the local needs and culture of the organizations. More faithful reproduction of what others are doing should serve as a clearer signal of compliance, and a better way of ensuring legitimacy.[6]

Empirical support for this intuition is provided by a study of the adoption of 20 different components of total quality management (TQM) programs by Westphal et al. (1997) based on survey and archival data from over 2000 hospitals. Consistent with arguments proposed by Tolbert and Zucker (1983), that earlier adopters of innovations are more likely to be driven by efficiency concerns, and later adopters more apt to be concerned with ensuring their legitimacy, they showed that, in describing their TQM programs, late-adopting hospitals were apt to report only elements that were most commonplace among other adopters; in contrast, early adopters were more likely to indicate selective incorporation of various practices as part of their TQM program. Moreover, their analysis suggested that the impact of strong network ties varied for early and late adopters: for early adopters, network connections facilitated exchange of information about the various components, leading to greater adaptation, while network connections reduced adaptation for later adopters, presumably because these now served largely to transmit norms of standardized components. Thus, the typical form of influence of other adopters on non-adopters (informational versus normative) may vary over time.

The idea that informational conformity is apt to be associated with greater adaptation is also supported by the study described earlier of the adoption of robotic surgery among Italian hospitals (Compagni et al., 2015). As the authors report, motivation to improve surgical practice and be at the cutting-edge of medicine was a key driver of the spread of robotics across hospitals even after the initial phase of adoption (Compagni et al., 2015, p. 258), encouraging practice adaptation across surgical units (spreading from cardiac surgery to urology, general and other areas).

Other work points out that motivation for adoptions is not perfectly related to timing of adoption (Kennedy & Fiss, 2009): those adopting later may be driven by informational conformity (perhaps, simply having higher standards for "evidence by numbers"), and those adopting earlier may seek the social status of being first movers, or innovators. (Note, though, that this motivation is not identical to that associated with coercive isomorphism; the latter involves compliance with relatively crystallized social expectations or demands.) Likewise, fidelity may be found during the early stages of practice adoption, sometimes as a result of a lack of knowledge about which options work best under which circumstances (Ansari et al., 2010). In general, though, we expect that in contexts of perceived threat – as is often the case with normative pressures – organizations are apt to cling rigidly to existing routines (Gilbert, 2005), therefore decreasing the likelihood of experimental adaption of a newly adopted innovation. Hence, we argue:

P2. Customization is more likely to occur when the adoption of formal structures is driven primarily by informational conformity pressures than normative.

Retention Versus Abandonment

Yet another post-adoption decision involves whether to retain changes after initial experiences with them. While decisions about decoupling or adapting are usually made soon after, if not simultaneously with the decision to adopt, decisions about retention or abandonment may be chronologically quite distant from the initial adoption. Studies of decisions to abandon existing formal structures have often been focused on structures that have been in place for many years and have become firmly accepted by both members of the organization and the larger society.

Thus, for example, Ahmadjian and Robinson (2001) examined the movement among Japanese firms in the 1990s to abandon systems of long-term (life-time) employment, systems that had been adopted by many firms more than half a century earlier as a way of addressing problems of productivity and labor unrest. By the late twentieth century, however, many firms had come to believe that the system was a liability for their global competitiveness, but because it had become institutionalized in the years since initial adoptions occurred, social and institutional pressures strongly limited decisions to abandon it via purposeful downsizing. Similarly, Briscoe and Murphy (2012) examined efforts by many large corporations at the turn of the twentieth century to abandon generous lifetime health insurance coverage for employees and families, practices that had spread in the US in post-WWII years as a means of attracting and retaining a motivated, stable workforce. As with lifetime employment systems in Japan, these benefit systems had become widely expected and accepted by employees and the general public, limiting firms' decisions about whether and how they could be abandoned (see also Fiss & Zajac, 2004). In each case, the long time span since adoption and the progressive institutionalization of the structures made abandonment happen at a slower pace – or not at all. Thus, the link between initial motivations for adoption decisions to retention decisions can be obliterated over time.

However, not all innovations become institutionalized (Tolbert & Zucker, 1996), and many have relatively short life spans after their initial adoption (Abrahamson & Eisenman, 2008). In this case, we propose that the motivations for adoption are apt to influence the likelihood of retention or abandonment. Ironically, because normative conformity is likely to result in less investment in implementing an innovation (greater decoupling), it may also lead to greater inertia in making decisions to either retain or abandon it. Insofar as its retention has relatively low costs and little effect on organizational operations, there is less pressure to eliminate it. Evaluating the impact of a given structure on public perceptions of the organization is likely to be difficult (though see Westphal & Zajac, 1998), also prompting inertia. Moreover, decision-makers may be concerned that even if an existing structure has relatively little signaling value, its *abandonment* could have symbolic consequences and entail legitimacy losses. Conversely, because adoption based on informational conformity, by definition, entails more specific, outcome-enhancing concerns, organizations are more likely to pay attention to these outcomes post-adoption. If the innovation is more fully implemented, its dysfunctions will be more readily apparent to decision-makers.

Several empirical studies provide evidence consistent with these points. One is Compagni et al.'s (2015) study of robotic surgery in Italian hospitals which, as described above, suggested the important role of informational conformity in adoption decisions. Not only did hospitals continue to adapt procedures and applications over time, but their analysis also indicates that 15 of 43 units that invested in the technology abandoned it after a few years due to concerns over economic sustainability. In line with this, examining the adoption and abandonment of matrix forms by hospitals between 1961 and 1978, Burns and Wholey (1993, p. 132) conclude:

> [...] (P)rior to adoption, organizations have little experiential knowledge about matrix management. They therefore turn to their environments for information or normative support. In the abandonment process, an organization can evaluate the matrix on the basis of its own experience.

Likewise, a study by Rao, Greve, and Davis (2001) suggested that information cascades among security analysts (Banerjee, 1992; Bikhchandani et al., 1992) often drove analysts' coverage decisions, leading them to overestimate future firm profitability. Subsequent revealing of the "true market value" led to post-decision regret and abandonment of coverage (Rao et al., 2001).

Thus, taking into account our previous caveats about potentially confounding effects of the institutionalization of structures over time, we expect that in the absence of this:

> *P3*: Abandonment is more likely to occur when the adoption of formal structures is driven primarily by informational conformity pressures than normative.

A Few Methodological Considerations

Empirically assessing whether an adoption decision reflects normative or informational conformity may be challenging, since both processes are consistent with an observed positive association between the proportion of prior adopters of an innovation at a given time point and the likelihood of subsequent adoptions by others. This does not seem an insurmountable challenge, however, and we offer some suggestions on possible ways to address it, with the aim of helping to spur further research.

First, in line with growing interest by institutional researchers in using experimental methods to explore the social psychological and interactional processes that underpin observed macro-level consequences of institutional pressure (Raaijmakers et al., 2015; Schilke, 2018), laboratory studies offer one promising avenue for research on this problem. We can envision designs similar to that used by Anderson and Holt (1997), in which subjects are provided with an adoption decision scenario, given private information on the likely "correct" decision, and information about others' – perhaps confederates' – differing choices. They could then be asked to make a public or private announcement of their decision (thus varying normative and informational conformity pressure). Following this, subjects who recommended adoption could be presented with choices involving post-adoption decisions, as the ultimate outcome variable.

Careful post-experimental surveys and manipulation checks can help to assess the underlying motives of subjects in making their decisions.

Outside of the laboratory, unstructured interviews with decision-makers who were involved in the decision to adopt a given innovation, similar to the approach taken by Compagni et al. (2015), could provide insights into decision-makers' general views and motives. As the authors of this study recognize, such accounts may be influenced by self-presentation biases – respondents' desire to present themselves or the organization as powerful, autonomous, rational actors (i.e., not at all prone to conformity of any type), but careful probing and triangulation across respondents and other archival records of the decision (e.g., email correspondence and meeting notes) could help minimize such distortions in accounts. These accounts could then be linked to information on whether and how an innovation was implemented (preferably collected prior to the interviews on the decision-making processes and from independent sources).

Even studies based strictly on archival data collection could benefit from more explicit consideration of the conditions surrounding adoption decisions as indicators of the likelihood that normative or informational conformity processes were operative. Insofar as coercive pressures are more likely to produce surface compliance (normative conformity), researchers could include indicators of the operation of such pressures in their analyses, such as newspaper accounts of social movement activities, organizations' annual reports or other public statements acknowledging pressures, the filing of lawsuits, etc. Some work has indicated that an organization's response to such pressures may depend on whether it is a direct target of the pressures or not. For example, research has shown that organizations facing discrimination law suits often show no change in their hiring of women and minorities, but those in the same industry and geographical area do increase their hires, presumably as a vicarious learning response (Hirsh, 2009). Existing research has not addressed the question of whether indirectly observed coercive pressure could also affect post-adoption decisions involving level of implementation, adaptation and whether to retain a practice, and this question deserves attention. In the absence of coercive forces at work, given evidence of social influence processes (i.e., the rate of prior adoption influences the likelihood of subsequent adoption), it seems reasonable to assume that informational conformity is dominant.

CONCLUSION

The central premise of institutional theory – that the adoption of practices and policies by organizations is strongly influenced by the actions of other organizations, regulatory measures, public opinion, and other external social pressures – rests on assumptions about processes of organizational decision-making. In this chapter, we have drawn upon classic work by social psychologists on conformity (Asch & Guetzkow, 1951) and more recent work by economists on herd behavior (Banerjee, 1992) to unpack these assumptions, illuminating and clarifying some core ambiguities in initial formulations of institutional theory (Meyer & Rowan, 1977). These ambiguities continue to be evinced in contemporary empirical research; therefore, resolving them is important for the development of future theorizing and research.

In this context, we argue for greater attention to long-standing distinctions from social psychology between normative and informational conformity, and correspondingly, between public and private behavior. Such distinctions not only offer important insights into different micro-level decision-making processes which institutional theory presumes, but also provide a foundation for both integrating extant empirical work based on this theoretical tradition and developing further studies. Here, we use these distinctions to offer a number of propositions about how different motivations for adopting new practices and policies affect different post-adoption behaviors and organizational outcomes: decoupling (e.g. Westphal & Zajac, 1994), customization (e.g., Fiss et al., 2012), and abandonment (e.g., Ahmadjian & Robinson, 2001). Specifically, we draw upon existing empirical findings in postulating that decoupling is more likely to occur when adoption reflects decision-making driven by normative conformity, while both customization and abandonment are more likely to occur when adoption reflects decision-making driven by informational conformity.

Our discussion of different types of conformity and organizational decision-making processes also has implications for long-standing concerns that institutional theory lacks a role for agency (DiMaggio, 1988; Heugens & Lander, 2009; Hirsch & Lounsbury, 1997). Interestingly, "agency" and "agentic behavior" are terms that are rarely explicitly defined. DiMaggio's (1988) initial plea for giving more attention to agency emphasized conscious interests as key when he suggested that agency involves "behavior…driven by and understandable in terms of the interests of human actors…" (p. 4), and again in referencing, "organized actors with sufficient resources…to realize interests that they value highly" (p. 14). In line with this, one might argue that decisions reflecting informational conformity – that is, those motivated by decision-makers' efforts to assess the "right" choice by using others as data points – are agentic, compared with normative conformity decisions which presumably lack voluntary choice. Yet, it is hard not to wonder: are organizational decision-makers truly being agentic when they make strategic choices that entail simply following the herd? Are normatively conforming decisions to avoid sanctions (and perhaps, secure additional resources) by complying with external demands really lacking in agency?

Heugens and Lander (2009, p. 63) more narrowly identify agency with protest, or "acts of resistance and deviance…to protest against dogmatically ordained and upheld social norms." This seems to exclude post-adoption decisions to decouple or customize adopted practices as agentic since these do not necessarily involve explicit rebellion against existing arrangements. Thus, application of the label of agency seems to be restricted to first-movers – those at the forefront of a diffusion process, or idiosyncratic adopters – and perhaps to organizations that initially abandon institutionalized practices. We note that individuals' thoughts are influenced by others even if they are not conscious of such influences. So, what then is the true litmus test for agency? To us, these complications suggest that the utility of focusing on agentic versus structurally driven action is moot. Rather, focusing on the nature of the underlying decision-making process is more useful for realizing both the theoretical advantages and limitations of institutional theory.

In this context, we note that a rather large hole in theorizing and research in this tradition involves the lack of integration between studies of intra-organizational conformity pressures and group dynamics in organizational decision-making (March & Simon, 1958; Cohen, March & Olson, 1992), and those of inter-organizational conformity or institutional pressures. Two lines of research, on organizational identity and on institutional logics, offer potential pathways to such integration. For example, an experimental study by Schilke (2018) found that strong organizational identification increases resistance to compliance with the external organizational environment, in part by deflecting attention from an external focus to an inward orientation. However, his study did not explore variations in the strength of external conformity pressures (whether normative or informational); this would be an important variable to consider in future studies. In general, investigating how conflicting internal and external conformity pressures may play out in influencing decisions would be useful in defining the scope conditions of institutional theory. Likewise, better integration of competing logics within organization (e.g., Zilber, 1992) with institutional theory's traditional emphasis on the need to respond to external pressure could extend our understanding of such post-adoption behaviors as decoupling, customization and abandonment.

In summary, we believe that exploring institutional theory through the lens of organizational decision-making – understanding the individual and small group processes that join observed conditions at the field level to observed organizational changes – offers important avenues for future research. More importantly, both theorizing and empirically examining microfoundational aspects of institutional theory, including assumptions about how individuals perceive and interpret external events, holds much potential for providing us with a better understanding of how organizations behave.

NOTES

1. Some scholars draw a theoretical distinction between processes leading to herd behavior and information cascades. For example, Celen and Kariv (2004, p. 484) note, "An informational cascade is said to occur when an infinite sequence of individuals ignore their private information when making a decision, whereas herd behavior occurs when an infinite sequence of individuals make an identical decision, not necessarily ignoring their private information." It is unclear whether this distinction is widely accepted. (See, e.g., Banerjee, 1992, p. 798.)

2. When a shift occurred such that subjects followed others in making an incorrect choice, it was coded as a "reverse cascade."

3. This analysis does, however, explicitly recognize agentic actions by different groups, such as social elites and lower-status immigrants, in the conflict over and ultimate institutionalization of civil service reform laws.

4. DiMaggio and Powell's types of isomorphic processes are similar to the distinctions drawn by Scott (2008) between three "pillars" of institutions – regulative, normative, and cultural-cognitive. The regulative pillar involves rules imposed on an organization by an

authoritative agency with sanctioning power (presumably producing coercive isomorphism). The normative pillar involves shared expectations of organizations held by social groups who generate informal pressures for compliance (similar to normative isomorphic forces). The cultural-cognitive pillar entails "shared conceptions that constitute the nature of social reality" (Scott, 2008, p. 57) – that is, collectively agreed-upon choices of "correct" behavioral choices.

5. This concept is similar to what Fiss, Kennedy, and Davis (2012) refer to as "extensiveness." At the risk of proliferating terms (a common academic problem), we prefer "implementation" because it seems to reflect better the underlying notion of genuine commitment and investment by an organization.

6. In this respect, decoupling and fidelity are likely to be related responses to normative pressure, since lack of adaptation makes it difficult to implement innovations without creating dysfunctional conflicts within the organization.

REFERENCES

Abbott, A. (1988). *The system of professions*. Chicago, IL: University of Chicago Press.

Abrahamson, E., & Eisenman, M. (2008). Employee-management techniques: Transient fads or trending fashions?. *Administrative Science Quarterly, 53*(4), 719–744. https://doi.org/10.2189/asqu.53.4.719

Ahmadjian, C. L., & Robinson, P. (2001). Safety in numbers: Downsizing and the deinstitutionalization of permanent employment in Japan. *Administrative Science Quarterly, 46*(4), 622–654. https://doi.org/10.2307/3094826

Aldrich, H. E., & Ruef, M. (2006). *Organizations evolving*. Thousand Oaks, CA: Sage.

Allen, V. L. (1965). Situational factors in conformity. In *Advances in experimental social psychology* (Vol. 2, pp. 133–175). New York, NY: Academic Press. https://doi.org/10.1016/S0065-2601(08)60105-7

Anderson, L. R., & Holt, C. A. (1997). Information cascades in the laboratory. *The American Economic Review, 87*(5), 847–862. Retrieved from https://www.jstor.org/stable/2951328

Ansari, S. M., Fiss, P. C., & Zajac, E. J. (2010). Made to fit: How practices vary as they diffuse. *Academy of Management Review, 35*(1), 67–92. https://doi.org/10.5465/amr.35.1.zok67

Asch, S. E. (1955). Opinions and social pressure. *Scientific American, 193*(5), 31–35. Retrieved from https://www.jstor.org/stable/24943779

Asch, S. E. (1956). Studies of independence and conformity: I. A minority of one against a unanimous majority. *Psychological Monographs: General and Applied, 70*(9), 1–70. http://dx.doi.org/10.1037/h0093718

Asch, S. E. (1951). Effects of group pressure upon the modification and distortion of judgments. In H. Guetzkow (Ed.), *Groups, Leadership, and Men*, (pp.177–190). Oxford, England: Carnetgie Press.

Banerjee, A. V. (1992). A simple model of herd behavior. *The Quarterly Journal of Economics, 107*(3), 797–817. https://doi.org/10.2307/2118364

Bikhchandani, S., Hirshleifer, D., & Welch, I. (1992). A theory of fads, fashion, custom, and cultural change as informational cascades. *Journal of Political Economy, 100*(5), 992–1026. https://doi.org/10.1086/261849

Blau, P. M. (1970). A formal theory of differentiation in organizations. *American Sociological Review, 35*(2), 201–218. https://www.jstor.org/stable/2093199

Briscoe, F., & Murphy, C. (2012). Sleight of hand? Practice opacity, third-party responses, and the interorganizational diffusion of controversial practices. *Administrative Science Quarterly, 57*(4), 553–584. https://doi.org/10.1177/0001839212465077

Briscoe, F., & Safford, S. (2008). The Nixon-in-China effect: Activism, imitation, and the institutionalization of contentious practices. *Administrative Science Quarterly, 53*(3), 460–491. https://doi.org/10.2189/asqu.53.3.460

Briscoe, F., Gupta, A., & Anner, M. S. (2015). Social activism and practice diffusion: How activist tactics affect non-targeted organizations. *Administrative Science Quarterly, 60*(2), 300–332. https://doi.org/10.1177/0001839215579235

Burns, L. R., & Wholey, D. R. (1993). Adoption and abandonment of matrix management programs: Effects of organizational characteristics and interorganizational networks. *Academy of Management Journal, 36*(1), 106–138. https://doi.org/10.5465/256514

Campbell, J. D., & Fairey, P. J. (1989). Informational and normative routes to conformity: The effect of faction size as a function of norm extremity and attention to the stimulus. *Journal of Personality and Social Psychology, 57*(3), 457–468.

Celen, B. & Kariv, S. (2004). Distinguishing informational cascades from herd behavior in the laboratory. *American Economic Review, 94*(3), 484–493.

Chandler, D. (2014). Organizational susceptibility to institutional complexity: Critical events driving the adoption and implementation of the ethics and compliance officer position. *Organization Science, 25*(6), 1722–1743. https://doi.org/10.1287/orsc.2014.0927

Child, J. (1972). Organizational structure, environment and performance: The role of strategic choice. *Sociology, 6*(1), 1–22. https://doi.org/10.1177/003803857200600101

Cohen, M. D., March, J. G., & Olsen, J. P. (1972). A garbage can model of organizational choice. *Administrative Science Quarterly, 17*(1), 1–25. doi:10.2307/2392088

Compagni, A., Mele, V., & Ravasi, D. (2015). How early implementations influence later adoptions of innovation: Social positioning and skill reproduction in the diffusion of robotic surgery. *Academy of Management Journal, 58*(1), 242–278. https://doi.org/10.5465/amj.2011.1184

David, R., Tolbert, P. S., & Boghossian, J. (Forthcoming). *Institutional theory. Oxford research encyclopedia of business and management*. Oxford: Oxford University Publishing.

Deutsch, M., & Gerard, H. B. (1955). A study of normative and informational social influences upon individual judgment. *The Journal of Abnormal and Social Psychology, 51*(3), 629–636. http://dx.doi.org/10.1037/h0046408

DiMaggio, P. J. (1988). Interest and agency in institutional theory. In L.G. Zucker (Ed.), *Institutional patterns and organizations: Culture and environment* (pp. 3–21). Cambridge, MA: Ballinger Publishing Co.

DiMaggio, P. J., & Powell, W. W. (1983). The iron cage revisited: Institutional isomorphism and collective rationality in organizational fields. *American Sociological Review, 48*(2), 147–160.

Dobbin, F., & Kelly, E. L. (2007). How to stop harassment: Professional construction of legal compliance in organizations. *American Journal of Sociology, 112*(4), 1203–1243. https://doi.org/10.1086/508788

Donaldson, L. (1996). Structure contingency theory. In S. Clegg, C. Hardy, & W. Nord (Eds.), *Handbook of organizational studies* (pp. 57–76). New York, NY: Sage.

Edelman, L. B. (1992). Legal ambiguity and symbolic structures: Organizational mediation of civil rights law. *American Journal of Sociology, 97*(6), 1531–1576. https://doi.org/10.1086/229939

Ferris, G. R., King, T, Judge, T., & Kacmar, K. M. (1991). The management of shared meaning in organizations: Opportunism in the reflection of attitudes, beliefs and values. In R. A. Giacolone, & P. Rosenfeld (Eds.), *Applied impression management* (pp. 41–65). Thousand Oaks, CA: Sage Publications.

Festinger, L. (1953). An analysis of compliant behavior. In M. Sherif & M. O. Wilson (Eds.), *Group relations at the crossroads* (pp. 232–256). New York, NY: Harper & Brothers.

Fiss, P. C., & Zajac, E. J. (2004). The diffusion of ideas over contested terrain: The (non) adoption of a shareholder value orientation among German firms. *Administrative Science Quarterly, 49*(4), 501–534. https://doi.org/10.2307/4131489

Fiss, P. C., Kennedy, M. T., & Davis, G. F. (2012). How golden parachutes unfolded: Diffusion and variation of a controversial practice. *Organization Science, 23*(4), 1077–1099. https://doi.org/10.1287/orsc.1110.0685

Freidson, E. (2001). *Professionalism: The third logic*. Chicago, IL: University of Chicago Press.

Gigerenzer, G., & Gaissmaier, W. (2011). Heuristic decision making. *Annual Review of Psychology, 62*, 451–482. https://doi.org/10.1146/annurev-psych-120709-145346

Gilbert, C. G. (2005). Unbundling the structure of inertia: Resource versus routine rigidity. *Academy of Management Journal, 48*(5), 741–763. https://doi.org/10.5465/amj.2005.18803920

Greve, H. R. (1996). Patterns of competition: The diffusion of a market position in radio broadcasting. *Administrative Science Quarterly, 41*(1), 29–60. doi:10.2307/2393985

Hardy, K. R. (1957). Determinants of conformity and attitude change. *The Journal of Abnormal and Social Psychology, 54*(3), 289–294. http://dx.doi.org/10.1037/h0048374

Heugens, P. P., & Lander, M. W. (2009). Structure! Agency! (and other quarrels): A meta-analysis of institutional theories of organization. *Academy of Management Journal, 52*(1), 61–85. https://doi.org/10.5465/amj.2009.36461835

Hewlin, P. F. (2009). Wearing the cloak: Antecedents and consequences of creating facades of conformity. *Journal of Applied Psychology, 94*(3), 727–741. http://dx.doi.org/10.1037/a0015228

Hewlin, P. F., Dumas, T. L., & Burnett, M. F. (2017). To thine own self be true? Facades of conformity, values incongruence, and the moderating impact of leader integrity. *Academy of Management Journal, 60*(1), 178–199. https://doi.org/10.5465/amj.2013.0404

Hirsh, C. E. (2009). The strength of weak enforcement: The impact of discrimination charges, legal environments, and organizational conditions on workplace segregation. *American Sociological Review, 74*(2), 245–271. https://doi.org/10.1177/000312240907400205

Hirsch, P. M., & Lounsbury, M. (1997). Ending the family quarrel: Toward a reconciliation of "old" and "new" institutionalisms. *American Behavioral Scientist, 40*(4), 406–418. https://doi.org/10.1177/0002764297040004004

Hodges, B. H., & Geyer, A. L. (2006). A nonconformist account of the Asch experiments: Values, pragmatics, and moral dilemmas. *Personality and Social Psychology Review, 10*(1), 2–19. https://doi.org/10.1207/s15327957pspr1001_1

Kelly, E. L. (2003). The strange history of employer-sponsored child care: Interested actors, uncertainty, and the transformation of law in organizational fields. *American Journal of Sociology, 109*(3), 606–649. https://doi.org/10.1086/379631

Kelman, H. C. (1961). Three processes of social influence. *Public Opinion Quarterly, 25*, 57–78.

Kennedy, M. T., & Fiss, P. C. (2009). Institutionalization, framing, and diffusion: The logic of TQM adoption and implementation decisions among US hospitals. *Academy of Management Journal, 52*(5), 897–918. https://doi.org/10.5465/amj.2009.44633062

Latané, B. (1981). The psychology of social impact. *American Psychologist, 36*(4), 343–356. http://dx.doi.org/10.1037/0003-066X.36.4.343

Levine, J. M. (1999). Solomon Asch's legacy for group research. *Personality and Social Psychology Review, 3*(4), 358–364. https://doi.org/10.1207/s15327957pspr0304_5

Lounsbury, M. (2001). Institutional sources of practice variation: Staffing college and university recycling programs. *Administrative Science Quarterly, 46*, 1.

Luchins, A. S., & Luchins, E. H. (1955). Previous experience with ambiguous and non-ambiguous perceptual stimuli under various social influences. *The Journal of Social Psychology, 42*(2), 249–270. https://doi.org/10.1080/00224545.1955.9921887

Mannes, A. E. (2009). Are we wise about the wisdom of crowds? The use of group judgments in belief revision. *Management Science, 55*(8), 1267–1279. https://doi.org/10.1287/mnsc.1090.1031

March, J. G., & Simon, H.A. (1958). *Organizations.* New York, NY: Wiley.

Meyer, J. W., & Rowan, B. (1977). Institutionalized organizations: Formal structure as myth and ceremony. *American Journal of Sociology, 83*(2), 340–363. https://doi.org/10.1086/226550

Mizruchi, M. S., & Fein, L. C. (1999). The social construction of organizational knowledge: A study of the uses of coercive, mimetic, and normative isomorphism. *Administrative Science Quarterly, 44*(4), 653–683. https://doi.org/10.2307/2667051

Nail, P. R., & Van Leeuwen, M. D. (1993). An analysis and restructuring of the diamond model of social response. *Personality and Social Psychology Bulletin, 19*(1), 106–116. https://doi.org/10.1177/0146167293191012

Oliver, C. (1991). Strategic responses to institutional processes. *Academy of Management Review, 16*(1), 145–179. https://doi.org/10.5465/amr.1991.4279002

Park, S., Sine, W. D., & Tolbert, P. S. (2011). Professions, organizations, and institutions: Tenure systems in colleges and universities. *Work and Occupations, 38*(3), 340–371. https://doi.org/10.1177/0730888411412725

Raaijmakers, A. G., Vermeulen, P. A., Meeus, M. T., & Zietsma, C. (2015). I need time! Exploring pathways to compliance under institutional complexity. *Academy of Management Journal, 58*(1), 85–110. https://doi.org/10.5465/amj.2011.0276

Rao, H., Greve, H. R., & Davis, G. F. (2001). Fool's gold: Social proof in the initiation and abandonment of coverage by Wall Street analysts. *Administrative Science Quarterly, 46*(3), 502–526. https://doi.org/10.2307/3094873

Raven, B. H. (1959). Social influence on opinions and the communication of related content. *The Journal of Abnormal and Social Psychology*, *58*(1), 119–128. http://dx.doi.org/10.1037/h0048251

Rosenberg, L. (1961). Group size, prior experience, and conformity. *The Journal of Abnormal and Social Psychology*, *63*(2), 436–437. http://dx.doi.org/10.1037/h0047007

Schilke, O. (2018). A micro-institutional inquiry into resistance to environmental pressures. *Academy of Management Journal*, *61*(4), 1431–1466. https://doi.org/10.5465/amj.2016.0762

Schoonhoven, C. B. (1981). Problems with contingency theory: Testing assumptions hidden within the language of contingency "theory". *Administrative Science Quarterly*, 349–377. Retrieved from https://www.jstor.org/stable/2392512

Scott, W. R. (1975). Organizational structure. *Annual Review of Sociology*, *1*(1), 1–20. https://doi.org/10.1146/annurev.so.01.080175.000245

Scott, W. R. (1995). *Institutions and organizations*. Thousand Oaks, CA: Sage Publishing.

Scott, W. R. & Davis, G. F. (2007). *Organizations: Rational, natural and open systems*. Upper Saddle River, NJ: Prentice Hall.

Tanford, S., & Penrod, S. (1984). Social influence model: A formal integration of research on majority and minority influence processes. *Psychological Bulletin*, *95*(2), 189–225. http://dx.doi.org/10.1037/0033-2909.95.2.189

Thompson, J. D. (1967). *Organizations in action: Social science bases of administration*. New York: McGraw-Hill Publishers. University of Illinois at Urbana-Champaign's Academy for Entrepreneurial Leadership Historical Research Reference in Entrepreneurship. Available at SSRN: https://ssrn.com/abstract=1496215

Tolbert, P. S. & Hall, R. H. (2009). *Organizations: Structures, processes and outcomes*. Upper Saddle River, NJ: Prentice Hall.

Tolbert, P. S., & Zucker, L. G. (1983). Institutional sources of change in the formal structure of organizations: The diffusion of civil service reform, 1880–1935. *Administrative Science Quarterly*, *28*(1), 22–39. doi: 10.2307/2392383

Tolbert, P. S., & Zucker, L. G. (1996). The institutionalization of institutional theory. In S. Clegg, C. Hardy, W. R. Nord (Eds.), *Handbook of organization studies* (pp. 175–190). London: Sage Publications.

Westphal, J. D., & Zajac, E. J. (1994). Substance and symbolism in CEO's long-term incentive plans. *Administrative Science Quarterly*, *39*(3), 367–390.

Westphal, J. D., & Zajac, E. J. (1998). The symbolic management of stockholders: Corporate governance reforms and shareholder reactions. *Administrative Science Quarterly*, 127–153. doi:10.2307/2393593

Westphal, J. D., & Zajac, E. J. (2001). Decoupling policy from practice: The case of stock repurchase programs. *Administrative Science Quarterly*, *46*(2), 202–228. https://doi.org/10.2307/2667086

Westphal, J. D., Gulati, R., & Shortell, S. M. (1997). Customization or conformity? An institutional and network perspective on the content and consequences of TQM adoption. *Administrative Science Quarterly*, 366–394. doi:10.2307/2393924

Zilber, T. B. (2002). Institutionalization as an interplay between actions, meanings, and actors: The case of a rape crisis center in Israel. *Academy of Management Journal*, *45*(1), 234–254. https://doi.org/10.5465/3069294

Zucker, L. G. (1977). The role of institutionalization in cultural persistence. *American Sociological Review*, 726–743. doi:10.2307/2094862

Zucker, L. G. (1986). The production of trust: Institutional sources of economic structure, 1840-1920. *Research in Organizational Behavior*, *8*, 53–111.

Zucker, L. G. (1987). Institutional theories of organization. *Annual Review of Sociology*, *13*(1), 443–464. https://doi.org/10.1146/annurev.so.13.080187.002303

Zucker, L. G. (1991). The role of institutionalization in cultural persistence. In W. W. Powell & P. J. DiMaggio (Eds.), *The new institutionalism in organizational analysis* (pp. 63–82). Chicago, IL: The University of Chicago Press.

INDEX

Note: Page numbers followed by "*n*" with numbers indicate notes.